AF881003

Beiträge zum ausländischen und internationalen Privatrecht

152

Herausgegeben vom

Max-Planck-Institut für ausländisches
und internationales Privatrecht

Direktorium:

Holger Fleischer, Ralf Michaels, Anne Röthel

Great Debates in German and Italian Company Law

Edited by

Holger Fleischer and Marco Speranzin

Mohr Siebeck

Holger Fleischer is Director at the Max Planck Institute for Comparative and International Private Law in Hamburg.

Marco Speranzin is a full professor of business law at the University of Padua and a practising lawyer.

Open Access funding provided by Max Planck Society.

ISBN 978-3-16-200537-3 / eISBN 978-3-16-200538-0
DOI 10.1628/978-3-16-200538-0

ISSN 0340-6709 / eISSN 2568-6577
(Beiträge zum ausländischen und internationalen Privatrecht)

The Deutsche Nationalbibliothek lists this publication in the Deutsche Nationalbibliographie; detailed bibliographic data are available at *https://dnb.dnb.de.*

Published by Mohr Siebeck Tübingen 2026.

© Holger Fleischer, Marco Speranzin (eds.); chapter: respective author.

This publication is licensed under the license "Creative Commons Attribution 4.0 International" (CC BY 4.0). A complete version of the license text can be found at: https://creativecommons.org/licenses/by/4.0/.

Any use not covered by the above license is prohibited and illegal without the permission of the author. The right to use the content of this volume for the purpose of text and data mining within the meaning of Section 44b UrhG (Urheberrechtsgesetz) is expressly reserved.

Printed on non-aging paper.

Mohr Siebeck GmbH & Co. KG, Wilhelmstraße 18, 72074 Tübingen, Germany
www.mohrsiebeck.com, info@mohrsiebeck.com

Preface

Great debates have spurred the development of company law in the past, and they continue to do so today. Building on an earlier publication (Fleischer/Koch/Schmolke, *Gesellschaftsrecht im Spiegel großer Debatten*, 2024), this conference volume examines classic controversies in German and Italian company law. New insights into company law and its traditions, doctrines, conceptual achievements, and discourse dynamics await from exploring these debates, their beginnings and endings, their participants, and the forums and discourse cultures in which they played out. In the introductory chapter and nine individual contributions that follow it, we invite readers to deepen their understanding of company law as an academic discipline and professional practice.

Many people have contributed to the creation of this book. First and foremost, we would like to extend our sincere thanks to all the authors for their insightful contributions. John A. Foulks, Ina Freisleben, Janina Jentz, and Anja Rosenthal at the Institute provided us with invaluable assistance during the editorial process.

Hamburg and Padova,
March 2026

Holger Fleischer
Marco Speranzin

Content

Abbreviations

AcP	Archiv für die civilistische Praxis
ADHGB	General German Commercial Code (Allgemeines Deutsches Handelsgesetzbuch)
AG	Public limited company (Aktiengesellschaft); Die Aktiengesellschaft
AI	Artificial intelligence
AJCL	American Journal of Comparative Law
AktG	Stock Corporation Act (Aktiengesetz)
Alb LRev	Albany Law Review
ALR	General State Laws for the Prussian States (Allgemeines Landrecht für die Preußischen Staaten)
An giur econ	Analisi Giuridica dell'Economia
ARUG II	Act Implementing the Second Shareholder Rights Directive (Gesetz zur Umsetzung der zweiten Aktionärsrechterichtlinie)
Banca borsa tit cred	Banca, borsa e titoli di credito
BB	Betriebs-Berater
BeckOGK	Beck'scher Online-Großkommentar
Berkeley Tech LJ	Berkeley Technology Law Journal
BGB	German Civil Code (Bürgerliches Gesetzbuch)
BGBl	Federal Law Gazette (Bundesgesetzblatt)
BGH	German Federal Court of Justice (Bundesgerichtshof)
BGHZ	Decisions of the German Supreme Court in civil matters (Entscheidungen des Bundesgerichtshofes in Zivilsachen)
BKR	Zeitschrift für Bank und Kapitalmarktrecht
BMF	Bundesministerium der Finanzen
BMJ	Bundesministerium der Justiz
BRIS	Business Registers Interconnection System
BT-Drs.	Printed matter of the German Federal Parliament (Bundestagsdrucksache)
BVerfG	German Federal Constitutional Court (Bundesverfassungsgericht)
BVerfGE	Decisions of the German Federal Constitutional Court (Entscheidungen des Bundesverfassungsgerichts)
Cass	Italian Supreme Court of Cassation (Corte di Cassazione)
Cath ULR	Catholic University Law Review
CBCI	Code of Business Crisis and Insolvency (Codice della crisi di impresa e dell'insolvenza)
CC	Civil Code (Codice Civile)
CDU	Christian Democratic Union of Germany (Christlich Demokratische Union)
CEO	Chief Executive Officer

cf	confer
CFSA	Consolidated Financial Service Act
Chi-Kent LRev	Chicago-Kent Law Review
CMU	Capital Markets Union
Colum Bus LRev	Columbia Business Law Review
Colum LRev	Columbia Law Review
COM	European Commission
confd.	confirmed
CONSOB	Italian National Commission for Companies and the Stock Exchange (Commissione Nazionale per le Società e la Borsa)
Contr impr	Contratto e impresa
Cornell LRev	Cornell Law Review
Corr giur	Corriere giuridico
Corte Cost	Constitutional Court of Italy (Corte Costituzionale)
CSDDD	Corporate Sustainability Due Diligence Directive
CSR	Corporate Social Responsibility
CUP	Cambridge University Press
DAC	Digital Administration Code
DAO	Decentralized autonomous organizations
DAV	Deutscher Anwaltverein
DB	Der Betrieb
Del JCorpL	Delaware Journal of Corporate Law
Dig disc priv, sez civ	Digesto delle discipline privatistiche, sezione civile
Dir comm int	Diritto del commercio internazionale
DJT	Association of German Jurists (Deutscher Juristentag)
DLT	Distributed Ledger Technology
D&O	Directors & Officers
DStR	Deutsches Steuerrecht
EBLR	European Business Law Review
EBOR	European Business Organization Law Review
ECFR	European Company and Financial Law Review
ECGI	European Corporate Governance Institute
ECJ	European Court of Justice
ECL	European Company Law
ECLI	European Case-Law Identifier
Econ Hist Rev	The Economic History Review
ed	editor
edn	edition
EDPB	European Data Protection Board
EEA	European Economic Area
eg	exempli gratia
EPRS	European Parliamentary Research Service
ESG	Environmental, Social and Governance
et seq	and those that follow
EU	European Union
EuZW	Europäische Zeitschrift für Wirtschaftsrecht
EWG	European Economic Community

FCA	Federal Court of Australia
Flex-KapG	Flexible Corporation (Flexible Kapitalgesellschaft)
Foro it	Il Foro italiano
GDPR	General Data Protection Regulation
GesRÄG	Corporate Law Amendment Act (Gesellschaftsrechts-Änderungsgesetz)
Giur comm	Giurisprudenza commerciale
Giur It	Giurisprudenza Italiana
Giust civ	Giustizia civile
GmbH	Private limited company (Gesellschaft mit beschränkter Haftung)
GmbH & Co. KG	Limited partnership with a limited liability company as general partner (Gesellschaft mit beschränkter Haftung & Compagnie Kommanditgesellschaft)
GmbHG	Limited Liability Company Act (Gesetz betreffend die Gesellschaften mit beschränkter Haftung)
GmbHR	Zeitschrift für Gesellschaftsrecht, Unternehmensrecht und Steuerrecht
HansRGZ	Hanseatische Rechts- und Gerichtszeitschrift
Harv JOLT	Harvard Journal of Law & Technology
Harv LRev	Harvard Law Review
Harv UP	Harvard University Press
HGB	Commercial Code (Handelsgesetzbuch)
Hist Pol Econ	History of Political Economy
ICT	Information and communications technologies
IDC	International Data Corporation
IDPL	International Data Privacy Law
ie	id est
IJLIT	International Journal of Law and Information Technology
InsO	Insolvency Code (Insolvenzordnung)
IPO	Initial Public Offering
IPRax	Praxis des internationalen Privat- und Verfahrensrechts
JAIR	Journal of Artificial Intelligence Research
JCMS	Journal of Common Market Studies
J Corp L	Journal of Corporation Law
J Fin Econ	Journal of Financial Economics
J Inst Econ	Journal of Institutional Economics
JZ	JuristenZeitung
KG	Limited partnership (Kommanditgesellschaft)
KGaA	Partnership limited by shares (Kommanditgesellschaft auf Aktien)
KonTraG	Act on Monitoring and Transparency of Enterprises (Gesetz zur Kontrolle und Transparenz im Unternehmensbereich)
KritZgR	Kritische Zeitschrift für die gesamte Rechtswissenschaft
L&E	Law & Economics
LG	German Regional Court (Landgericht)

LLC	Limited Liability Company
Lodo arb	Lodo arbitrale
M&A	Mergers & Acquisitions
MBCA	Model Business Corporation Act
MiFID II	Markets in Financial Instruments Directive II
MLR	Modern Law Review
MoMiG	Act to modernize the law of private limited companies (Gesetz zur Modernisierung des GmbH-Rechts und zur Bekämpfung von Missbräuchen)
MoPeG	Act to modernize the law of partnerships (Gesetz zur Modernisierung des Personengesellschaftsrechts)
MP	Member of Parliament
NJOZ	Neue Juristische Online-Zeitschrift
NJW	Neue Juristische Wochenschrift
Nuove leggi civ	Le nuove leggi civili commentate
NUS	National University of Singapore
NYU JL&Bus	New York University Journal of Law & Business
NZG	Neue Zeitschrift für Gesellschaftsrecht
ÖBA	Österreichisches Bankarchiv
OECD	Organisation for Economic Co-operation and Development
OJLS	Oxford Journal of Legal Studies
Okla LRev	Oklahoma Law Review
OLG	German Higher Regional Court (Oberlandesgericht)
OS	Organization Studies
OUP	Oxford University Press
Oxf Econ Pap	Oxford Economic Papers
Pac Econ Rev	Pacific Economic Review
para	Paragraph
Princ UP	Princeton University Press
RabelsZ	Rabels Zeitschrift für ausländisches und internationales Privatrecht
R&D	Research & Development
Rev soc	Revue des sociétés
RGBl	Official Law Gazette of the German Reich (Reichsgesetzblatt)
RGZ	Decisions of the Supreme Court of the German Reich in civil matters (Entscheidungen des Reichsgerichts in Zivilsachen)
Riv corp gov	Rivista Corporate Governance
Riv dir civ	Rivista di Diritto Civile
Riv crit dir lav	Rivista critica di diritto del lavoro
Riv dir comm	Rivista del Diritto Commerciale
Riv dir comp	Rivista di diritto comparato
Riv dir soc	Rivista di Diritto Societario
Riv dott comm	Rivista dei dottori commercialisti
Riv giur lav	Rivista giuridica del lavoro e della previdenza sociale
Riv it scienze giur	Rivista Italiana per le Scienze Giuridiche

Riv ODC	Rivista Orizzonti del Diritto Commerciale
Riv soc	Rivista delle società
Riv trim proc civ	Rivista trimestrale di diritto e procedura civile
RIW	Recht der internationalen Wirtschaft
R not	Rivista notarile
ROHG	Reichsoberhandelsgericht
ROHGE	Entscheidungen des Reichsoberhandelsgerichts
RuW	Verlagsgesellschaft Recht und Wirtschaft
S.a.R.L.	Société à responsabilité limitée
SchiedsVZ	Zeitschrift für Schiedsverfahren
SE	Societas Europaea
SEBI	Securities and Exchange Board of India
SJZ	Schweizerische Juristen-Zeitung
SLIM	Simpler Legislation for the Internal Market
SME	small and medium-sized enterprises
SPA	Sale and Purchase Agreement
S.p.A.	Public limited company (Società per azioni)
SPAC	Special Purpose Acquisition Company
SPE	Societas Privata Europea
SPV	Special Purpose Vehicle
SRD	Shareholder Rights Directive
S.r.l.	Limited liability company (Società a responsabilità limitata)
Stan LRev	Stanford Law Review
TFEU	Treaty on the Functioning of the European Union
Trib	Tribunale
U Cal P	University of California Press
U Chi LRev	University of Chicago Law Review
UCITS	Undertakings for collective investment in transferable securities
UCLA LRev	UCLA Law Review
UCP	University of Chicago Press
UG	Unternehmergesellschaft
UK	United Kingdom
U Pa LRev	University of Pennsylvania Law Review
U Pitt LRev	University of Pittsburgh Law Review
US	United States
USC	United States Code
UTLJ	University of Toronto Law Journal
Va LRev	Virginia Law Review
VC	Venture Capitalist
Vita not	Vita notarile
VS	Verlag für Sozialwissenschaften
Wash LRev	Washington Law Review
WM	Zeitschrift für Wirtschafts- und Bankrecht
WPg	Die Wirtschaftsprüfung

WpHG	Wertpapierhandelsgesetz
WpÜG	Wertpapiererwerbs- und Übernahmegesetz
Yale LJ	Yale Law Journal
ZEuP	Zeitschrift für Europäisches Privatrecht
ZfgG	Zeitschrift für das gesamte Genossenschaftswesen
ZfPW	Zeitschrift für die gesamte Privatrechtswissenschaft
ZGH	Zeitschrift für das gesamte Handelsrecht
ZGR	Zeitschrift für Unternehmens- und Gesellschaftsrecht
ZHR	Zeitschrift für das gesamte Handelsrecht und Wirtschaftsrecht
ZInsO	Zeitschrift für das gesamte Insolvenz- und Sanierungsrecht
ZIP	Zeitschrift für Wirtschaftsrecht
ZRG	Zeitschrift der Savigny-Stiftung für Rechtsgeschichte: Germanistische Abteilung
ZSR	Zeitschrift für Schweizerisches Recht
ZVglRWiss	Zeitschrift für Vergleichende Rechtswissenschaft

Great Debates in Company Law

A Research Outline

Holger Fleischer[*]

I. Introduction

Anyone who wishes to delve deeper into company law and its professional culture has various points of entry. One can take a closer look at the preferred re-

---

[*] This article first appeared in German in [2023] JZ 365. It was written at the beginning of the research program and has been slightly revised for this introductory chapter.

search topics and methods,[1] examine the key protagonists and their interactions,[2] or trace the development of company law scholarship in specific eras.[3] It is also conceivable to devote oneself to the *grands arrêts* of the field[4] or to inspect the great masterpieces of draughtsmanship.[5]

Another key to better understanding company law lies in familiarizing oneself with the major historical as well as with today's major debates in the field. This essay sets forth the program for a new project that takes up this line of research. The first case study has already been published.[6] Inspired by two slim edited volumes on English law[7] and expected to fill about twenty chapters, it will examine the flashpoints of German company law in context. Novices and experts alike can look forward to valuable insights from his 'cartography of controversies,'[8] such as about the essence of company law, its traditions and dogmas, its intellectual achievements, and its discourse culture.

Part II of the following research outline first amplifies the potential of systematically studying any discipline's crucial controversies. Part III provides orientation in the form of a brief chronology of major debates in company law. Part IV follows with observations on how these debates began and how they were resolved or ended. Part V makes observations on the formation of theories as the debates matured. Subsequently, Part VI maps important debates in company law accord-

---

[1] For more details on the topics and methodological approaches of all habilitation theses on company law, see Holger Fleischer, 'Gesellschaftsrecht im Spiegel seiner Habilitationsschriften' (2022) 51 ZGR 191; specifically on methodological theory in company law, see Peter O Mülbert, 'Einheit der Methodenlehre? Allgemeines Zivilrecht und Gesellschaftsrecht im Vergleich' (2014) 214 AcP 188.

[2] See Hans-Ueli Vogt, Holger Fleischer and Susanne Kalss (eds), *Protagonisten im Gesellschaftsrecht* (Mohr Siebeck 2020).

[3] Thought provoking is Friedrich Kübler, 'Wirtschaftsrecht in der Bundesrepublik. Versuch einer wissenschaftshistorischen Bestandsaufnahme' in Dieter Simon (ed), *Rechtswissenschaft in der Bonner Republik* (Suhrkamp 1994); Jan Thiessen, 'In neuer Gesellschaft? Handels- und Gesellschaftsrecht in der Berliner Republik' in Thomas Duve and Stefan Ruppert (eds), *Rechtswissenschaft in der Berliner Republik* (Suhrkamp 2018); Tobias Tröger, 'Vom Rheinischen Kapitalismus zum Kapitalmarktrecht (und wieder zurück?' in ibid.

[4] See Holger Fleischer and Jan Thiessen (eds), *Gesellschaftsrechts-Geschichten* (Mohr Siebeck 2018); for a didactic approach, see Jan Lieder and Martin Bialluch, *Handels- und Gesellschaftsrecht in 100 Leitentscheidungen* (Mohr Siebeck 2022).

[5] See Holger Fleischer and Sebastian Mock (eds), *Große Gesellschaftsverträge aus Geschichte und Gegenwart* (De Gruyter 2021).

[6] See Holger Fleischer, 'Große Debatten im Gesellschaftsrecht: Fiktionstheorie versus Theorie der realen Verbandspersönlichkeit im internationalen Diskurs' (2023) 87 RabelsZ 5. The complete book has since been published: Holger Fleischer, Jens Koch and Klaus Ulrich Schmolke (eds), Gesellschaftsrecht im Spiegel großer Debatten (De Gruyter 2024).

[7] See Andrew Johnston and Lorraine Talbot, *Great Debates in Commercial and Corporate Law* (Red Globe Press 2020); Lorraine Talbot, *Great Debates in Company Law* (Hart 2014).

[8] Bruno Latour, 'Von der „wissenschaftlichen Wahrheit" zur Kartographie von Kontroversen' in Wolf-Andreas Liebert and Marc-Denis Weitze (eds), *Kontroversen als Schlüssel zur Wissenschaft?* (transcript 2006).

ing to their main topics before Part VII turns to look at the debate participants, the forums, and the discourse culture. Finally, Part VIII sorts out which of these discourses in company law were or are of purely national interest and which of them also had or have international components or relevance.

II. Insights from the Study of Controversies

For the scientific community, major debates are centres of gravity that command attention in many disciplines. Thus the topic of great debates itself has attracted interest not only in the natural sciences but also in the humanities, cultural studies, and social sciences.[9] One can list the edited volumes devoted to salient controversies in the fields of history,[10] philosophy,[11] sociology[12] and literature.[13] Read together they suggest there is much insight to be gained from the systematic study of controversies.

1. Milestones

Major debates encapsulate the history of a discipline. Some fields consist entirely of one or more major debates.[14] That would probably be an exaggeration in the

---

[9] See, for example, Wolf-Andreas Liebert and Marc-Denis Weitze, 'Kontroversen als Schlüssel zur Wissenschaft – Probleme, Ideen und künftige Forschungsfelder' in Liebert and Weitze (n 8) 12: 'We believe – and this is the starting point of this book – that controversies are an essential part of knowledge about science, that they play such a central role in science that they can be considered a key to science.' For a view from popular science, cf Hal Hellman, *Great Feuds in Science* (Trade Paper Press 1998); Hal Hellman, *Great Feuds in Mathematics* (Trade Paper Press 2006).

[10] See Jürgen Elvert and Susanne Krauß (eds), *Historische Debatten und Kontroversen im 19. und 20. Jahrhundert* (Franz Steiner 2003); Klaus Große Kracht, *Die zankende Zunft. Historische Kontroversen in Deutschland nach 1945* (Vandenhoeck & Ruprecht 2005); Hartmut Lehmann (ed), *Historikerkontroversen* (Wallstein 2000); Martin Sahrow, Ralph Jessen and Klaus Große Kracht, *Zeitgeschichte als Streitgeschichte. Große Kontroversen nach 1945* (CH Beck 2003); The Rohr Jewish Learning Institute, *Great Debates in Jewish History* (Jewish Learning Institute 2017).

[11] See Kurt Flasch, *Kampfplätze der Philosophie. Große Kontroversen von Augustin bis Voltaire* (2nd edn, Vittorio Klostermann 2009); Bernward Gesang and Julius Schälike (eds), *Die großen Kontroversen der Rechtsphilosophie* (Brill 2011); see also Marcelo Dascal, *Gottfried Wilhelm Leibniz: The Art of Controversies* (Springer 2008).

[12] See Georg Kneer and Stephan Moebius, *Soziologische Kontroversen* (Suhrkamp 2010).

[13] Cf Ralf Klausnitzer and Carlos Spoerhase, *Kontroversen in der Literaturtheorie/Literaturtheorie in der Kontroverse* (Peter Lang 2007).

[14] See Georg Kneer and Stephan Moebius, 'Vorwort' in Kneer and Moebius (n 12) 8: 'We believe that sociology owes its (incidentally, constantly changing) identity, if not exclusively, then to a considerable extent to a series of fundamental theoretical conflicts and far-reaching methodological debates.' See also Lutz Niethammer, 'Über Kontroversen in der Geschichtswissenschaft' (1989) 43 Merkur 73: 'Because of this dual role as scientific research into tradi-

case of company law. Like most other legal disciplines company law largely owes its identity to a regulatory framework. But major debates do provide a good way to trace the history of company law as a subject. Its major debates alone capture in time-lapse fashion the paths as well as the detours that the discipline, as we know it today, took as knowledge accumulated and various research questions were pursued. Such a longitudinal view also provides a basis for critical self-reflection and an assessment of the current state of affairs in the discipline.[15]

2. *A Legacy of Traditions*

In addition, major debates are part of the traditional heritage of every discipline. Reconstructing them and mapping them out fulfils an important archival function, preventing knowledge from being permanently lost.[16] A compendium of fundamental debates in company law, past or present, introduces beginner researchers to established traditions of thought[17] and prevents them from mistakenly characterizing something as new that has actually long been known and that past scholars have already thoroughly fleshed out. And even experienced scholars can benefit, because with experience often comes the ability to see the classic debates in a new light,[18] much like someone reading Goethe's *Faust* or Thomas Mann's *The Magic Mountain* will respond differently depending on whether they are 17

tion and as a basis of public discourse, controversies in history are constitutive and not, as in other sciences, merely incidental, namely related to the stimulation and integration of innovations and to the honor of fellow members of the profession.' See also Jürgen Elvert, 'Zur Einführung' in Elvert and Krauß (n 10) 9: 'This volume deals with the significance of historical debates and controversies for historical knowledge in the narrower scientific and broader public sense. It aims to recall the tradition of scientific debates and controversies as a whole that have shaped the history of historical science since Ranke at the latest.'

[15] For a detailed discussion of self-reflection in company law, see Holger Fleischer, 'Selbstreflexion im Gesellschaftsrecht: „Hottest Game in Town" oder „Death of Corporate Law"?' (2022) 51 ZGR 466.

[16] For examples of a loss of knowledge in the related field of business administration, see Klaus Brockhoff, *Betriebswirtschaftslehre in Wissenschaft und Geschichte* (5th edn, Springer Gabler 2017) 41f.

[17] See also, in general, Marcelo Dascal, 'Die Dialektik in der kollektiven Konstruktion wissenschaftlichen Wissens' in Liebert and Weitze (n 8) 36f: 'In addition, prospective scholars must at least be familiarized with the most important controversies that have been debated in their respective fields in the past and present.'

[18] For a view on the 'potentially creative function of re-reading the classics' from a sociological perspective, see Robert K Merton, *Social Theory and Social Structure* (Free Press 1968) 37: 'For just as new knowledge has a retroactive effect in helping us to recognize anticipations and adumbrations in earlier work, so changes in current sociological knowledge, problems, and foci of attention enable us to find *new* ideas in a work we had read before. The new context of recent developments in our own intellectual life or in the discipline itself brings into prominence ideas or hints of ideas that escaped notice in an earlier reading.'

or 70 years old.[19] However, despite all justified respect for tradition, one caveat is in order: Erudition must not inhibit scientific originality,[20] nor must it lead later generations to uncritically glorify the discipline's classic texts.[21]

3. A Repository of Ideas, Doctrines, and Dogmas

Furthermore, a close examination of major debates will help scholars achieve an understanding of the doctrinal and intellectual history of their fields. Today this is actually a pressing necessity in company law, in which the history of the science so far has been beggared and marginal.[22] The topic of great debates has found no real home in the ubiquitously dominant commentary literature, and the great textbooks that have long done outstanding service in this area[23] are probably a dying species. An edited volume on fundamental debates in the field, by contrast, seems an ideal forum in which to shed light on the historical, theoretical, and economic conditions that have propelled the main currents in company law. It is precisely through the sharp juxtaposition of rival explanations and schools of thought – the 'agonistic discourse formations'[24] – that doctrines diverge and material differences of assessment become more apparent. Moreover, a more diligent search for clues can help scholars identify intellectual breaks and continuities in the history of company law, revivals of earlier doctrine, and 'prediscovery' formulations of what would later become doctrine.[25]

---

[19] Example based on Merton (n 18) 37: 'Just as the *Song of Songs* is different when it is read at age 17 and at age 70, so Weber's *Wirtschaft und Gesellschaft* or Durkheim's *Suicide* or Simmel's *Soziologie* differ when they are read at different times.'

[20] See Merton (n 18) 30ff under the subheading 'Erudition Versus Originality'.

[21] See Merton (n 18) 30: 'uncritical reverence toward almost any statement made by illustrious ancestors'.

[22] See Holger Fleischer, 'Unternehmensinteresse und intérêt social: Schlüsselfiguren aktienrechtlichen Denkens in Deutschland und Frankreich' (2018) 47 ZGR 703, 704: 'Publications on company law usually revolve around individual legal provisions or court decisions. This is immediately obvious, because our field has always thrived on dealing with practical problems. Nevertheless, it is also worth reflecting on theoretical concepts here, even if this does not provide any immediate answers to questions of day-to-day company law.' See also Eckart Bueren, *Short-termism im Aktien- und Kapitalmarktrecht* (Mohr Siebeck 2022) 4: 'This work closes this gap in basic research by examining the controversy surrounding short-termism and thus the protection of the functioning of stock corporations as one of the "great debates in company law" for the first time in its entirety from the perspective of legal and intellectual history, comparative law, and law and economics.'

[23] For an appreciation of this genre of literature in German corporate law, see Holger Fleischer, 'Gesellschaftsrecht' in Dietmar Willoweit (ed), *Rechtswissenschaft und Rechtsliteratur im 20. Jahrhundert* (CH Beck 2007) 493f.

[24] Kneer and Moebius (n 14) 8: 'agonale Diskursformationen'.

[25] Merton (n 14) 9.

4. Drivers of Progress

Finally, following *Karl Raimund Popper*,[26] the internal debates in any field of science can be considered an engine of scientific progress.[27] In his fallibilistic model of science, the critical debates that play out within the scientific community are central tests of scientific knowledge. New claims and hypotheses are put to the test in a 'friendly but also fiendish competition between scientists'.[28] The extent to which this linear concept of progress in the natural sciences can be transferred to jurisprudence in general, much less to company law, is yet to be examined in detail.[29] Prominent voices contributing to the development of legal doctrine do consider such progress to be achievable.[30] In company law, the maturation of basic categories such as the recognition of corporate personhood comes to mind as a possible example of such progress.[31] Diving into these and other debates will help us understand how they contributed to our field and its most important intellectual achievements.

---

[26] See Karl Popper, *Logik der Forschung* (1st edn, Springer 1935, 11th edn, Mohr Siebeck 2005), English: *The Logic of Scientific Discovery* (1st edn, Basic Books 1959).

[27] In the present context, Andrea Hamp, *Der praktische Sinn in wissenschaftlichen Diskussionen* (Springer VS 2017) 14; Kneer and Moebius (n 14) 8f.

[28] Franz Kreuzer (ed), Karl R Popper and Konrad Lorenz, *Die Zukunft ist offen: das Altenberger Gespräch, mit den Texten des Popper Symposiums* (Piper 1985) 51.

[29] See Holger Fleischer, 'Gesellschaftsrechts-Innovationen: Eine Gedankenskizze' in Christian Deckenbrock and others (eds), *Arbeit, Wirtschaft, Recht. Festschrift Henssler* (CH Beck 2023) (distinguishing between legal inventions, discoveries, and innovations); see also Frank Saliger, 'Intra- und Interdisziplinarität: Wie kommt das Neue in die Rechtswissenschaft?' in Eric Hilgendorf and Helmuth Schulze-Fielitz (eds), *Selbstreflexion der Rechtswissenschaft* (2nd edn, Mohr Siebeck 2021) 120: 'Regardless of any optimism or skepticism about progress, the following article avoids explaining the issue in terms of the idea of progress. The reason for this is that any talk of progress presupposes a reference to an evaluation criterion that can come under pressure from contingency' (raising but not answering the question).

[30] See Robert Alexy, *Theorie der juristischen Argumentation* (Suhrkamp 1978) 328; for a more detailed discussion from a criminal-law perspective, see Björn Burkhardt, 'Hauptreferat. Geglückte und folgenlose Strafrechtsdogmatik' in Albin Eser, Winfried Hassemer and Björn Burkhardt (eds), *Die deutsche Strafrechtswissenschaft vor der Jahrtausendwende* (CH Beck 2000) 124ff; Heinz Müller-Dietz, 'Gibt es Fortschritt im Strafrecht?' in Heike Jung (ed), *Perspektiven der Strafrechtsentwicklung* (Nomos 1996) 31.

[31] On the concept of 'legal entity' as a creation of doctrine and legislation in the 19th and 20th centuries, see Filippo Ranieri, 'Die Rechtskategorie „Juristische Person" als Schöpfung von Doktrin und Gesetzgebung im 19.–20. Jahrhundert. Zugleich ein Kapitel aus der neueren Geschichte des kontinentalen Zivil- und Handelsrechts' in Herbert Kronke, Heinz-Peter Mansel and Marc-Philippe Weller (eds), *Liber Amicorum Giuseppe B Portale* (Nomos 2019) 109ff with further references.

III. A Brief Chronicle of Great Debates in Company Law

A first impression of the wealth of debates in company law can be gained from a diachronic review of the available material. However, it will not be possible, nor will it make sense to try, to cover all the fundamental debates past and present in a single edited volume. An informed selection must be made, which inevitably involves subjective value judgments. The dictum that history is a construct will also apply to a chronicle of company law. The aim is to achieve a healthy balance that ranges from the classic to the current controversies and also covers the doctrinal, theoretical, and policy disputes that have left their marks in stock corporation, GmbH, partnership, and association law. Debates about major court decisions have already been extensively studied elsewhere and are thus omitted.[32] Furthermore, as far as terminology is concerned, no distinction will be made and none is intended at the analytical level between debates, discussions, disputes, or controversies;[33] these terms are used interchangeably.

1. Generational Issues

It is often said that each successive generation of company law scholars has its own row to hoe. This is also reflected in the chronology of major debates. The 'golden generation' of great company lawyers, who became professors in the 1960s, focused largely on the inclusion of concerns or groups of companies in company law,[34] inspired by the world's first codification of a body of statutes applicable to them in the German Stock Corporation Act of 1965.[35] This was followed in the 1970s by wrangling over legal policy with respect to an overarching 'enterprise law'[36] and co-determination, and by the doctrinal analysis, in essays and commentaries, of the Co-Determination Act of 1976.

The leading scholars during the 1980s devoted themselves primarily to systems and principles,[37] transforming the disorder of individual laws from different

---

[32] See the individual chapters in Fleischer and Thiessen (n 4).

[33] For a subdivision into three ideal main types (discussion, dispute, controversy), see Dascal (n 17) 24ff.

[34] See Wolfgang Zöllner, 'Alfred Hueck als Arbeitsrechtler' in Claus-Wilhelm Canaris and others (eds), *Gedächtnisreden auf Alfred Hueck* (1976) 17, 22; Herbert Wiedemann, *Die Unternehmensgruppe im Privatrecht* (Mohr Siebeck 1988) 10: 'The objective and systematic integration of the group of companies into company law – a task for our generation – is no less radical than the step taken at the beginning of the modern era from the individual merchant to the association of persons.'

[35] See Ernst Geßler, 'Probleme und Wege der Aktienrechtsreform' [1966] JBl 169, 179 (taking pride: 'This provision has no parallel in the world's stock corporation legislation. It should be regarded as the reformist achievement of the German Stock Corporation Act of 1965').

[36] See BMJ (ed.), *Bericht über die Verhandlungen der Unternehmensrechtskommission* (1980). This commission met from 1972 to 1980.

[37] See, eg, Herbert Wiedemann, *Gesellschaftsrecht*, vol I: Grundlagen (CH Beck 1980); Karsten Schmidt, *Gesellschaftsrecht* (1st edn, Heymanns 1986, 4th edn 2002).

eras into an authoritative canon of general doctrine.[38] Thematically, significant debates revolved around crisis-related company and enterprise law[39] and the law on shareholder contributions in lieu of equity investment.[40] In the second half of the 1990s, the duties and liability of members of executive and supervisory boards came into focus as favoured topics and were the subject of countless dissertations and habilitation monographs.

In the first decade of the new millennium, three major tasks awaited the quite populous Baby Boomer generation of company lawyers.[41] The German Corporate Governance Code of 2002 was an unmistakable signal that the time was ripe for broad discussions about corporate governance, focusing particularly on listed companies. At the same time, the relationship between company and capital market law commanded considerable attention, especially after the German Securities Acquisition and Takeover Act (WpÜG) came into force in 2002.[42] Finally, the realignment of the private international law of companies following decisions by the European Court of Justice became prominent in the interdisciplinary discourse between company law, private international law, and European law. As a ripple effect of this discourse, there was also a lively debate about reforming the statutory capital system for AGs and GmbHs.

It appears that the latest cohort of company law scholars, more than ever of whom are women,[43] will focus, in this era of ESG, primarily on elements of the sustainability debate as well as the implications of digitalization and artificial intelligence for company law.

2. *Eternal Issues*

In addition to debates that began and ended at some point, including any lead-up and follow-up to them,[44] some debates in company law, or in jurisprudence in

---

[38] For an appreciation of this enormously fruitful research program on 'institutional development', see Fleischer (n 23) 493f.

[39] See, eg, the topics of the 54th Association of German Jurists convention in 1982 (corporate restructuring) and of the 55th in 1984 (measures, particularly in company and capital market law, to improve the equity base of companies long-term).

[40] See a summary by Peter Hommelhoff, 'Das Gesellschafterdarlehen als Beispiel institutioneller Rechtsfortbildung' (1988) 17 ZGR 460.

[41] On the record number of 43 postdoctoral theses on company law between 2000 and 2009, see Fleischer (n 1) 197.

[42] See Fleischer, 'Das Aktiengesetz von 1965 und das neue Kapitalmarktrecht' [2006] ZIP 451 (on capital market law and the German Stock Corporation Act at 40); Katja Langenbucher, '50 Jahre Aktiengesetz – Aktienrecht und Kapitalmarktrecht' in Holger Fleischer and others (eds), 50 Jahre Aktiengesetz (De Gruyter 2016).

[43] On the low proportion of women and habilitation monographs by woman company law scholars, see Fleischer (n 1) 199 with further references.

[44] On sociological controversies, see Kneer and Moebius (n 14) 13.

general for that matter,[45] never die and can be traced throughout the history of the subject. One of these perennial issues is 'interest of the enterprise' ('Unternehmensinteresse' in German).[46] For more than a century, the concept of the corporate interest has been a vehicle for fleshing out problems both old and new, such as the enterprise-in-itself ('Unternehmen an sich') problem, the stakeholder versus shareholder debate, and corporate social responsibility. One may mock the concept as an 'egg of Columbus for lawyers'[47] or condemn it as an 'an ideology that obscures the true connections'[48]; nevertheless, it is a constant companion topic to discussions of stock corporation law.[49]

Ever since the advent of the BGB, the German Civil Code, another debate has persisted about the legal nature of the 'Gesamthand' or joint ownership. Since the legislature at the time did not think to establish a doctrinal foundation for this concept,[50] scholars throughout the twentieth century disputed joint ownership[51] in increasingly vehement terms.[52] In some combination of reverence and perplexi-

---

[45] See, eg, Wolfgang Loschelder, 'Religiöse Unterweisung als Merkmal kultureller Identität. Die Auseinandersetzung über Religionskunde und Religionsunterricht für Muslime in Deutschland 1970 bis heute' in Lothar Gall and Dietmar Willoweit (eds), *Judaism, Christianity, and Islam in the Course of History* (Oldenbourg 2011): 'In jurisprudence, there are "eternal topics" that can be discussed again and again – and profitably – in a professional context [...].'

[46] Similarly, Peter Hommelhoff, 'Das Unternehmensrecht vor den Herausforderungen der Globalisierung' in Uwe H Schneider and Peter Hommelhoff (eds), *Festschrift für Markus Lutter* (O Schmidt 2000) 103: 'marks a fundamental, century-long problem in the history of German stock corporation law'.

[47] Hans-Joachim Mertens, 'Der Aktionär als Wahrer des Rechts? – Aktuelle Probleme der Durchsetzung von Aktionärsrechten' [1990] AG 49, 54.

[48] Wolfgang Zöllner, 'Das Unternehmensinteresse – eine ideologische Leerformel?' AG 2003, 2, 8.

[49] See Fleischer (n 22) 704; see also Philip JS Fendt, 'Der Aufsichtsrat in der Mitverantwortung einer interessenpluralistischen. Formalzielbestimmung' [2017] AG 99: 'Please, not another debate about the "interest of the enterprise". After more than 40 years of abstract and tiresome theoretical debates about the supreme maxim of action for capital market-oriented stock corporations, these could truly be scaled back if recurring corporate turmoil and scandals did not keep reviving this topic.'

[50] See Protokolle, in Benno Mugdan (ed), *Die gesammten Materialien zum BGB für das Deutsche Reich*, vol II (1899) 900, according to which 'a statement on the scientific dispute about the nature of joint ownership should be avoided'.

[51] See Andreas Dieckmann, *Gesamthand und juristische Person* (Mohr Siebeck 2019); Alexander Wilhelm, *Das Recht der Gesamthand im 21. Jahrhundert* (Mohr Siebeck 2021).

[52] See, eg, Holger Altmeppen, 'Kritischer Zwischenruf zum „Mauracher Entwurf"' [2020] NZG 822; Wolfgang Zöllner, 'Rechtsfähigkeit der BGB-Gesellschaft – ein Sachverstands- oder Kommunikationsproblem?' in Günther Hönn (ed), *Festschrift für Alfons Kraft* (Luchterhand 1998) 701.

ty, they referred to joint ownership as an 'unknown creature',[53] an 'enigma',[54] a 'mystery play',[55] or even as an 'inscrutable *mysterium tremendum*'.[56]

Another topic in company law that simply will not rest is multiple-voting shares.[57] Section 252(1)(4) of the German Commercial Code of 1897 expressly permitted them as a separate class of shares; as protection against foreign ownership during the Weimar Republic, one-third of all listed stock corporations featured multiple-voting shares, sometimes with 500 times the voting rights of regular shares.[58] Section 12(2)(1) of the Stock Corporation Act of 1937 then generally abolished multiple-voting shares, but the statute's next sentence permitted the government's Minister for Economic Affairs to allow exceptions if the welfare of the company or macroeconomic interests so required.[59] The reforms enacted in the 1965 Stock Corporation Act stipulated, in s 5(1) of the former Stock Corporation Implementation Act (EGAktG) (now superseded), that multiple-voting rights created before the Stock Corporation Act took effect would continue to be valid. In 1998, the Bundestag passed an 'Act on Monitoring and Transparency of Enterprises' (known as the 'KonTraG'), after which s 12(2) of the Stock Corporation Act (now superseded) declared tersely that 'multiple voting rights are not permitted.' Recently the latest twist has now materialized in legislation called the 'Zukunftsfinanzierungsgesetz' (or the Act on financing investments in the future), which has allowed multiple-voting shares once again (see s 135a of the Stock Corporation Act) under certain conditions.[60]

---

[53] Peter Ulmer, 'Die Gesamthandsgesellschaft – ein noch immer unbekanntes Wesen?' (1998) 198 AcP 113.

[54] Karsten Schmidt, 'Erbteilsabtretung, Miterbenabfindung und Anwachsung bei der Erbengemeinschaft: Nachdenken über § 2033 BGB und die Struktur der Erbengemeinschaft' (2005) 205 AcP 305, 312.

[55] Heinrich Weber-Grellet, 'Die Gesamthand – ein Mysterienspiel?' (1982) 182 AcP 316.

[56] Alexander Schall, 'Zur Rechtsnatur der rechtsfähigen Personengesellschaft nach dem MoPeG – Abschied vom „guten alten Recht"?' in Burkhard Gehle, Heribert Hirte and Daniel Lochner (eds), *Festschrift für Thomas Heidel* (Nomos 2021) 155, 162.

[57] See Sebastian Mock and Jean Mohamed, 'Goodbye One Share One Vote? – Welcome Dual-Class Shares!' [2022] NZG 1275: 'Multiple voting rights shares are a phenomenon of stock corporation law that has been discussed repeatedly in German legal history for over 85 years.' See also Julia Nicolussi, 'Mehrstimmrechtsaktie: Renaissance auf europäischer und auf nationaler Ebene' (2022) 67 AG 753.

[58] See Sebastian Mock and Christoph Beckmann, '§ 13 Von der privaten zur staatlichen Aktiengesellschaft – die Satzung der Hamburger Hochbahn AG' in Fleischer and Mock (n 5) 651ff with further references (discussing the example of Hamburger Hochbahn AG, in which the City of Hamburg held a share with 48,900 votes).

[59] See Holger Fleischer, 'Die Siemens AG: Rechtliche Wegmarken von der Familien- zur Publikumsgesellschaft' (2019) 64 AG 481, 489 (examining the case of Siemens AG).

[60] BGBl 2023 I No. 354; see, eg, Tim Florstedt, 'Das Zukunftsfinanzierungsgesetz – Börsenmantelaktiengesellschaft und Mehrstimmrechtsaktie' [2024] NZG 139; Mock and Mohamed (n 57) ('Goodbye One Share One Vote? – Welcome Dual-Class Shares?'); see also Matthias Casper, 'Das Zukunftsfinanzierungsgesetz – Zwischen Griff in die historische Mottenkiste und behutsamer Fortentwicklung der Unternehmensfinanzierung' (2023) 187 ZHR 5, 17ff.

Predatory shareholders are a fourth phenomenon that at various times has occupied legislators, courts, and legal scholars. The topic may be traced all the way back to the legislative materials for the 1884 stock corporation law amendments, which state, presciently, that actions to set aside resolutions of the general meeting are a 'double-edged sword which opens the door to harassment and blackmail'.[61] Experienced practitioners at the beginning of the twentieth century, whether in-house, in private practice or on the bench, confirmed as much: *Julius Flechtheim* reported that actions to set aside in a very large number of cases were used to 'extort' stock corporations;[62] *Max Hachenburg* noted that it was an 'open secret' that actions to set aside 'are usually only brought to achieve other purposes';[63] and as *Albert Pinner* wrote, 'especially for professional representatives at annual general meetings, the trade stands them in good stead'.[64] Subsequent waves of abusive actions to set aside, from the 1980s to the present day, as well as the response of courts and legislature, are comprehensively documented.[65]

IV. The Beginning and End of the Debates

Both the beginning and end of a debate are particularly appealing subject matter for the insight they offer into the anatomy of academic controversies.

1. What Sparks Debate

Debates in company law are often sparked by a sensational court ruling. The *ARAG/Garmenbeck* case, decided by the German Federal Court of Justice (the BGH) in 1997,[66] sparked a debate about directors' and officers' liability that has not yet ebbed. The German Federal Constitutional Court's judgment in *DAT/Altana* judgment from 1999[67] prompted much introspection about the significance of share price in determining fair value in merger scenarios; the *Centros* ruling by the European Court of Justice (ECJ) in 1999[68] triggered unexpected rounds of debate on international company law.

[61] Begründung zu dem Entwurf eines Gesetzes, betreffend die KGaA und AG, 1884, reprinted in Werner Schubert and Peter Hommelhoff (eds), *Hundert Jahre modernes Aktienrecht* (De Gruyter 1985) 467.

[62] Julius Flechtheim, 'Das Urteil auf Ungültigkeitserklärung eines Generalversammlungsbeschlusses' in *Festschrift für Ernst Zitelmann* (Duncker & Humblot 1913) 5.

[63] Max Hachenburg, 'Aktiengesellschaft und Volkswirtschaft' [1918] JW 16, 17.

[64] Albert Pinner, 'Die stillen Reserven der Aktiengesellschaft' [1914] LZ 226, 229.

[65] See, eg, Walter Bayer, 'Fehlerhafte Beschlussfassung in Hauptversammlung, Aufsichtsrat und Vorstand' in Fleischer and others (n 42) 203ff; see also Dagmar Mathieu, *Der Kampf des Rechts gegen erpresserische Aktionäre: Bestandsaufnahme, Kritik und Perspektiven* (Peter Lang 2014).

[66] BGH 21 April 1997, II ZR 175/95, 135 BGHZ 244.

[67] BVerfG 27 April 1999, 1 BvR 1613/94, 100 BVerfGE 289.

[68] CJEU 9 March 1999, C-212/97 *Centros*, ECR 1999 I-1459, ECLI:EU:C:1999:126.

Occasionally the legislature has forged ahead and presented scholars as well as the courts with the task of putting loosely defined, cursory concepts, such as joint ownership or de facto groups of companies, on a firmer footing. The invention of the 'GmbH & Co. KG' type of business organization purely through draughtsmanship by corporate lawyers as well as other non-typical forms of organization has also fuelled specific debates, as has the mischief of locust investors.

While publications may often spark controversies in the field of history, they have only rarely done so in company law. *Walther Rathenau*'s short treatise *Vom Aktienwesen* (On stock companies) from 1917 comes to mind;[69] its author is considered to have single-handedly originated[70] the shareholder/stakeholder debate in Germany.[71] Then there are *Marcus Lutter*'s original but highly controversial theses on German group law, which were updated by his academic disciples but also met with fierce opposition from scholars as well as the bench.[72] More recently, *Peter Mülbert*'s highly regarded though not universally accepted plea for a more capital market-oriented formulation of shareholder rights in setting up or restructuring groups of companies comes to mind.[73]

2. When Debates Conclude

Conclusions of debates are just as interesting. General theoretical reflection about what it means to conclude a scientific discourse are rare.[74] A highly regarded article in the natural sciences distinguishes between three possible outcomes: the

---

[69] Walter Rathenau, *Vom Aktienwesen. Eine geschäftliche Betrachtung* (Fischer 1917); see, eg, Hachenburg (n 63) 16 (review) and *Richard Passow*, Weltwirtschaftliches Archiv 12 (1918) (review) 353; see also Holger Fleischer, 'Walther Rathenau: Vom Aktienwesen – Eine geschäftliche Betrachtung (1917)' [2017] JZ 991 (retrospective on the work's 100th anniversary).

[70] See Fleischer (n 22) 704: 'historical starting point and *locus classicus*'.

[71] Cf Martin Gelter, 'Taming or Protecting the Modern Corporation? Shareholder-Stakeholder Debates in a Comparative Light' (2011) 7 NYU JL & Bus 641, 683: 'often seen as a defining moment for the German debate (i.e. comparable to the role of the Berle-Dodd debate in the US)'; cf also Thilo Kuntz, 'German Corporate Law in the 20th Century' in Harvell Wells (ed), *Research Handbook on the History of Corporate and Company Law* (Edward Elgar 2018) 214: 'commonly considered as the seminal work'; Michael Jürgenmeyer, *Das Unternehmensinteresse* (Recht und Wirtschaft 1984) 51: 'The discussion about the "Unternehmensinteresse" began in the context of the discussion about the catchphrase "the enterprise as such". Before that, as far as can be seen, the term "corporate interests" was not in use.'

[72] For details on this and the Lutter school of company law, see Holger Fleischer and Elke Heinrich, 'Holzmüller – Ungeschriebene Hauptversammlungszuständigkeit' in Fleischer and Thiessen (n 4) 351f with further references.

[73] Peter O Mülbert, *Aktiengesellschaft, Unternehmensgruppe und Kapitalmarkt* (CH Beck 1995).

[74] See Peter Weingart, Wissenschaftssoziologie (Transcript 2003) 62ff (chapter on social factors in the closure of scientific discourses).

resolution of a problem, 'closure', and the abandonment of debate.[75] In company law, but also in law more generally, controversies can rarely be resolved in the fashion of Newton's *experimentum crucis* or by analysing the empirical evidence. The end of a debate in law is often more like a secular version of 'Roma locuta, causa finita' (*Abbé de Grécourt*),[76] in which the Federal Court of Justice stands in for the Pontiff. Sometimes, a landmark decision is followed closely by a codification of the rule.[77] A case in point is the century-long debate about the legal nature of joint ownership, which the Federal Court of Justice ended with its spectacular ruling on the legal capacity of civil-law partnerships vis-à-vis third parties in 2001.[78] Statutory reform has now arrived with the 'Act to modernize the law of partnerships' (called the *MoPeG*), which has introduced s 705(2) of the German Civil Code, and which has scrapped joint ownership.[79]

Not every academic controversy ends with a winner and a loser.[80] Sometimes the result is an unsatisfactory if temporary draw. Case in point is the heated debate about the benefits and drawbacks of statutory capital as an instrument for protecting creditors.[81] Triggered by criticism from the ECJ and its advocates general regarding the minimum capital requirement[82] and far-reaching proposals for reforming the EU Capital Directive,[83] scholars have expended a great deal of energy attempting to demonstrate the superiority of either the Continental or the English approach. Comparing entire creditor protection systems ('macrocompari-

---

[75] Cf Ernan McMullin, 'Scientific Controversy and its Termination' in H Tristram Engelhardt and Arthur L Caplan (eds), *Scientific Controversies: Case Studies in the Resolution and Closure of Disputes in Science and Technology* (CUP 1989) 49, 77ff.

[76] See Claus Leggewie and Elke Mühlleiter, *Die akademische Hintertreppe. Kleines Lexikon des wissenschaftlichen Kommunizierens* (Campus 2007) 163f ('Kontroversen').

[77] For details see Holger Fleischer and Frauke Wedemann, 'Kodifikation und Derogation von Richterrecht' (2009) 209 AcP 597.

[78] BGH 29 January 2001, II ZR 331/00, 146 BGHZ 341.

[79] See explanatory memorandum in BT-Drucks. 19/27635, 48; see also Holger Fleischer, 'Änderungen des KG-Rechts im Regierungsentwurf eines Gesetzes zur Modernisierung des Personengesellschaftsrechts' [2021] DStR 430, 435.

[80] See Kneer and Moebius (n 14) 9 (attribution of winner or loser status itself dependent on perspective and context).

[81] For details see Holger Fleischer, 'Grundfragen der ökonomischen Theorie im Gesellschafts- und Kapitalmarktrecht' (2001) 30 ZGR 1, 12ff with further references ('argumentative stalemate').

[82] See Advocate General La Pergola, *Centros* (n 68) para 21 (minimum capital in the *Centros* case as an 'idolum theatri'); Advocate General *Alber*, CJEU 30 September 2003, C-167/01 *Inspire Art*, ECR 2003 I-10155, ECLI:EU:C:2003:512, para 141 et seq (denying that minimum capital would protect creditors in *Inspire Art*).

[83] See Luca Enriques and Jonathan R Macey, 'Creditors Versus Capital Formation: The Case against the European Legal Capital Rules' (2001) 86 Cornell L Rev 1165; Jonathan Rickford, 'Reforming Capital: Report of the Interdisciplinary Group on Capital Maintenance' (2004) 15 EBLR 919.

son') like this continues to pose insurmountable difficulties.[84] It is therefore not surprising that a study commissioned by the European Commission did not reveal a clear preference from a cost perspective for either the existing or for any other capital protection system.[85]

Furthermore, some debates simply dead-end: they do not arrive at doctrinal innovation, nor suggest policy reforms, but rather result in negative findings. The epistemic gain is there, of course. The ambitious attempt to institutionalize unwritten barriers to the freedom of contract in company law is one example of such an outcome. For a while, this methodological approach was en vogue, inspiring three habilitation monographs alone in 1970[86] whose conclusions cast a wet blanket over the notion.[87] As a result of the 'disillusioning course'[88] of the discussion, the doctrine of 'statutory typology' has been abandoned.[89] It had long been 'obsolete'[90] anyway, when the Federal Court of Justice dealt it a final blow by recognizing the GmbH & Co. KGaA.[91] Thus – with a few exceptions – hybrid organi-

---

[84] For details see Holger Fleischer, in Lutz Michalski and others (eds), *Kommentar zum Gesetz betreffend die Gesellschaften mit beschränkter Haftung* (4th edn, CH Beck 2023) Syst. Darst. 5 para 82 et seq; Sergei A Davydenko and Julian R Franks, 'Do Bankruptcy Codes Matter? A Study of Defaults in France, Germany, and the U.K.' (2008) 63 Journal of Finance 565 (empirical comparison of insolvency law in France, England, and Germany).

[85] See KPMG, *Feasibility Study on an Alternative to the Capital Maintenance Regime Established by the Secondary Company Law Directive* (2008); Wienand Schruff and Georg Lanfermann, 'EU-Machbarkeitsstudie für ein alternatives Kapitalschutzsystem' [2008] WPg 1099.

[86] Manfred Nitschke, *Die körperschaftlich strukturierte Personengesellschaft* (Gieseking 1970); Arndt Teichmann, *Gestaltungsfreiheit in Gesellschaftsverträgen* (CH Beck 1970); Harm Peter Westermann, *Vertragsfreiheit und Typengesetzlichkeit im Recht der Personengesellschaften* (Springer 1970).

[87] See reviews by Konrad Duden, 'Grenzen der Vertragsfreiheit im Recht der Personengesellschaften. Eine Besprechung der Monographien von Teichmann, Huber, H. P. Westermann und Ott' (1973) 2 ZGR 360, Johann Georg Helm, 'Theorie und Sachanalyse im Recht „atypischer" Gesellschaften. Eine Besprechung der Habilitationsschriften von Immenga und Nitschke' (1973) 2 ZGR 478, and Hermann Schultze-von Lasaulx, 'Zur Frage der Gestaltungsfreiheit für Gesellschaftsverträge. Eine Bestandsaufnahme. Abschied von Illusionen' (1971) 21 ZfgG 327.

[88] K Schmidt (n 37) 119: 'desillusionierende[r] Verlauf'; similarly, the subtitle of the review by Schultze-von Lasaulx (n 87) 327: 'Farewell to Illusions'.

[89] For details see Felix Hey, *Freie Gestaltung in Gesellschaftsverträgen und ihre Schranken* (CH Beck 2004) 233ff; Herbert Wiedemann, *Gesellschaftsrecht*, vol II: Recht der Personengesellschaften (CH Beck 2004) 38f: 'The theory ultimately failed due to the vagueness of the concept of type; it also came too late for the precautionary practice that had already moved beyond it. People have resigned themselves to distinguishing between typical and atypical manifestations [...].'

[90] Helmut Andreas Graf, *Die Kapitalgesellschaft & Co. KG auf Aktien* (Müller 1993) 158: 'obsolet'.

[91] See BGH 24 February 1997, II ZB 11/96, 134 BGHZ 392.

zations and other atypical structures are not only allowed but are characteristic of German company law.[92]

Some major debates have ground to a halt when they lost their practical relevance. A prime example is the debate about the nature of corporate personhood. Long fought over 'with great acuity, ingenuity, and persuasiveness',[93] the debate gradually 'subsided' after the BGB took effect.[94] One leading legal historian is less guarded: 'the discussion about the nature of legal personhood in Germany ended at the beginning of the 20th century. It was not actually concluded; one could sooner say it was abandoned.'[95] One of the main reasons was that the German Civil Code itself clarified essential questions about corporate personhood, minimizing the need for theoretical discussion.[96] When the topic is broached in more recent scholarship, it has become like a 'compulsory exercise',[97] whereas the great theoretical debate is regarded as a 'child of the late 19th and early 20th centuries'.[98]

Ultimately, scholars sometimes cease to debate a topic because the hope to change legal policy appears futile. Co-determination is one such case. This stagnation also affects related areas of law and policy, because parity-based co-determination – as in *Dostoevsky*'s *Demons* – surfaces as the 'elephant in the room'.[99] Businesses are responding with evasive manoeuvres, such as by organizing as SEs and KGaAs, which are proliferating at record rates.[100]

---

[92] See Holger Fleischer, 'Ein kleiner Fremdenführer durch das deutsche Gesellschaftsrecht: Charakteristika – Besonderheiten – Eigenarten' in Thomas Ackermann und Johannes Köndgen (eds), *Privat- und Wirtschaftsrecht in Europa, Festschrift für Wulf-Henning Roth* (CH Beck 2015) 131: 'Finally, a characteristic feature of the range of corporate forms in Germany is that combinations of types and mixtures of basic types are very popular.'

[93] Marie Theres Fögen, '„Mehr Sein als Schein"? Anmerkungen zur juristischen Person in Theorie und Praxis' (1999) 95 SJZ 393: 'Gedankenschärfe, Konstruktionslust und Argumentationskraft'.

[94] Karl Larenz, *Allgemeiner Teil des deutschen Bürgerlichen Rechts* (7th edn, CH Beck 1989) 133.

[95] Helmut Coing, *Europäisches Privatrecht*, vol II (CH Beck 1989) 343.

[96] See, eg, Gottlieb Planck, *Kommentar zum BGB*, vol I (1913, reprint, 4th edn, De Gruyter 2020) § 21, p 55: 'Opinions on the nature and concept of a legal entity vary greatly. A closer examination of this controversial issue is not necessary for understanding the provisions of the BGB.'

[97] Werner Flume, *Die juristische Person* (Springer 1983) 24: 'Pflichtübung'.

[98] Wiedemann (n 37) 191.

[99] Christoph Teichmann, 'Mitbestimmungsschutz bei grenzüberschreitenden Umwandlungen – Zugleich ein Rückblick auf die Beratungen der „Informal Company Law Expert Group" (2014–2018)' in Stefan Grundmann and others (eds), *Festschrift für Klaus J. Hopt* (De Gruyter 2020).

[100] See Walter Bayer, Jan Lieder and Thomas Hoffmann, 'Bundesweite Rechtstatsachen zum Unternehmens- und Gesellschaftsrecht (Stand 1.1.2023)' [2023] GmbHR 709 para 18 (with numbers).

V. Course of Debates and Theory Formation

Competing views are developed into 'theories', or are at least referred to as such, in many debates on company law.[101] Typically there are two diametrically opposed theories: fiction versus real entity theory, unity versus separation theory, real seat versus incorporation theory. Occasionally, following a common pattern in legal theory,[102] a mediating view emerges. But company law is also subject to an old rule of thumb: 'At four theories per problem, legal discourse seems to reach a saturation point. More is rarely offered.'[103] An exception to this is piercing the corporate veil, on which different theories abound.[104] Most of these theories are doctrinal and take an internal perspective on company law.[105] It is hard to qualify piercing the veil as a major debate because none of them can be readily disproved.[106] Critical voices see irreconcilable differences between doctrinal theories and empirical theories,[107] while others entertain that there must be a specifically legal mode of verifying theories.[108] In (company) law, clarity regularly turns either on consensus or on a determination by a recognized authority,[109] namely through a supreme court ruling.[110]

VI. Key Points of Debate

In substance, major debates can also be categorized according to their subject matter and main thrust.[111]

---

[101] For details see Holger Fleischer, 'Rundgang durch die Landschaft gesellschaftsrechtlicher Theorien' [2023] NZG 243.

[102] For general information on the development of mediating theories, see Hans-Martin Pawlowski, *Methodenlehre für Juristen* (3rd edn, Müller 1999) para 764.

[103] Joachim Rückert, '„Große" Erzählungen, Theorien und Fesseln in der Rechtsgeschichte' in Tiziana J Chiusi, Thomas Gergen and Heike Jung (eds), *Festschrift für Elmar Wadle* (Duncker & Humblot 2008) 963, 964.

[104] See Georg Bitter, in Franz Scholz, *Kommentar zum GmbH-Gesetz* (13th edn, Otto Schmidt 2022) § 13 para 116: 'As an alternative, a large number of different piercing doctrines have been developed, which are difficult to classify because even the terminology is not uniform.'

[105] For details see IV.1.

[106] See Fleischer (n 101) 244f; Nils Jansen, 'Dogmatik, Erkenntnis und Theorie im europäischen Privatrecht' [2005] ZEuP 750, 769ff.

[107] Cf, eg, Klaus F Röhl and Hans Christian Röhl, Allgemeine Rechtslehre (3rd edn, Carl Heymanns 2008) 164.

[108] See Claus-Wilhelm Canaris, 'Funktion, Struktur und Falsifikation juristischer Theorien' [1993] JZ 377, 386f (suggesting 'legal falsificationism').

[109] See Jansen (n 106) 776.

[110] See the text around fn 76.

[111] For a striking contrast from the field of history, see Lutz Niethammer, 'Über Kontroversen in der Geschichtswissenschaft' (1989) 43 Merkur 73, 74ff (distinguishing 'legend killers', 'horizon shifts', and 'work on myths' as basic controversy types).

1. Doctrine

Doctrinal debates make up a large part of the discourse on company law. This should come as no surprise. Company law was a latecomer to the core civil law subjects that had Roman beginnings, and its doctrines had to mature. Theory here has to contend with a rapidly growing body of material in an effort to advance concepts and establish systems and principles.[112] Discussions about corporate personhood, joint ownership, groups of companies, and atypical organizational forms fall into this category.

2. Ethics

Debates about how better to protect individuals and minority shareholders are more oriented toward legal ethics than doctrine. In line with a broader trend toward substantive rather than formal considerations, which German refers to as 'materialization', in private law,[113] one may also speak of substantive issues cropping up in company law.[114] This is exemplified by long-standing debates on termination and severance clauses in partnership and GmbH law, which courts evaluate through the lenses of unconscionability or usury.[115] In stock corporation law, too, a broad body of literature has called for a 'breakthrough to responsibility ethics'[116] in the assessment of majority–minority conflicts, and the Federal Court of Justice has responded; both in the *Kali-und-Salz* judgment (on the substantive justification for the exclusion of subscription rights[117]) and in the *Linotype* and *Girmes* judgments on reciprocal duties of loyalty among shareholders,[118], the court has hybridized elements of legal ethics into its rulings. Some currents now

---

[112] See Holger Fleischer, 'Gesellschafts- und Kapitalmarktrecht als wissenschaftliche Disziplin – Das Proprium der Rechtswissenschaft' in Christoph Engel and Wolfgang Schön (eds), *Das Proprium der Rechtswissenschaft* (Mohr Siebeck 2007) 55ff.

[113] See, eg, Claus-Wilhelm Canaris, 'Wandlungen des Schuldvertragsrechts –Tendenzen zu seiner „Materialisierung"' (2000) 200 AcP 273 (the law of obligations); Marietta Auer, *Materialisierung, Flexibilisierung, Richterfreiheit* (Mohr Siebeck 2005).

[114] This terminology is used by Christine Windbichler, 'Gibt es ein „Sozialmodell" des Gesellschaftsrechts?' in Antje GI Tölle and others (eds), *Selbstbestimmung: Freiheit und Grenzen. Festschrift für Reinhard Singer* (Berliner Wissenschafts-Verlag 2021).

[115] See Klaus Ulrich Schmolke, *Grenzen der Selbstbindung im Privatrecht* (Mohr Siebeck 2014) 534ff, 557ff.

[116] Herbert Wiedemann, 'Rechtsethische Maßstäbe im Unternehmens- und Gesellschaftsrecht, Rektoratsrede' (1980) 9 ZGR 147, 155.

[117] BGH 13 March 1978, II ZR 142/76 *Kali und Salz*, 71 BGHZ 40; see Jan Lieder and Valentin Müller, '§ 8 – Kali und Salz AG – Kapitalerhöhung mit Bezugsrechtsausschluss' in Fleischer and Thiessen (n 4) 285, 293ff.

[118] BGH 1 February 1988, II ZR 75/87, 103 BGHZ 184; BGH 20 March 1995, II ZR 205/94 *Girmes*, 129 BGHZ 136; see Ulrich Schmolke, '§ 13 – Girmes. AG – Treuepflicht des Minderheitsaktionärs' in Fleischer and Thiessen (n 4) 435ff.

want to 'put company law on an ethical footing'[119] within the debates on corporate social responsibility, corporate purpose, and ESG.[120] Since 2017, the German Corporate Governance Code has even enshrined the model of the honourable businessperson in its preamble.[121]

3. Policy

Though its practitioners may like to tell themselves differently, company law goes beyond providing an objective framework for organizing businesses and instead – openly or not, consciously or not – regularly wades into legal policy debates.[122] Of course some debates are highly political. Co-determination is a prime example; its expansion and elaboration in the Co-Determination Act of 1976 precipitated a battle of expert opinions before the German Federal Constitutional Court. On one side was the 'Frankfurt Report' commissioned by the German government (*Kübler*, *Schmidt*, *Simitis*) and other reports commissioned by the states controlled by the SPD (*Zweigert*, *Kappler*); on the other side were the 'Cologne Report' commissioned by large stock corporations and the management lobby (*Badura*, *Rittner*, *Rüthers*).[123] Here was one of those rare legal controversies that play out in public; unlike for example the field of history,[124] company law is not normally a 'public science'. Another debate with major legal and economic policy implications revolved around depositary voting rights as a pillar of 'banking power' – a discussion that never completely died down after the 1965 stock corporation law reforms and came back in force over Deutsche Bank's role in the 1989 mega-merger of Daimler-Benz and the aerospace company MBB;[125] there was a public outcry and numerous legislative initiatives in the mid-1990s.

---

[119] Windbichler (n 114) 731: 'ethisch[e] Fundierung oder Überformung des Gesellschaftsrechts'.

[120] Jens Koch, *Aktiengesetz* (17th edn, CH Beck 2023) § 76 para 35ff (summary).

[121] See Holger Fleischer, 'Ehrbarer Kaufmann – Grundsätze der Geschäftsmoral – Reputationsmanagement: Zur „Moralisierung" des Vorstandsrechts und ihren Grenzen' [2017] DB 2015 (criticizing this).

[122] See Fleischer (n 15) 477; Ulrich Seibert, 'Politik und Gesellschaftsrecht – Gibt es vermehrt sozialpolitisch motivierte Eingriffe der Politik in das Gesellschaftsrecht und wenn ja, warum?' in Hans-Ueli Vogt, Holger Fleischer and Susanne Kalss (eds), *Protagonisten des Gesellschaftsrechts* (Mohr Siebeck 2020) 171.

[123] See BVerfG 1 March 1979, 1 BvR 532/77 and others, 50 BVerfGE 290, 303ff, 310ff.

[124] For details see Helmuth Trischler and Marc-Denis Weitze, 'Kontroversen zwischen Wissenschaft und Öffentlichkeit: Zum Stand der Diskussion' in Liebert and Weitze (n 8) 69ff (numerous examples).

[125] For details see Jessica Schmidt, 'Das Depotstimmrecht als Säule der „Bankenmacht" – 61. DJT (1996)' in Walter Bayer (ed), *Gesellschafts- und Kapitalmarktrecht in den Beratungen des Deutschen Juristentages* (Jenaer Wissenschaftliche Verlagsgesellschaft 2010) 496ff with further references.

VII. Debate Participants, Discussion Forums, and Discourse Culture

Company law debates are brought to life by their participants, who meet in the field's leading forums and cultivate a characteristic discourse culture.

1. Participants

In the German tradition of 'professorial law',[126] the premier scholars have always led the important debates. One need only recall the controversy surrounding the nature of corporate personhood, in which *Friedrich Carl von Savigny* and *Otto von Gierke*, two of the most famous law professors of all time, duked it out intellectually. The great *Werner Flume* animated the debate over joint ownership; his 'group theory' attracted enormous attention, and '[t]his was, of course, due to the aura of the author, whose confident style of argumentation still captivates readers today and made doubters appear small-minded'.[127] *Alfred Hueck* dominated company law from the late 1930s to the 1970s:

> 'In his sixth and seventh decades of life, without the slightest decline in his mental faculties, he is the undisputed master of [labor and company law], not only in the eyes of practitioners, but also of academics. Such a status is rarely achieved, even more rarely is it beyond doubt, and even more rarely is it uncontested.'[128]

Influence in the next generation was spread among half a dozen leading figures, and today, in part because there are so many more chairs in commercial and company law,[129] the gatekeepers are neither singular nor few. Today's field is multipolar.

At the practical level, the voice of the justices on the Second Civil Senate of the German Federal Court of Justice is even more important. They act as arbiters of victory in scholarly disputes. In academic circles, the justices who chair the panel have always been omnipresent as well as public figures[130] who are conscious of their great responsibility but who also exercise humility. Surely they all would have signed on to what *Justice Jackson* once remarked about the Supreme Court of the United States: 'We are not final because we are infallible, but we are infallible only because we are final'.[131] This shows when the Federal Court of Jus-

---

[126] See Raoul C Van Caenegem, *Judges, Legislators and Professors, Chapters in European Legal History* (CUP 1992) 67ff.

[127] Schall (n 56) 163.

[128] Zöllner (n 34) 17, 21.

[129] These figures are from Lilly Gerstorfer and Jan Thiessen, 'Unternehmensrechtliche Lehrstühle in der Berliner Republik' (2018) Max Planck Institute for European Legal History, Research Paper Series 2018/04.

[130] For details see Holger Fleischer, 'Gesellschaftsrechts-Honoratioren: Schlüsselfiguren im Gesellschaftsrecht und ihr diskursives Zusammenwirken' [2019] NZG 921, 923.

[131] *Brown v Allen* 344 US 443, 540 (1953).

tice reverses course, sometimes but not always when the composition of the panel changes.[132] Scholars' willingness to revise their own positions has tended to be less evident. In this respect, one is reminded of *Max Planck*'s bon mot in the natural sciences: 'A new scientific truth does not prevail when its opponents become convinced and acknowledge its merit, but rather as they gradually die off'.[133]

Practicing attorneys and notaries are still among the influential debaters. As skilled draftsmen and with their intimate knowledge of economic life, their contributions to company law have been significant. In legal policy, they make their voices heard primarily through the Commercial Law Committee of the German Bar Association, which has been providing commentary and proposing legislation in commercial, company, and capital market law since its founding in 1948.[134]

Participants from government have also been highly influential. The role of legislative aides in practice is 'hard to overestimate'[135] because of their enormous expertise and close connections with both interest groups and legal scholars.[136] The German Bundestag as the highest legislative body in cooperation with the Bundesrat is of course formally responsible for legislation in company law.[137]

2. Forums

The German Jurists' Conference (Deutscher Juristentag) has traditionally been one of the most important company law venues. For more than 160 years, it has frequently addressed issues relating to company and capital market law[138] to con-

---

[132] See Holger Fleischer, in Holger Fleischer and Wulf Goette (eds), *Münchener Kommentar zum Gesetz betreffend die Gesellschaften mit beschränkter Haftung* (5th edn, CH Beck 2025), Introduction, para 132ff; Frank Weber, *Anlässe und Methoden der Rechtsrückbildung im Gesellschaftsrecht* (Nomos 2003).

[133] Max Planck, *Wissenschaftliche Selbstbiographie* (Barth 1948) 22. For details see Martin Carrier, 'Erkenntnisziele, Beurteilungskriterien und epistemische Exzellenz' in Ulrich Arnswald and Hans-Peter Schütz (eds), *Rationalität und Irrationalität in den Wissenschaften* (VS 2011) 79ff.

[134] See Michael Hoffmann-Becking (ed), *Stellungnahmen des Handelsrechtsausschusses des DAV* (CH Beck 2016).

[135] *Hans-Joachim Mengel*, Gesetzgebung und Verfahren, 1997, p 288; Reinhard Zimmermann, 'Text und Kontext – Einführung in das Symposium über die Entstehung von Gesetzen in rechtsvergleichender Perspektive' (2014) 78 RabelsZ 315, 319.

[136] For more details, see Fleischer (n 132) 923.

[137] For more details, see Heribert Hirte, 'Wer „setzt das Recht" im Gesellschaftsrecht? Unabhängigkeitsfragen bei Stakeholdern im Gesetzgebungsprozess' in *Festschrift für Thomas Heidel* (n 56) 58ff.

[138] Overviews in Friedrich Kübler, 'Die fachliche Arbeit der Deutschen Juristentage und ihre Wirkungen auf dem Gebiet des Handels-, Gesellschafts- und Wirtschaftsrechts' in Felix Busse (ed), *Festschrift 150 Jahre Juristentag* (CH Beck 2010) (commercial, company, and economic law); Michael Hoffmann-Becking, 'Die fachliche Arbeit der Deutschen Juristentage und ihre Wirkungen auf dem Gebiet des Aktien-, Konzern- und Kapitalmarktrechts' in ibid (stock corporation, groups of companies, and capital market law).

siderable impact[139] on topics ranging from the end of the concession requirement for stock corporations (1869) to the standardization of German and Austrian GmbH law (1912, 1914), directors' and officers' liability reform (2014), and partnerships (2016). They have also addressed the restructuring of companies (1982), equity capital (1984), depositary voting rights of banks (1996), and on several occasions, groups of companies (1957, 1992) and investor protections in capital market law (1884, 1976, 2002). Their carefully prepared reports, in-depth presentations, and expert deliberations are particularly valuable to scholars.

Additional forums are the annual ZGR and ZHR symposia, whose significance is perhaps comparable to the meetings of the Association of Constitutional Law Teachers (the Staatsrechtslehrervereinigung),[140] with the important difference that members of the latter must have habilitated through a university, while the leading representatives of all the professions in the field of company law come together in the former. Another well-attended gathering is the annual conference of the Society for Company Law (Gesellschaftsrechtliche Vereinigung).

3. *Discourse Culture*

The 'German approach'[141] in company law is characterized by an elaborate discourse culture.[142] As early as 1969, the preeminent *Robert Fischer*, former panel chair and president of the German Federal Court of Justice, spoke of the 'unique and excellent interaction between contracts, legal scholarship, and jurisprudence'[143] in advancing company law. Other prominent scholars have issued similar appraisals.[144] There still has not been a detailed study of the 'règles de formation' (*Foucault*)[145] of a discourse. Any worth its salt would have to account not only for the epistemic but also to non-epistemic facts as formants of the debate.[146]

---

139 For a comprehensive overview, see Bayer (n 125) 6: 'The contributions thus convey, in fast motion over almost 150 years, a significant excerpt of the central legal policy issues in the field of German company and capital market law.'

140 See Helmuth Schulze-Fielitz, *Die Wissenschaftskultur der Staatsrechtslehre im Spiegel der Geschichte ihrer Vereinigung* (Mohr Siebeck 2022).

141 Based on Christoph Schönberger, *Der „German Approach". Die deutsche Staatsrechtslehre im Wissenschaftsvergleich* (Mohr Siebeck 2015).

142 See Fleischer (n 132) 924 (for details on the German discourse culture and the elements that promote it).

143 Robert Fischer, 'Zur Methode revisionsrichterlicher Rechtsprechung auf dem Gebiet des Gesellschaftsrechts' in Kurt Ballerstedt (ed), *Recht und Rechtsleben in der sozialen Demokratie. Festgabe für Otto Kunze* (Duncker & Humblot 1969).

144 See, eg, Wiedemann (n 89) 40: 'The discourse between supreme court jurisprudence and academic scholarship, which is constantly renewed in many symposia and conferences and is based on mutual respect, has been an integral part of German-speaking legal culture since the establishment of the Federal Supreme Court.' See also Mülbert (n 1) 291.

145 Michel Foucault, *L'archéologie du savoir* (Gallimard 1969) 53.

146 See McMullin (n 75) 60: 'Among the more obvious sorts of nonepistemic factors are personality traits (e.g., ambition, laziness, sensitivity to criticism, carelessness); institutional

Compared to the relentless harping of the so-called 'historians' dispute'[147] and other forms of trench warfare in the 'quarrelsome guild'[148] of historians, major debates in company law are markedly civilized, getting by without personal attacks and insults. When it does get harsh, it lingers; see *Lutter*'s tirade against the *Siemens/Nold* decision on 'authorized capital'[149] or *Flume*'s polemic against the notorious *Video* judgment on 'qualified' de facto groups.[150] One explanation for this relative harmony is probably that company lawyers tend to be homogeneous and share a set of fundamental convictions. This makes it even more important to allow outsiders into the discourse. Even in company law, there can be no progress unless fundamental assumptions are open to challenge.[151]

The spirit of 'Rhineland capitalism' (*modèle rhénan*)[152] continues to permeate the legal policy arena. This emphasizes class solidarity and consensus building among all participants in the company law discourse. One place this is most evident is in equal representation on major reform commissions such as the Enterprise Law Commission (1972–1980), the Government Commission on Corporate Governance (2000–2001), and the Biedenkopf Commission on the Modernization of German Corporate Co-determination (2005–2006).

VIII. Debates at the National and International Level

In terms of scope, some debates are limited to the German legal sphere, while others are also carried on abroad or are incipiently international.

---

pressures (loss of research funding, changing university needs); political influences (e.g., tipping a controversy in favor of the side with stronger political backing); hostility between scientists, directed along national lines; "chance" events (e.g., an unplanned meeting at a railroad station, a longtime friendship between two of the protagonists; the fact that someone trained at Cambridge rather than at Berkeley, death or illness of a major protagonist).'

147 See, eg, Klaus Große Kracht, 'Der Historikerstreit: Grabenkampf in der Geschichtskultur' in Große Kracht (n 10).

148 See the book title by Große Kracht (n 10): 'Die zankende Zunft'.

149 Marcus Lutter, 'Anmerkung zu BGH, Urteil v. 23.6.1997 – II ZR 132/93' [1998] JZ 50, 53: 'This ruling is a tragedy. […] Truly, this ruling is a tragedy.'

150 Werner Flume, 'Das Video-Urteil und das GmbH-Recht' [1992] DB 25, 27: '"evident breach of GmbH law" in "disregard of Art 20 (3) GG"'; Werner Flume, 'Das Video-Urteil als Entscheidung des II. Senats des BGH aus dessen Selbstverständnis der Innehabung gesetzgeberischer Gewalt' [1992] ZIP 817, 818 (details on unconstitutionality of the *Video* ruling); cf Herbert Wiedemann, 'Entwicklungen im Kapitalgesellschaftsrecht' [1993] DB 141, 151: 'One may fear being ignored if one does not describe a scandal or at least point to a breach of the constitution.'

151 See, in general, Karl R Popper, *Conjectures and Refutations: The Growth of Scientific Knowledge* (Routledge and Paul 1963) 316.

152 Michel Albert, *Kapitalismus contra Kapitalismus* (Campus 1992) 25 (on the term).

1. National Idiosyncrasies

Comparative lawyers know that every jurisdiction has its own peculiarities, idiosyncrasies, and path dependencies that astonish and amaze outsiders.[153] In partnership law, the notion that joint ownership is a 'construction of German philology'[154] is one of these. There were significant obstacles to its acceptance in other legal systems. These ranged from the terminological (because the German word, 'Gesamthand', is difficult to translate) to the substantive (because the drafters of the German Civil Code only vaguely defined it).[155] Thus little attention has been paid outside Germany to the fundamental debate about the 'nature' of joint ownership in Germany. Depending on their temperament, the few interested scholars could be dismissive or diplomatic. In his theory of corporate personhood, *Francesco Ferrara*, famous law professor from Pisa, ridiculed the lack of abstraction in German law, which he said had sealed itself off from the idea that an entity could be independent of its shareholders.[156] The great French jurist *Raymond Saleilles* noted that the concept of joint ownership was unknown in domestic business transactions and customs, and the fact that partnerships were classified as legal entities on the other side of the Rhine did not render it necessary.[157] Other introverted debates in German partnership law revolve around the 'Publikums-KG', a product of transactional drafting brought on by tax law,[158] as well as the GmbH & Co. KG, which is permissible *de jure* in most foreign legal orders but has nowhere been accepted as a local type.[159]

A defining element of stock corporation law is strict adherence to the articles of association pursuant to s 23(5) of the German Stock Corporation Act. This rigid legal framework applies equally to listed and unlisted companies and has been compared to an 'iron vice'.[160] No other jurisdiction even comes close to Ger-

---

[153] See Fleischer (n 92) 125 (short guide to German company law); Holger Fleischer, 'Der Zoo der Gesellschaftsformen in Deutschland' [2023] ZIP 1505 (on the 'zoo of corporate forms in Germany'); Michael J Ulmer, *Harmonisierungsschranken des Aktienrechts* (Winter 1998) (specifically about stock corporation law, identifying the dual board system (17ff), co-determination (52ff), and seat theory in international company law (84ff) as rooted in German legal culture).

[154] Ulrike Seif, 'Die Gesamthand als Konstruktion der Germanistik' (2001) 118 ZRG (GA) 302: 'Konstruktion der Germanistik'.

[155] See Holger Fleischer, 'Idiosynkrasien im deutschen Personengesellschaftsrecht: Allmähliche Erosion oder erfolgreiche Exportartikel?' [2020] NZG 601, 602f.

[156] See Francesco Ferrara, *Teoria delle persone giuridiche* (2nd edn, E Marghieri 1923) 45.

[157] See Raymond Saleilles, *De la personnalité juridique* (2nd edn, Rosseau & Co 1922) 177 et seq.

[158] See Fleischer (n 155) 607f (limited response abroad).

[159] See Holger Fleischer and Till Wansleben, 'Die GmbH & Co. KG in den Auslandsrechten – Zirkulation eines gesellschaftsrechtlichen Regelungsmodells' [2017] GmbHR 633, 634ff (comparative law analysis).

[160] Hans-Joachim Mertens, 'Satzungs- und Organisationsautonomie im Aktien- und Konzernrecht' (1994) 23 ZGR 426: ('eiserne Klammer').

many in terms of this strictness of the articles of association,[161] and so the recurring debate in Germany about the freedom of contract, at least for close stock corporations,[162] has no analogue abroad. The debate about abusive actions to set aside shareholder resolutions has also remained a purely domestic issue. This does not come as a surprise, since the importance of the Continental concept of defective shareholder resolutions is often overlooked in the Anglo-American discourse,[163] and so far our neighbours have been spared the plague of predatory shareholders.[164] The strongly path-dependent[165] system of parity-based co-determination is also unique, meaning that the discussion in Germany has resonated little elsewhere. It has happened, as recently in *Elizabeth Warren*'s Accountable Capitalism Act and *Bernie Sanders*' Corporate Accountability and Democracy Plan, but in those cases the legal, social, and institutional differences between Germany and the United States were misunderstood.[166]

Other specifically German debates have revolved around the 'secondary purpose privilege'[167] in non-profits and the rules for shareholder contributions in lieu of equity[168] in GmbHs. However, Austria has since 2003 had its own Equity Replacement Act, and case law from the US has provided helpful tests for distinguishing between equity and debt.[169]

---

161 See Holger Fleischer, 'Der Einfluß der Societas Europaea auf die Dogmatik des deutschen Gesellschaftsrechts' (2004) 204 AcP 502, 517: 'From comparative law, we know that the rigid strictness of s 23(5) of the Stock Corporation Act, though it may stand alone internationally, is certainly not outstanding.'

162 See, eg, Gerald Spindler, 'Regeln für börsennotierte vs. Regeln für geschlossene Gesellschaften – Vollendung des Begonnenen?' [2008] AG 598, 600ff; see also Susanne Kalss and Holger Fleischer, 'Neues zur Lockerung der Satzungsstrenge bei nicht börsennotierten Aktiengesellschaften: ein Grundsatzbeschluss des österreichischen OGH und seine Implikationen für das deutsche Recht' [2013] AG 693, 699ff (after an Austrian Supreme Court ruling on unlisted companies); Bayer, *Gutachten E zum 67. Deutschen Juristentag 2008*.

163 For details see Holger Fleischer, 'Reformperspektiven des aktienrechtlichen Beschlussmängelrechts im Lichte der Rechtsvergleichung' [2012] AG 765, 768ff; Martin Gelter, 'Why Do Shareholder Derivative Suits Remain Rare in Continental Europe?' (2012) 37 Brooklyn J Int L 843.

164 See Fleischer (n 163) 779 (calling it 'a German disease').

165 See BVerfG 1 March 1979, 1 BvR 532/77 and others, 50 BVerfGE 290, 294 (on co-determination originating early in industrialization and being anchored in the Weimar Constitution) (with further references).

166 For details see Jens Dammann and Horst Eidenmüller, 'Codetermination: A Poor Fit for U.S. Corporations' (2020) 3 Colum Bus L Rev 870.

167 See, eg, Lars Leuschner, in Claudia Schubert (ed), *Münchener Kommentar zum Bürgerlichen Gesetzbuch* (9th edn, CH Beck 2021) § 22 para 51 et seq.

168 See, for example, Bitter (n 104), Appendix § 64 GmbHG para 1 et seq.

169 For details see Holger Fleischer, *Finanzplankredite und Eigenkapitalersatz im Gesellschaftsrecht* (Heymann 1993) 117 et seq.

2. Transnational Legal Discussions

Other debates have had a transnational dimension from an early stage. A prime example was the theoretical dispute over the nature of corporate personhood.[170] Picked up by foreign students in Berlin, Bonn, and Heidelberg, fiction theory and real entity theory gained a foothold not only in France and Italy but also in England and the United States in the late 19th and early 20th centuries,[171] where they were eagerly consumed.[172] The mediators of real entity theory in England were *Frederic Maitland*, the most important legal historian of his time, who had translated parts of *Gierke*'s theory of cooperation,[173] and German-born *Ernst Freund* in the United States, who became a professor at the University of Chicago Law School.[174]

Decades later, the German debate on statutory typology in company law had been taken up primarily by Romanic legal scholars. The text and footnotes of major monographs such as *La tipicità delle società* by *Paolo Spada* (1974)[175] and *La atipicidad en derecho de sociedades* by *Luis Fernández de la Gándara* (1977),[176] are full of the names and arguments of the German theorists.

In this millennium, a pan-European debate has erupted over the effectiveness of Continental-style capital protection. It was celebrated in Germany as a monumental 'cultural achievement of the first order' in company law,[177] while others (particularly in England) called for its overthrow.[178] Capital protection was enacted throughout the EU in 1976 in the Second Directive on stock corporations. A report published by an interdisciplinary research group led by *Jonathan Rickford* in 2004 on reforming the capital maintenance regime in the European Union caus-

---

170 See Ron Harris, 'The Transplantation of the Legal Discourse on Corporate Personality Theories: From German Codification to British Political Pluralism and American Big Business' (2006) 63 Wash & Lee L Rev 1421, 1425: 'It was rare for legal discourse in that era to have such a dimension.'

171 For details see Fleischer (n 6) 20ff.

172 See Morton J Horwitz, 'Santa Clara Revisited: The Development of Corporate Theory' (1985) 88 W Va L Rev 173, 217: 'Beginning in the 1890s and reaching a high point around 1920, there is a virtual obsession in the legal literature with the question of legal personality.'

173 Otto von Gierke, *Political Theories of the Middle Age* (CUP 1900), translated with an introduction by Frederic W Maitland.

174 Ernst Freund, *The Legal Nature of Corporations* (University of Chicago Press 1897); see also Horwitz (n 172) 218: 'Influenced by the work of Gierke on the nature of the corporation, Freund sought to translate Gierke's Hegelian analysis for a practical-minded and anti-metaphysical American Bar.'

175 Paolo Spada, *La tipicità delle società* (Cedam 1974).

176 Luis Fernández de la Gandara, *La atipicidad en derecho de sociedades* (Pórtico 1977).

177 Wiedemann (n 37) 588.

178 Markus Lutter, *Sicherung der Kapitalaufbringung und Kapitalerhaltung in den Aktien- und GmbH-Rechten der EWG* (Müller 1964); see Holger Fleischer, 'Kapital, Sicherung der Kapitalaufbringung und Kapitalerhaltung in den Aktien- und GmbH-Rechten der Europäischen Union' [2020] ZIP 2478 (review of).

ed a particular furore.[179] It concluded that the fixed capital system was expensive and superfluous, and the British government heeded its call for the abolition of the Second Directive and began lobbying the European Commission. The response from Germany was quick. A working group called 'Capital in Europe' set up by *Marcus Lutter* presented a nearly 800-page edited volume in German and English.[180] Its core message was that abolishing fixed capital would be imprudent until alternative instruments had been reliably tested.[181]

An international debate has been alive for more than a century about the best connecting factor in the private international law of companies. Two theories, real seat theory (*Sitztheorie, théorie du siège réel*) and incorporation theory (*Gründungstheorie, théorie du siège statutaire*), are in contention almost everywhere. These were not conceived in Germany; incorporation theory was born in 18th-century England, whereas real seat theory emerged in France[182] and Belgium[183] in the late 19th century. In the wake of the *Centros* decision by the ECJ, German courts saw no other choice but to abandon their long adherence to real seat theory[184] in favour of incorporation theory for companies falling within the scope of the freedom of establishment.[185]

German debates too have been significantly influenced from abroad, particularly by Anglo-American 'legal transplants'.[186] One of the best-known from the United States is piercing the corporate veil, which entered German discourse in the early post-war period through a few highly regarded treatises.[187] Since the late 1990s, the courts[188] and the Bundestag[189] have established a business judgment rule based on the US model, steering the German debate on directors' and officers' liability. The German Corporate Governance Code, the subject of a lively debate

---

[179] Jonathan Rickford (ed), 'Reforming Capital, Report of the Interdisciplinary Group on Capital Maintenance' (2004) 15 EBLR 919.

[180] Markus Lutter (ed), *Das Kapital der Aktiengesellschaft in Europa* (De Gruyter 2006).

[181] Markus Lutter, 'Das (feste Grund-)Kapital der Aktiengesellschaft in Europa – Zusammenfassung der Überlegungen des Arbeitskreises „Kapital in Europa"' in Lutter (n 180) 2, 6.

[182] See French Court of Cassation, Civil Chamber 20 June 1870, S 1870 I, 373.

[183] See Articles 128 and 129 of the Belgian Commercial Companies Act of 1873.

[184] RG 29 November 1904 – Rep. VII 192/04, JW 1904, 231.

[185] BGH 13 March 2003, VII ZR 370/98, 154 BGHZ 185; but see BGH 27 October 2008, II ZR 158/06, 178 BGHZ 192 (retention of seat theory for companies from outside the EU).

[186] For details see Holger Fleischer, 'Legal Transplants im deutschen Aktienrecht' [2004] NZG 1129; Jan von Hein, *Die Rezeption US-amerikanischen Gesellschaftsrechts in Deutschland* (Mohr Siebeck 2008).

[187] See, eg, Ulrich Drobnig, *Haftungsdurchgriff bei Kapitalgesellschaften* (Metzner 1959) and Rolf Serick, *Rechtsform und Realität juristischer Personen* (Mohr Siebeck 1955) (both written at the Max Planck Institute for Comparative and International Private Law).

[188] See BGH 21 April 1997, II ZR 175/95, 135 BGHZ 244; Klaus J Hopt, 'Die Haftung von Vorstand und Aufsichtsrat – Zugleich ein Beitrag zur corporate governance-Debatte' in Ulrich Immenga (ed), *Festschrift für Ernst-Joachim Mestmäcker* (Nomos 1996) (preparatory work).

[189] BGBl 2005, I-2802; see Holger Fleischer, 'Das Gesetz zur Unternehmensintegrität und Modernisierung des Anfechtungsrechts' [2005] NJW 3525, 3527f.

since its introduction in 2002, is based on the British Cadbury Code of 1992 (now the UK Corporate Governance Code (2010)), with its 'comply or explain' mechanism.[190]

Comparison between the monistic or administrative board model and German stock corporation law's dualistic organizational model remains an ubiquitous topic in corporate governance[191] and was given new impetus by the 2001 Statute of the European Company.[192] Its greatest innovation is probably that it leaves it up to whoever drafts the bylaws.[193] But the debate in Germany and elsewhere has lost momentum: The main arguments have been stated, and people broadly agree that neither model is *a priori* superior.[194] Instead, convergence is everywhere: The monistic model has adopted a functional separation between executive and non-executive directors, and it is regarded as advisable that the CEO and the chairman of the board should not be the same person. The dualistic model is trying to better coordinate between management and supervisory board.[195]

Finally, academic debates everywhere have been sparked by the purpose of the corporation: *Rathenau* versus *Haussmann* in the Weimar Republic, *Berle* versus *Dodd* during the Great Depression in the United States, *Schluep* versus *Bär* in Switzerland in the 1950s.[196] The international as well as interdisciplinary debate on corporate purpose and ESG orientation is a continuation of this classic debate under a new label.[197] *Plus ça change, plus c'est la même chose.*[198]

---

[190] Jens Koch, '20 Jahre Deutscher Corporate Governance Kodex — Missverständnisse auf hohem Niveau' [2022] AG 1 (20th anniversary of the code); Klaus J Hopt and Patrick C Leyens, 'Der Deutsche Corporate Governance Kodex 2020' (2019) 48 ZGR 929 (for details).

[191] See Klaus J Hopt and Patrick C Leyens, 'Board Models in Europe – Recent Developments of Internal Corporate Governance Structures in Germany, the United Kingdom, France, and Italy' [2004] ECFR 135; Klaus J Hopt and Patrick C Leyens, 'The Structure of the Board of Directors: Boards and Governance Strategies in the US, the UK and Germany' in Afra Afsharipour and Martin Gelter (eds), *Comparative Corporate Governance* (Edward Elgar 2021).

[192] For details see Fleischer (n 161) 521ff.

[193] See Fleischer (n 161) 528 (for an open-choice principle *de lege ferenda* in stock corporation law); Koch (n 120) § 76 AktG para 4 (caution).

[194] See Fleischer (n 161) 527; Patrick C Leyens, 'Deutscher Aufsichtsrat und U.S.-Board: ein- oder zweistufiges Verwaltungssystem? Zum Stand der rechtsvergleichenden Corporate Governance-Debatte' (2003) 67 RabelsZ 57, 96; Christoph Teichmann, 'Corporate Governance in Europa' (2001) 30 ZGR 645, 675.

[195] See Fleischer (n 161) 527f; Klaus J Hopt, 'Der Aufsichtsrat' (2019) 48 ZGR 507, 517ff.

[196] For details see Holger Fleischer, 'Shareholders vs. Stakeholders: Aktienrechtliche Fragen' in Peter Hommelhoff, Klaus J Hopt and Axel von Werder (eds), *Handbuch Corporate Governance* (2nd edn, Schäffer-Poeschel 2009) 206 et seq (further references).

[197] See, eg, Holger Fleischer, 'Corporate Purpose: A Management Concept and its Implications for Company Law' [2021] ECFR 161.

[198] Alphonse Karr, *Les Guêpes* (1848) vi.

IX. Conclusion

Major debates are centres of gravity in company law, having contributed significantly to its development and continuing to do so. But they are largely uncharted territory as a topic in themselves. This contribution has been an introduction to an upcoming series of individual studies that should help identify prototypical characteristics of company law disputes, their substantive and methodological focal points, and their discursive dynamics. These studies will also explore how knowledge has and continues to accumulate in company law, how the field is changing, and which ideas, concepts, and theories are part of its intellectual traditions.

Artificial Intelligence, Legal Personality and Corporate Governance

Marco Cian and Claudia Sandei[*]

I. Digital Technology and Company Law: Some Inceptive Issues and Insights

The use of digital tools in a company's procedures has been well established for many years. Examples in Italy include the regulation of e-voting in general meetings in 2010 and publication of the notice of call on the company's website; for at least fifteen years, it has been mandatory to digitally transmit communications between intermediaries and issuers concerning shareholders rights. What artificial intelligence changes in this regard is that technology is no longer simply a labour-saving technique at the service of humans, but in the case of AI actually replaces humans and what they do.

These events were in some ways envisaged in dystopian literature: seventy years ago, the American novelist *Kurt Vonnegut* imagined a society where machines not only replaced humans at all manual work but were also ready to take their place in every intellectual occupation. In the same year, another well-known novelist, *Jack Williamson*, depicted a world governed by robots that took care of political, economic and social matters, whilst humans devoted themselves to chess and philosophy.

[*] This paper reflects the shared views of Marco Cian and Claudia Sandei. It should nonetheless be noted that Section I was authored exclusively by *Marco Cian*, while the remaining sections were written by *Claudia Sandei*.

Fortunately, we don't live in such a world (yet). However, the substitution of AI applications for human activities in running a business and consequently in the government and control of a company is not a matter for science fiction writers but a topic for legal scholars and practitioners.

A necessary caveat at this stage is that the concept of artificial intelligence used in this paper could be judged by an IT specialist as non-technical. For instance, we will include under 'AI' some digital tools that specialists working in that field may classify differently. This being said, such inaccuracy has no impact from a legal point of view. First, it is necessary to make clear where and how AI can be employed in the company's internal procedures.

All the company's bodies are involved.

As far as the general meeting is concerned, a digital tool could hypothetically have different roles: it could be assigned service tasks, operate as a member of the company or as an advisor to or representative of a member, or have decisional powers in regard to the meeting instead of the company's members. The first hypothesis we could refer to as the AI clerk, to the second as the AI attendee, and to the third as vicarious AI.

As regards the board of directors, we can more or less replicate the same situations: AI could cooperate with the directors on secretarial services (drafting minutes, for instance) or could have a role in analysing data and working out proposals as an advisor. We should also consider the hypothesis of AI acting as a director (maybe an independent director) within the board or running the company's business instead of a board of human beings (as a sole manager or member of a board solely composed of AIs).

The same roles could be assigned to a software with audit functions.

Obviously, instead of every imaginable use of AI having to be consistent with the legal framework of corporate governance, AI should be seen in the context of the key rules of company law. However, it seems incorrect to proceed in this assessment from the basic legal concepts as they are traditionally intended. For example, the impossibility of categorising AI as a representative does not entail that a shareholder should not be allowed to entitle it (AI) to attend the general meeting on his/her behalf (art 2372 of the Italian civil code, 'CC'). The interpretation of the law in an evolutive perspective requires proceeding in reverse order, ie, the legal concept should be adapted to the modern tool offered by technical development, and the suitability of this tool to the law should not depend on any previous, ante-digital meaning the law might have had.

The extent and impact of AI's involvement with company law in corporate governance has therefore to be considered from three different points of view.

A first aspect concerns the subjective element of the corporate bodies: the members of the general meeting and boards are individuals or legal entities; can AI be a member too?

The second aspect is related to the role covered by the members of all bodies: the shareholders' right to attend the general meeting, the director's duty to manage the company and the auditor's duty to check the management's conduct are aimed to fulfil specific purposes (*ie*, each role pursues specific economic interests); can AI satisfy this condition?

Finally, the third aspect is a matter of the rules established for membership in the different bodies: for example, the directors of a bank or a financial intermediary must declare that they have sufficient professional experience in the relevant field of business; how can AI fulfil these requirements?

These questions raise jointly varying issues.

First of all, membership in a corporate body is affected by the problem of legal personality. Nevertheless, the question requires different approaches, depending on the corporate body implied.

As regards the general meeting, legal persons are entitled to membership in the company: shareholders may be individuals or legal entities. Therefore, it is only possible to have AI attend a meeting as a member of the company if we can classify AI as a legal entity subject to certain conditions. The issue does not depend on the rules concerning corporate governance. Indeed, it goes beyond company law.

For that same reason, to have an AI substitute for the general meeting appears inconsistent with the general meeting's function within the corporate governance structure as well as with the economic interest underlying its powers. Indeed, the general meeting expresses the interests of the investors and company's owners; for that reason, any decision taken by a different body (or by a digital application such as an AI) conflicts with the view of shareholders as the company's owners. Therefore, the hypothesis we termed 'vicarious AI' lies outside the possible uses of such a digital tool in a corporation.

Every other role is characterized simply by a service function, namely directors managing the company, auditors checking the management, representatives acting on behalf of the members, notaries certifying the corporate decisions and so on. This enables us to ask whether these 'ancillary' services can be performed by software just as well as by persons.

The discussion requires an examination of the rules of each function, which are significant in at least two aspects.

First, many rules restrict assigning a certain role in the company's procedures to an AI because the affected role can only be performed by an individual, ie, the rules impose a subjective condition. For example, with regard not only to extraordinary general meetings but also to certain decisions by the directors, a notary is required to draft the minutes (CC, art 2375), and according to current law an AI cannot fulfil the requirement. The same hurdle concerns all the personal requirements for directors and particularly for auditors: an AI can only fulfil requirements consisting in the absence of personal relationships (eg, in an auditor not having family ties with the directors: CC, art 2399); it cannot satisfy the rule as regards professional experience or the qualifications required to practice a certain profession (for instance, professorship).

A second group of rules is based on the mandatory nature and on the consequent responsibility connected with the position of a board member. A director or auditor is a legal person while an AI is a digital process. What does this imply? When an AI is used to support the management or audit function in an advisory role, it raises a simple problem concerning the due diligence required of managers and auditors: does their reliance on AI release them from liability? On the contrary, when the direct assignment of a directing or auditing role to an AI is hypothesised, then no legal relationship would be established with the company and no one would be liable for mismanagement or inadequate audit activities, a situation that would not be in accordance with the legal principles on corporate governance.

In conclusion, the obstacles emerging from the hypothetical use of AI relate to its participation as a board member or its hypothetical activity in place of a company's board: in short, they relate to the substitution of an AI for a corporate body or a member of one. In fact, corporate law is entirely conceived with reference to the personality of the membership of all bodies of the corporation while artificial intelligence is a digital process. However, AI's role in simply supporting the members of the general meeting or the board of directors or the auditors poses very different issues.

Obviously, our comments here are related to current company law in Italy. A future reform of the law may modernise this system of law in order to extend the permissible scope of application of artificial intelligence in corporate procedures. For instance, an AI satisfying certain conditions in the field of software development or of functionality may be considered equivalent to the professional multi-annual experience expected of directors of companies acting as intermediaries in financial markets. Similarly, a reform could shift director liability to the AI developer or its licensor.

II. The Rise of AI. Digitalization *vs* Automation – AI as a Disruptive Technology

It is beyond doubt that digital technologies hold great promise for improving corporate governance.[1] It is therefore not a surprise that within the last decade, at the European level, we have witnessed ambitious digitalization legislative initiatives.

The first and most remarkable is Directive 2007/36/EC (Shareholder Rights Directive – SRD)[2], as amended by Directive (EU) 2017/828 as regards the en-

[1] For the purpose of this article, we define corporate governance as 'the system by which companies are directed and controlled [...] as the composite of ownership, boards, incentives, company law, and other mechanisms' (Cadbury Report on Financial Aspects of Corporate Governance in the UK, 1992, 15).

[2] Directive 2007/36/EC of the European Parliament and of the Council of 11 July 2007 on the exercise of certain rights of shareholders in listed companies [2007] OJ L184/17.

couragement of long-term shareholder engagement (Shareholder Rights Directive 2 – SRD2)[3], and the Commission Implementing Regulation (EU) 2018/1212[4]. The Directive provides guidance on a range of shareholder rights issues including electronic voting.

In this regards, art 8 of the SRD stipulates in para 1 that 'Member States shall permit companies to offer to their shareholders any form of participation in the general meeting by electronic means […]'. It also establishes in para 2 that

> '[t]he use of electronic means […] may be made subject only to such requirements and constraints as are necessary to ensure the identification of shareholders and the security of the electronic communication, and only to the extent that they are proportionate to achieving those objectives'.

Thus the SRD recognizes the importance of electronic voting as a means of enhancing shareholder participation and improving corporate governance.

Again, recital 4 of the Commission Implementing Regulation (EU) 2018/1212 underlines that

> '[i]n order to facilitate the exercise of shareholders rights and make it more efficient, particularly across borders, the use of modern technologies in communication between issuers and their shareholders and by intermediaries, including other service providers which are deployed for these processes, should be encouraged. Any communication between intermediaries should, to the extent possible be transmitted using machine-readable and standardised formats which are interoperable between operators and which allow straight-through processing […]'.

Despite the emphasis on virtual tools, it is worth noticing that the SRD *i)* concerns only 'listed companies', meaning companies whose shares are admitted to trading on a regulated market; *ii)* merely provides companies the option of allowing electronic shareholder participation without establishing a shareholder right to individually require the company to allow them to participate electronically in a general meeting if this kind of participation is not envisaged by the company itself (eg, in its articles of association or bylaws) or in national law (eg, national legislation adopted during or after the pandemic); *iii)* does not explicitly mention (allow) purely virtual general meetings.

Nevertheless, it cannot be disregarded that the EU is still working to adapt EU company law to continuing digital developments.[5]

---

[3] Directive (EU) 2017/828 of the European Parliament and of the Council of 17 May 2017 amending Directive 2007/36/EC as regards the encouragement of long-term shareholder engagement [2017] OJ L132/1.

[4] Commission Implementing Regulation (EU) 2018/1212 of 3 September 2018 laying down minimum requirements implementing the provisions of Directive 2007/36/EC of the European Parliament and of the Council as regards shareholder identification, the transmission of information and the facilitation of the exercise of shareholders rights [2018] OJ L223/1.

[5] A general overview of the activities in this field is provided at <https://commission.europa.eu/business-economy-euro/doing-business-eu/company-law-and-corporate-governance_en>.

First, in 2019, as a part of the 'EU Company Law Package', the Digitalization Directive[6] adopted common rules on the use of digital tools and processes in company law (eg, online formation of companies and registration of branches).

Second, in 2021, the European Commission launched the new company law initiative called 'Upgrading digital company law'[7], followed shortly by a public consultation[8]. The initiative, which recently resulted in a proposal for a new directive[9], aims at assessing four highlighted areas of concern: enhancing the transparency of company data through national business registers and via the Business Registers Interconnection System (BRIS) across the Single Market; removing barriers to and difficulties in the use of the company information available from business registers in cross-border administrative or judicial procedures; expanding, via BRIS, the application of the once-only principle to permit subsidiaries or branches to be set up in other Member States; and enhancing the digitalization of company law procedures and addressing new digital developments.

Third, the Staff Working Document, issued in December 2022[10], seems to have paved the way for a new EU-level intervention committed to 'facilitating shareholders' voting using digital means' (see Recommendation 9 of the High Level Forum to the Commission and Member States for advancing the CMU)[11].

After all, COVID-19 accelerated enterprise digital transformation and forced us to realise how valuable the use of electronic devices can be, also in managing corporations.

However, one might observe that while the use of information and communications technologies (ICTs) can increase efficiency by reducing costs and speeding

[6] Directive (EU) 2019/1151 of the European Parliament and of the Council of 20 June 2019 amending Directive (EU) 2017/1132 as regards the use of digital tools and processes in company law [2019] OJ L186/80.

[7] <https://ec.europa.eu/info/law/better-regulation/have-your-say/initiatives/13055-Upgrading-digital-company-law_en>.

[8] The results of the consultation (closed on 8 April 2022) are available here: <https://ec.europa.eu/info/law/better-regulation/have-your-say/initiatives/13055-Upgrading-digital-company-law/public-consultation_en>.

[9] Commission, 'Proposal for a Directive of the European Parliament and of the Council amending Directives 2009/102/EC and (EU) 2017/1132 as regards further expanding and upgrading the use of digital tools and processes in company law' (Proposal) COM (2023) 177 final.

[10] Commission Staff, 'On possible national regulatory barriers to the use of new digital technologies in the interaction between investors, intermediaries and issuers' (Action 12 of 2020 Capital Markets Union Action Plan) (Commission Staff Working Document) SWD(2022) 447 final, <https://commission.europa.eu/system/files/2023-01/SWD_2022_447_F1_STAFF_WORKING_PAPER_EN_V3_P1_2467629%20%283%29.PDF>.

[11] *A New Vision for Europe's Capital Markets. Final Report of the High Level Forum on the Capital Markets Union* (June 2020) <https://finance.ec.europa.eu/system/files/2020-06/200610-cmu-high-level-forum-final-report_en.pdf>.

up processes,[12] digitalization and artificial intelligence (AI) applications in particular provide advanced capabilities for decision-making in corporate boardrooms, as well as in the general meeting, potentially helping corporations to become more profitable, reliable and effective. For the first time, computers are no longer merely executing detailed, pre-written instructions but are capable of arriving at dynamic solutions to problems based on data patterns that humans may not even be able to perceive. This means that with AI, it is not simply the how (doing things faster or more cheaply etc.) but the what (doing better) that changes.

III. What is AI. Definitions, Types and Capabilities. Pros and Cons of AI for Corporate Governance

Before exploring some important applications of AI for corporate governance, and in order to discuss select legal issues derived from them, just what does AI mean? Because AI covers a broad range of evolving technologies and fields of study, pinning down a precise definition of AI becomes problematic.[13]

In the simplest terms, AI is any computer software that mimics the ways that humans think in order to perform complex tasks that historically could only be done by humans, such as analysis, reasoning, and learning from prior experiences. Indeed, while automated machines and systems merely follow a set of instructions and dutifully perform them without change, AI-powered ones can learn from

---

[12] 'The advantages of digitalization and of the internet can be quickly summoned and sketched: Any form of communication is extremely facilitated, transaction costs decrease enormously, at the same time participants of communication – here in particular shareholders – can be addressed individually. The border between mass and individual communication disappears and may be varied as necessary. Along with this a much better transparency is achieved, where all information can be personalized, including a real time availability' (Gerald Spindler, 'Digitalization and Corporate Law – A View from Germany' (2019) 16 ECFL 106).

[13] As 'there is no general definition of AI that enjoys widespread consensus', all articles, position papers or even regulatory proposals begin by providing a sort of definition of what is meant by 'AI' in that specific context. In this regard it bears notice that unlike the doctrinal approach, the regulators' approach is more focused on AI's functional characteristics rather than on its abilities. For instance, according to the Consultation presented to Parliament by the Secretary of State for Science, Innovation and Technology by Command of His Majesty on 29 March 2023 in the UK ('A Pro-innovation Approach to AI Regulation' 22, <www.gov.uk/government/publications/ai-regulation-a-pro-innovation-approach>), AI is 'defined by reference to the two characteristics that generate the need for a bespoke regulatory response', which is to say, 'adaptivity' and 'autonomy'. Similarly Article 3 (1) of the AI Act defines an AI system as follows: 'AI system means a machine-based system that is designed to operate with varying levels of autonomy and that may exhibit adaptiveness after deployment, and that, for explicit or implicit objectives, infers, from the input it receives, how to generate outputs such as predictions, content, recommendations, or decisions that can influence physical or virtual environment' (see also Commission 'Guidelines on the definition of an artificial intelligence system established by Regulation (EU) 2024/1689 (AI Act)', C(2025) 5053 final).

their interactions to improve their performance and efficiency. Machine learning, in particular, is built on the ability to create a model from historical data and then generate predictions for the future.

In this perspective, although 'general AI' has not been created yet[14], meaning that the ability of any current AI is limited to achieving a certain, stipulated goal or set of goals ('narrow or weak AI'), it is undeniable that AI can contribute to improving process robustness and so to strengthening corporate governance in several ways.

First, AI can streamline everyday business practices and activities: by automating tasks, companies can reduce the time and costs of performance and lower the risk of mistakes, allowing mainly directors and auditors to focus more on core business activities that require a high degree of human commitment. Plus, with inherent process standardization, the results are highly traceable and auditable.[15]

Second, AI can enhance decision-making processes: AI can be used to analyse large volumes of data, classify information and provide knowledgeable insights (predictions, forecasts, interpretations, …) that support better decisions. For example, AI can help identify patterns in financial data as well as in consumer behaviour and/or in past incidents that may not be immediately apparent to human analysts. By providing extensive analytics and pattern predictions, AI can bolster a company's ability to identify opportunities, predict failures and allow planned interventions, resulting in better management and greater risk control.[16] Furthermore, as AI does not have feelings, in theory it can make decisions and collate data without emotions or bias getting in the way.

More generally speaking, while the vast majority of applications are meant to boost productivity and profitability, it has been argued that the use of AI can also

---

[14] According to EPRS, *General-Purpose Artificial Intelligence* (March 2023) <www.europarl.europa.eu/RegData/etudes/ATAG/2023/745708/EPRS_ATA(2023)745708_EN.pdf>, general AI, also referred to as strong AI, 'are machines designed to perform a wide range of intelligent tasks, think abstractly and adapt to new situations' which 'are trained by scraping, analysing and processing publicly available data from the internet'. Although the recent launch of ChatGPT may suggest that general AI is already available today, notice that systems like ChatGPT can only perform specific tasks, such as generating text or other natural language processing tasks (including language translation, summarisation and responding to questions). Many experts believe that it will take many years (more than forty) before AI replaces humans in all tasks (Katja Grace and others, 'Viewpoint: When Will AI Exceed Human Performance? Evidence from AI Experts' (2018) 62(1) JAIR 729).

[15] Jingchen Zhao, 'Artificial Intelligence and Corporate Decisions: Fantasy, Reality or Destiny' (2022) 71 Cath ULR 663.

[16] In a recent decision, Justice Middleton of the Federal Court of Australia found that if a director is provided with too much information in regards to a company, so that he/she cannot understand all its workings, then the director must decrease the volume of information provided to them or increase the amount of time prescribed to absorb the information. The volume of information to process cannot allow directors to simply 'go through the paces' when signing off on financial statements. See *ASIC v Healey* [2011] FCA 717.

contribute to democratizing corporate governance and to reducing 'short-termism' in companies.

In fact, by providing shareholders with up-to-date, detailed information and prediction, AI has the potential to lower the costs associated with voting, which constitutes one cause of the thorny problem of retail investors apathy. Thanks to AI, shareholders have the chance to reduce information asymmetry, thus leading to an improvement of their capacity to limit managerial discretion and to initiate important governance changes. At the same time, analytics provided by AI can assist the board in personalising concise communication aligned to individual and grouped stakeholders, supporting genuine interaction and engagement strategies.

In other words, not only may an AI system highlight issues that humans may have omitted to consider, but it can also put forth a view that humans may have been hesitant to voice because they preferred not to rock the boat.[17]

In the same vein, it has also been hypothesized that AI could make corporate decision-making more humane: the cognitive capabilities of artificial intelligence can be used to implement intuitive, psychological and other components of internal mental activity of a person when making decisions.[18] Paradoxically, where adequately governed, AI could contribute to overcoming group-think or conflicts of interests and other biases and could consequently give momentum to humans' needs,[19] providing companies with the opportunity to benefit from many perspectives and experiences and so to align their decisions both with shareholders' and stakeholders' expectations.[20]

Obviously with all these pros also come certain cons (risks). But as the value of AI continues to grow (especially in the EU),[21] and as surveys find that executive confidence in AI is on the rise,[22] it seems reasonable to expect that AIs will definitively be at the centre of corporate decision-making in the near future, which

---

17 Akshaya Kamalnath and Umakanth Varottil, 'A Disclosure-Based Approach to Regulating AI in Corporate Governance' (2022) NUS Law Working Paper 2022/001, 2.

18 Michael R Siebecker, 'Making Corporations More Humane Through Artificial Intelligence' (2019) 45(1) J Corp L 95.

19 Akshaya Kamalnath, 'The Perennial Quest for Board Independence – Artificial Intelligence to the Rescue?' (2019) 83 Alb LRev 4.

20 Muzaffer Eroğlu and Meltem Karatepe Kaya, 'Impact of Artificial Intelligence on Corporate Board Diversity Policies and Regulations' (2022) 23 EBOR 541.

21 A new UN Trade and Development (UNCTAD) report projects the global AI market will soar from $189 billion in 2023 to $4.8 trillion by 2033 – a 25-fold increase in just a decade. By then, AI could quadruple its share of the global frontier technology market, rising from 7% to 29% and emerging as the sector's dominant force. See 'Technology and Innovation Report 2025: Inclusive Artificial Intelligence for Development' (<https://unctad.org/system/files/official-document/tir2025_en.pdf>).

22 See Teneo's 2023 Global CEO and Investor Outlook Survey. It shows that half (48%) of CEOs from the world's leading public companies have already adopted AI into their operating models, with another 58% actively investing to strengthen their AI capabilities, <www.teneo.com/app/uploads/2022/12/Teneo-Vision-2023-CEO-Investor-Survey.pdf>.

brings up the question of whether and to what extent corporate bodies in general can resort to AI within the framework of existing legislation.

In this regard it is worth noticing that despite significant advances in the capabilities of AI technologies in recent years, so far only a few national statues, mostly in the US, have passed to explicitly amend company law in order to make way for algorithmic management. For example, Wyoming[23] recently passed a law that for the first time in US history formally gives decentralised autonomous organisations ('DAOs') the same legal rights as limited liability companies, providing even that a DAO may be (fully) algorithmically managed.[24] None of this has happened in Europe yet; specifically, no hard or soft company law (corporate governance code) in Italy, Germany or Spain even mentions AI.[25] But we know that the fact that something is not explicitly regulated does not mean that it is forbidden; nor it could be said that the use of AI today operates in a 'legal vacuum'. The truth is that we need to distinguish the different roles played by AI and consider each separately in light of the existing principles and rules set forth in corporate law as well as in privacy law and in the emerging field of data/robot law.

IV. Robo-board and Directors' Duties. From OECD Principles to GDPR

There is no doubt that the advent of AI technology has brought us to reconsider conventional legal thought about anthropocentrism – the worldview in which the legal order is subordinate and dedicated exclusively to the interests of human beings. From cars driven by automated systems to robots sitting in on a company's weekly meetings, technology has undoubtedly blurred legal reality between persons and objects.

From this point of view, the current debate shows similarities to a question many EU countries (Italy included) are now specifically addressing: whether it would be possible to appoint a company as a director of another company.[26] Dealing with the problem of endowing AI with legal subjectivity, it has been argued that the crucial difference between a corporation and a AI system is that corpo-

---

[23] On 21 April 2021, Wyoming Governor Mark Gordon signed Bill 38 (<www.wyoleg.gov/Legislation/2021/SF0038>) into law allowing Wyoming to recognize decentralized autonomous organizations (DAOs) as limited liability companies. The bill was sponsored by Wyoming's Select Committee on Blockchain, Financial Technology and Digital Innovation Technology and takes effect 1 July 2021.

[24] Carla L Reyes, 'Autonomous Corporate Personhood' (2021) 96 Wash LRev 1453.

[25] Actually, AI is now mentioned in the G20/OECD Principles of Corporate Governance, 2023, p 12, as a powerful means of supervision that can enhance authorities' oversight capacity (Principle I.F.), rather than as a corporate governance tool.

[26] Sergio Alberto Gramitto Ricci, 'Artificial Agents in Corporate Boardrooms' (2023) Cornell LRev 869.

rations always act through humans.[27] Humans sit on boards whose actions are attributed to the corporation. This leads to the conclusion that robots are inherently different from both natural and legal persons and should be treated as such.

However, if we assume an AI that shares the same degree of autonomy as a human being, what is the rationale for distinguishing among robots and humans? In this light we have to admit from a theoretical point of view that nothing stands in the way of granting legal personality to an AI. Legal personality is only a concept that designates an entity's ability to have rights and obligations. It does not imply that a legal person is akin to a human being, that it has a free will or a conscience or that it must enjoy all the rights granted to human beings. It is no more unthinkable to grant legal personality to an AI than to a company,[28] giving both the chance to be considered as a 'fictional' person.[29]

The question is not whether it is possible to confer legal personhood on an AI but whether it is desirable and to what extent.[30]

However, if major legal reform would be needed in Italy and *a fortiori* in Germany (and in other countries such as Australia[31] and the US[32] where company law restricts directorship to 'natural persons') before a robot could occupy a seat at the boardroom table, the use of assistive (or augmented) solutions does not call into question the fundamental nature of corporate governance, nor does it deprive board members of power. Rather, it promises to provide amplified decision-making capabilities, thus raising a number of legal issues regarding the board's duties when using AI.

1. Transparency and Explainability

As noted above, the AI commonly used today is based on deep learning, a technology used to identify hidden correlations through machine learning of data. While it is helpful in discovering what a human can hardly recognise, humans

---

[27] Horst Eidenmüller, 'The Rise of Robots and the Law of Humans' (2017) Oxford Legal Studies Research Paper No 27/2017 <https://ssrn.com/abstract=2941001>.

[28] Gyandeep Chaudhary, 'Artificial Intelligence: The Personhood Conundrum' (2021) <https://ssrn.com/abstract=3804265>.

[29] On the fictional nature of corporate personality, see Ben Allgrove, 'Legal Personality for Artificial Intellects: Pragmatic Solution or Science Fiction?' (2004) <https://ssrn.com/abstract=926015>.

[30] Every legal system envisages some legal persons with fewer legal rights and different obligations than others. For instance, whereas under US federal law the term person is defined to include corporations (Dictionary Act, 1 U.S.C. 1.), according to Delaware Corporations Law, art 141(1)(b) ('The board of directors of a corporation shall consist of 1 or more members, each of whom shall be a natural person.') as well as California Corporations Code 2020, art 164(1) ('Directors means natural persons […]'), directors need to be human. Legal and natural persons in those states are therefore not treated equally.

[31] Australian Corporation Act 2001, s 201B(1): 'Only an individual who is at least 18 may be appointed as a director of a company'.

[32] See n 30.

find it difficult to review how an AI has reached a decision, still less to control its decision-making. Furthermore, the AI continues learning after the developer delivers the system to the user, making its decisions even less controllable. A salient feature of AI systems (in contrast with non-autonomous systems) is then the difficulty of knowing or predicting how they will behave in novel situations or contexts (the black-box problem).[33] So one might ask whether directors must disclose how they reached a decision (transparency) and in particular what role artificial intelligence may have played (explainability).[34]

On one hand, the duty of disclosure could be inferred from the shareholders' right to choose, on a fiduciary basis, the company's directors. Simply put, it could be argued that if directors could outsource their ultimate decisions to an AI without sharing this fact with shareholders it would *de facto* negate the relevance of a choice by the company's members. To be more explicit, imagine that the shareholders had appointed a distinguished, very skilled and experienced person. Now, what if this person could elect to be 'augmented' (guided) by a beta testing app (that is, by an experimental app with limited experience in that specific field of activity)?

While it is clear that robot and human reasoning may often diverge, leading to different decisions, it bears notice that generally speaking there is no legal rule setting forth how directors should exercise their powers of decision, meaning that directors are free to decide how to decide, be it alone or by relying on professional or, eventually, on algorithmic advice. Obviously, the duty of care requires that directors use the same degree of diligence, inquiry and skill in performing their duties as a prudent person would use in similar circumstances. And breaching this duty can give rise to personal liability and eventually provide a 'just and reasonable cause' for removing a director. But far from demonstrating that directors cannot rely on AI, this confirms that directors can fail to reach the best decision for the company no matter why. Shareholders' interest in good governance is protected through the provision of an *ex post* liability remedy.

If corporate law seems not to support an (*ex-ante*) obligation of disclosure, it has been noticed that securities regulation may furnish an analogy.[35] Based on the G20/OECD Principle of Corporate Governance, according to which

[33] Yavar Bathaee, 'The Artificial Intelligence Black Box and the Failure of Intent and Causation' (2018) 31(2) Harv JOLT 889.

[34] More precisely it has been argued that AI's opacity can arise from various sources. Sometimes institutions or corporations fail to communicate that they have relied on AI systems or to report how these systems work. Alternatively, those who are entitled to transparency might lack the expertise to understand the explanations at hand. Finally, due to the increasing reliance on machine learning, even the most expertly trained humans might fail to grasp the algorithm in full detail (Bram Vaassen, 'AI, Opacity, and Personal Autonomy' (2022) 35 Philosophy & Technology 88).

[35] Kamalnath and Varottil (n 17) 10ff.

'[t]he corporate governance framework should ensure that timely and accurate disclosure is made on all material matters regarding the corporation, including the financial situation, performance, sustainability, ownership, and governance of the company',[36]

some commentators have inferred that since AI can somehow restructure the decision-making process and the related risks, at least for listed companies it should be mandatory that the use of AI in their governance must be transparent, especially if AI is used in investment decisions. To support their view, they refer to a recent regulation by the Indian Financial Markets Authority (SEBI) that expressly requires the board of Indian listed companies to make a disclosure regarding 'Any other information/event viz. major development that is likely to affect business, e.g. emergence of new technologies' and 'brief details thereof', if this becomes 'necessary to enable the holders of securities of the listed entity to appraise its position and to avoid the establishment of a false market'[37].

The meaning of the foreign rule is far from crystal clear. However, if we consider that according to OECD AI Principles 'AI Actors should commit to transparency', thus 'disclosing when AI is being used (in a prediction, recommendation or decision, or that the user is interacting directly with an AI-powered agent, such as a chatbot)'[38], it does not seem amiss to interpret the new provision as forcing Indian listed companies to declare any AI usage.

Anyway, while it remains debatable whether listed companies (especially EU companies) should disclose any AI usage in corporate governance and thus whether investors (meaning both actual and potential shareholders) may claim a right to know how, when, and for what purposes an AI system is being used in corporate governance, such a right seems to have been granted already under privacy law (GDPR)[39].

---

[36] In the EU this principle is expressed in art 20 of the Directive 2013/34/EU of the European Parliament and of the Council of 26 June 2013 on the annual financial statements, consolidated financial statements and related reports of certain types of undertakings, amending Directive 2006/43/EC of the European Parliament and of the Council and repealing Council Directives 78/660/EEC and 83/349/EEC [2013] OJ L182/19.

[37] SEBI LODR Regulations, schedule III, pt A.

[38] The quotation is of Principle 1.3 (<https://oecd.ai/en/ai-principles>). Adopted in May 2019, the OECD's Principles on AI provide sound policy guidance for governments and stakeholders around the world who are working to advance responsible, human-centred AI. The OECD's view that AI must be fair, explainable and secure.

[39] Regulation (EU) 2016/679 of the European Parliament and of the Council of 27 April 2016 on the protection of natural persons with regard to the processing of personal data and on the free movement of such data, and repealing Directive 95/46/EC (General Data Protection Regulation) (Text with EEA relevance) [2016] OJ L119/1 (GDPR).

2. Processing of Personal Data in the Context of AI Models

It is well known indeed that the GDPR already extensively regulates the processing of personal data by AI systems.[40] Generally speaking this means that during both the training and use phases of an AI, data controllers need to rely on one of the six legal bases for processing set out under art 6(1) of the GDPR for all processing of personal data using AI systems[41]. Most commonly, controllers rely on consent, legitimate interests, legal obligation or contractual necessity. There are various requirements associated with these legal bases, but all of them need to comply at least with certain general principles, which include transparency.

In this regard it must be recalled that under art 5(1)(a) of the GDPR, controllers are required to process personal data lawfully, fairly and transparently. Articles 13 and 14 also set out various notice requirements specifying what individuals should be informed of before their personal data is processed.

In particular, as the GDPR requires the data controller to tell individuals what information it holds about them and how it is being used, this means that if the controller is going to use artificial intelligence to process someone's personal data, it normally needs to tell them about it.

Differently from what is provided by art 22 (and art 13(2)(f), 14(2)(g) and 15(1)(h)) for automated decision making that might significantly affect the data subject, when the scope of AI is to support humans, not to replace them, no 'meaningful information about the logic involved' is required.

Indeed, while generic information on the use of AI is normally sufficient to comply with data protection (in line with its risk-based approach), art 22 of the GDPR imposes additional requirements on decisions based on automated processing and/or profiling that have legal or similarly significant effects on individuals.

The nature of art 22 of the GDPR has been heavily debated in academia and recently also within the ECJ.[42]

One crucial question is whether art 22(1) of the GDPR contains an in-principle prohibition of automated decision-making or whether it enshrines a right which must be invoked by the affected data subject. According to the European Data Protection Board (WP 29),[43] art 22(1) establishes a general prohibition for decision-making based solely on automated processing. This prohibition applies

---

[40] As stated by the EDPB, '[a]ny processing of personal data through an algorithm falls within the scope of the GDPR' (EDPB Response to the MEP Sophie in Veld's letter on unfair algorithms, <https://edpb.europa.eu/sites/default/files/files/file1/edpb_letter_out2020_0004_intveldalgorithms_en.pdf>.

[41] See EDPB Opinion 28/2024 on certain data protection aspects related to the processing of personal data in the context of AI models, 2024.

[42] See ECJ 7 December 2023, C-634/21, *OQ v SCHUFA Holding AG*, ECLI:EU:C:2023:957 regarding automated credit-scoring for the purpose of obtaining a loan.

[43] Guidelines on Automated individual decision-making and Profiling for the purposes of Regulation 2016/679, 2018.

whether or not the data subject takes an action regarding the processing of their personal data.

In summary, Article 22 provides that:

(i) as a rule, there is a general prohibition on fully automated individual decision-making, including profiling that has a legal or similarly significant effect;
(ii) there are exceptions to the rule;
(iii) where one of these exceptions applies, there must be measures in place to safeguard the data.

However, the Article 22(1) prohibition only applies in specific circumstances when a decision based solely on automated processing, including profiling, has a legal effect on or similarly significantly affects someone, as explained further in the guidelines.

Another crucial question concerns the granularity of information given to the data holder, which affects how far the controller of automated individual decision-making applications has to go to fulfil certain explanation requirements. The GDPR imposes special explanation requirements on the data controller for certain cases of automated data processing. According to art 13(2)(f) and 14(2)(g), when collecting personal data, the data controller must provide the data subject with information on 'the existence of automated decision-making pursuant to art 22(1) and (4) and – at least in these cases – meaningful information about the logic involved and the scope and intended effects of such processing for the data subject'. Article 15(1)(h) provides for a corresponding right of access.

There has been broad discussion on whether art 15 should be read as granting data subjects the right to obtain an individualised explanation of automated assessments and decisions.

Unfortunately, the formulation of art 15 is very ambiguous, and that ambiguity is reflected in recital 63. In particular, it is not specified whether the obligation to provide information on the 'logic involved' only concerns providing general information on the methods adopted in the system or whether it instead concerns specific information on how these methods where applied to the data subject.

According to some commentators, because recital 71(4) mentions the 'explanation of the decision reached' as part of the 'suitable safeguards' for automated processing, this should lead us to accept the existence of a case-by-case requirement to provide detailed, specific explanations of processing operations (known as *post-hoc* explainability)[44] and consequently to accept that only fully explainable AI may be used for automated processing of personal data.

---

[44] Notably Bryan Casey, Ashkon Farhangi and Roland Vogl, 'Rethinking Explainable Machines: The GDPR's "Right to Explanation" Debate and the Rise of Algorithmic Audits in Enterprise' (2019) 34 Berkeley Tech LJ 143; Maja Brkan, 'Do Algorithms Rule the World? Algorithmic Decision-making and Data Protection in the Framework of the GDPR and Beyond' (2019) 27 IJLIT 91.

However, others have noticed a non-univocal reference between the already mentioned 'appropriate measures' expressly established (but not better specified) by art 22 (3) and the 'adequate guarantees' mentioned in Recital 71 of the GDPR, which include 'specific information to the interested party and the right to obtain human intervention, to express their opinion, to obtain an explanation of the decision reached after such assessment and to challenge the decision'. Given that such a 'whereas' is not binding and is used by operators as an interpretative tool, some scholars maintain the systematic interpretation of the GDPR and recognize only one right of access and information but not a right to explanation.[45]

Obviously the 'right-to-explanation' debate regarding the GDPR is too lively and extensive to be addressed now in this article, especially considering on one hand that after decades of existence the right not to be subject to automated decision-making is finally going to be considered for the first time before the European Court of Justice ('ECJ')[46] but on the other hand that the vast majority of corporate decision-making is also likely to (directly) affect persons other than natural persons.

Should this be the case, however, then directors should be very attentive to GDPR obligations that provide parties who are directly affected by the use of an AI system with 'appropriate information'.[47] In this regard it is worth recalling that, according to the European Data Protection Board, in order to comply with high information standards it may not be sufficient if the information received is not comprehensible to the recipient given the complexity of the automated decision-making process(es). Therefore it would be appropriate to provide not so much an explanation on how the algorithm works but rather complete information, communicated in a simple way, about the elements used and about the relative weighting of factors in the procedure in order to allow the interested parties ('intended audience') to understand the reasons for the decision and possibly to dispute it.[48]

V. Conclusive Remarks

Finally, to conclude this section on the regulatory framework applicable to AI-augmented corporate bodies and especially to the board of directors, it is worth no-

---

45 Sandra Wachter, Brent Mittelstadt and Luciano Floridi, 'Why a Right to Explanation of Automated Decision-Making Does Not Exist in the General Data Protection Regulation' (2017) 7 IDPL 76.

46 See n 42.

47 On the importance of providing 'appropriate transparency and explainability', see the UK Consultation on 'A Pro-innovation Approach to AI Regulation' (n 13) 28, according to which AI disclosure should be 'proportionate to the risks […] recognising that consumers, users and regulators will require different information'.

48 Guidelines on Automated individual decision-making (n 43) 25.

ticing that according to the AI Act[49], high-risk AI systems must be interpretable in order to ensure human oversight (art 29(4)). Recital 71 and art 13(1) indeed state that the high-risk AI systems listed in Annex III must be designed and developed in such a way that their operation is comprehensible to those who deploy them. Deployers of such a system should be able (a) to interpret its output and (b) to use it in an appropriate manner.

From this perspective it seems that as deployers are vested with greater responsibility, the explanation due to them should be more technical and more detailed, so directors as 'deployers' are to be equipped with specific AI skills (AI Literacy, Art 4 AI Act). In this perspective the choice to benefit from the useful insights of an AI would come with a price.

As an old saying goes, 'all that glitters is not gold': AI certainly has many pros for corporate governance, but it also has drawbacks in terms of additional duties, especially for the board of directors, for whom, considering that the analytical capabilities of AI may be superior to those of humans on a number of specific tasks, the ubiquitous expectation that directors must act on a well-informed basis may very well evolve into the duty to rely on the output of AI.[50]

---

[49] Regulation (EU) 2024/1689 of the European Parliament and of the Council of 13 June 2024 laying down harmonised rules on artificial intelligence and amending Regulations (EC) No 300/2008, (EU) No 167/2013, (EU) No 168/2013, (EU) 2018/858, (EU) 2018/1139 and (EU) 2019/2144 and Directives 2014/90/EU, (EU) 2016/797 and (EU) 2020/1828 (Artificial Intelligence Act) (Text with EEA relevance) [2024] OJ L2024/1689.

[50] Floris Mertens, 'The Use of Artificial Intelligence in Corporate Decision-Making at Board Level: A Preliminary Legal Analysis' (2023) Financial Law Institute Working Paper Series 2023-01 <https://papers.ssrn.com/sol3/papers.cfm?abstract_id=4339413>.

Rules and Standards on Corporate Control Transactions

Marco Speranzin

I. Introduction: Private Legal Transplants and the Debate Concerning Corporate Control Transactions

The transfer of 'control' (ie, of the controlling shareholding or block of shares) has been a major topic of debate in commercial and company law since the last century.[1]

Despite the widespread nature of this debate,[2] discordant views exist as to the definition of a corporate control transaction[3] and the specific feature of the share-

---

[1] See Lorraine Talbot, 'Shareholders and Directors: Entitlements, Duties and the Expansion of Shareholder Wealth' in Andrew Johnston and Lorraine Talbot (eds), *Great Debates in Commercial and Company Law* (Red Globe Press 2020) 128 (on discussion of the nature of the share) (see infra, § II).

[2] In the American scholarship, see William D Andrews, 'The Stockholder's Right to Equal Opportunity in the Sales of Shares' (1965) 78 Harv LRev 505; in German scholarship, see Herbert Wiedemann, *Minderheitenschutz und Aktienhandel. Eine rechtsvergleichende Studie zum amerikanischen und deutschen Recht* (Enke 1968) 51 ff; in the Italian scholarship, see Lorenzo Mossa, 'La vendita dell'impresa sociale' in Annuario dir. comparato (1932) III, 158 ff; furthermore Giovanni E Colombo, 'La cessione dei pacchetti di controllo: considerazioni per una discussione' [1978] Riv soc 1443, and the monographic work of Mario Stella Richter jr, *'Trasferimento del controllo' e rapporti tra soci* (Giuffrè 1996) 3 ff: transfer of control as a 'problematic area'; in the French scholarship, see Daniel Roux, 'La spécificité des cessions de contrôle' [1980] Rev soc 49.

[3] In many languages, the word 'control' (*controllo* in Italian or *Kontrolle* in German, from the Latin *contra-rotulum*) has the double meaning of directing or dominating (*dominio* or *Herr-*

holding that determines dominance over the company, which is not always exercised by the majority stake.[4]

The transfer of controlling shareholdings raises various 'internal' issues, usually connected to the relationship between the parties buying and selling shares – the seller and the buyer[5] – even though the controlling shareholdings could be acquired through specific company transactions such as a capital increase or a merger.

Specific legal issues are also connected to the transfer of the controlling shareholdings *mortis causa* due to the relationship (and often, disputes) among heirs, foremost the material problems of the succession law applicable to the case,[6] and therefore of legal certainty in the transfer, which is why a specific regulation has been introduced in the Italian system that applies to the heirs (calling for either a share deal or an asset deal).[7]

The transfer of controlling shareholdings raises many 'external' issues as well, in particular questions of company law regarding the relationship between majority and minority shareholders and the relationship between shareholders and directors;[8] questions of financial law regarding the rules applicable to public offers or the regulation of market abuse; questions of antitrust law connected with the relevance of the acquisition and the eventual triggering of Golden Powers regulations; questions of specific national (or sometimes, supranational) rules regarding employee protections and taxation.[9]

---

schaft or *Beherrschung*) on one side and monitoring (*verifica* or *Aufsicht*) on the other side: Stella Richter (n 2) 38 fn 84.

[4] The answer to that legal question depends on the type of legal business entity (for example, it differs between public and private companies) and its specific by-laws. In general, controlling shareholdings could be considered that which allows for *dominant influence* over the legal entity, usually through the appointment or removal of members of the board of directors, as provided by art 2359(1) and (2) of the Italian civil code. See Carlo Angelici, 'La partecipazione azionaria nella società per azioni' in Pietro Rescigno (ed), *Trattato di diritto privato*, vol 16 (Utet 1985) 333.

[5] Legal practice usually refers to the sale and purchase agreement as an SPA; the agreement could be drafted as an asset deal or a share deal (the latter object of this paper), with material differences that are discussed infra in the article. In the Italian literature, see Giorgio De Nova, *Il Sale and Purchase Agreement: un contratto commentato* (4th edn, Giappichelli 2021).

[6] See, in the Italian scholarship, Mengoni, 'La divisione del pacchetto azionario di maggioranza tra gli eredi dell'azionista' [1959] Riv soc 428; *Alessio Zaccaria*, 'La collazione delle partecipazioni sociali diverse dalle azioni' (2016) 2 Riv dir civ 418.

[7] The regulation of the so-called *patti di famiglia*: art 768-*bis* ff of the Italian civil code. See on the issue Marco Cian, 'La nozione di "partecipazioni societarie" nella disciplina dei patti di famiglia' (2008) 4 Riv dir soc 767.

[8] In general, the corporate control transaction (the transfer between seller and buyer) should be considered immaterial to the company and its shareholders (as a phenomenon of *Individualrecht*); but it is well asserted that this conclusion is not correct and that the sale has *sozialrechtliche* consequences (or a relevance *causa societatis*): Wiedemann (n 2) 58; Carlo Angelici, 'Parità di trattamento degli azionisti' (1987) 1–4 Riv dir comm 16.

[9] For a detailed examination of the main problems connected with corporate control transactions, see Stella Richter (n 2) 5 ff.

The specific focus of this article is the *private* transfer-of-control transaction (as opposed to the rules applicable to public M&A transactions),[10] and the article's focus is limited to the relationship between seller and buyer (the internal issues) and to certain company law questions (the external issues).

Before going through these specific legal problems, some general remarks are required regarding the practice of acquisitions.

First of all, sale and purchase agreements are usually drafted following specific models imported from Anglo-American practice, often written in English (even though the parties are from the same national system), and adapted to the particular national context,[11] which raises some interesting and problematic issues that we will outline later on. This phenomenon is common to other innovations of the legal marketplace[12] that have been widely discussed in scholarship and in case law: the performance bond or *Garantievertrag*, recognized by the Corte di Cassazione as part of an international uniformity trend in private law;[13] the Russian roulette or shoot-out clauses inserted into shareholder agreements or company charters and by-laws, usually following a joint-venture project, recently upheld by the Italian Supreme Court;[14] the clauses venture capital funds insert into investment agreements for the financing of start-ups, such as tag-along, drag-along and anti-dilution provisions or liquidation preferences.[15]

We could also speak about the circulation of legal models[16] or just as well about other private legal transplants[17] or even a new *lex mercatoria*.[18] Such con-

[10] On public corporate control transactions, see Duccio Regoli, 'Tutela delle minoranze e circolazione del controllo' in Francesco Barachini (ed), *La tutela del socio e delle minoranze. Studi in onore di Alberto Mazzoni* (Giappichelli 2018) 177.

[11] See *ex multis* Hanno Merkt, 'Grundsatz- und Praxisprobleme der Amerikanisierungstendenzen im Recht des Unternehmenskaufs' in Klaus Peter Berger and Werner F Ebke (eds), Festschrift Otto Sandrock (Recht und Wirtschaft 2000); Jochen Vetter, 'Kautelarpraxis und M&A Verträge' (2018) 82 RabelsZ 274.

[12] On legal innovation, discovery or invention see Holger Fleischer, 'Juristische Entdeckungen im Gesellschaftsrecht' in Georg Bitte and others (eds), *Festschrift für Karsten Schmidt* (Schmidt 2009); Stefan Grundmann and Florian Möslein, *Innovation und Vertragsrecht* (Mohr Siebeck 2020).

[13] Cass 1 October 1987, no 7341, following Giuseppe B Portale, 'Fideiussione e "Garantievertrag" nella prassi bancaria' (1977) 1–2 JUS 3.

[14] Cass 25 July 2023, no 22375. On such clauses in a comparative perspective Holger Fleischer and Stephan Schneider, 'Shoot-Out Clauses in Partnerships and Close Corporations' (2012) 9 ECFR 35.

[15] Paolo Giudici, Peter Agstner and Antonio Capizzi, 'The Corporate Design of Investments in Startups: A European Experience' (2022) ECGI – Law Working Paper 662/2022 <https://papers.ssrn.com/sol3/papers.cfm?abstract_id=4256344>; Thilo Kuntz, *Gestaltung von Kapitalgesellschaften zwischen Freiheit und Zwang* (Mohr Siebeck 2016).

[16] See Rodolfo Sacco, 'Circolazione e mutazione dei modelli giuridici' (1988) 2 Dig disc priv, sez civ 365; Rodolfo Sacco, *La comparaison juridique au service de la conaissance du droit* (Economica 1991) 158.

[17] Heike Schweitzer, 'Private Legal Transplants in Negotiated Deals' (2007) 4 ECFR 79.

[18] For recent Italian scholarship, see Francesco Galgano, 'Lex mercatoria' Enc dir, Agg, vol 5 (Giuffrè 2001) 721; Carlo Angelici, 'La lex mercatoria e i problemi dei codici di com-

tract models address the main legal needs of the parties (usually entrepreneurs) and set forth what has been defined as a *proper law* of acquisitions, which to a certain extent creates a private body of autonomous rules that are different from what applies to general contracts in continental European legal systems.[19] This phenomenon is also generally described as part of the 'commercialization' of civil law principles.[20]

Secondly, the role of corporate law firms[21] is well established in the field of acquisitions, in particular the role of international law firms or of national ones with established foreign connections. Therefore, this is an area where practitioners or transactional lawyers, more so than judges, legislators and professors, are the real protagonists of law development.[22]

On one hand, this phenomenon relates to the origin of the proper law we are discussing, and to the lack of specific rules on controlling shares or business acquisitions in most of the legal systems.[23] In fact, the general provisions of the law of sales that the private or commercial codes provide (in particular the legal warranty: see infra) are not equipped to solve the problems connected with a complex and dynamic good, considering the marked information asymmetry between the parties.[24] On the other hand, the big law firms are often better suited to offer-

---

mercio' (2010) 1 Giur comm 361; Mario Libertini, 'Le fonti private del diritto commerciale. Appunti per una discussione' (2008) 1 Riv dir comm 614.

[19] Italian scholars have defined these agreements as 'alien' from a strict civil law perspective. See Giorgio De Nova, *Il contratto alieno* (2nd edn, Giappichelli 2010) 2. This terminology has been recently followed by the Italian Supreme Court with reference to the Russian roulette clause. See Cass 25 July 2023, no 22375.

[20] For an early discussion see George Ripert, 'La commercialization du droit civil français' in *Mélanges Maurovic* (Belgrade 1934); in the Italian literature Galgano (n 18) 725; Mario Libertini, 'La c.d. commercializzazione del diritto privato' (2022) Special Issue, Riv it scienze giur 283.

[21] See Yves Dezalay and Bryant G Garth, *Law as Reproduction and Revolution* (U Cal P 2021) (on the role of US corporate law firms in a 'legal revolution').

[22] Specifically in reference to the M&A practice, see Ronalöd J Gilson, 'Value Creation by Business Lawyers: Legal Skills and Asset Pricing' (1984) 94 Yale LJ 239; Jacek Jastrzebski, 'Value Creation in Negotiations of Contractual Warranties and Indemnification' (2019) 6 ECFR 273. In general, see Holger Fleischer, 'Kautelarpraxis und Privatrecht: Grundfragen und gesellschaftsrechtliche Illustrationen' (2018) 82 RabelsZ 239, and Vetter (n 11) 281; Hans-Ueli Vogt, Holger Fleischer and Susanne Kalls (eds), *Protagonisten im Gesellschaftsrecht* (Mohr Siebeck 2020).

[23] For example, Italian law expressly regulates only the asset deal (*trasferimento di azienda*: CC, art 2555 ff), if only in reference to the relationship with third parties. The share deal is not regulated, with the exception of the necessary formalities towards the company. See CC, art 2355 (public company) and CC, art 2470 (private company). Therefore, these features of Italian law raise the question of whether the general law of sale can be enforced. See infra, II. and III.

[24] Acquisition agreements have therefore become longer and more complicated in order to comply with this information asymmetry and with the complexity of the management of the company. See John C Coates IV, 'Why have M&A Contracts grown? Evidence from Twenty

ing legal advice on all aspects of an acquisition (as mentioned above: contracts, company law, antitrust and so on), and hiring an elite law firm to advise on corporate transactions is considered to be an exercise of due care by directors and managers and not to be challenged under the business judgment rule safe harbor.

Thirdly, share sale and purchase agreements for company shares are usually subject to arbitration clauses, even where disputes are otherwise to be decided by specialized courts, as is the case in Italy[25] or as is projected for Germany.[26] Arbitrators (in particular those appointed by international arbitration courts, who are usually company or business law professors)[27] are deemed better prepared to enforce the specific rules such agreements provide, and debate and much discussion of private legal transplants has often originated in their decisions.[28]

In an important Italian Supreme Court decision, the proper law generated by international practice and enforced by arbitration courts has also been recognized as belonging to an international and transnational practice that is to be upheld on one hand;[29] but on the other hand, this proper law discourages the establishment of new, specific legal provisions in the national private or commercial codes. Such provisions may not fully comply with this international practice or proper law.[30]

Years of Deals' (November 2016) ECGI Law Working Paper 333/2016 <https://papers.ssrn.com/sol3/papers.cfm?abstract_id=2862019>. In the Italian literature, see De Nova (n 9) 9; in the German literature, see the *incipit* to the essay by Ulrich Huber, 'Die Praxis des Unternehmenskaufs im System des Kaufrechts' (2002) 202 AcP 179: 'Das zentrale Rechtsproblem des Unternehmenskaufs ist ein Informationsproblem'; see also Klaus J Hopt, 'M&A, Due Diligence und Kautelarpraxis' (2022) 186 ZHR 10.

[25] By judges appointed to the Tribunale delle imprese, which is competent to hear disputes regarding the transfer of shares (of public and private companies).

[26] See the legislative project (approved on 16 August 2023) focused on establishing commercial chambers at the Court of Appeals; disputes (mostly regarding *Unternehmenskauf*) are to be heard in English. See Hilmar Raeschke-Kessler, 'Schiedgerichtsbarkeit und Commercial Courts' [2023] SchiedsVZ 158.

[27] This is the norm in Italy; for Germany, see Holger Fleischer, 'Große Debatten im Gesellschaftsrecht: Eine Forschungsskizze' [2023] JZ 372 (the Supreme Court judges decide as well as an arbitrator).

[28] In reference to drag-along provisions (and the possibility to insert them into company by-laws by a majority shareholders' resolution) Lodo arb 29 July 2008 (Prof Mazzoni), (2009) 2 Banca borsa tit cred 493. In reference to questions about share and purchase agreements, see Lodo arb 25 May 2022 (Prof Portale, Rescigno e Roppo), (2023) 2 Banca borsa tit cred 151, with a critical note by Andrea Tina, 'Note in materia di trasferimento di partecipazioni societarie (di controllo e rilevanti) e tutela dell'acquirente, tra responsabilità precontrattuale, dolo incidente e integrazione del contratto secondo buona fede e correttezza.'

[29] Cass 24 July 2014, no 16963, which is particularly important regarding representations and warranties: see infra, III. Recently, see also Cass 25 July 2023, no 22375.

[30] This issue has been discussed in Italy upon presentation – through the initiative of an international law firm – of a legislative project to regulate representations and warranties in company acquisitions (project of law no 1610/2014, commented by Marco Speranzin and Andrea Tina, 'Una recente proposta legislativa in tema di trasferimento di aziende e partecipazioni sociali' (2014) 3 Società 261). The project was put aside after the above-mentioned Supreme

II. Internal Issues: Agreements for the Sale and Purchase of Shares and Buyer's Protections

Considering the first internal issue, the relationship between the vendor and acquirer in the sale of shares, a preliminary question regards whether the sale of the controlling block of shares is special, and therefore whether there is a difference between share and asset deals as a form of *Unternehmenskauf*, in particular from the perspective of the law of sales.

This debate has always been connected with the nature of the share, its form as property and its transferability;[31] the above-mentioned difference (share or asset deal) could be fundamental with reference to protecting the purchaser regarding the stability of the company's business. In other words: Could the buyer of a controlling block of shares seek a remedy if the asset values are less than expected due to the past management of the company?

On this issue, the Italian history in practice and case law is characterized by a cyclical trajectory[32] or by an inter-generational debate[33] evolving from an initial period (dated 1930–1960) to a second period (1960–1990) and finally to a third, more recent one (1990–present).[34]

During the initial period, agreements for the sale and purchase of shares were very short, without representations and warranties, and the Supreme Court as well as a number of scholars recognized that the share deal should be considered as an asset deal in order to protect the buyer under the terms of a legal warranty – provided by the sales law – not only with reference to the shares she was buying (for example: shares without voting rights; shares of a company already insolvent), but also with reference to the company's assets.[35] This position was supported by the prevalence of the notion of economic substance over form: the acquirer of the controlling shareholding should be considered as the buyer of the business. But the opposite opinion was nevertheless already receiving support: from a legal point of view, the transfer of shares (even if they represented 100% of the share capital) could not be considered to be a transfer of assets that belonged to the company, and therefore the buyer (who actually purchased the shares)

Court decision in 2014. In Germany as well, an initiative to regulate acquisition is under discussion, but it has been sharply criticized: see Jörg Risse, 'Kodifizierung des Unternehmenskaufrechts – wirklich keine gute Idee!' [2023] NZG 721.

[31] Talbot (n 1) 128.

[32] See Brian R Cheffins, The Trajectory of (Corporate Law) Scholarship (2003) 42ff <https://ssrn.com/abstract=429624>, on the Corporate Law Cycles.

[33] See Fleischer (n 27) 367 on the *Generationsthemen*.

[34] See Franco Bonelli, 'Acquisizioni di società e di pacchetti azionari di riferimento: le garanzie del venditore' [2007] Dir comm int 293.

[35] See Corte del Regno d'Italia 27 July 1933 (so called *Raggio* case) (1935) 2 Riv dir comm 121; for a prominent voice in the literature, see Mossa (n 2) 158ff.

was not entitled to recover on the basis of a legal warranty if the company's assets were not as valuable as expected.[36]

During the second period, agreements for the sale of shares became longer and, following what has become the leading opinion in the literature and case law, contained a number of synthetic, general representations and warranties; the buyer could not be protected with respect to the company assets without such clauses because she was not a new owner of the assets, and therefore share and asset deals were to be treated differently.[37]

Finally, the boom of acquisitions, the development of financial markets and the expansion of international (and in particular American and English) law firms in continental Europe was followed by the third period in this company law debate. The agreements were now usually sophisticated, with pages of representations, warranties and indemnity clauses.

A minority opinion still considers – in some extreme cases – that notwithstanding a lack of representations and warranties, the acquirer could be protected even in reference to the company's assets; these cases would usually involve sales of almost the entire quota or lesser economic relevance (usually transactions in partnership interests or the shares in small private companies); this opinion is based on legal standards such as the piercing of the corporate veil theory or the good faith principle (CC, art 1375), which serves as the source of an implied legal warranty referring to the company's assets.[38]

However, Italian Supreme Court case law does not share this general opinion: from a legal point of view, transfers of shares are to be considered to be different from transfers of assets.[39] Unless the agreement provides contractual business warranties or in the event of fraud or malice on the part of the vendor (rare in this kind of litigation), the acquirer is not entitled to recover on the basis of a company's assets valuing below expectations.

Although the German Federal Court of Justice appears (with some doubts) to adhere to the opposite position,[40] the leading opinion in the Italian literature and case law seems preferable for two main reasons.[41]

---

[36] See Cass 4 August 1941, no 2736; Cass 22 September 1959, no 2598. Prominent in the literature, along with Mossa (n 2), is an essay by Paolo Greco, 'Le società di comodo e la vendita delle loro azioni' (1935) 2 Riv dir comm 123, 132 ff.

[37] Cass 16 February 1977, no 721.

[38] See Francesco Galgano, 'Cessione di partecipazioni sociali e superamento della alterità soggettiva fra socio e società' [2004] Contratto e impr 537. The Italian Supreme Court cases followed: Cass 9 September 2004, no 18181 (case *Varese Football Club*), and the *obiter dicta* (buyer's claim rejected in both cases) of Cass 20 February 2004, no 3370 (case *Hotel*); Cass 12 September 2019, no 22790.

[39] *Ex multis*: Cass 27 September 1999, no 10669; Cass 19 July 2007, no 16031; Cass 13 March 2019, no 7183; Cass 10 June 2022, no 18755; Cass 27 April 2025, no 11076.

[40] BGH 26 September 2018, VIII ZR 187/17, [2018] NZG 1305.

[41] See the essays in Franco Bonelli and Mario De Andrè (eds), *Acquisizioni di società e di pacchetti azionari di riferimento* (Giuffrè 1990); for a broader explanation the monographic

Firstly, the parties are usually financially sophisticated entrepreneurs and should enjoy a broad freedom of contract; despite information asymmetries, the paternalistic approach of protecting the acquirer on the basis of an implied warranty appears inadvisable, and it also goes against the general *caveat emptor* principle. Secondly, legal certainty and predictability is an important feature. The minority opinion fails at demonstrating *when* the theory of piercing of the corporate veil or the good faith principle is the source of an implied legal warranty.[42] Additionally, the minority opinion fails at demonstrating *how* such theories could work; it is unclear what the implied warranties and their consequences are.[43] Therefore, the opposite, prevalent – and from a comparative perspective, established theory – is to be followed: share deals and asset deals are different from the perspective of protecting the acquirer.[44]

---

works Marco Speranzin, *Vendita della partecipazione di "controllo" e garanzie contrattuali* (Giuffrè 2006) in particular 91 ff, and Andrea Tina, *Il contratto di acquisizione di partecipazioni societarie* (Giuffrè 2007) in particular 294 ff.

[42] Does it occur only when the 100% shareholding is sold? Or is the majority stake enough? Or could the minority stake also suffice if specific rights connected with the appointment of the board are provided for?

The difficulties connected with the above-mentioned question are well demonstrated by the unsettled German debate on when a share deal could be considered as an asset deal with reference to the legal warranty before the *Schuldrechtsmodernisierung*. See the case law (three decisions: BGH 23 November 1979, V ZR 123/76, [1980] DB 679; BGH 2 June 1980, VIII ZR 64/79, [1980] NJW 2408; BGH 1 August 1980, VIII ZR 218/78, [1980] WM 284) and scholarship at (1982) 11 ZGR (in particular Claus-Wilhelm Canaris, 'Leistungsstörungen beim Unternehmenskauf' (1982) 11 ZGR 395). Since the *Schuldrechtsmodernisierung*, discussion has been based on the new § 453 BGB but is still not finally settled. See BGH 26 September 2018, VIII ZR 187/17, [2018] NZG 1305 (sale of the 50% shareholding in a *GmbH* to the other shareholder as an asset deal) and, in the literature, Claus-Wilhelm Canaris, 'Leistungsstörungen und Gewährleistung beim Unternehmenskauf nach der Reform des deutschen Schuldrechts' in Michael Stathopoulos (ed), *Festschrift für A Georgiades* (Beck 2005).

[43] As mentioned before, significant on one hand is that the buyer's claim has been upheld in the case of *Varese Football Club*, in which the company whose shares were sold was already insolvent at closing; therefore, in this case the *legal* warranty was already applicable (see Marco Speranzin, 'Compravendita "non convenzionalmente garantita" di partecipazioni sociali di "controllo"' (2019) 1 Giur comm 468).

On the other hand, the buyer's claim was rejected in the other two cases (apparently based on minority opinion) by the Italian Supreme Court (case *Hotel*; Cass 12 September 2019, no 22790), though the court did state it was following minority opinion as an *obiter dictum*. The lower Italian courts (in particular the important *Tribunale delle imprese* of Milan) also recognized that the main opinion is the only one which provides the legal certainty that acquisition practice needs. See for example Trib Milano, sez imprese 29 September 2020, no 5675.

[44] Share and asset deals could be treated as the same under other legal perspectives or in reference to specific legal topics, for example antitrust law, labour law, or competition limitations on the seller under Italian law, in reference to the application of art 2557 CC. See Giovanni E Colombo, *L'azienda e il mercato* (CEDAM 1979) 194; Marco Cian, *Dell'azienda* (Giuffrè 2018) 157.

III. Representations and Warranties

As mentioned in the previous paragraph, the prevailing opinion holds that the buyer is not entitled to recover in reference to the company's assets unless the agreement provided for representations and warranties.

Therefore, the representations and warranties are fundamental to protecting the purchaser and addressing the substantial gap between seller's and buyer's information concerning the target company.[45] The legal qualification of such representations and warranties is important in order to understand what the applicable rules are, in particular when the contract is not complete. Usually, agreements for the sale and purchase of shares are self-governing and extremely detailed, but problems can always arise owing to language that is misleading due to the origin of the clauses or that was left intentionally vague in order to leave broad interpretive discretion to the court.[46]

In Italy, the issue of the correct qualification of representations and warranties[47] was debated until 2014, on one hand in terms of literature and arbitration case law, and on the other hand in terms of judicial case law. The courts considered representations and warranties as a specification of the general warranty provided by the (much discussed) law of sales in the Italian civil code (art 1497).[48] Therefore, such clauses were also subject to the mandatory provision that establishes a limitation period of one year from the execution of the agreement (CC, art 1495) in which to bring claims against the vendor based on these clauses. A much-discussed case decided by the Milan Court of Appeal declared an arbitral tribunal's decision invalid due to a violation of this provision.[49] Following this

---

[45] *Ex multis*, Cass 19 July 2007, no 16031.

[46] Albert H Choi and George G Triantis, 'Strategic Vagueness in Contract Design: The Case of Corporate Acquisitions' (2010) 119 Yale LJ 848, 876ff.

[47] In this paper we assume representations and warranties have the same meaning and function, even though the two terms have (at least in some jurisdictions) a different meaning. See Mark Paul Gergen and Jacek Jastrzebski, 'Representation, warranty and indemnity' in *Le parole del diritto. Scritti in onore di C Castronovo*, vol 3 (Jovene 2018) 1491.

[48] Cass 10 February 1967, no 338, (1967) 1 Foro it 966; Cass 20 February 2004, no 3370; Cass 13 December 2006, no 26690.

The legal warranty provided by the law of sales since Roman law times has been defined as the *crux* of the civil law provisions. See Luigi Mengoni, 'Profili di una revisione della teoria sulla garanzia per i vizi nella vendita' (1953) 1–2 Riv dir comm 3 (discussing the seminal work of Werner Flume, *Eigenschaftsirrtum und Kauf* (Regensberg 1948) 187, who also proposed the application of the legal warranty to the sale of shares due to his interpretation of § 459 BGB (old formulation before the 2001 reform of the German private law)).

[49] The tribunal's decision granted indemnity to the buyer due to the violation of an environmental warranty even though the claim had been raised more than one year after the execution of the agreement; as discussed before, arbitration case law in Italy is usually *Professorenrecht*, and the arbitration court followed the leading opinion from scholarship. However, the Milan Court of Appeal (App Milano 21 November 2008, no 3138) considered the arbitration tribunal's decision to have gone against the mandatory provision of art 1495 of the Italian

case, a legislative proposal was presented, with support from academics and an international firm, to introduce a new, specific rule for representations and warranties in acquisition agreements:[50] the general limitation period of one year for warranties was considered by these advocates to be inconsistent with international standards and was deemed an unacceptable limitation on the freedom of contract.[51]

Before this initiative could be discussed in the parliament, the Italian Supreme Court overruled its previous case law in a decision that represented a turning point in acquisition practice[52] and whose *ratio decidendi* is specifically based on the role of international commerce and markets (*lex mercatoria*).

In the decision, the Italian Supreme Court first outlines its view that these representations and warranties (and indemnity) serve an insurance or security function: they allocate to the seller certain risks connected with the previous management of the business. The buyer is entitled to this indemnity even if the vendor could not be considered liable under the general principle of the law of obligations (*Garantiehaftung* or *garanzia*).[53] Of course, some of the vendor's undertakings could be also drafted so as to be less stringent depending on the seller's (best) knowledge[54] or requiring certain additional factors such as a material adverse effect on the company's assets.[55]

Second, the Corte di Cassazione followed the leading scholarship as well as the leading opinion in the arbitration case law: representations and warranties are autonomous provisions of the agreement and are not subject to legal warranty rules such as Article 1495 and its limitation period.[56] Therefore, the parties are

---

civil code because the claim was been raised more than one year after the execution of the agreement.

[50] Project of law no 1610/2014, with comments by Speranzin and Tina (n 30). Germany has experienced the same thing since the *Schuldrechtsmodernisierung* and the interpretation of § 444 BGB. See Vetter (n 11) 281.

[51] Actually, environmental claims as well claims under tax and labour law are usually enforceable even after a period of one year.

[52] Cass 24 July 2014, no 16963. On this decision see Pietro Trimarchi, 'Le garanzie contrattuali nell'acquisto di partecipazioni sociali' (2016) 1 Giur comm 5.

[53] Hanno Merkt, 'Haftung des Verkäufers bei M&A-Transaktionen in der US-amerikanischen Vetragspraxis' (2019) 1–2 RIW 2. On the warranty as a different undertaking from an obligation, see generally an early article by Mengoni (n 48) 23, and more recently Luigi Regazzoni, *La garanzia nel diritto dei contratti* (Giuffrè 2022).

[54] De Nova (n 9) 153.

[55] Choi and Triantis (n 46) 865.

[56] Cass 24 July 2014, no 16963; see also the more recent Cass 16 June 2021, no 17053 ('the business warranty is a product of the freedom of contract which allows the parties to increase or reduce the protection in order to connect the shares' value to the value of the company's assets'), and Cass 27 April 2025, no 11076 (with an ambiguous reference to the legal warranty).

free to specifically provide for the matter as well as to establish a suitable period within which the buyer may raise the claims provided by the agreement.[57]

This opinion is mainly based on *three* different legal points: as already discussed, the legal warranty concerns the shares rather than the company' assets;[58] the legal warranty (and limitation period) provided by art 1490ff CC should concern only material goods, not rights (ie, should relate to a *Sachkauf* and not to a *Rechtskauf*);[59] and the principle of freedom of contract allows the parties to establish specific contractual provisions without being constrained by rules that do not comport with the information asymmetry and the object of the sale, which is a 'complex and dynamic' good.[60]

IV. Due Diligence

Due diligence by the purchaser and her advisors can be considered as an internationally established practice in company acquisitions, no less so in Europe.[61] The importance of due diligence pertains not only to what we have defined as the internal issues of company acquisitions but also to the external ones.

First, in many legal systems the information the seller is obligated to divulge when negotiating an SPA is still subject to debate. Continental case law does not strictly adhere to the traditional *caveat emptor* principle; the information asymmetry between the parties and the closer relationship established by due diligence could be the source of a broader duty on the part of the vendor to divulge information even though the extent of such a duty is not completely clear.[62] Another

---

[57] See again Cass 24 July 2014, no 16963. Usually the period is longer, and it is often five years in reference to environmental, tax and labour matters, with a short notice period of 30–90 days from when buyer learned of the claim in order to inform the seller that a claim has arisen.

[58] In other words, if the company's assets, as stated before, are not the object of the agreement, legally speaking, then they cannot become part of the legal warranty when specific clauses are granted by the agreement.

[59] In the German literature, see Canaris in *Festschrift Georgiades* (n 42); Martin Zimmermann, 'Die Sachmängelgewährleistung beim Rechtskauf' (2013) 213 AcP 652. In the Italian literature, see Trimarchi (n 52) 7 ff.

[60] Freedom of contract is also the basis of the discussion of other important clauses in agreements for the sale and purchase of shares, such as exclusive remedy or entire agreement clauses. See De Nova (n 19) 97, and infra, IV.

[61] Hopt (n 24) 30; Antonio Morello, *Diritto alla due diligence e doveri degli amministratori* (Giuffré 2023) 1.

[62] The general principle of negotiating in good faith (CC, art 1337) could be the reason why the vendor must disclose more detailed information to the buyer during due diligence. See Tina (n 28) 193; in Germany BGH 26 September 2018 (n 26): 'gesteigerte Aufklärungspflicht'; Jan Möller, 'Offenlegungen und Aufklärungspflichten beim Unternehmenskauf' [2012] NZG 841, 843.

much-discussed topic is whether a violation of this duty has a material effect (and whether the buyer can recover damages) despite having executed the agreement.[63]

Experience with case law, however, shows that the special relationship between the parties at the due diligence stage can sometimes reduce, rather than increase, the seller's obligation to disclose material circumstances regarding the company's business.[64]

Second, due diligence – as a fundamental legal tool to overcome information asymmetries – is the source of the buyer's knowledge (real or potential) of certain facts related to the target company; as a default rule, at least in the UK and in continental Europe, such knowledge prevents the acquirer from pursuing a claim against the vendor (see art 1491 of the Italian civil code; § 442 BGB)[65]. Under US law the question is surprisingly unsettled in many jurisdictions.[66]

The main problem in acquisition practice is whether so-called 'sandbagging' clauses (under which the buyer is entitled to recover despite her knowledge that some of the seller's representations or warranties were incorrect) are enforceable. Some scholars are against sandbagging clauses because they consider them *a venire contra factum proprium* (in breach of the good faith principle, which is mandatory).[67] Other scholars – and this interpretation seems preferable – consider the rule provided by the European codes to be a default rule rather than mandatory: the buyer is fully entitled to protect herself from events ascribed to the past

[63] This has been a topic in private law in Italy following the case of *Cir v Fininvest*, Cass 17 September 2013, no 21255. Recently on this matter, see Giovanni D'Amico, 'La responsabilità precontrattuale' in Vincenzo Roppo (ed), *Trattato del contratto*, vol 5 (Giuffrè 2022) 1297. On the seller's disclosure duty in agreements for the sale and purchase of shares, see Lodo arb 25 May 2022 (n 28) 151.

[64] The seller who lets the acquirer or her advisors perform due diligence is often considered to have complied with the good faith principle *ipso facto*. See Speranzin (n 43) 474 (with the relevant Italian case law on the matter); Roel Fluit, 'What a US Buyer Should Expect in a Dutch M&A Transaction' (2017) 14(1) ECLJ 31 (mentioning the case of *Hoog Catharijne*, Dutch Supreme Court 22 December 1995 which stated that due diligence could increase the buyer's duty to ask for information).

[65] See Gergen and Jastrzebski (n 47) 1492 (deeming that the default rule in Europe and the UK is better than the one in the US because it reduces information and transaction costs.

[66] Charles K Whitehead, 'Sandbagging: Default Rules and Acquisition Agreements' (2011) 36 Del JCorpL 1081, 1082 (noting that the traditional default rule is complaint with the European one, even though some jurisdictions (such as Delaware and New York) follow the opposite principle).

[67] Fluit (n 64) 32; Jastrzebski (n 22) 292 fn 77.

The same discussion is also ongoing with reference to entire agreement or merger clauses, which aim to limit what the parties have discussed (and the representations they have made) before the execution of the agreement. It is doubtful whether such a clause could exclude pre-contractual liability based on statements made prior to closing that are later found to have been incorrect. For a critical opinion, see De Nova (n 19) 97; Steven L Schwarcz, 'Representations & Warranties, Fraud, and Risk Shifting: An Analytical Framework' (2022) Duke Law School Public Law & Legal Theory Series 2022-56, <https://ssrn.com/abstract=4256322>.

management of the company.[68] In any case, the pro-sandbagging clause is considered to be relatively unusual in European practice.[69]

Third – and starting now to look to what we have called the external issues of acquisition – it is not completely settled whether the target's board of directors is entitled to let a third party (the buyer) perform due diligence or whether the company's confidentiality must prevail. Under the business judgement rule, due diligence prevails even though the board's decision could be challenged.[70] Therefore, the directors should consider the potential buyer (competitor or not), the seller's shareholdings (majority or control) as well as other specific circumstances (business sector; industrial or intellectual property rights; *et cetera*).[71] In certain, specific cases, however, the business judgement rule either does not apply or judicial oversight could be tighter (for example, if some member of the board has even a minority shareholding in the target company).[72]

V. External Issues: The Role of the Majority Shareholder Towards Minority Shareholders in the Transfer of Control

It has been discussed whether the seller – as a dominant shareholder – has a fiduciary duty of care or good faith (or a trust relationship) toward the minority shareholder(s) in choosing to whom to sell.

The majority shareholder is generally widely recognized to have a fiduciary duty (*obbligo fiduciario* or *Treuepflicht*) vis-à-vis the company and the minority shareholders.[73] A fiduciary duty is also recognized in corporate control transactions in reference to the looting or stripping of assets and the conversion of cor-

---

[68] See generally Speranzin (n 41) 332.

[69] See Gergen and Jastrzebski (n 47) 1495.

[70] The board's business judgement rule on due diligence is discussed in Roberto Sacchi, 'Due ipotesi di asimmetria informativa consentita nelle s.p.a. non quotate' in Federico Ghezzi, Piergaetano Marchetti and Roberto Sacchi (eds), *Il caleidoscopio dell'informazione nel diritto societario e dei mercati* (Giuffrè 2020) 52; Hopt (n 24) 33; Morello (n 61) 67.

[71] Italian case law has rejected a minority shareholder's claim against the board of directors that had allowed the potential buyer of her shareholding to perform due diligence: Trib Bologna 23 July 2018, [2018] Società 1380. See the above-mentioned work of Morello (n 61) 67 ff (required is the shareholding that allows for control under CC, art 2359 no 1: the shareholdings necessary to appoint the members of the board of directors, usually 50.1% of the share capital)).

[72] OLG Düsseldorf 16 June 2016, I-22 U 14/17, [2017] NJOZ 202 ('vorzeitig übergehende Loyalität').

[73] In the United States, see *Jones v H.F. Ahmanson* (Cal. 1969). In Germany, see Marcus Lutter, 'Theorie der Mitgliedschaft' (1980) 180 AcP 84; Marcus Lutter, 'Die Treuepflicht des Aktionärs' (1989) 18 ZGR 446 ff; BGH 1 February 1988, II ZR 75/87, *Linotype*, [1989] JZ 43, with note Herbert Wiedemann (47). In Italy, see Cass 12 December 2005, no 27387.

porate business opportunities.[74] There is also reference to a duty on the majority shareholder's part to inform minority shareholders about the sale and the potential buyer.[75]

Some authors have tried to extend the fiduciary duty to a pro-rata, 'equal opportunity' rule, even in unlisted companies, that would support a legal tag-along right of the minority shareholders or a right to sell their shares to the buyer on the same terms.[76] The European Court of Justice rejected this position in the *Audiolux* case, stating that there is no evidence that a general principle of equal treatment of minority shareholders exists and therefore that there is no corresponding obligation on the dominant shareholder in European company law.[77]

Recent, specific Italian legal provisions outline the role of a change in the majority shareholder even outside the regulation of listed companies. Article 2497-*quater CC* provides minority shareholders with an exit right at market prices when a group of companies is established (thus under a *Konzernbildung* hypothesis)[78] and as well when the controlling shareholder changes; but this exit right is not triggered if a fairly priced offer is extended to all shareholders, even through a private offering.[79] Crowdfunding investors in an Italian *società a responsabilità limitata*'s (and therefore in a private company's) shares are afforded a mandatory exit or tag-along right in case the founders sell their controlling shareholdings within three years of the crowdfunding offer.[80]

---

[74] See *ex multis* Alfred Hill, 'The Sale of Controlling Shares' (1957) 70 Harv LRev 986; F Hodge O'Neal, 'Sale of a Controlling Corporate Interest: Bases of Possible Seller Liability' (1976) 38 U Pitt LRev 9 ff; Colombo (n 2) 1454; Herbert Wiedemann, *Gesellschaftsrecht*, vol 1 (CH Beck 1980) 451; Martin Weber, *Vormitgliedschaftliche Treubindungen* (CH Beck 1999) 249.

[75] Andrea Vicari, 'Sui doveri del socio di controllo in caso di vendita della partecipazione sociale' in *Amministrazione e controllo nel diritto delle società. Liber amicorum Antonio Piras* (Giappichelli 2010); Regoli (n 10) 181.

[76] See Andrews (n 2) 505 ff; broad analysis in Stella Richter (n 2) 268ff.

[77] See CJEU 15 October 2009, C-101/08 *Audiolux SA and others v Groupe Bruxelles Lambert SA (GBL) and others*, ECLI:EU:C:2009:626. On this decision Frederico Mucciarelli, 'Equal Treatment of Shareholders and European Union Law' (2010) 7 ECFR 158; in general Mathias Habersack and Dirk A Verse, *Europäisches Gesellschaftsrecht* (5th edn, CH Beck 2019) para 92, 268.

[78] In Germany, see Marcus Lutter, 'Treuepflichten und aktuelle Anwendungsprobleme' (1998) 162 ZHR 174; already discussed in Colombo (n 2) 1479.

[79] On this provision, see Trib Milano 21 July 2015 (*Pomellato* case) and Paolo Piscitello, 'Note critiche in tema di recesso nei gruppi di società' in Guiseppe A Rescio and Marco Speranzin (eds), *Patrimonio sociale e governo dell'impresa. Dialogo tra giurisprudenza, dottrina e prassi in ricordo di Colombo* (Giappichelli 2020) 384.

[80] See the regulation of the Italian Financial Authority on the matter at art 24 of the Regolamento Consob no 18592/2013. On the issue, see Marco Cian, 'S.r.l. PMI, s.r.l., s.p.a.: schemi argomentativi per una ricostruzione del sistema' [2018] Riv soc 835 (considering the provision more as a rule of financial market law than of company law).

However, at the practical level drag-along clauses regarding the transfer of shares further illustrate developments in the area of freedom of contract or private ordering. These clauses, as is well known, can be and frequently are inserted into private equity and venture capital deals or in the articles of associations or shareholders' agreements, and the established sale price has been considered (firstly, once again, in arbitration case law and only then by the courts) fair at market prices.[81] Some recent scholarship (inspired by arbitration case law) requires that drag-along clauses are to comply with the good faith-principle (or other general shareholder's fiduciary duties), which means that not only the price but also the other provisions of SPA agreements (in particular, any representations and warranties) offered to all the shareholders should be fair in order to equally protect minority shareholders.[82]

Therefore, even if the rules provided by the takeover regulation are generally not considered to be applicable to private sales,[83] we could probably conclude that both statutory and contractual rules are giving rise to a standard for the transfer of control,[84] and the seller has a specific duty of good faith towards minority shareholders in corporate control transactions.[85]

---

[81] See the already mentioned Lodo arb 29 July 2008 (n 28); Trib Milano 24 March 2011, (2013) 2 Banca borsa tit cred 65; Trib Milano 22 December 2014, <www.giurisprudenzadelleimprese.it>.

[82] Alberto Mazzoni, 'Patti di co-vendita e doveri fiduciari' in Antonio Crivellaro (ed), *Trasferimenti di partecipazioni azionarie. Linee evolutive dopo il convegno di Portofino del 1989* (Giuffrè 2017) 211ff.

[83] See Peter O Mülbert, 'Entwicklung des Übernahmerechts' in Rüdiger Veil, Hans C Grigoleit and Mathias Habersack (ed), *Öffentliche Unternehmensübernahmen* (Mohr Siebeck 2022) 21. Broad discussion on the issue since the Italian regulation of the public offering was provided by law no 149, 18 February 1992 is found in Stella Richter (n 2) 44 and 347ff.

[84] On the alternatives between rules and standards see, *ex multis*, Louis Kaplow, 'General Characteristics of Rules' in *Encyclopedia of Law and Economics*, vol 5 (Edward Elgar 2000) 502.

[85] A fiduciary duty *on the buyer* is generally ruled out. See Andreas Cahn, 'The Shareholders' Fiduciary Duty' in Hanne S Birkmose (ed), *Shareholders' Duties* (Kluwer Law 2017); but see Weber (n 74); Peter O Mülbert and Roger Kiem, 'Der schädigende Beteiligungserwerb' (2013) 177 ZHR 819.

Legal Capital

Alexander Schall

I. The Concept of Legal Capital

Legal capital consists of two pillars. To incorporate a company, a substantial minimum capital must be raised (*Kapitalaufbringung*, capital procurement).[1] This is the 'subscribed capital' or 'stated capital'. It must not be returned to the shareholders (*Kapitalerhaltung*, capital maintenance).[2] Legal capital must be safeguarded by exit liabilities that apply when insolvency is looming. This is because the capital maintenance principle does not prevent the capital from being diminished or lost in the course of trading; it only forbids its return to the shareholders. That is why additional rules must be in place to counter the risk of directors op-

[1] Marcus Lutter, 'Legal Capital of Public Companies in Europe' in Marcus Lutter (ed), Legal Capital in Europe (ECFR Special Volume 1/1, 2006) 6–8. For public companies see eg AktG, § 7 (50,000 EUR); CC, art 2327 (50,000 EUR); for private companies see, eg, GmbH Act, § 5(1) (25,000 EUR); but note that private companies with only 1 EUR worth of assets are permissible in both Germany (the 'Unternehmergesellschaft' or 'UG' under GmbH Act, § 5a I) and Italy (CC, art 2463).

[2] AktG, §§ 57, 62; GmbH Act, §§ 30, 31; CC, art 2445–2447; cf Lutter (n 1) 8–11.

portunistically trading behind the backs of creditors. This is the task of the Member States.[3]

Each of the two pillars of legal capital is free-standing. For example, England has always enforced capital maintenance,[4] but it never required a minimum capital before it was forced to by the Second Directive 77/91/EEC. Conversely, it would theoretically also be possible to set a high minimum capital as an entry barrier to limited liability but allow distributions merely on solvency tests regardless of the amount of subscribed capital. But only the combination of the two pillars adds up to a coherent system of legal capital.[5]

Legal capital was first established as a coherent system based on raising and maintaining subscribed capital in the German GmbH; with that, it spread all over the world.[6] The late Marcus Lutter conceptualized the function of legal capital in his fundamental comparative habilitation thesis *Kapital, Sicherung der Kapitalaufbringung und Kapitalerhaltung in den Aktien- und GmbH-Rechten der EWG* (1964). His work gained much traction at the national and European levels. It resulted in the extension of legal capital rules to all public companies through the Second Directive. The core idea is that legal capital provides legal certainty for the shareholders as well as for the directors running a business with limited liability.[7] If the rules of procuring and maintaining the company's capital are complied with, the shareholders will avoid any further liability. This is not only so in large public companies but also in close corporations, in which the shareholders are typically involved in the conduct of the business. If the company becomes insolvent, the directors will be obliged to stop trading and enter into insolvency proceedings through exit liabilities like the German duty to file for insolvency (*Insolvenzantragspflicht*, § 15a of the Insolvency Code – InsO) or the prohibition of outgoing payments from insolvent companies (*Zahlungsverbot*, InsO, § 15b). The long and short of it is that legal capital is the quid pro quo of limited liability.

> 'Die Sicherstellung der Kapitalaufbringung ist Voraussetzung für die Zulassung von Körperschaften […], bei denen die Haftung […] beschränkt ist'.[8]
>
> [Securing the raising of capital is a prerequisite for the registration of corporations […] for which liability […] is limited.]

---

[3] Lutter (n 1) 11–12.

[4] Cf, eg, *Trevor v Whitworth (1887)* 12 App Cas 409, at 423–424 on share buy-backs. According to Lord Watson, the law prohibits '[…] every transaction between a company and a shareholder, by means of which the money already paid to the company in respect of his shares is returned to him […]'; cf Eva Micheler, 'Gläubigerschutz im englischen Gesellschaftsrecht' (2004) 33 ZGR 324.

[5] Similarly Lutter (n 1) 6; Jan P Brosius, in Peter Kindler and Jan Lieder (eds), European Corporate Law (Nomos, Beck, Hart 2021) art 45 para 7: 'minimum capital not a necessary element'.

[6] Lutter (n 1) 3.

[7] Lutter (n 1) 4 sub 8 (3).

[8] BGH 18 February 1991, II ZR 104/90, 113 BGHZ 335 = [1991] NJW 1754, 1758.

'Zweck der Gründungsvorschriften ist es in erster Linie, die reale Aufbringung der gesetzlich vorgeschriebenen Mindestkapitalausstattung der Gesellschaft im Zeitpunkt ihres Entstehens als Ausgleich für die Beschränkung ihrer Haftung auf das Gesellschaftsvermögen sicherzustellen'.[9]

[The purpose of the incorporation provisions is primarily to ensure that the company' statutory minimum capitalisation is actually raised at the time of its formation as compensation for the limitation of its liability to the company's assets.]

Legal capital provisions can be 'goldplated'. For example, German stock corporation law prohibits not only the return of the subscribed capital (the 'capital yardstick'), but also of all accumulated legal reserves.[10] The MBCA in the US supplements strict maintenance of the stated capital with an equitable solvency test.[11] Meant as an additional safeguard, this test was turned into the main criterium by which to allow distributions. That was a prelude to the capital debate (see below at V.).

II. The Origins of Legal Capital

1. The Aktiengesellschaft after 1884

When modern companies emerged in the course of the nineteenth century, the concept of legal capital had not yet been developed. At stake in these large companies was investor protection, not creditor protection. Company acts would usually prohibit the return of subscribed and paid-up capital,[12] but the raising of capital was largely subject to private ordering. In Germany, this became a particularly pressing problem after the system of state concessions (art 208 of the German General Commercial Code – ADHGB 1861) was abolished in 1870.[13] Henceforth, everyone was entitled to set up a company to pursue whatever purpose they wished, provided they complied with the legal provisions. This soon resulted in the *Gründerschwindel* ('founder's fraud') and the ensuing *Gründerkrach* ('founder's crash') of 1873 – a belated German South Sea Bubble that was fuelled by an influx of funds after the victory over France in the Franco-Prussian War of 1870–1871.

---

[9] BGH 16 March 1992, II ZB 17/91, 117 BGHZ 323 = [1992] NJW 1824, 1825.

[10] Alexander Schall and Jan Machunsky, in Andrea Vicari and Alexander Schall (eds), *Company Laws of the EU* (CH Beck 2020) part 2 (Germany) ch 2 paras 117ff.

[11] MBCA, §§ 45–46 and 66–70 (1969) (amended 1980).

[12] ADHGB 1861, art 216(2); as to England, see above at n 4.

[13] Alexander Schall, in Vicari and Schall (n 10) part 2 (Germany) ch 1 paras 14ff. The connection between the abolition of the concession system and the *Gründerkrach* is generally accepted though not entirely certain, because the surviving concession system in Austria did not prevent a similar crash, cf Jan Lieder, 'Die 1. Aktienrechtsnovelle vom 11. Juni 1870' in Mathias Habersack and Walter Bayer, *Aktienrecht im Wandel*, vol 1 (Mohr Siebeck 2007) paras 109ff; Walter Bayer, 'Die Entstehung und Fortentwicklung der Kapitalschutzvorschriften' in Bayer and Habersack (this note) vol 2 paras 36–37.

In response, Germany enacted the *Gesetz betreffend die Kommanditgesellschaft auf Aktien und die Aktiengesellschaft* of 18 July 1884.[14] This act marked the birth of modern German company law – and of legal capital. The general principle was self-help instead of state help[15] (no 'corporate police'). It contained various protective measures like, eg, strict disclosure of privileges granted to the incorporators.[16] Through our modern lenses we would link most of those instruments with legal capital and creditor protection. But in truth, they started as investor protection tools.[17]

All contributions had to be transferred to the free disposal of the directors.[18] That excluded any agreed kick-backs to the incorporators or the involved banks. Contributions in cash had to be fully subscribed and paid up to 25% (previously 10%).[19] Netting by the incorporator was prohibited.[20] Contributions in kind had to be disclosed and were subject to expert evaluation.[21] To avoid evasion, the new rules on *Nachgründung* (substantial subsequent acquisitions) were introduced.[22] The minimum amount per share was set at 1,000 marks. For a mandatory number of five incorporators, the result was a de facto minimum capital of 5,000 marks. Again, this was done to protect investors by keeping out inexperienced retail investors (not to protect creditors). There had been no official minimum capital for stock corporations prior to the Stock Corporation Act (the 'AktG') of 1937, which copied the concept from the GmbH Act.

The 1884 act added core elements of the first pillar (procurement of capital) to the existing rules of capital maintenance to give birth to legal capital. But it was not implemented with a view to creditor protection but rather to support self-help by shareholders. This perspective did not change until the introduction of the GmbH in 1892.

2. The GmbH Act of 1892

The first coherent system of legal capital for the purpose of creditor protection was introduced with the GmbH Act of 1892. The safeguards in the ADHGB of 1884 were aimed at investor protection, but this priority shifted when Germany decided to introduce a small private company from scratch. This top-down ap-

[14] For details see Sibylle Hofer, 'Das Aktiengesetz von 1884 – ein Lehrstück für prinzipielle Schutzkonzeptionen' in Bayer and Habersack (n 13) vol 1; Markus Söhnchen, *Die historische Entwicklung der rechtlichen Gründungsvoraussetzungen von Handels- und Aktiengesellschaften* (Duncker & Humblot 2005).

[15] Hofer (n 14) paras 18ff with references to the antecedent debate of this issue.

[16] ADHGB 1884, art 209b; today AktG, § 26.

[17] Lutter (n 1) 2; Walter Bayer, 'Die Entstehung und Fortentwicklung der Kapitalschutzvorschriften' in Bayer and Habersack (n 13) vol 2.

[18] ADHGB 1884, art 210(3); today AktG, § 36(2).

[19] ADHGB 1884, art 210(3); today AkG, § 36a(1).

[20] ADHGB 1884, art 184; today AktG, § 66(1)(2).

[21] ADHGB 1884, art 209b, 209f, 209h; today AktG §§ 27(1), 33(2) no 4; 34(1) no 2.

[22] ADHGB 1884, art 213f; today AktG, § 52.

proach countered the bottom-up emergence of the English small companies[23] that had spread across the world via the British colonies. In those small entities, limited liability came with far greater and more concrete perils for creditors. The German legislator reacted by implementing the two pillars of legal capital. A considerable minimum capital of 20,000 gold marks (today, about 160,000 euros[24]) posed an entry barrier and counterbalanced the wide scope of party autonomy under the articles. Sections 30 and 31 of the GmbH Act ordained that the capital yardstick set by the subscribed capital of at least 20,000 gold marks was to be maintained. Legal capital was born.

The system in its youth was still weak. There was no state oversight over the raising of capital yet. The incorporators were allowed to self-evaluate their contributions in kind. But over time, the rules were tightened, and as the next chapter will show, more and more safeguards were put in place.

III. The Rise of Legal Capital

1. Evolution at the National Level

Once the ADHGB of 1884 had installed the initial safeguards under German law to enforce the effective raising of capital and supplemented the existing rules on capital maintenance, legal capital in the stock corporation was almost complete. It is true that no minimum capital was introduced prior to the Stock Corporation Act of 1937, but it never played an important role anyway.[25] More importantly, capital maintenance in the German stock corporation is very strict. Disguised distributions are absolutely prohibited because the shareholders are only entitled to dividends (AktG, § 57(3)). Any financial advantage to shareholders at the expense of the company is deemed a disguised distribution.

For an extreme example, see BGH – *Telekom III*[26]: Under US law, unlike under German law, only the issuer was liable for providing false information in the prospectus. Shareholders selling their existing shares in the course of an IPO are not. As a result, the company is not only liable for the damage with respect to the fresh shares, but also for the damage from existing shares sold in the issue. The BGH held that the shareholder (the Bundesrepublik Deutschland) should have granted indemnity from liability arising from the prospectus insofar as its old shares were sold. Not doing so was considered an unlawful return of capital.

---

[23] Cf Ron Harris, 'The Private Origins of the Private Company: Britain 1862–1907' (2013) 33(2) OJLS 339.

[24] <www.bundesbank.de/resource/blob/615162/94b87ff6d25eceb84c9cfb801162b334/mL/kaufkraftaequivalente-historischer-betraege-in-deutschen-waehrungen-data.pdf> accessed December 2025.

[25] Lutter (n 1) 7.

[26] BGH 31 May 2011, II ZR 141/09, 190 BGHZ 7.

By contrast, legal capital in the GmbH suffered from structural weakness because it did not provide sufficient safeguards to prevent evasion of the law.[27] This was particularly true for the first pillar, the raising of capital. But it did not remain so. After initial steps by the Reichsgericht, the Bundesgerichtshof continuously strengthened the legal capital concept in private companies. The rules on *verdeckte Sacheinlagen* (hidden contributions in kind) furnished the paradigm. Former § 19(2)(2) of the GmbH Act prevented shareholders from offsetting their liability to pay up on the share capital against counterclaims, while former § 19(3) of the GmbH Act, more specifically, forbade netting the duty to pay up against claims arising from a sale of assets to the company unless the sale transaction was disclosed pursuant to § 5(4) of the GmbH Act, ie, as a contribution in kind. Owing to unclear wording, a debate arose whether the prohibition under § 19(3) was also (like § 19(2)(2)) restricted to set-offs initiated by the shareholder or whether the prohibition covered netting agreements and set-offs by the company as well. The Reichsgericht took the latter view because the ability to raise capital in general had to be ensured.[28] The BGH developed this idea further and prohibited a cash contribution that was only formally paid up from being returned immediately to the shareholder as the purchase price for an asset.[29] This so-called *Hin- und Herzahlen* (back-and-forth payment) of the cash invalidated both the contribution and the purchase – even if the transaction was actually at fair value.[30] The pro-

[27] See Jonathan Rickford, 'Reforming Capital, Report of the Interdisciplinary Group on Capital Maintenance' (2004) 15 EBLR 919 (criticising the concept due to the 'bypassibility' of the rules); see also Paul L Davies, *Gower and Davies' Principles of Company Law* (7th edn, Sweet & Maxwell 2003) 230. However, this criticism is too superficial, because it overlooks the antidotes. The true criticism was the cost of these legal instruments. See below.

[28] RG 2 March 1915, II 471/14, 86 RGZ 291, 293–294; confd. RG 20 June 1933, II 41/33, 141 RGZ 204, 209ff (to prevent circumvention).

[29] BGH 10 November 1958, II ZR 3/57, 28 BGHZ 314 = [1959] NJW 383; RG 5 March 1938, II 104/37, 157 RGZ 213, 2 (earlier ruling in regard to stock corporations).

[30] BGH 10 November 1958 (n 29): 'Grundsätzlich genügt allerdings zur Erfüllung der Einlageschuld, daß die Leistung des Gesellschafters in die freie Verfügungsgewalt des Geschäftsführers gelangt. Das kann aber nicht für eine Leistung gelten, die zwar ernstlich, aber in der Absicht bewirkt wird, aus ihr die eigene Forderung aus einer Übernahmeabrede befriedigt zu erhalten. Eine solche Leistung des Einlageschuldners gleicht einem geworfenen Ball, der an einem Gummiband hängt und wieder zurückschnellt. Sie scheidet nur vorübergehend aus dem Vermögen des Leistenden aus und soll nur zeitweilig der Gesellschaft gehören, aber wieder, wenn auch zur Erfüllung der Vergütungsforderung, ausgekehrt werden.'

[For the fulfilment of the obligation to contribute, in principle it is sufficient that the shareholder's remittance be placed at the managing director's disposal. However, this cannot apply to a payment that, while made in earnest, is intended to go to satisfying the shareholder's own claim arising from a premeditated agreement. Such a performance by the shareholder is like him throwing a ball attached to a rubber cord. It bounces back. It is only temporarily not among his assets; it is supposed to belong to the company temporarily, to be paid out again in fulfilment of the [shareholder's] claim to compensation.]

For more on this, cf BGH 2 December 2002, II ZR 101/02, 153 BGHZ 107 = [2003] NZG 168; BGH 7 July 2003, II ZR 235/01, 155 BGHZ 329 = [2003] NZG 867; BGH 16 January hibition of the disguised contribution in kind was born. The underlying principle is called the *Grundsatz der realen Kapitalaufbringung*. The company must receive precisely those assets it was promised as a contribution to its free disposal. It is not sufficient that the value of the assets should be enough to cover the subscribed capital on the balance sheet. The rule on this *verdeckte Sacheinlage* was codified in 2008 (but also mitigated, see below) for both the GmbH (GmbH Act, § 19(4)) and the AG (AktG, § 27(3)).

GmbH Act, § 19(4)(1):
'Ist eine Geldeinlage eines Gesellschafters bei wirtschaftlicher Betrachtung und aufgrund einer im Zusammenhang mit der Übernahme der Geldeinlage getroffenen Abrede vollständig oder teilweise als Sacheinlage zu bewerten (verdeckte Sacheinlage), so befreit dies den Gesellschafter nicht von seiner Einlageverpflichtung.'

[If, upon economic consideration and on the basis of an agreement reached in connection with the taking over of a contribution in cash, a contribution in cash made by a shareholder is to be regarded either fully or partly as a contribution in kind ('hidden contribution in kind'), this does not exempt the shareholder from the obligation to pay a capital contribution.][31]

Beyond this signature development, there have been several other legislative and jurisdictional interventions over the decades to tighten the system of legal capital. They were usually introduced with a view to the GmbH even though the new instruments, once established, were extended to the *Aktiengesellschaft*, too.[32] That happened either immediately or over time.

In 1980, the power of the Registergericht (court of registry) to examine the value of contributions in kind (GmbH Act, § 9c) was introduced. It was flanked by a liability on the part of the contributing shareholders to pay up any shortfall in cash (GmbH Act, § 9(1) – *Differenzhaftung*).

The Bundesgerichtshof, disappointed by the low levels of equity in private companies and the practice of financing them via shareholder loans, had introduced the *Eigenkapitalersatzrecht* (law on capital replacing shareholder loans) back in 1959.[33] At the same time, the justices rejected piercing the corporate veil for material undercapitalisation.[34] They did not want to make the shareholders

2006, II ZR 76/04, 166 BGHZ 8 = [2006] NZG, 344; BGH 16 March 1998, II ZR 303/96, [1998] NJW 1951.

31 Translation available at <https://www.gesetze-im-internet.de/englisch_gmbhg/>.

32 Take for example the transfer of the rules on subordination for equity-replacing loans (*Eigenkapitalersatzrecht*) in BGH 26 March 1984, II ZR 171/83, 90 BGHZ 381 = [1984] NJW 1893, *BuM*; or, see the academic discussion on application of *Existenzvernichtungshaftung* in AGs. On both issues, cf Alexander Schall, '„Durchgriffshaftung" im Aktienrecht – haften Aktionäre für existenzvernichtende Eingriffe, qualifiziert faktische Konzernierung oder materielle Unterkapitalisierung?' in Mathias Habersack, Karl Huber and Gerald Spindler (eds), *Festschrift für Eberhard Stilz* (CH Beck 2014) 542ff.

33 BGH 14 December 1959, II ZR 187/57, 31 BGHZ 258 = [1960] NJW 285, *Lufttaxi*. For a case narrative, see Jan Thiessen, '§ 5 – Lufttaxi' in Holger Fleischer and Jan Thiessen (eds), Gesellschaftsrechts-Geschichten (Mohr Siebeck 2018).

34 Confirmed in BGH 4 May 1977, VIII ZR 298/75, 68 BGHZ 312 – *Fertighaus*; BGH 28 April 2008, II ZR 264/06, 176 BGHZ 204 – *Gamma*.

pay up the company's debts like partners. But they did want to keep funds in the company that the shareholders had actually contributed to the company's finances. In the 2008 MoMiG (an act to modernise the law of GmbHs), this case law was replaced by a general subordination of shareholder loans (sub VI.).

The BGH disallowed the immediate return of the cash contribution as a loan to the shareholder.[35] This practice, called 'simple payment back and forth' (*einfaches Hin- und Herzahlen*), was once widespread and since 2008 has been codified (and under certain conditions, legalised) in § 19(5) of the GmbH Act. Before, such payments could never discharge the duty to pay up. The doctrinal starting point was the same as for the *verdeckte Sacheinlage*. The cash is not at the free disposal of the directors.[36] Nevertheless, what is called the 'simple payment back and forth' does not amount to a hidden contribution in kind. The transaction does not disguise the transfer of another asset to the company, but rather it merely 'dodges' the receipt of the cash. In essence, the promise to contribute cash is replaced with the promise to repay a loan.[37] The company's claim becomes much weaker because it is not secured by subsidiary joint and several liability on the part of the other incorporators under § 24 of the GmbH Act, and it is subject to the regular limitation period of three years (BGB, § 195) as opposed to ten years for claims to contributions (of the GmbH Act, § 19(6)). That is why the BGH refused to allow the duty to pay up to be discharged in those cases, too, even though no disclosure obligations were being circumvented (unlike in the case of disguised contributions).

In the beginning of the new millennium, the acquisition of both (new) shelf companies[38] and (old) shell companies[39] in order to run a business was restricted by case law.[40] The BGH treated such transactions as *wirtschaftliche Neugründung* ('economic incorporation'), meaning that not only did the directors have to register the company's new activity by modifying the 'objects' clause, they al-

[35] BGH 21 November 2005, II ZR 140/04, 165 BGHZ 113 = [2006] NZG 24; BGH 24 January 2006, XI ZR 384/03, 166 BGHZ 84 = [2006] NZG 227; BFH, 27 September 2001, V R 32/00, [2002] NZG 54.

[36] See above, at n 30. See also BFH, 27 September 2001 (n 35).

[37] That is why a minority view assumes it to be a disguised contribution in kind, a claim based on the loan instead of on the cash contribution. Cf Tim Drygala, 'Zweifelsfragen im Regierungsentwurf zum MoMiG' [2007] NZG 561, 563–564. But the legislator followed the majority and distinguished *einfaches Hin- und Herzahlen* in § 19(5) of the GmbH Act (and AktG, § 27(4)) from the *verdeckte Sacheinlage* in § 19(4) of the GmbH Act (and AktG, § 27(3)).

[38] So-called *Vorratsgründung*, ie, agents incorporating companies for future use. Activity only commences when they are acquired later. A *Vorratsgründung* is only permissible if its purpose is openly declared (*offene Vorratsgründung*), because it is illegal to incorporate on a pseudo-purpose, as was decided in BGH 16 March 1992 (n 9). It follows that the objects clause must be modified when the company launches.

[39] So-called *Altmantelverwendung*, ie, defunct companies, depleted of all assets and liabilities, which are not liquidated but rather sold as a vehicle for a new business.

[40] BGH 9 December 2002, II ZB 12/02, 153 BGHZ 158 = [2003] NZG 170, *Vorratsgründung*; BGH 7 July 2003, II ZB 4/02, 155 BGHZ 318 = [2003] NZG 972, *Altmantelverwendung*.

so had to provide new assurances that the subscribed (minimum) capital of the company was at their free disposal (GmbH Act, § 8(2)). If not, limited liability for both directors and shareholders would be jeopardised by a duty to pay up the minimum capital and make good any losses.[41] Again, this was done to safeguard against evasion of the minimum capital requirement.

The BGH created case law on *Existenzvernichtungshaftung* to mitigate two specific shortcomings of the capital maintenance rules for GmbHs.[42] First, the static balance sheet test under §§ 30–31 of the GmbH Act makes no provision for impending payments on current contracts. As long as they did not disturb the capital yardstick, the *Geschäftsführer* or managing director(s) could legally withdraw a million euros worth of wages the day before pay day, ruining the company, but would still escape liability simply by filing for insolvency on time. Second, the consequence of an unlawful return of capital is merely the restoration of that amount. The damage caused by ruining the company (particularly the loss caused by the shift from going concern to break-up value) was left uncompensated. These gaps in the law motivated the BGH to introduce *Existenzvernichtungshaftung*.[43] It applies where shareholders abuse their powers to deplete the assets of the company and thereby cause or deepen its insolvency. Originally, it was construed as a true piercing of the corporate veil.[44] But in 2007, the basis for the claim was shifted to tort law under § 826 of the BGB.[45] It is now very similar to the French crime of 'abus des biens sociaux'; according to the BGH, this tort's specificity was that the victim was not the creditors but the company itself.

In November 2004, the BGH tightened its capital maintenance rules in a highly problematic way.[46] In spite of the balance sheet neutrality of the loan, the court said it assumed a loan extended by an ailing company to a (perfectly solvent) shareholder could amount to an unlawful return of capital. Sufficient was that the loan depleted the company's liquid assets and that these assets did not exceed the

---

[41] BGH 6 March 2012, II ZR 56/10, 192 BGHZ 341 = [2012] NZG 539 (considerably restricting those risks by looking at the company's balance sheet retrospectively on the day when the registration should have happened instead of the day of the actual insolvency).

[42] The fundamental justification was delivered by the then-chair of the corporate law chamber Volker Röhricht, 'Die GmbH im Spannungsfeld von wirtschaftlicher Dispositionsfreiheit ihrer Gesellschafter und Gläubigerschutz' in Karlmann Geiß (ed), *Festschrift aus Anlass des fünfzigjährigen Bestehens von Bundesgerichtshof, Bundesanwaltschaft und Rechtsanwaltschaft am Bundesgerichtshof* (Heymanns 2000) 103ff.

[43] The first case was BGH 17 September 2001, II ZR 178/99, 149 BGHZ 10 = [2002] NZG 38, *Bremer Vulkan*, for an account of which see, eg, Thomas Liebscher, in *Münchener Kommentar GmbHG*, vol 1 (4th edn, CH Beck 2022) Anhang § 13 para 539ff.; on further developments, see Alexander Schall, *Kapitalgesellschaftsrechtlicher Gläubigerschutz* (CH Beck 2009) 216ff; see also, eg, Jan Lieder, in Lutz Michalski and others (eds), Kommentar zum Gesetz betreffend die Gesellschaften mit beschränkter Haftung, vol 1 (4th edn, CH Beck 2023), § 13 para 434ff (criticising the principle and preferring true veil-piercing).

[44] BGH 24 June 2002, II ZR 300/00, 151 BGHZ 181 = [2002] NZG 914, *KBV*.

[45] BGH 16 July 2007, II ZR 3/04, 173 BGHZ 246 = [2007] NZG 667, *Trihotel*.

[46] BGH 24 November 2003, II ZR 171/01, 157 BGHZ 72.

subscribed capital. This mirrored the system of *reale Kapitalaufbringung* with a hitherto unheard-of element of *reale Kapitalerhaltung*, medicine that was administered to prevent the looting of cash from ailing companies. But the side effect was a massive blow to central cash management, because every transfer to the central account now necessitated a balance sheet test. That result was overly burdensome, which is why the legislator of the MoMiG explicitly overruled the precedent of this infamous *Novemberurteil* (see below VI.).

2. Expansion Throughout Europe

Following the influential comparative work of Marcus Lutter, the concept of legal capital gained traction at the European level. It was extended to all European stock corporations via the Second Company Law Directive 77/91/EEC in 1977. The directive was based on the principle of minimum protection and therefore is less rigid in some parts than German and Italian stock corporation law.[47] Today, we find the following rules on the raising of capital in the Company Law Directive (EU) 2017/1132:

- Article 45 requires a minimum capital of 25,000 euros, whereas Germany and Italy require 50,000 euros[48] – which is nonetheless negligible for a 'true' – ie, listed – public company.
- Article 46 requires that the assets forming the subscribed capital must be capable of economic assessment and prohibits undertakings to perform work or supply services.[49]

  Contrary to widespread opinion,[50] such assets must be accounted for on the left side of the balance-sheet ('assets') to qualify as contributions. This restriction does not derive directly from the wording ('capable of economic assessment') but from the context, because otherwise the contributed asset could not 'form the subscribed capital'. Put even more precisely, the asset need not be accounted for (yet) on the balance sheet of the subscriber (if any), but it must be accounted for on the balance sheet of the company.
- Article 47 prohibits issues of shares below par value ('sub pari').[51] This does not refer to any premium (*agio*) reflecting the 'true value' of the share, and so is practically irrelevant.
- Article 48 requires 25% of a cash contribution to be paid up immediately.[52] Contributions in kind have to be transferred within five years, whereas Germany and Italy insist on immediate conferral.[53]

---

[47] For details see Lucia Folladori, in Vicari and Schall (n 10) part 3 (Italy) ch 2 paras 91ff.

[48] AktG, § 7; CC, art 2327.

[49] AktG, § 27(2); CC, art 2342(5).

[50] Jessica Schmidt, in Walter Bayer, Marcus Lutter and Jessica Schmidt, *Europäisches Unternehmens- und Kapitalmarktrecht* (6th edn, De Gruyter 2018) para 19.52.

[51] AktG, § 9(1); CC, art 2346(4).

[52] AktG, § 36a(1); CC, art 2342(2).

[53] AktG, § 36a(2); CC, art 2342(3).

- Article 49 makes an independent expert report on contributions in kind mandatory (subject to the derogation in art 50).[54]
- Article 52 makes substantial acquisitions subsequent to incorporation (*Nachgründung*) subject to expert valuation in order to avoid circumvention of art 49.[55]
- Beyond lawful capital reductions, art 53 prohibits any release of the shareholder from the obligation to pay the contribution.[56]

As to capital maintenance, a similar picture materialises.

- Article 56(1) prohibits distributions that would undercut the capital yardstick (plus mandatory reserves). Article 56(3) limits distributions to accumulated net profits (plus sums drawn from reserves available for distribution). Italy basically mirrors these rules,[57] while Germany provides, more restrictively, that prior to liquidation shareholders are only entitled to balance-sheet profits.[58] It follows that German shareholders must not receive any value from the company. This is the doctrinal basis prohibiting all 'disguised distributions', as exemplified above. It also prevents snow-ball systems, in which dividends are paid from the premium on new shares (*Agiotage* = stockjobbing).[59]

  It is not settled whether the broad German understanding of distribution applies under European law as well.[60] The better answer is no.[61] For starters, the thesis of German authors that *European law* prohibits the distribution of any reserves[62] clearly contradicts the wording of Art 56(1), which remits the issue to the law of the Member States: '[…] no distribution to shareholders may be made […] when the net assets would become […] lower than the amount of the subscribed capital plus those reserves which may not be distributed under the law or the statutes of the company.' This also defeats the related thesis that European law prohibits any disguised distributions. On closer look, it becomes apparent that unlike § 57(3) of the AktG, art 56 does not restrict the share-

[54] AktG, § 33(2) no 4; CC, art 2343.

[55] AktG, § 52; art 2343-*bis*.

[56] AktG, § 66.

[57] CC, art 2344.

[58] AktG, § 57(3): 'Vor Auflösung der Gesellschaft darf unter die Aktionäre nur der Bilanzgewinn verteilt werden.' [Prior to the dissolution of the company, only the balance sheet profit may be distributed among the shareholders.]

[59] Lutter (n 1) 5, sub 7; Peter O Mülbert and Max Birke, 'Legal Capital – Is *There a Case* against *the* European Legal Capital Rules?' (2002) 3 EBOR 695, 704; contrast Mathias Habersack and Dirk A Verse, *Europäisches Gesellschaftsrecht* (5th edn, CH Beck 2019) § 6 para 42; Rickford (n 27) 954 et seq; Ellis Ferran, 'The Place for Creditor Protection on the Agenda for Modernisation of Company Law in the European Union' (2006) 3(2) ECFR 178, 198; Schall (n 43) 35.

[60] See Holger Fleischer, 'Disguised Contributions and Capital Maintenance in European Company Law' in Lutter (n 1) 98–100; Brosius (n 5) art 56 para 6; Schall (n 43) 31ff.

[61] Schall (n 43) 31ff; Tilman Bezzenberger, *Das Kapital der Aktiengesellschaft* (O Schmidt 2005) 259ff.

[62] Lutter (n 1) 5 sub 7.

holders from receiving from the company the (accumulated) net balance-sheet profits absolutely. It merely protects the capital yardstick (plus mandatory reserves, if any). It is therefore more like §§ 30–31 of the GmbH Act.[63] In the GmbH, 'disguised distributions' that do not diminish the stated capital are lawful and only interest the taxman as *verdeckte Gewinnausschüttung*. National law may be stricter, as is the case with Germany. But the Company Law Directive does not demand it, because, first, it only requires minimum protection.[64] Second, there are other legal instruments available to fight unlawful gratuitous transfers of value to shareholders, eg, director's duties, the principle of equal treatment of shareholders (art 85), limits on related-party transactions, insolvency law (*actio Pauliana*) and criminal statutes like the *abus des biens sociaux*, *Untreue* (§ 266 of the Penal Code, the 'StGB') or *Bankrottdelikte* (§§ 283ff of the StGB). The Directive relies on them in the same way it relies on national insolvency laws to step in when the legal capital has evaporated.[65]

Finally, it should be noted that a broad understanding of distributions would probably delegitimise German *Konzernrecht*.[66] Derogation from the capital maintenance rules under § 291 of the AktG raises doubts because the Company Law Directive does not provide for an exception. The traditional German argument that the then-Second Directive did not aim to regulate group situations because such issues were supposed to be covered by the Ninth Directive, which never materialised,[67] is hard to maintain in light of the *Kefalas* jurisprudence, which denied the existence of any unwritten 'area exemptions' under the Second Directive (in that case, for insolvency law).[68] In this context, the broad understanding of distributions would leave no room for § 291 of the AktG at all, whereas the narrow understanding would only disallow open distributions that diminish the stated capital plus reserves.

- Article 59 prohibits any subscription of the company's own shares.
- Articles 60ff limit the acquisition of the company's own shares.[69] In particular, under art 60(1)(b) together with art 56(1) and (2), such acquisitions must not reduce the stated capital below the capital yardstick (plus reserves).

[63] Compare this with Habersack and Verse (n 59) § 6 para 42, who distinguish the regimes on the basis that art 56(3) requires a shareholder resolution to draw on the available reserves. But the same is true in the GmbH. See Jens Ekkenga, in *Münchener Kommentar GmbHG*, vol 1 (4th edn, CH Beck 2022) § 30 para 34.

[64] Henrik Drinkuth, *Die Kapitalrichtlinie – Mindest- oder Höchstnorm* (O Schmidt 1998) 124; Schall (n 43) 36. It is therefore not persuasive to demand complete protection like, eg, Fleischer (n 60) 100; Habersack and Verse (n 59) § 6 para 43; Schmidt (n 60) para 19.96.; Brosius (n 5) art 56.

[65] See above, at p 64–65.

[66] Schall (n 43) 32–33; Fleischer (n 60) 109ff (also sceptical).

[67] Cf, eg, Mathias Habersack, 'Das Konzernrecht der „deutschen" S.E.' (2003) 32 ZGR 724, 733, Rüdiger Veil, 'Das Konzernrecht der Europäischen Aktiengesellschaft (SE)' [2003] WM 2169, 2171.

[68] CJEU 12 May 1998, C-367/96 *Kefalas*, ECLI:EU:C:1998:222.

[69] AktG, § 71; CC, art 2357.

- Article 64 prohibits the company from providing financial assistance to third parties in acquiring its shares.[70]

  The prohibition was not an integral part of legal capital, but rather originated in England, where it was positioned against asset stripping by corporate raiders[71] like Richard Gere's Edward Lewis in 'Pretty Woman'. However, it can be related to legal capital as well. If the company enforces repayment against the third party, it risks being left with nothing but its own shares as seizable assets. Accordingly, this prohibition, which was absolute prior to 2006, was relaxed and made subject to capital-related safeguards in the SLIM initiative.[72]
- Articles 73ff regulate the procedure and safeguards for reductions of subscribed capital.[73] The right of unsecured creditors to demand security for their debts (art 75) makes capital reductions rare and onerous procedures.

The European harmonisation was restricted to public companies because they were deemed more important for cross-border trade in the common market. The exemption of private companies left the door open for the regulatory competition that was sparked by the ECJ's *Centros* jurisprudence (see below).

IV. Setbacks for the Concept of Legal Capital

1. *International Level*

The first major setback for the concept of legal capital originated on the other side of the Atlantic Ocean. As said in the beginning, the Model Business Corporation Act 'goldplated' capital maintenance by inserting the dynamic element of an equitable solvency test based on the cash flow prognosis. But in the early eighties, the view spread that for purposes of creditor protection, the solvency prognosis was actually the only relevant parameter. Corporate finance is provided by debt and equity. Bank loans are based on income. And so too should be the level of equity. One active promoter of this new perspective was Bayless Manning, who (in)famously compared the amount of the legal capital to a number from a telephone book:[74]

> 'A corporation's "legal capital" is a wholly arbitrary number, unrelated in any way to any economic facts that are relevant to a creditor. [...]. from his standpoint the stated capital is simply a fortuitously-derived number that could as well have been taken from a telephone directory as from a series of unconnected and irrelevant historical events.'

This criticism falls short because it presupposes that legal capital is *only* meant to protect the creditors. Even if we accept that the stated capital bears no relationship to how much money the company will need in the future, there is no

70 AktG, § 71a; CC, art 2358.

71 John Armour, 'Share Capital and Creditor Protection: Efficient Rules for a Modern Company Law' (2000) 63 MLR 355, 368.

72 See below at n 91.

73 AktG, §§ 222–240; CC, art 2445–2447.

74 Bayless Manning and James J Hanks, *Legal Capital* (3rd edn, Foundation Press 1990) 92.

reason why shareholders should be allowed to claw back the consideration they gave for the receipt of shares with rights to vote and to collect a dividend. The venerable principle of *pacta sunt servanda* suggests otherwise. It is noteworthy that Delaware, the only American jurisdiction that matters for large corporations, has continuously upheld legal capital. Nevertheless, this polemic fell on fertile ground during a period in which American lawyers seemed all too keen on cutting their ties to their European roots and going their own way. The MBCA of 1984 adopted the new approach.[75] It made the equitable solvency test the decisive determiner of distributions by eliminating the stated capital from the balance-sheet test and lowering that threshold to zero. Under the MBCA, the level of reserves in the company is steered, indirectly, by the avoidance provisions on *fraudulent transfers*, a standard of federal bankruptcy law. Distributions can be clawed back if they leave the company with an *unreasonably small capital*.[76]

The emergence of this alternative system of creditor protection in the US was the fuel academics used to ignite the debate on legal capital at the turn of the century. Proponents of Law & Economics (L&E) tarnished legal capital as an outdated concept and advocated for the modern approach of the solvency test. The rules of legal capital were said to be costly and inefficient. They would cause high transaction costs and impede value-creating transactions like, eg, leveraged buyouts or mergers. At the same time, they were not even fit for the purpose because they did not reflect the future income streams. When this criticism was picked up by the European regulator, it led to a fierce debate about the future of legal capital at the European level (see below).

2. National Level

The criticism of legal capital in Germany was of a different nature. Instead of being a fundamental attack on capital maintenance as such, it played out within the system. And like the majority of the L&E attacks, it was Janus-faced instead of one-sided.[77] On the one hand, many proponents of legal capital deemed the

[75] MBCA 1984, § 6.40(c), current unmodified version dated 25 April 2025, available at <https://www.americanbar.org/content/dam/aba/administrative/business_law/corplaws/mbca-202504.pdf> accessed December 2025.

'No distribution may be made if, after giving it effect

(1) the corporation would not be able to pay its debts as they become due in the usual course of business; or

(2) the corporation's total assets would be less than the sum of its total liabilities plus (unless the articles of incorporation permit otherwise) the amount that would be needed, if the corporation were to be dissolved at the time of the distribution, to satisfy the preferential rights upon dissolution of shareholders whose preferential rights are superior to those receiving the distribution.'

[76] 11 USC, § 548(a)(1)(B)(i) and (ii)(II).

[77] But compare this with Christoph Kuhner, 'The Future of Creditor Protection through Capital Maintenance Rules in European Company Law – An Economic Perspective' in Lutter (n 1) 342ff (seeing no clear advantages on balance).

level of creditor protection too low. For starters, the minimum capital of 25,000 euros was just a sixth of what 20,000 gold marks was worth in 1892! Also, it was more and more recognised that the strictly formal rules of legal capital were not fit to prevent the malicious causation of insolvency.[78]

On the other hand, critics of legal capital deplored the burdens from overreaching safeguards. The critics particularly focused on the minimum capital and the safeguards for its enforcement. The virtue of a minimum capital for creditor protection had become more and more doubtful, because it could nevertheless be dissipated in the course of the business. Against that background, the downsides of the strict controls over the procurement of capital loomed large. They produced high costs in terms of long incorporation periods, often necessitated expert opinions and liability traps, and generated little (if any) return. This can be demonstrated with regard to the paradigm of the *verdeckte Sacheinlage*.[79]

In principle it is understandable that specific disclosure rules for contributions in kind must be protected against evasion – or else they would not make sense. Who would declare a contribution in kind and subject himself to the scrutiny of the registrar if he could instead contribute cash and 'sell' his asset to the company a few days later? The problem with the case law was its misdirected side effects. The original purpose was to guarantee that the subscribed (minimum) capital at the time of registration was raised in an orderly fashion. But disguised contributions in kind were not normally detected until several years later when the company was in insolvency. The extremely long limitation period of 10 years allowed the liquidator to sue the shareholder to pay up the cash contribution, while the opposed unjust enrichment claims for the use of the asset that had actually been transferred as a 'disguised contribution in kind' would fail due to the insolvency of the company, and the claims also could not be netted (GmbH Act, § 19(2)). This resulted in a 'double contribution' by the shareholder, who would lose both cash and the asset. That was perceived as an undeserved 'punishment' alien to private law, so much the more since the initial evasion of the disclosure rules at the time of incorporation was not normally the cause of the company later entering into insolvency. While theoretically justified as creditor protection, practically the BGH's case law produced windfall profits for the insolvency practitioners.

---

78 Röhricht (n 42) 103ff.

79 Tim Drygala, 'Stammkapital heute – zum veränderten Verständnis vom System des festen Nennkapitals und seinen Konsequenzen' (2006) 35 ZGR 587, 615; Barbara Grunewald, 'Rechtsfolgen verdeckter Sacheinlagen' in Gerd Pfeiffer (ed), Festschrift Rowedder (CH Beck 1994) 114ff; Martin Heidenhain, 'Katastrophale Rechtsfolgen verdeckter Sacheinlagen' [2006] GmbHR 455; Detlef Kleindiek, 'Referat zur Reform des Gesellschaftsrechtlichen Gläubigerschutzes' in *Verhandlungen des 66. Deutschen Juristentages Stuttgart 2006*, vol II/1 – Sitzungsberichte (CH Beck 2007) P 52ff; Wienand Meilicke, *Die „verschleierte" Sacheinlage – eine deutsche Fehlentwicklung* (Schaffer 1989); Martin Winter, 'Die Rechtsfolgen der „verdeckten" Sacheinlage – Versuch einer Neubestimmung' in Peter Hommelhoff, Peter Rawert and Karsten Schmidt (eds), *Festschrift für Hans-Joachim Priester* (O Schmidt 2007); Jan Wilhelm, 'Cash-Pooling, Garantiekapital der GmbH und die GmbH-Reform' [2006] DB 2729, 2732–2733.

Even more problematically, the doctrine of *verdeckte Sacheinlage* prevented the company from paying pre-existing debts (*Altschulden*) to its shareholders[80] – despite the fact that the payment of debts is a typical purpose of raising new capital.[81] The reason is again to be found in the legalistic requirements for raising capital. German law – unlike, eg, English law[82] – does not allow the netting of debts against the duty to pay up a cash contribution (GmbH Act, § 19(2)). Rather, it perceives the payment of a debt to the shareholder as a contribution in kind. The argument is that instead of being discharged, the claim could (and should) have been assigned to the company so that the extinction of the debt would have been achieved by confusion. The payment of the debt is therefore deemed a circumvention of the correct procedure, ie, the transfer of the debt to the company as a contribution in kind. It follows that the claim of the shareholder against the company is liable to evaluation. For purposes of evaluation, German law ignores the value of the debt for the company (whose balance sheet is relieved at the full nominal value) and only looks at the value of the debt in the hands of the shareholders. If the company is in crisis, the nominal value will therefore have to be discounted. This amounts to a considerable complication of debt–equity swaps.

In the *Aktiengesellschaft*, the additional issue arose whether the rules on substantial acquisitions after incorporation (now art 52) finally settled the issue of circumvention for public companies in a way that left no room for gold-plating by the Member States. This was the view of domestic critics.[83] The BGH held the opposite view and even invoked the 'acte clair' doctrine to avoid referral to the ECJ under art 256(3) and 267 of the TFEU.[84] Subsequently, the Landgericht of Hannover stepped in and referred another case to the ECJ. Advocate General Tesauro shared the scepticism toward the legitimacy of the *verdeckte Sacheinlage* (thus casting severe doubt on the BGH's 'acte claire' solution).[85] However, the ECJ sniffed at the test case that it was and declined to decide the 'hypothetical question'.[86] Alas, it has remained unresolved to this day.

Germany's slow but steady renegation of the case law safeguards for legal capital picked up momentum with the emergence of central cash management (in Anglicised German, *Cash Pool* or *Cash Pooling*) in groups of companies. In these structures, the parent (or a SPV directly owned by it) creates a central account where the funds of the group are accumulated in order to maximise liquidity and to save banking costs. The subsidiaries continuously remit receipts to the central

[80] BGH 18 February 1991 (n 8); BGH 4 March 1996, II ZR 89/95, 132 BGHZ 133; BGH 16 September 2002, II ZR 1/00, 152 BGHZ 37 = [2002] NJW 3374.

[81] Wilhelm (n 79) 2732–2733.

[82] Companies Act 2006, s 583(3)(c).

[83] See, most notably, Meilicke (n 79); Wienand Meilicke, 'Verschleierte Sacheinlage und EWG-Vertrag' [1990] DB 1173.

[84] BGH 15 January 1990, II ZR 164/88, 110 BGHZ 47 = [1990] NJW 982 Leitsatz.

[85] ECJ 8 April 1992, C-83/91 *Meilicke v ADV/ORGA* – Opinion of AG Tesauro, ECLI:EU:C:1992:178;.

[86] ECJ 8 April 1992, *Meilicke* (n 85).

account and in turn can draw on it on demand. Even though the 'cash pool' made a bad entry onto the German stage,[87] it was generally accepted as good commercial practice.

The case law of the BGH impeded cash pooling because the subsequent transfer of the cash contribution back into the central cash management amounted to a prohibited payment back and forth between company and shareholder. If the retransfer created a claim to the central account on the part of the subsidiary against the parent, it was a case of a simple payment back and forth (*einfaches Hin- und Herzahlen*, see above).[88] If the retransfer happened at a time when the subsidiary was indebted vis-à-vis the parent to pay into the central account, it was a hidden contribution in kind (*verdeckte Sacheinlage*) because an existing debt was being paid.[89] In both cases, the procurement of capital would be invalidated and both the directors and the shareholders could have been liable under civil and criminal law (§§ 9a, 82 I nos 1 and 2 of the GmbH Act).

Owing to the *Novemberurteil* of 2004 (above), the disruption of the cash pool extended even beyond capital procurements. If the company's assets did not exceed its debts plus subscribed capital, the loan created by the remittance of the funds to the parent would be deemed an unlawful return of capital under §§ 30–31 of the GmbH Act such that the transfer to central cash management was prohibited. To avoid that risk, the daily clearing of the subsidiary's account required accompanying balance sheet tests.

It was obvious that the disruption of central cash management was not the purpose but rather a negative side effect of the case law. That is why academics and practitioners started opposing it. The BGH nevertheless refused to recognize a 'cash pool exception'.[90] In the end, the legislator in Berlin stepped in (below at VI.).

V. Beginning and End of the *Kapitaldebatte* (Debate on Legal Capital) in the First Decade of the New Millennium

1. *The Cocktail of Causes Igniting the Kapitaldebatte*

The academic criticism of legal capital gained traction when it was picked up by European Union as well as national regulators. As far as Germany is concerned, there were three coinciding, closely interwoven reasons, of independent origin, for the debate:

[87] In BGH 17 September 2001, *Bremer Vulkan* (n 43), EU subsidies to the group's shipyards in East Germany disappeared into the central cash pool to the benefit of the West German parent. The case became known for introducing the case law on *Existenzvernichtungshaftung*, which replaced the previous concept of piercing the corporate veil for running a *qualifiziert faktischer Konzern*.

[88] BGH 21 November 2005 (n 35); BGH 24 January 2006 (n 35); BFH, 27 September 2001 (n 35).

[89] BGH 16 January 2006 (n 30).

[90] BGH 16 January 2006 (n 30).

- The EU initiatives to modernise European company law: After the Simpler Legislation for the Internal Market (SLIM) initiative led by Eddy Wymeersch from Ghent proposed some initial relaxations of the Capital Directive,[91] the Report of the High Level Group of Company Law Experts (the 'Winter Group') put the alternative solvency test on the reform agenda.[92]
- The jurisprudence of the ECJ in C-212/97 *Centros*, C-208/00 *Überseering* and C-167/01 *Inspire Art* opened the door to letter-box companies from other Member States and sparked regulatory competition in Europe.
- The German plan to reform the law of private companies was initially motivated by abuses of the GmbH law, particularly so-called *GmbH-Bestattungen* ('GmbH interments'), in which, after a series of sales of shares during which all the company's books would somehow get lost, a hapless, penniless director would be solely appointed to file for liquidation.[93]

2. The Subsequent Debate on Two Levels

These three factors were crucial to the incitement of an intense debate about legal capital both at the European and at the national level. Voices at the European level fundamentally challenged the system of legal capital. The question here was between legal capital and an solvency test. At the national German level, fixed capital as such had never been questioned;[94] the focus was on the minimum capital of private companies. The jurisprudence of the ECJ had put pressure on national minimum capital requirements because they could now easily be circumvented through letter-box companies. The question here was whether to lower or dispense with minimum capital. The massive influx of tens of thousands foreign letter-box companies since 2003 turned up the heat on the national reform debate.

a) The Debate at the European level

The European discussion gained traction after Jonathan Rickford, the English representative within the group of experts, published a paper entitled 'Reform-

[91] Eddy Wymeersch, 'European Company law: The Simpler Legislation for the Internal Market (SLIM) Initative of the EU Commission' (August 2000) Financial Law Institute Working Paper Series 2000-09 <https://financiallawinstitute.ugent.be/index.php/wps/european-company-law-the/> accessed December 2025.

The proposals were implemented in Directive 2006/68/EC, including *inter alia* relaxation of the previously absolute prohibition against financial assistance that had been brandished as a major hurdle for leveraged buyouts.

[92] *Report of the High Level Group of Company Law Experts on a Modern Regulatory Framework for Company Law in Europe* (2002) 78–81; available at <www.ecgi.global/sites/default/files/report_en.pdf> accessed December 2025.

[93] See BGH 22 December 2005, IX ZR 190/02, 165 BGHZ 343; for a detailed account, see Heribert Hirte, 'Die organisierte „Bestattung" von Kapitalgesellschaften: Gesetzgeberischer Handlungsbedarf im Gesellschafts- und Insolvenzrecht' [2003] ZInsO 833.

[94] Lutter (n 1) 2.

ing Capital' in (2004) 15 EBLR 919, in which he voiced his interdisciplinary research group's plea for the solvency test to replace legal capital. In Germany, opposition formed. Marcus Lutter gathered the 'Arbeitskreis Kapital', a group of high-profile academics and practitioners, which published a extensive bilingual defence of legal capital: *Das Kapital der Aktiengesellschaft in Europa/Legal Capital in Europe* (2006). There were several conferences and high-profile papers in addition to these two fundamental publications, most notably the Munich conference of 2005.

The L&E-fuelled attack saw legal capital as costly and superfluous.[95] Echoing Bayless Manning's 'telephone number' polemic, the critics painted the picture of an 'outdated concept'[96] that came with high costs and few if any benefits.[97] The costs drove up the transaction costs of incorporating and of capital measures on one hand (expert opinions, public oversight, delays) and overall economic costs (prevention of reasonable transactions and distributions) on the other. Their verdict of superfluity was built on the fact that the capital yardstick could not prevent insolvencies and was not the right instrument by which to predict an organization's future need for funds in the first place. Those defending legal capital countered that the system was well-established and working smoothly, while the prospective costs of changing the system were considerable and the advantages of vague prognosis-based limits on distributions doubtful.[98] There was also a wide range of opinion between the two extremes of scrapping legal capital completely or leaving everything unchanged.[99]

---

[95] Succinctly put by Lutter (n 1) 2.

[96] *Armour*, Legal Capital: An Outdated Concept, 2006 EBOR 5.

[97] Besides Rickford and Armour (n 96), see, eg, Ferran (n 59); Luca Enriques and Jonathan R Macey, 'Creditors Versus Capital Formation: The Case against the European Legal Capital Rules' (2001) 86 Cornell LRev, 1165; Luca Enriques and Martin Gelter, 'Regulatory Competition in Europe and Creditor Protection' (2006) 7(1) EBOR 417; Alain Pietrancosta, 'Capital zéro ou zéro capital' in Alain Couret and Hervé Le Nabasque (eds), *Quel avenir pour le capital social?* (Dalloz 2004); Marcel Kahan, 'Legal Capital Rules and the Structure of Corporate Law: Some Observations on the Differences Between European and U.S. Approaches' in Klaus J Hopt and Eddy Wymeersch (eds), Capital Markets and Company Law (OUP 2003); Friedrich Kübler, 'The Rules of Capital Under Pressure of the Securities Markets' in Hopt and Wymeersch (this note); Mülbert and Birke (n 59) 708ff; Hanny Schutte-Veenstra, Hylda Boschma and Marie-Louise Lennarts, *Alternative Systems for Creditor Protection* (Wolters Kluwer 2005) 4ff.

[98] See Lutter (n 1) 4–6, counting 12 specific points in favour of legal capital and concluding: 'All of these aspects of legal capital cannot be wrong'; Rüdiger Veil, 'Capital Maintenance – The Regime of the Capital Directive versus Alternative Systems' in Lutter (n 1) 92–93; Kuhner (n 77).

[99] Cf, eg, Massimo Miola, 'Legal Capital and Limited Liability Companies: The European Perspective' (2005) 2(4) ECFR 413; Francesco Denozza, 'Different Policies for Corporate Creditor Protection' (2006) 7 EBOR 409; Wolfgang Schön, 'The Future of Legal Capital' (2004) 5(3) EBOR 429; Hanno Merkt, 'European Company Law Reform: Struggling for a More Liberal Approach' (2004) 1 ECFR 3; Hanno Merkt, 'Creditor Protection and Capital Maintenance from a German Perspective' (2004) 15 EBLR 1045. On a supplementary solvency test associated

At the European level, the debate concluded after a study by KPMG commissioned by the Commission was inconclusive.[100] Basically, KPMG found that the costs of capital measures on both sides of the Atlantic were similar. With no pressing case for a systemic change,[101] the system of legal capital under the Company Law Directive remained unchanged. It should however be noted that the findings of the KPMG study did not defeat the criticism of the economic costs of impeding efficient transactions – they were beyond the scope of the analysis. For example, the strict legal capital rules had hitherto excluded the use of the *Aktiengesellschaft* as a SPAC on the German capital market even as these new vehicles were attracting billions of dollars of investment in the US.[102]

Personally, I think that the outcome of the debate was not right from a purely doctrinal perspective. The existence of an equally effective system to control distributions under the MBCA can hardly be doubted. That being so, the principles of minimum protection and subsidiarity would have called for introducing options to the Member States. It was not necessary to show that the solvency test was superior in order to make a case for change. However, if the EU preferred to hold on to the high level of harmonisation that had been achieved this field, a compromise might have been to relax the limits for capital reductions. This would have answered the criticism of inefficient overcapitalisation.[103] Capital reductions seem too tightly restricted under art 75. Since the subscribed capital can be dissipated in the course of business, the unsecured creditors cannot rely on it anyway. So why should they be granted security if surplus capital is returned to the shareholder? A solvency test, maybe with additional claw-back provisions, might well be sufficient.

b) The Debate in Germany

The debate in Germany took a different turn due to the pressure of regulatory competition. Also, the required minimum capital was much harder to defend than balance-sheet capital maintenance.[104] As a consequence, rather than petering out,

with IFRS accounting, see Bernhard Pellens and Thorsten Sellhorn, 'Improving Creditor Protection through IFRS-Reporting and Solvency Test' in Lutter (n 1) and Veil (n 98) 92–93.

[100] KPMG, 'Feasibility study on an alternative to the capital maintenance regime established by the Second Company Law Directive 77/91/EEC of 13 December 1976 and an examination of the impact on profit distribution of the new EU-accounting regime – main report' (2008), available at <https://ec.europa.eu/docsroom/documents/42762?locale=en> accessed December 2025.

[101] Along these lines, see also Kuhner (n 77); Veil (n 98) 92–93.

[102] David Günther, *Special Purpose Acquisition Companies und die Ineffizienz des Kapitalsystems* (De Gruyter 2021) 16. But note that the SPACs are now available as *Börsenmantelgesellschaft* in §§ 44–47b of the BörsG as introduced by the 'Zukunftsfinanzierungsgesetz' of 2023. Also note that it was only German stock corporation law that previously stood in their way; European law has always allowed redeemable shares (art 81, 82).

[103] Cf Lutter (n 1) 7 sub III.2. (deeming only German law rather than European law overly restrictive).

[104] Cf in particular Schön (n 99).

the debate led to the largest reform of the GmbH Act since its enactment in 1892 with the *Gesetz zur Modernisierung des GmbH-Rechts und zur Bekämpfung von Missbräuchen* (MoMiG).

The course toward reform had been set at the sixty-sixth conference of the Deutscher Juristentag in Stuttgart 2006, a highly influential association of legal practitioners and academics that holds biannual assemblies in the capitals of the German states. The topics it chooses and the discussion it organises often set the agenda for legal reform. Representatives of the executive branch of the German government are practically obliged to attend. Stuttgart 2006 was a particular highlight with respect to company law. The written expert opinion delivered by *Ulrich Haas*,[105] fervently supported by the expert presentation of *Heribert Hirte*,[106] made it clear that the decisive tool for creditor protection in private companies was strict, well-defined exit liability. If that condition was met, the procurement of a minimum capital would be of no consequence. Since such capital could be 'traded away', it did not matter whether the company started with 25,000, 10,000, 7,000 or even 0 euros. Strict exit liability would suffice to prevent the incorporators from starting out with too little investment. This assumption accorded with observations from France, where incorporators voluntarily raised 3,000 euros on average after the abolition of the 7,000 euro minimum capital requirement for an S.a.R.L.[107]

The defenders of minimum capital granted that it did not secure sufficient funds to protect the creditors. They tried to justify it instead as an entry barrier that signalled the seriousness of the incorporators. (Put your money where your mouth is!) *Detlef Kleindiek* emphasised this argument at the conference in his opposing expert presentation.[108] It was – and still is – persuasive.[109] However, the accessibility of the UK limited company exerted too much pressure. ECJ C-212/97 *Centros* ruled that the incorporation of foreign letter-box companies for that purpose *did not constitute abuse*, but rather was a legitimate expression of the freedom of establishment. ECJ C-208/00 *Überseering* held that Germany had to accept the legal personality of companies from other Member States regardless of where they had their real seat. ECJ C-167/01 *Inspire Art* added a prohibition against specific safeguards against pseudo-foreign companies like what had been in place in the Netherlands. This judicial trilogy led to tens of thousands of UK limited companies that had a 'real seat' in Germany. The mass abandonment of domestic corporate law proved too hard to sustain. Germany budged. But it did not follow the French example of simply striking the minimum capital requirement over-

---

105 Ulrich Haas, 'Reform des Gesellschaftsrechtlichen Gläubigerschutzes, Gutachten E' in *Verhandlungen des 66. Deutschen Juristentags* (n 79) vol I.

106 Heribert Hirte, 'Referat zur Reform des Gesellschaftsrechtlichen Gläubigerschutzes' in *Verhandlungen des 66. Deutschen Juristentags* (n 79) vol II/1, P 11.

107 Isabelle Urbain-Parléani, 'Working Group on the Share Capital in Europe – French Answers to the Questionnaire' in Lutter (n 1) 484–485.

108 Kleindiek (n 79).

109 Even Jonathan Rickford told me so privately after the dust had settled.

night. Rather, the legislator seized the opportunity for a large and thorough reform that also took care of overly burdensome issues so eloquently criticised in an expert presentation by corporate lawyer *Jochen Vetter* at the same conference.[110]

VI. The Modernisation of Legal Capital: Germany after the MoMiG

On the surface, the MoMiG struck a compromise between the opposing poles. The traditional system of legal capital including the minimum capital requirement remained in place, even though the rules were softened and streamlined. But the cut was deeper, because Germany introduced the *Unternehmergesellschaft* (the 'UG'), a 'small' GmbH that can be incorporated for one euro (§ 5a I of the GmbH Act).

Originally, the UG was conceived as a new form of business organization after a proposal by Jürgen Gehb, a member of the CDU and head of the Rechtsausschuss, the parliamentary committee on legal affairs.[111] It piggy-backed on a similar proposal for a 'FlexCap' that had been made a year earlier by the present author and his colleague *Andre Wetshoff* when they were both researchers at the chair of *Heribert Hirte*.[112] The idea was to grant barrier-free access to limited liability and cut out the tailor-made safeguards without profoundly disturbing the legal underpinnings of the one million GmbHs that already existed at the time. Interestingly, this idea has been picked up (albeit with considerable delay) by Austria and is now being touted for introduction in Germany![113]

However, the original proposal of the UG was met with broad resistance, even from adversaries of minimum capital.[114] It was widely assumed that a completely new organizational form would bring massive legal uncertainty because no judicial guidance existed and the scope of the case law on existing companies would be debatable in every single instance. That seemed an undesirable prospect for business.[115]

---

[110] Jochen Vetter, 'Referat zur Reform des Gesellschaftsrechtlichen Gläubigerschutzes' in *Verhandlungen des 66. Deutschen Juristentags* (n 79) vol II/1, P 75; with a view to the *verdeckte Sacheinlage* also Kleindiek (n 79) P 52ff.

[111] Jürgen Gehb, Günter Drange and Martin Heckelmann, 'Gesellschaftsrechtlicher Typenzwang als Zwang zu neuem Gesellschaftstyp' [2006] NZG 88.

[112] Alexander Schall and André Westhoff, 'Warum Deutschland eine neue Kapitalgesellschaftsform braucht' [2004] GmbHR R 381; Alexander Schall and André Westhoff, 'Die Neuwahlen zum deutschen Bundestag liegen hinter uns – kommt jetzt die „UGG"?' [2005] GmbHR R 357 (revisiting Gehb's proposal).

[113] Eveline Artmann, 'Die Flexible Kapitalgesellschaft („FlexCo") in Österreich: Vorbild für Deutschland?' (2024) 53 ZGR 482.

[114] The 66th Deutsche Juristentag rejected it. See Alexander Schall, 'Tagungsbericht' [2006] JZ 239.

[115] The same argument holds true against the introduction of any new European organizational form, eg, an SPE or an SES.

The breakthrough came with the idea of integrating the new UG into the GmbH Act. On the surface, this left the system of legal capital in GmbHs unchanged. The waiver of legal capital for UGs is compensated by specific safeguards and certain adaptions to the general rules in § 5a I–V of the GmbH Act. The gist is that a UG can operate indefinitely on little capital but must build reserves from a quarter of its annual earnings until the equity reaches 25,000 euros. However, on closer look it becomes evident that this minimum capital can no longer justify limited liability when it is available for one euro.[116] That made the case for an overdue relaxation of the case law-based protections that the business community had so desired.

In particular, the legislator intervened in three ways to facilitate cash pooling. It legalised *Hin- und Herzahlen* under certain conditions as long as it was disclosed (GmbH Act, § 19(5); AktG, § 27(4)). The original plan to legalise the *verdeckte Sacheinlage* as well was dropped because it would have rendered the disclosure provisions dead-letter law. However, the risk of double contributions was eliminated by mandating that the actual value of the asset at the time it was transferred to the company as a hidden contribution in kind was to be deducted from the undischarged duty to pay up in cash (GmbH Act, § 19(4)(3); AktG, § 27(3)(3)). Lastly, the legislator took the rare step of explicitly overruling a BGH judgement, namely the notorious *Novemberurteil* (GmbH Act, § 30(1)(2); AktG, § 57(1)(3)), and reinstated a purely value-oriented balance-sheet test. The danger of depleting cash payments was countered instead by extending the *Zahlungsverbot* (prohibition of payments) to payments *to shareholders* such that would inevitably lead to insolvency (*zur Zahlungsunfähikgeit führen musste*). This version of director's liability covered the cases the *Novemberurteil* was meant to address. It also flanked shareholder liability under *Existenzvernichtungshaftung*. Originally enshrined in § 64 sentence 3 of the GmbH Act and § 92(2)(2) of the AktG, this extended *Zahlungsverbot* was also incorporated into § 15b of the InsO at the beginning of 2021.

Finally, it should be noted that the overcomplicated *Eigenkapitalersatzrecht* was replaced by a general subordination of shareholder loans and an additional clawback clause covering repayments made up to one year prior to insolvency (InsO, §§ 37(1) no 5 and 135). This shift to insolvency law followed a proposal by *Ulrich Huber and Mathias Habersack*.[117] The law cut the ties between the subordination of shareholder loans and capital maintenance (GmbH Act, § 30(1)(3); AktG, § 57(1)(4)), which finalised a development that had begun with the often-criticised extensions of case law beyond the original notion of *falsa demonstratio*.

[116] Cf Schall (n 43) 101ff (the central thesis of the author's habilitation monograph); Alexander Schall, 'Kapitalaufbringung nach dem MoMiG' (2009) 35 ZGR 126.

[117] Ulrich Huber and Mathias Habersack, 'GmbH-Reform: Zwölf Thesen zu einer möglichen Reform des Rechts der kapitalersetzenden Gesellschafterdarlehen' [2006] BB 1. See also Ulrich Huber and Mathias Habersack, 'Special Rules for Shareholder Loans: Which Consequences Would Arise for Shareholder Loans if the System of Legal capital Should be Abolished' in Lutter (n 1).

VII. Conclusion

Any future debate should concentrate on the financial need for long term sustainability. Neither legal capital nor the solvency test could have saved retail chains from being 'raided' in the most recent golden era before e-commerce started to kill off High Street/Main Street. The money needed to transform ours into a climate-friendly and sustainable economy while keeping abreast of technological progress must remain in the corporation. It does not belong in the hands of investors. This will pose new questions on the steering of distributions. But the old battle is over. The concept of legal capital has survived the onslaught of critics both at the national German and the European level. However, it did evolve under the pressure of criticism. Most importantly, minimum capital is not a mandatory entrance fee to limited liability anymore – not in Germany, Italy, France or many other Member States. This was regulatory competition at work, set in motion by the ECJ, which may or may not have overstepped its brief by doing so. But in this case, the outcome is not to be deplored. Looking back, it seems unlikely that minimum capital would have been abolished in Germany at that time anyway. Still, the UG has become a success story – as was to be expected in the light of the positive experience of France. This shows the added value of the European level. It is good for any domestic jurisdiction to have an outside perspective that forces us to reconsider old convictions now and then. But the benefits go both ways. A coherent system of legal capital is a cultural achievement[118] that has surely enriched European law.

---

[118] Herbert Wiedemann, *Gesellschaftsrecht*, vol 1 (CH Beck 1980) 558 ('Kulturleistung ersten Ranges').

Review of Shareholder Resolutions and Director Compensation

Vincenzo Antonini

I. Shareholder Resolutions: Freedom to Vote and Majority Rule

The exercise of voting rights in joint stock companies expresses an individual's right to participate in the life of the company and is therefore subject to the free will of the shareholder, who may independently choose whether to participate in a meeting or to vote for or against each proposed resolution. Indeed, the regulations governing access to voting and its manifestations only prescribe when and in what form this relative freedom may be exercised, without however saying what the shareholder should decide. This is the reason the right is often referred to as a 'procedurally empty' voting right.[1]

When they attend shareholder meetings, shareholders are beholden to none other than their own individual interest. In fact, a joint stock company is also characterised by the plurality of interests of the shareholders: such pluralism of interests is the basis of equity investment.[2] Precisely for this reason, each share-

[1] Paolo Spada, 'Riflessioni conclusive' in Laura Schiuma (ed), *Governo societario ed esercizio del diritto di voto* (Cedam 2015) 340.

[2] Carlo Angelici, 'Note minime su "La libertà contrattuale e i rapporti societari"' (2009) I Giur comm 258; Vincenzo Calandra Buonaura, 'Funzione amministrativa e interessi sociali'

holder is free to pursue their own interest and to express by vote what they deem most appropriate for their investment.[3] The rule by which to resolve this dialectic is expressed by the principle of majority: the prevailing interest is the one favoured by the majority.[4] The primacy of the will of the majority over the minority also finds its grounds in the concept of risk, which can be summarised in the assumption that the resolution that receives the most votes represents the vote of those who have the prevailing economic interest and therefore run the greater risk.[5] However, if on the one hand the regulatory framework of majority rule is a technical tool that guarantees the efficiency and promptness of the company's operations, on the other hand it means that the minority remains exposed to the danger of seeing its rights sacrificed for the exclusive advantage of the controlling group, as it is subject to the abusive exercise of the power of the majority.[6]

For such reasons, it is necessary to provide checks of some form on the application of majority rule,[7] with the awareness that, in the event of an appeal against the resolutions of the shareholders, judicial authorities are in any case precluded from any review on the merits of the suitability or timeliness of the resolution; instead they are (only) allowed to verify whether the resolution is unlawful.[8] However, review of the mere legitimacy of resolutions does not mean that the right to vote can be exercised absolutely freely or unquestionably. In fact, joint stock companies constitute organisations that overall aim to pursue a pre-established purpose represented by the 'company interest' and made up of the sum of the individual interests of the shareholders.

Here it is appropriate to recall the maxim that 'the judge may annul a resolution which no reasonable person could consider useful to the company'[9]: the fact that a resolution in the eyes of any reasonable person appears pointless for the company is assumed as presumptive evidence of an abuse of the right to vote. In

---

in *L'interesse sociale tra valorizzazione del capitale e protezione degli stakeholders. In ricordo di Pier Giusto Jaeger* (Giuffrè 2010) 103.

[3] Pier Giusto Jaeger, *L'interesse sociale* (Giuffrè 1972) 183f; Giuseppe Ferri, 'Poteri della maggioranza e diritti del socio' (1952) II Banca borsa tit cred 162ff; Ariberto Mignoli, 'L'interesse sociale' (1958) Riv soc 725, 740f.

[4] Francesco Galgano, *La forza del numero e la legge della ragione* (Mulino 2007) 203f.

[5] Tullio Ascarelli, *Studi in tema di società* (Giuffrè 1952) 150.

[6] With regard to the different forms of checks on majority rule, see Agostino Gambino, *Il principio di correttezza nell'assemblea delle società per azioni* (Giuffrè 1987) 1ff; Marco Cassottana, *L'abuso di potere a danno della minoranza assembleare* (Giuffrè 1991) 1ff.

[7] Disiano Preite, *L'«abuso» della regola di maggioranza nelle deliberazioni assembleari delle società per azioni* (Giuffrè 1992) 3.

[8] See Cass 30 October 1970, no 2263, (1971) I Foro it 1999. On the limits of judicial review, see Carlo Angelici, 'La società per azioni. Principi e problemi' in Antonio Cicu and Francesco Messineo (eds), *Trattato di diritto civile e commerciale* (Giuffrè 2012) 110 fn 65; Gambino (n 6) 270.

[9] See for example Francesco Galgano, *Diritto civile e commerciale*, vol. 3/II (2nd edn, Cedam 1994) 201; Francesco Galgano, 'Il nuovo diritto societario' in Francesco Galgano (ed), *Trattato di diritto commerciale e di diritto pubblico dell'economia*, vol. 29 (Cedam 2003) 232.

essence, according to an approach that also seems to be shared in German jurisprudence, not only decisions of the directors but also shareholder resolutions are subject to the business judgement rule.[10] In fact, it is possible to infer the existence of a general clause summarised in the principle of business purpose, that is, in economic reasonableness as a criterion by which to distinguish legitimate corporate activities from abusive ones.[11]

II. The (External) Limits of Majority Rule: The General Prohibition of Abuse of the Right to Vote

The shareholder's freedom to vote is subject to a double external limit: on the one hand, the company interest; on the other hand, the duty of fairness and good faith.[12] In terms of the company interest, a resolution is considered voidable if a shareholder voted to support a particular interest in conflict with that of the company and potentially harmful to the company itself. The shareholder therefore has an interest contrary to that of the company: there is an 'external conflict' between the interest of the shareholder and the company interest. In terms of the duty of fairness and good faith, a resolution is considered voidable if passed by the majority to the harm not of the company itself but of the minority shareholders. A shareholder has an interest in pursuing purposes that go beyond the normal dialectic among the shareholders, and hence this is an 'internal conflict' between shareholder interests.

From these two situations, a general principle of the Italian corporate system is derived: a shareholder resolution is voidable when the right to vote is exercised in an abusive manner. In Italy this principle is set out at the doctrinal and jurisprudential level,[13] while in other legal systems it is provided by an express provision of positive law,[14] which is the case for example in the German legal system (§243 of the Stock Corporation Act, the 'AktG').

As mentioned, in Italy this general principle needs to be specified, however, and certain appropriate distinctions need to be made. Depending on which limit

[10] Peter Agstner, 'Interesse sociale tra contrattualismo e istituzionalismo nella giurisprudenza del Supremo Tribunale Federale tedesco: Viel Lärm um wenig?' (2017) III Riv dir soc 949, referred to BGH 12 April 2016, II ZR 275/14 (OLG München); in the German literature, Kai Wallisch, *Unternehmerische Entscheidungen der Hauptversammlung* (Nomos 2014) 69ff.

[11] Paolo Montalenti, 'L'abuso del diritto nel diritto commerciale' (2018) I Riv dir civ 873.

[12] For further references see also Aurelio Mirone, Il sistema tradizionale: l'assemblea, in Marco Cian (ed), *Diritto commerciale. Diritto delle società*, vol 3 (4th edn, Giappichelli 2024) 455ff.

[13] Pietro Rescigno, 'L'abuso del diritto' (1965) I Riv dir civ 205ff.

[14] With regard to the lack of a specific positive provision dedicated to the abuse by the majority in shareholder resolutions under Italian law, see Disiano Preite, 'Abuso di maggioranza e conflitto di interessi del socio nelle società per azioni' in Giovanni E Colombo and Giuseppe B Portale (eds), *Trattato delle società per azioni*, vol 3/2 (Utet 1993) 3.

is violated, and therefore on whether a shareholder has voted for an external interest or for an interest detrimental to that of another shareholder, there are two different remedies. In the situation of an external interest, there may be a conflict of interest, while the vote detrimental to another shareholder's interest may constitute an abuse of majority. There are thus two different assumptions governed by different bodies of rules. But both represent an external limit to the power of the majority as forms of abuse of shareholder voting in a broader sense.

III. The 'Company Interest': Institutionalism Versus Contractualism

In any case, both the aforementioned theories accord a certain relevance to the 'company interest'. In the case of a conflict of interest, the corporate interest is in conflict with the particular interest of a shareholder. In an abuse of majority case, the corporate interest becomes a parameter by which to assess whether there are grounds to find an infringement of the minority's rights.

It is known that the debate on institutionalism and contractualism has always represented a dilemma of legal philosophy, and not only in Italy. Originally, the distinction pertained to the legal qualification of a joint stock company either as a contract or an institution.[15] When the contractual origin of the company was no longer in question (including in light of art 2247 of the Italian Civil Code), the problem shifted to the definition of the company interest.[16]

Traditionally, the institutional theory would see the company interest as the interest of the company as an independent subject and – as this is an interest proper to the company as a legal person – as different from and superior to the interests of individual shareholders. In this perspective, the right to vote is granted to a shareholder for the primary purpose of pursuing the corporate interest (which is completely separate from that of the shareholders). Therefore, exercising the right to vote for a different purpose or based on self-interest should imply that such an exercise is not valid, and the resulting resolution may be annulled. This theory has recently evolved towards more moderate positions (we speak of 'weak neo-institutionalism'), which sees the company interest in the efficiency and profitability of the company.[17]

---

[15] On this debate (also in reference to the historical context), see Jaeger (n 3) 13ff.

[16] For a survey of the multiple nuances of each thesis and for further references in doctrine, see Preite (n 14) 8ff; Preite (n 7) 83ff; Francesco Galgano and Riccardo Genghini, 'Le nuove società di capitali e cooperative' in Francesco Galgano (ed) (n 9) 56ff.

[17] Mario Libertini, 'Ancora in tema di contratto, impresa, società. Un commento a Francesco Denozza, in difesa dello "istituzionalismo debole"' (2014) I Giur comm 664ff; Mario Libertini, 'Scelte fondamentali di politica legislativa' (2008) I Riv dir soc 201ff. For a critique of the thesis, see Francesco Denozza, 'Logica dello scambio e «contrattualità»' (2015) I Giur comm 18ff.

On the other hand, the corporate interest according to the contractual theory merely follows one or more of the shareholders' own interests, traditionally identified as the common interest in running a business in order to share in the profits.[18] According to this concept, the company interest represents a limit on the actions of the group in control of the company. Consequently, a resolution may be challenged when the majority shareholders have pursued purposes that are contrary to those of the shareholders overall. In this regard, it should be noted that it is possible to distinguish 'typical' interests that lawmakers have expressly provided (such as interests in profit maximisation, the receipt of dividends, influencing management etc.) from 'atypical' interests. Atypical interests are ones the shareholders would have expressly agreed to if they had foreseen every development in their future relationship. These interests are relevant as they constitute a translation of the general principles of good faith and fairness into the corporate field.[19] Today, the contractualism theory has prevailed after gradually establishing itself in case law, which for a long time had remained rooted in traditional institutionalist theories.[20]

IV. Conflicts of Interest, Abuse by the Majority Shareholder and Related Assumptions

As mentioned above, an important reference in the development of theories on the abuse of the right to vote is traditionally constituted by the normative rule on conflicts of interest (CC, art 2373).[21] The norm expresses a principle whereby the corporate interest applies as a limit to the right to vote and has the function of ensuring that the majority shareholders do not use their power to obtain private benefits from their position of power.[22] In particular, the conflict occurs when

[18] In accordance with contractualist theory see, for example, Gambino (n 6) 231ff.

[19] Preite (n 14) 27s, according to which the principle of good faith is suitable for establishing the balance not only of the company interests but also of the interests that the parties would have expressed in their contract if they had foreseen the need and if indicating them had not been too onerous. In this regard, see also Giuseppe Zanarone, 'Società a responsabilità limitata' in Francesco Galgano (ed), *Trattato di diritto commerciale e di diritto pubblico dell'economia*, vol 8 (Cedam 1985) 150. The thesis complies with the prevailing opinion in German doctrine and Anglo-Saxon jurisprudence. See, respectively, Marcus Lutter, 'Theorie der Mitgliedschaft' (1980) 180 AcP 105ff, and the ruling *In re Westbourne Galleries Ltd.* (1972) 2 WLR, 1289 per Wilberforce LJ.

[20] With reference to institutionalist theories, see Cass 20 June 1958, no 2148, (1959) I Giur It 330, the principles of which were later abandoned in Cass 26 October 1995, no 11151, (1996) II Giur comm 329ff.

[21] According to the majority opinion, the provision represents a textual hypothesis of repression of the abuse of the vote. On this see, among many others, Francesco Galgano, Diritto commerciale. Le società (18th edn, Zanichelli 2012) 295.

[22] See Floriano d'Alessandro, 'Il conflitto d'interessi nei rapporti tra socio e società' (2007) I Giur comm 5ff.

the personal interest of a shareholder is opposed to the interests of the company. This happens when a shareholder is placed in a position in which they must choose either the company's interest or their own. But even if established objectively and decisively, a shareholder's personal interest does not matter unless it objectively contrasts with the company's interest (cf *Sondervorteile zum Schaden der Gesellschaft*, AktG, §243, para 2).

In essence, the law does not require a shareholder to generally use their vote in the best pursuit of an objective company interest. The law does not even require a shareholder to participate in meetings or vote, even when a particular resolution is vital for the company. Moreover, the law does not deal with the situation in which a shareholder uses their vote to pursue an extra-corporate interest as long as this interest does not conflict with the corporate interest. Hence, what is relevant is a conflict between the company interest and the vote of a shareholder pursuing a particular (other) interest. In such a case, the conflict is cause for annulment of the resolution as long as the following additional conditions are also met: the vote must be decisive; and the resolution must have the potential to harm the company.[23]

A different situation arises when the majority adopts a resolution not to harm the company but to harm minority shareholders. The assumption that arises then is commonly classified as abuse by the majority. Indeed, 'control by the majority is an indispensable legal instrument in the life of commercial businesses. But, as in all things, it can serve good and evil'[24].

The range of conceivable cases is very wide, but the most common occurrence is that a capital increase is approved without a specific interest on the part of the company and for the sole purpose of reducing the holdings of minority shareholders who are not given an opportunity to subscribe to the newly issued shares.[25] Another instance is when the majority never decides to distribute annual profits even if the company's capitalisation needs do not require it and with the evident purpose of inducing the minority to sell their shares at a low price.

As mentioned, in Italy has no rule similar to §243 of the AktG, and abuse of majority is an 'untyped' legal doctrine developed through case law. Although it

---

[23] These are constitutive elements of the case in question. See Fabrizio Guerrera, *La responsabilità deliberativa nelle società di capitali* (Giappichelli 2004) 182ff; Francesco Denozza, 'L'interesse sociale tra coordinamento e cooperazione' in *L'interesse sociale tra valorizzazione del capitale e protezione degli stakeholders. In ricordo di Pier Giusto Jaeger* (Giuffrè 2010) 27.

[24] Francesco Carnelutti, 'Eccesso di potere nelle deliberazioni dell'assemblea delle anonime' (1926) I Riv dir comm 181ff.

[25] The leading case is Cass 12 May 1951, no 1177, (1951) I Foro it 694, con nota di Scialoja, 'Sui poteri del giudice nel procedimento di impugnazione di deliberazioni assembleari di società (Oss. a sent. Cass., 12 maggio 1951, n. 1177)'. According to the ruling, in judging a challenge by dissenting shareholders to a shareholder resolution of a joint stock company, the court must not limit itself to reviewing its formal legitimacy but may examine the financial situation of the company to determine whether or not the measures approved by the shareholders are to be considered fraudulent and detrimental to the interests of the minority.

is evidently impossible to provide a particularly clear picture of the evolving lines of jurisprudence, two fundamental judgments have been rendered, one in 1995[26] and the other in 2005[27]. The cases are founded in a violation of the general principle of fairness and good faith in the execution of the articles of association; as previously mentioned, pursuant to art 1375 of the Civil Code, this acts as an external limit to the otherwise unquestionable freedom to exercise the right to vote.

The theory of abuse of majority is grounded in the following provisions and principles. Article 1175 of the Italian Civil Code requires the parties to an obligatory relationship to behave according to fairness standards; this rule expresses a principle of social solidarity under art 2 of the Italian Constitution, which imposes on the parties a mutual duty of collaboration. Furthermore art 1375 of the Italian Civil Code establishes that a contract must be executed in good faith, that is, with a commitment to cooperation that requires each party to behave in a manner that meets the legitimate expectations of the other party. The latter principle applies to all contracts. The company itself is a contract under CC, art 2247, in which the shareholders vote in meetings, thereby executing the contract such that the shareholder's vote is subject to the principles of articles 1175 and 1375; this is explained by our legal system's increased sensitivity to the need to protect individuals facing off against organised communities.

In other words, the principle is similar to *Treuepflicht* in the German legal system, recognised among shareholders[28] in awareness of the approach that the more stable the majority, the more stringent the duty.[29]

---

[26] Cass 26 October 1995 (n 20), according to which a meeting resolution adopted by and for the exclusive benefit of the majority shareholders of a joint stock company to the detriment of a minority (for the sole purpose of ousting a shareholder, it was assumed) is illegitimate and contestable pursuant to CC, art 2377, as art 1375, according to which the contract must be executed in good faith, given that the decisions of the members must be considered to all intents and purposes as real acts of execution of the associative relationship because they are preordained for the best implementation of the company bylaws.

[27] Cass 12 December 2005, no 27387, (2007) II Giur comm 86ff, according to which an abuse of majority is cause for annulment of a shareholder resolution when the resolution finds no justification in the interests of the company (for the vote was inspired the majority shareholders' pursuit of a personal interest antithetical to the corporate one) or is the result of intentional fraudulent activity by the majority shareholders aimed at infringing on the participation rights and other property rights of the minority shareholders *uti singuli*; outside of these hypotheses, any possibility of judicial review of the reasons behind the majority vote to dissolve the company early is ruled out, the needs relating to the individual finances of the shareholder being unquestionable and which may have led him to vote for this dissolutive solution.

[28] BGH 1 February 1988, II ZR 152/87, [1988] ZIP 201; Giuseppe B Portale, '"Uguaglianza e contratto": il caso dell'aumento del capitale sociale in presenza di più categorie di azioni' (1991) I Riv dir comm 735.

[29] Lutter (n 19) 102ff; Marcus Lutter, 'Die Treupflicht des Aktionärs' (1989) 153 ZHR 452.

As stated in case law,[30] the principle applies such that abuse of majority is cause for annulment of a shareholder resolution when: *(i)* there is no justification for the resolution in the interest of the company, but rather the resolution is in pursuit of the personal interests of the majority and opposed to the corporate interest; or, alternatively, *(ii)* the resolution is the result of intentional fraudulent activity by the majority shareholders aimed at infringing against the individual rights of minority shareholders.

To base the abuse of majority theory on such principles avoids having to resort to an uncertain identification of the company interest. Indeed, the interest of the company should be used as a 'negative' evaluation criterion to determine whether or not a case of abuse of law is occurring.[31] In other words, the pursuit of the corporate interest legitimises the prejudice caused to the individual interests of a shareholder. Otherwise, a similar conclusion could not be reached in the event that harming a shareholder's individual interest was not counterbalanced by a benefit to the company. In conclusion, the case law has observed that the vote of a majority shareholder is abusive when it consciously supports the adoption of a resolution detrimental to the interests of the other shareholders without pursuing the company's interests.

V. Evidence of Abuse and Limited Judicial Review

The issue of evidence is key to understanding an abuse of majority theory. The burden of proving an abuse by the majority rests on the person contesting the resolution, who must be able to demonstrate its unlawfulness in reference to concrete elements and whose allegations must go beyond the conclusory. From the point of view of the defendant company, on the other hand, its ability to justify the resolution as in the business interest of the company and to prove the transaction's economic rationale suffices to rule out abuse in relation to any alleged harm to the claimant's protected interests.[32] Evidence that an individually pro-

---

[30] This is the principle stated in Cass 12 December 2005 (n 27) and later widely taken up by jurisprudence. See, for example, Cass 17 July 2007, no 15942, [2009] R not 640ff; Cass 29 September 2020, no 20625, [2020] Riv dott comm 596.

[31] Trib Milano 30 January 2017, no 1157, <www.dirittobancario.it>.

[32] With particular reference evaluating the economic rationality of operations in relation to the management strategies of the company, see Paolo Montalenti, 'L'interesse sociale: una sintesi' (2018) Riv soc 319; in jurisprudence it has been stated that the discriminating element for the existence of the abuse (due to violation of the duty of fairness and good faith) consists in the company interest: if ascertained based on sufficient elements of a normally presumptive nature, the concrete divergence of the adopted resolution from the company interest may constitute arbitrary and unjustified prejudice to the minority, unlike when a superior social interest justifies the minority's sacrifice. See Trib Venezia 31 October 2018, [2020] II Giur comm 633ff, according to which, in relation to a resolution to increase share capital below accounting parity, an abuse of majority rule must be examined not only from the general contours of concrete

tected shareholder interest was jeopardised is therefore not enough to satisfy the plaintiff's burden of proof, since the plaintiff must also persuade the court that there is no concomitant interest on the part of the company.

On the other hand, if the resolution is manifestly unreasonable or incongruous in regard to the concretely inferred corporate interest, it may constitute an objective confirmation of the conflict between such corporate interest and the interest of the majority of voters. In such a case, the unreasonableness or incongruity of the resolution would sufficiently reveal the lack of a concomitant corporate interest underpinning the shareholder resolution. The plaintiff in that case would not be required to concretely identify the possible contours of the company's interest in adopting the contested resolution. Conversely, the defendant company would have to counteract the (presumptive) evidence produced by the plaintiff and thereby demonstrate the existence of a specific business interest capable of justifying the sacrifice of the disadvantaged shareholder interests.

In assessing the legitimacy of the resolution, it is therefore possible to distinguish between two types of cases. The first case is where a resolution can only be contested by alleging abuse, that is, an intention behind the resolution to take advantage of a specific extra-corporate situation of the minority (as in the typical case of early dissolution resolutions), requiring the minority to produce evidence of abuse by the majority. The second case is where a resolution contributes to furthering the company's business but also has the potential to alter the balance within the company, and therefore those who believe in the resolution's lawfulness are required to justify it.[33] In any case, the variety of concrete cases and the different ways in which the relationship between majority and minority can develop across the different corporate types makes it impossible, in terms of evidence, to define a certain set of elements as relevant *a priori*.

As mentioned, the underlying principle is that the substance of shareholder resolutions is not called into question. Indeed, a common view holds that the court – for its lack of adequate specialized background – is not a suitable institution to formulate assessments in a field such as business, which requires appropriate technical knowledge.[34] Moreover, abuse of majority is an issue that, while it does concern relations between shareholders, cannot be properly addressed without dealing with issues pertaining to business operations.[35]

---

utility and the company's interest in the capital increase but also in light of the company's concrete interest, embodied in the resolution, in the increase according to approved methods, ie, by issuing new shares below accounting parity. In the present case, the court considered that the issue of shares with a nominal value markedly lower than the previous accounting parity could excessively compress the interests of the minority shareholders who dissented from the procedure.

33 Angelici (n 8) 120.

34 Jaeger (n 3) 110.

35 With reference to the judge's assessment of individual acts (such as meeting resolutions) and not of its entrepreneurial activity as a whole, see Denozza (n 23) 23.

Also, the case law oscillates on this issue between different statements of principle: some rulings are limited to affirming the non-reviewable character of the substance of shareholder resolutions;[36] others consider review on the merits to be admissible in order to assess whether a resolution is unlawful; yet another prevailing approach considers assessment on the merits to be possible only in cases of blatant breach or, in another formulation, after a preliminary assessment whether there is evidence of abuse, which, if affirmed, would allow an assessment of the substance of the resolution.[37] In summary, it could be said – to use an effective expression that has gained a certain following in the literature – that the judge is called to perform a 'legitimacy check carried out through an assessment of the merits'.[38]

VI. The Consequences of Abuse by the Majority (and the Issue of Negative Resolutions)

The consequences of abuse of majority have been the subject of extensive debate. Some scholars have drawn a general principle of law analogous to art 2373 of the Italian Civil Code in terms of annulment of a resolution. However, as already mentioned, the basis of the abuse assumption is not the regulatory framework on conflicts of interest but the duty of fairness and good faith the violation of which implies, first of all, a form of liability in the company's obligation to compensate the aggrieved shareholders; according to a certain approach, the majority shareholders also bear this liability. In fact, the legal personality of the joint stock company is not an appropriate element by which to rule out that the rules also apply to shareholders. It follows that both the company and the majority shareholders are obliged to pay compensation, notwithstanding the company's right to levy charges against the majority shareholders.[39] Secondly, a violation of the duty of fairness and good faith entails the annulment of the offending resolution pursuant to art 2377 of the Italian Civil Code for failure to comply with the law. The violation of the duty of good faith and fairness indeed entails a such a violation of the law.[40] As a result, the resolution lapses, and the directors are obliged to adopt the consequent measures.[41]

---

36 Cass 29 May 1986, no 3628, (1987) 2 Giur comm 572.

37 Cass 12 December 2005 (n 27); Cass 7 February 1963, no 195, (1964) 2 Riv dir comm 93.

38 Walter Bigiavi, 'Elezione di nuovi amministratori con il voto di amministratori revocati in seguito ad azione sociale di responsabilità' (1956) I Giur it 488; Paolo Ferro-Luzzi, *La conformità delle deliberazioni assembleari alla legge ed all'atto costitutivo* (Giuffrè 1993) 164.

39 Preite (n 7) 151.

40 Giuseppe Ferri, 'Diritto agli utili e diritto al dividendo' (1963) 1 Riv dir comm 412.

41 See, among many others, Giorgio Meo, *Gli effetti dell'invalidità delle deliberazioni assembleari* (Giuffrè 1998) 207ff; Giuseppe Zanarone, 'L'invalidità delle deliberazioni assembleari' in Giovanni E Colombo and Giuseppe B Portale (eds), *Trattato delle società per azioni*,

In terms of consequences, an appeal against a so-called 'negative' shareholder resolution represents a controversial case. As is known, this is a situation in which a proposed resolution is submitted to the shareholder meeting but is illegitimately rejected in a case of one or more shareholders abusively exercising their right to vote.[42]

In the German legal system, if the judge determines that the resolution was not actually adopted owing to abusive voting activity by a decisive percentage of shareholders, such resolution can be replaced by a converse 'positive' resolution.[43] In the case of partnerships, this principle even receives explicit mention in §115 of the Commercial Code (the 'HGB') following the enactment of the *Gesetz zur Modernisierung des Personengesellschaftsrecht* (as of 1 January 2024).

The availability of this solution in the Italian legal system is far from obvious. Originally, the Italian system regarded it as controversial whether the rejection of a proposal even qualifies as a shareholder resolution. The negative resolution thesis was based on a contractual conception of the resolution, according to which a failure to approve a proposal could not constitute a shareholder decision because the will of the corporation cannot be considered to be truly developed in such a case.[44] However, this view has been superseded by the now-prevailing opposite approach, which emphasises organisational and corporate viewpoints rather than contractual ones. According to the latter approach, rejecting a proposed resolution constitutes an activity of the meeting that expresses a legally relevant will at the conclusion of a sub-procedure of the same.[45] Therefore, whether the shareholder resolution is negative or positive appears to be irrelevant to whether it legally qualifies as a resolution.[46]

Consequently, today it is commonly believed that a negative resolution can be challenged and annulled. At the same time, however, it is also believed that the cancelled resolution cannot be replaced with a positive ruling by the judicial

---

vol 3/2 (Utet 1993), 185ff; Roberto Sacchi, 'Tutela reale e tutela obbligatoria della minoranza' in Pietro Abbadessa and Giuseppe B Portale (eds), *Il nuovo diritto delle società. Liber amicorum Gian Franco Campobasso*, vol 2 (Utet 2006) 135ff.

[42] Among Italian authors, see Vincenzo Pinto, 'Il problema dell'impugnazione della delibera negativa nella giurisprudenza delle imprese' (2016) I Riv dir civ 901ff, with emphasis on the discrepancy between Italian positive law and substantial needs worthy of protection.

[43] See for example BGH 12 April 2016, II ZR 275/14 (OLG Munich), (2017) III Riv dir soc 945ff; OLG Munich 23 June 2016, 23 U 4531/15, [2016] GmbHR 925.

[44] Giuseppe Ferri, 'Le società' in Filippo Vassalli (found), *Trattato di diritto civile italiano*, vol 10/3 (Utet 1987) 650ff; Roberto Weigmann, 'Società per azioni' (1997) 14 Digesto comm 396ff; in case law: Trib Milano 29 November 2003, [2004] Giur it 1459ff.

[45] Carlo Angelici, 'Società per azioni e in accomandita per azioni' in Enc dir, vol XLII (Giuffrè 1990) 987; Marco Cian, *La deliberazione negativa dell'assemblea nelle società per azioni* (Giappichelli 2003) 71ff; Marco Cian, 'Abus d'égalité, tutela demolitoria e tutela risarcitoria' (2008) Corr giur 399ff.

[46] Ferro-Luzzi (n 38) 50ff.

authority.[47] This means that the only further consequence in the event of annulment consists in the directors' obligation to reconvene the meeting with the same item on the agenda, this time with (at most) an aggravation of liability on the part of the shareholder who repeats an abusive vote on the new resolution. Despite this approach, the preferable solution, suggested in a minority segment of Italian scholarship and case law, appears to support a more extensive solution similar to the German one.[48] In fact, from a practical point of view, this solution best protects the interest of the shareholders who have suffered the abuse and avoids discrepancies between the treatment of positive and negative shareholder resolutions.

VII. Determining Abuses of Power and the Related Issue of the Motivation of Shareholder Resolutions

Alongside references to abuse of majority shareholder power, the case law often (and indifferently) uses other terms such as 'abuse of power' or 'excess of power', which as legal determinations originally belonged to administrative law.[49] According to the majority of opinion, 'excess of power' represents merely an obsolete reference or (from the perspective of case law in any event) a terminological nuance used to define a case of abuse of majority. However, to a minority it seems possible to identify a conceptual difference:[50] the legal determination of abuse requires proof of specific wilful misconduct by majority shareholders to the detriment of minority shareholders; the legal determination of excess of power, on

[47] On the dominant view and more generally on the debate about this topic, see Camillo Patriarca, sub art 2377, in Pietro Abbadessa and Giuseppe B Portale (eds) *Le società per azioni. Codice civile e norme complementari*, vol 1 (Giuffrè 2016) 1057; Mirone (n 12) 446; Cass 26 August 2004, no 16999, [2005] Società 599ff, according to which the proclamation of the results of the vote has a constitutive nature and therefore cannot be replaced by judicial verification of the erroneous counting of votes; Trib Roma, 14 December 2020, (2021) II Riv dir soc 412.

[48] With reference to cases of conflict of interest, see Preite (n 14) 120s, provided that the rejection of the resolution is potentially harmful to the company; Cian (n 45) 140ff; on the limits of this thesis, see, however, Vincenzo Meli, sub art 2373, in Abbadessa and Portale (eds) (n 47) 1006, with further references in the literature and jurisprudence. With regard to the abuse of majority in line with the aforementioned minority opinion, see Lodo arb, 2 July 2009, (2010) II Giur comm 911ff, with comments by Alberto De Pra, 'Deliberazione negativa votata in conflitto d'interessi e divieto di voto del socio amministratore'; Trib Milano 28 November 2014, (2016) II Riv dir soc 146, according to which the judge having ascertained the illegitimacy of the vote in the deliberative quorum also ascertains that the proposal on the agenda was approved (positive resolution) and not rejected (negative resolution).

[49] Giuseppe Ferri, 'Eccesso di potere e tutela delle minoranze' (1934) I Riv dir comm 725ff; Aurelio Candian, *Nullità ed annullabilità di delibere di assemblea delle società per azioni* (Giuffrè 1961) 109ff; Carnelutti (n 24) 176ff.

[50] See Mirone (n 12) 448s.

the other hand, requires proof of the objective impossibility of invoking a reasonable corporate interest in the resolution. This arises when the resolution is absolutely and objectively incompatible with any criterion of efficient management of a for-profit company.

However, what it does not entail is a general requirement to justify acts of the corporation; in fact, the general rule is that shareholder resolutions are presumed to be in the interest of the company until proven otherwise.[51]

In the Italian legal system, only a limited number of resolutions are subject to an explicit obligation to give reasons, and as a rule, shareholders are free to decide on votes without automatically stating the reasons for their decisions,[52] an obligation that exists only in particular cases, such as when the right of pre-emption is ruled out in connection with a capital increase.[53]

This means that the evidentiary path in matters of abuse of majority presents differently depending on whether or not shareholders are obligated to state reasons for the resolution.[54]

In the event such an obligation is provided, the contending minority may prove the abuse by simply contesting the motivation provided by the company or, in the most serious cases, by asserting the absence of a motivation. On the other hand, while the company and majority shareholders can certainly maintain the fairness of the motivation, they cannot adopt reasons other than those already stated in support of the resolution.[55] In summary, if stating the reason for a certain resolution is mandatory by law, the review of whether the resolution complies with the fairness standard must necessarily be subject to a verification of the congruity and completeness of the reason.[56]

On the other hand, in the case of resolutions that raise no obligation to state reasons, the contesting minority is free to submit any elements deemed useful to demonstrate the existence of abuse by the majority; however, the evidence from

---

[51] Francesco Galgano, 'La società per azioni' in Francesco Galgano (ed) *Trattato di diritto commerciale e di diritto pubblico dell'economia*, vol 7 (2nd edn, Cedam 1988) 385.

[52] Cass 26 January 2018, no 2037, (2018) 1 Foro it 864ff. However, this does not rule out that the shareholder meeting can spontaneously put forward a resolution with the aim of demonstrating that it is being taken in the exclusive interest of the company.

[53] For a comparative perspective, see Marco Speranzin, 'Aumento del capitale delegato con esclusione «semplificata» del diritto di opzione: tutela dell'azionista dal punto di vista informativo e della parità di trattamento' (2020) II Giur comm 701ff. However, a motivation is not necessary in the case of a sole resolution to increase the capital: Angelici (n 8) 122ff; Cass 22 July 2020, no 15647, [2021] Le società 267ff.

[54] About the motivation of shareholder resolutions, see Alessio Diego Scano, *La motivazione delle decisioni nelle società di capitali* (Giuffrè 2018) 244ff, mentioning the function of formulating shareholder interests and reaching an agreement between majority and minority.

[55] Galgano (n 51) 385, refers to shifting the burden of proof, as the burden of proving that the resolution (eg, to exclude the right of option) is justified by specific needs of the company lies with the majority.

[56] Alessio Diego Scano, 'La motivazione della giusta causa di revoca degli amministratori di s.p.a. (con una postilla sull'azione sociale di responsabilità)' [2020] Riv soc 968ff,

which it deduces an abuse of majority cannot be based either on the mere absence of reasons or on the mere assertion that a motivation that (although not required) is contained in the text of the contested resolution is illogical. And the company and the majority shareholders for their part are equally free to submit any elements in defence of the resolution as adopted, including reasons other than those contained in the minutes.

VIII. A Specific Case of Abuse: Disproportionate Remuneration of Directors

The above observations prompt a reference to resolutions that concern the remuneration of directors. Frequently, such resolutions lead to a conflict between majority and minority shareholders,[57] in particular when the composition of the management body does not reflect a balance between shareholders. This conflict mainly occurs in the following two cases.

(i) Firstly, substantial remuneration of directors may have an impact on the interests of minority shareholders, as revenues under such circumstances may not leave room for an operating profit to be distributed to the shareholders. There are two relevant interests: that of the managing shareholder in compensation for their work and that of the company obliged to pay. In short, according to the case law there is no conflict of interest solely because the managing shareholder supported, with a decisive vote, a resolution on their own remuneration; directors are in fact entitled to remuneration in any case.[58] What the case law does not tolerate is excessive or unreasonable remuneration, as better explained in the following paragraph.

(ii) Secondly, in companies in which the majority shareholders also have a mandate as directors, it is not uncommon[59] for the majority to decide to allocate profits to reserves. Consequently, the minority does not enjoy the benefit of the profits of the business even as the majority shareholders do; these do not receive profits as distributions to the shareholders but instead benefit in the form of compensation for a management position. In this second case, disproportionate remuneration of the directors represents a symptom of other abuse

[57] As well as, obviously, among shareholders and directors. See, for instance, Lorraine Talbot, 'Shareholders and Directors: Entitlements, Duties and the Expansion of Shareholder Wealth' in Andrew Johnston and Lorraine Talbot (eds), *Great Debates in Commercial and Corporate Law* (Red Globe Press 2020) 126ff, also with regard to high executive pay considered as a 'modern-day scandal'.

[58] Cass 21 March 2000, no 3112, [2001] Foro it 2329; Trib Milano 22 February 2022, no 1554, <www.giurisprudenzadelleimprese.it>.

[59] With specific reference to director compensation (in Spanish law), see Fernando Marin de la Bárcena, 'Shareholder Control over Executive Pay' in Holger Fleischer, Andrés Recalde and Gerald Spindler (eds), *Family Firms and Closed Companies in Germany and Spain* (Mohr Siebeck 2021) 171ff.

situations. In other words, regardless of the ability of the minority shareholders to challenge the resolution on remuneration on grounds of abuse of majority, the same minority can point to this circumstance as evidence of abuse by the majority in relation to the resolution on the (non-)distribution of profits.[60]

In either case, the judge is implicitly required to scrutinise the substance of the resolutions and to quash those that are outside the scope of reasonableness.[61]

Already a subject of historical debate in company law, not only in Italy,[62] the issue of remuneration of directors has recently channelled media attention (due to the ethical and social impacts of the problems involved) onto well-known events held by large industrial groups, and these were also involved in certain caselaw rulings.[63] Moreover, remuneration is one of the most important corporate governance issues. The relevant rules are established (for joint stock companies, expressly so) in the public interest to ensure orderly conduct of the country's commercial and industrial activities.[64] At the same time, the subject is of particular interpretative complexity, also involving limited liability companies, due to the regulatory void that characterises its positive regulation.[65] The practical impact is even greater if the concept of remuneration is considered in an all-encompassing

---

[60] Jurisprudence has examined various cases on this second aspect. See, for example, Trib Venezia 15 October 2016, <www.giurisprudenzadelleimprese.it>, which assessed very high compensation of the chairman of the board compared to market values, including a specific variable component in proportion to accrued (but not distributed) operating profits, as symptomatic of the existence of abuse in the non-distribution of profits.

[61] Roberto Weigmann, 'Compensi esagerati agli amministratori di società a base ristretta' (1991) 1 Giur it 799.

[62] With regard to works that address the subject transversally, see, among many other monographs, Anna Laura Bonafini, *I compensi degli amministratori di società per azioni* (Giuffrè 2005) *passim*; Andrea Pilati, *Lavoro e funzione negli amministratori di società per azioni* (Edizioni Scientifiche Italiane 2012) *passim*; see also the various contributions in Carlo Amatucci (ed), *La remunerazione degli amministratori nelle società di capitali* (Giuffrè 2010); among commentaries, see Gianvito Giannelli and Antonio Dell'Osso, sub art 2389, in Abbadessa and Portale (eds) (n 47) 1313ff; among manuals, Pierpaolo M Sanfilippo, 'Gli amministratori' in Cian (ed) (n 12) 532ff.

[63] See, for example, Trib Roma 8 June 2020, [2021] Società 934ff, with comments by Michele Perrino, 'Compensi e "buonuscita" dell'amministratore delegato di S.p.a.: problemi di competenza'; Trib Roma 15 May 2019, no 10212, <www.dejure.it>. From German courts, see BGH 24 September 2019, 4 StR 368/19, [2020] NJW 679 with specific reference to the variable components of the remuneration of a *Vorstandsmitglied*; see also (in relation to criminal penalties) BGH 21 December 2005, 3 StR 470/04, [2006] NZG 141 on the *Mannesmann* case (see Thilo Kuntz, '§ 18 – Mannesmann' in Holger Fleischer and Jan Thiessen (eds), Gesellschaftsrechts-Geschichten (Mohr Siebeck 2018). Among many other authors, see Mario Campobasso, 'I compensi degli amministratori di società quotate: l'esperienza italiana' (2011) Riv soc 702ff.

[64] Cass, sez. un. 29 August 2008, no 21933, in accordance with Cass 4 September 2013, no 20265.

[65] Vincenzo Antonini, 'Amministratori di s.r.l. e diritto al compenso' (2022) I Riv dir civ 777ff and 797ff, with specific reference to the quantification (even excessive) of the compensation.

sense;[66] therefore, the issue is not limited to 'basic remuneration' of the directors merely as compensation for their services but is extended to other items, which actually tend to predominate, namely the bonuses paid to them and their end-of-term fees (severance pay).

IX. The Quantification of Remuneration and Unreasonable or Excessive Amounts as Abuse Cases

In Italian law, the regulatory framework for limited liability companies provides no rule on quantifying remuneration. It follows in principle that the decision is left to the relevant body, as lawmakers set no limits in this regard. This might seem surprising, at least in the eyes of non-Italian literature, considering the naturally burdensome nature of the director's assignment.[67] In fact, once the management relationship is established upon acceptance of an appointment, remuneration is legally due to the incumbent director, so much so that in the event of a failure to determine the remuneration, the director (although unable to provide for self-payment[68]) has a right to obtain the same in court.[69]

The freedom to determine the amount of remuneration is certainly confirmed when one asks about minimum remuneration thresholds in relation to the activity performed. There are in fact no downward limits in terms of minimum remuneration, to the point that remuneration of directors can be objectively inadequate with respect to their performance but will not be questioned provided that they have (even tacitly) consented.[70] Moreover, the director has a right to remuneration and as such it is subject to waiver: a director who did not complain of inadequate

[66] AktG, §87 refers to the concept of *Gesamtbezüge*; see, among many others, Uwe Hüffer and Jens Koch (ed), Aktiengesetz (16th edn, CH Beck 2022) §87 para 2ff.

[67] The view that the director's task is 'naturally' a paid one is now unanimous in Italy with regard to joint stock companies, and has been since before the 2003 reform. See, among many others, Giovanni Caselli, 'Vicende del rapporto di amministrazione' in Giovanni E Colombo and Giuseppe B Portale (eds), *Trattato delle società per azioni*, vol 4/12 (Utet 1991) 49; Anna Laura Bonafini, Divagazioni sul credito retributivo dell'amministratore di s.p.a., (2004) II Giur comm 310 fn 15. However, isolated support for the contrary thesis (the natural gratuitousness of the task) is found in Giancarlo Frè, sub art 2389, in Antonio Scialoja and Giuseppe Branca (eds) *Commentario del Codice civile*, vol 1 (6th edn, Zanichelli 1997) 818. See also Cass 24 February 1997, no 1647 (compensation as a natural element of the management relationship characterized by the nature of a perfect subjective right of the director); Cass 9 August 2005, no 16764, [2006] Giur it 295; Cass 26 January 2021, no 1673, <www.dejure.it>.

[68] Paying oneself constitutes an illicit act, at least in the event that the amount paid is excessive; see Trib Roma 23 January 2017, <www.ilcaso.it>.

[69] Cass 23 June 2016, no 13058, <www.dejure.it>; Cass 16 September 2014, no 8897, [2014] Riv dott comm 579; Paolo Spada, 'Preposizione e assunzione dell'amministratore di società per azioni' in Amatucci (ed) (n 62) 62.

[70] Trib Roma 21 February 2017, no 3422, <www.giurisprudenzadelleimprese.it>.

remuneration when taking office has tacitly accepted it and is therefore precluded from appealing the pertinent shareholder resolution.[71] It is a common-ground solution, not so much because it is the result of a free negotiation between the company and the director, but because there is no risk of harm to the interests of minority shareholders or of a conflict of interest in the event that the shareholder who determines the amount of remuneration is also a director – precisely because of the limited (or even non-existent) economic burden borne by the company.

It is precisely the contemplation of the latter two situations that leads to diverging conclusions where the amount of the remuneration is disproportionately high in comparison with the performance of the management task. Indeed, the case law in this case is, understandably, generally oriented toward justifying appeals against disproportionate remuneration upon the occurrence of certain parameters referring in particular to the rules governing the conflict of interest in the case of a managing shareholder and abuse of voting rights by the majority.[72]

Certain important judgments advance the alternatives of a conflict of interest versus majority abuse without distinction and without adopting a position on either one; the cases limit themselves to indicating that the key issue is the disproportionate remuneration.[73] In any case, according to the prevailing theory a resolution adopted thanks to a decisive vote by the managing shareholder can be annulled if it pursues extra-corporate interests to the detriment of the company (that is, when the remuneration is excessive or unjustified with respect to the tasks to be fulfilled).[74] However, for purposes of annulment it is not sufficient merely that the decisive vote should have been cast by the conflicted shareholder.[75] The same applies in the (different) case of majority abuse and even if the resolution is not considered contrary to the corporate interest: the resolution that rewards a direc-

---

[71] Trib Milano, 18 January 2022, no 256, <www.dejure.it>; Cass 24 May 2010, no 12592, [2010] Riv crit dir lav 854; Cass 17 March 1981, no 1554, [1981] Rep Foro it, «Società», 175.

[72] See Daniele U Santosuosso, 'Il rapporto di amministrazione. Il compenso degli amministratori' in Michele Vietti (ed), *La governance nelle società di capitali: a dieci anni dalla riforma* (EGEA 2013) 17ff, Daniele U Santosuosso, 'La remunerazione degli amministratori: norme per "sanare" le cattive prassi' (2010) I Riv dir soc 349s.

[73] Cass 3 December 2008, no 28748, (2009) 2 Giur comm 1131.

[74] Cass 3 December 2008 (n 73); Cass 21 March 2000, no 3312, [2001] Foro it 2329; Lodo arb, 30 March 2009 (Arb. Cagnasso), (2010) II in Riv dir comm 87ff; Trib Milano 5 September 2016, n. 9893, <www.giurisprudenzadelleimprese.it>; Trib Bologna 19 October 2020, no 1448 (annulment due to a conflict of interest of a resolution approved by the exclusive and decisive vote of the conflicted managing partner as harmful to a company that never had profit margins such as to allow the attribution of compensation to the administrator). See BGH 21 July 2008, II ZR 39/07, [2008] NZG 783ff. Among Italian authors, see further references in Anna Maria Bentivegna, 'Il problema dei compensi. Eccessività sopravvenuta e possibili rimedi' (2014) I Riv dir soc 510ff.

[75] In fact, the thesis according to which a conflict of interest was recognizable *in re ipsa* in the sole vote of the shareholder in conflict has been abandoned regardless of any assessment of the (disproportionate and unjustified) amount of the compensation; see, eg, Trib Milano 20 March 1980, (1980) II Giur comm 396ff.

tor with excessive remuneration is in any case liable to be annulled if it is the result of a breach of the obligation of objective good faith or fairness and to the detriment of a minority shareholder.[76]

This is an interpretative result that in the German legal system is expressly governed by §87 of the AktG, which imposes proportionality between the remuneration of the directors, the tasks they concretely carry out, and the financial situation of the company. It is a norm that aims at reasonably protecting the assets of the company and therefore the *Unternehmensinteresse*.[77]

Moreover, according to Italian case law, to avoid an excessive degree of discretion, the reasonableness of the remuneration must be measured *ex ante* according to a so-called relational criterion, which looks at the following parameters: *(i)* the commitment required of management and the extent of the tasks concretely entrusted to the directors; *(ii)* current market remuneration for similar services in companies of similar size; *(iii)* turnover, yearly profit, and the economic-financial dimension of the company (also on a forward-looking basis); *(iv)* economic performance of the company and any increase in the volume of business generated by the directors.[78]

In conclusion, the judge does not aim to ascertain the appropriateness of the resolution in the interest of the company (it would constitute illegitimate interference by the judge in decisions that are the responsibility of the shareholder meeting). On the contrary, the aim is to establish whether there is an element of illegitimacy in unreasonable compensation. If the remuneration is found to be excessive, a violation of the duty of good faith may be found, either in terms of objectiveness or fairness; such a resolution is in pursuit of personal interests unrelated to the business relationship and damaging to other shareholders. In any case, however, the annulment of the resolution does not result in outright non-payment of remuneration to the director, who, upon request for judicial liquidation, will be entitled to reasonable remuneration in any case, to be equitably determined by the judge, as well as to reimbursement of any expenses, at least per analogous application of the regulations on the mandate provided in art 1720 of the Italian Civil Code.

[76] Cass 17 July 2007 (n 30); Trib Milano 29 April 2008, (2009) III Riv dir soc 181 (annulment due to abuse of majority of a meeting resolution that awarded the majority shareholder directors annual compensation such as to fully absorb the operating profits with consequent exclusion of the non-director minority shareholder from participating in the profits).

[77] The rule, as is known, was examined in the *Mannesmann-Vodafone* case.

[78] On these parameters, see Cass 17 July 2007 (n 30); Anna Laura Bonafini, 'Note in tema di quantificazione del compenso dell'amministratore sociale' [2006] Giur it 300ff; Lodo arb 30 March 2009 (n 74); Bentivegna (n 74) 505ff.

The Concept of Limited Liability

Justification and Critique in the Debates of the Past and Present

*Klaus Ulrich Schmolke**

I. Introduction

1. Limited Liability as a Perpetual Subject of Debate

The principle of limited shareholder liability has been continuously applied to corporate (and limited partnership) law in Western jurisdictions since the nineteenth century. Limitation of liability gained broad acceptance during and after

* Translations into English are by the author unless otherwise indicated.

the industrial revolution, and many even consider it to have been a critical factor in the dazzling dynamism of the industrial age.[1] The proponents of limited liability therefore praise it in the highest terms. For example, *Stephen Bainbridge* and *M Todd Henderson* state in their treatise on the topic:

'Limited liability is one of mankind's greatest ideas. Creating artificial entities [...] and using it as a mechanism of risk taking was the key legal innovation that drove much of the economic growth that created our modern world.'[2]

However, not everyone joins in the praise of limited liability. On the contrary, the feature of limited shareholder liability has always met with criticism. Recently some German scholars have bemoaned a 'lack of critical discussion' of the concept and have subsequently endeavoured to fill the gap.[3] In short, the principle of limited shareholder liability has always stirred emotions and sometimes prompted commentators to harsh words. In an article published around the turn of the millennium, *David L Cohen* summarises this controversial reception:

'For it is limited liability that sets a corporation apart from regular business partnerships and which provokes the greatest ire in its critics and praise in its defenders.'[4]

As a consequence of such opposing views, the concept of limited liability sparked one of the core debates in corporate law that has transcended the generations.[5] One of the peculiarities of the debate on limited liability is that since its establishment in corporate law, this (non-)liability principle has never come under lasting pressure – at least not when the corporate group[6] is out of the picture. On the contrary, the – ultimately unsuccessful – criticism ebbs and flows in waves. We are currently on the crest of such a wave again. Just as the foundations of the market economy in the Western world are currently facing increased criticism from 'anticapitalists', doubts are also being raised about limited shareholder liability. Indeed, limited liability is seen as a legal manifestation or even a prerequisite of the capitalist system they criticise.[7]

---

[1] Admittedly, this has been increasingly doubted in recent times. See below under IV.3.a).

[2] Stephen M Bainbridge and M Todd Henderson, *Limited Liability* (Edward Elgar 2016) 302.

[3] See, for example, Chris Thomale, 'Kapital als Verantwortung' (2018) 218 AcP 685 (in German) (in the original German: 'verbreitete Kritikarmut'); similarly Andreas Conow, *Vertragsbindung als Freiheitsvoraussetzung* (Mohr Siebeck 2015) 280 (in German): 'unilateral willingness of lawyers to receive' ('einseitige Rezeptionsbereitschaft der Juristen'); see also the critical review by Klaus Ulrich Schmolke, (2016) 180 ZHR 136 et seq (in German).

[4] David L Cohen, 'Theories of the Corporation and the Limited Liability Company. How Should Courts and Legislatures Articulate Rules for Piercing the Veil, Fiduciary Responsibility and Securities Regulation for the Limited Liability Company' (1998) 51 Okla LRev 427, 428.

[5] In contrast to 'generational issues', see Holger Fleischer, 'Große Debatten im Gesellschaftsrecht: Eine Forschungsskizze' [2023] 78 JZ 365, 368 et seq (in German).

[6] See the recent articles in Alfred Bergmann and others (eds), *Vom Konzern zum Einheitsunternehmen* (ZGR Special Issue 22, De Gruyter 2020) (in German)).

[7] See, for example, Katharina Pistor, *The Code of Capital* (Princ UP 2019) 54 et seq; also Conow (n 3) 199 et seq (with a focus on the statutory minimum capital pursuant to GmbHG, § 5(1)).

The following discussion provides a structured depiction of this 'perpetual debate' about limited shareholder liability and examines it for lasting insights and advances in the understanding of this concept. The closely related debate over suspending the principle in certain scenarios ('piercing the veil'), by contrast, will only be touched upon in passing, if only for reasons of space. The discussion also excludes issues of entity shielding and 'economic unity' in corporate group liability.[8]

2. Necessary Distinctions and Revenants haunting the Debate

Before outlining the debate over limited shareholder liability, it seems appropriate to distinguish the limited liability referred to here from other related concepts in corporate law: (a) so-called 'entity separateness' and (b) the association's legal capacity or 'legal personhood'.[9] Attempts have been made in Germany to use both of these concepts as fundamental building blocks of limited liability. Today, however, these efforts can be considered a failure.[10]

a) Entity separateness

The formation of a corporation, be it a joint stock corporation or a limited liability company, creates a legal entity that is distinct and separate from its founders.[11] This 'corporate' separateness is a prerequisite of limited liability. *Thomale* calls it the 'essential structuralist basis' (*wesentliche strukturalistische Grundlage*) of limited liability.[12] However, to understand limited liability as a logical consequence of entity separateness goes too far. It is not even a convincing basis by which to legitimise it. For this reason, one current critique of limited liability, which accuses its proponents of relying on an understanding of entity separateness that turns out to be a misinterpretation of Savigny's fiction theory[13], misses the point.[14]

---

[8] Only on more recent times, cf Peter Hommelhoff, 'Ein Europäisches Gruppenrecht für den Binnenmarkt' in Stefan J Geibel, Christian Heinze and Dirk A Verse (eds), *Binnenmarktrecht als Mehrebenensystem* (Nomos 2023) 159 et seq (in German) under the heading 'Risiko- und Haftungssegmentierung im Konzern' (Risk and liability segmentation in the group).

[9] See also Bainbridge and Henderson (n 2) 4 et seq on this approach. 'Entity shielding', ie, shielding companies from liability, is not discussed in detail here. See, for example, Bainbridge and Henderson (n 2) 7 et seq, with further references.

[10] See Bernhard Großfeld, Aktiengesellschaft, Unternehmenskonzentration und Kleinaktionär (Mohr Siebeck 1968) 104 et seq (in German). More on this in the text.

[11] Bainbridge and Henderson (n 2) 5; Thomale (n 3).

[12] Thomale (n 3) (pointing out that entity separateness (*Trennungsprinzip*) and limited liability are often used synonymously; see, eg, Hommelhoff (n 8) 159 et seq).

[13] See Holger Fleischer, 'Große Debatten im Gesellschaftsrecht: Fiktionstheorie versus Theorie der realen Verbandspersönlichkeiten im internationalen Diskurs' (2023) 87 RabelZ 5, 12 et seq (in German) on the debate conducted in this regard.

[14] See Thomale (n 3) 686. On this and the general contemporary criticism of limited shareholder liability, see IV.3. In the 1970s and 80s, Hans Kiefner, 'Personae vice fungitur? Juristische Person und industrielle Corporation im System Savignys' in Wolfgang Hefermehl, Rudolf

The debate on limited liability in English corporate law in the nineteenth century shows that such conceptual-dogmatic considerations played no significant role.[15] Statements by German corporate law scholars at the end of the nineteenth century also clearly show that the concept of limited liability was derived from other sources. *Karl Lehmann* refers to the Code de Commerce of 1807/08.[16] However, it was not until 1840 that *Savigny* developed his 'fiction theory' within his system of modern Roman law.[17] The recently amended law of private partnerships in the German Civil Code (the 'BGB') also provides a compelling argument against the assumption that limited liability is a necessary consequence of entity separateness. As amended, section 705 (2) of the code grants 'legal capacity' (*Rechtsfähigkeit*) to the private partnership as a consequence of entity separateness, while section 721 provides for the unlimited liability of the partners for the debts of the partnership.

b) Legal personhood

'Legal personhood', legal subjectivity or the legal capacity of the association of persons is generally understood as an implication of entity separateness.[18] Re-

Gmür and Hans Brox (eds), *Festschrift für Harry Westermann* (CF Müller 1974) 263 et seq (in German) and Theodor Baums, *Gesetz über die Aktiengesellschaften für die Königlich Preußischen Staaten vom 9. November 1843* (Scientia 1981) 38 et seq (in German) were already arguing, convincingly, that Savigny could not be taken into service for such an interpretation; more recently, for example, Justus Meyer, *Haftungsbeschränkung im Recht der Handelsgesellschaften* (Springer 2000) 260, 261 et seq (in German).

[15] On this debate, see Frank H Easterbrook and Daniel R Fischel, 'Limited Liability and the Corporation' (1985) 52 U Chi LRev 89.

[16] Karl Lehmann, *Das Recht der Aktiengesellschaften*, vol 1 (Scientia 1898) 1 et seq: 'Thus we must also accept a certain concept of the joint-stock company as fixed, […]. This concept can only be the French one of the Code de Commerce, which focuses on the limited liability of the members up to the amount of their capital contribution. For the principle which the Code de Commerce established as the first code of law has been adopted over time by the legislation of other countries.' (In the original German: 'So müssen auch wir einen bestimmten Begriff der Aktiengesellschaft als festen hinnehmen, […]. Dieser Begriff kann uns nur der französische des Code de commerce sein, dessen Schwerpunkt in der beschränkten Haftung der Mitglieder auf den Betrag ihrer Vermögenseinlage liegt. Denn das Prinzip, welches der Code de commerce als erstes Gesetzbuch aufstellte, ist im Laufe der Zeit von den Gesetzgebungen der anderen Länder übernommen worden.') See III.1. below on the Code de Commerce.

[17] See once again Fleischer (n 13) 5, 9 et seq.

[18] See, for example, Bainbridge and Henderson (n 2) 5 et seq: 'The first implication of corporate separateness is that corporations have a legally recognized personhood separate and distinct from its shareholders and other shareholders.'; cf also Thomale (n 3) 686 on the basis of a (merely) 'technical' understanding of entity separateness: 'As a result, all that remains of entity separateness is the technical bundling effect that emanates from the legal subjectivity of the corporation as such.' (in the original German: 'Im Ergebnis bleibt somit vom Trennungsprinzip lediglich die technische Bündelungswirkung übrig, die von der Rechtssubjektivität der Kapitalgesellschaft als solcher ausgeht.').

ferring to *Thomale*'s definition of entity separateness,[19] it can be put more precisely that legal personhood in the corporation is widely regarded as a defining component of entity separateness. If the former is to be sharply distinguished from the latter, entity separateness has to be reduced to the distinction between the company's and the shareholders' assets. Vesting the company with legal capacity is then to be regarded merely as a technical means of implementing this separation of assets. Another means of separating these assets would be joint ownership of the association's assets (*Gesamthand*).[20] For present purposes, however, it is only of importance that, while the corporation's legal personality may technically serve as a conceptual basis for limited shareholder liability, it cannot materially legitimise limited liability.[21] The example, already referred to, of partnerships that possess legal capacity but that come with unlimited liability for the partners, is illustrative.[22]

II. Historical References: From Ancient Times to the Late Eighteenth Century

A significant political (as well as academic) debate on limited liability in Europe did not develop until the nineteenth century, when legislative activity began to unfold in the field of company and partnership law.[23] Since the late nineteenth century, this debate in Western jurisdictions has evolved before the backdrop of a widely shared (at least in its key features) historical narrative about the origins of limited liability. At least until the late eighteenth and early nineteenth centuries, history speaks of a 'common European narrative' to which the American corporate law literature also refers.[24] The common roots of limited liability from ancient times through the early modern period point with striking regularity to the protection of financiers of (highly) risky business ventures who stood to share in the project's profits.[25]

---

[19] Thomale (n 3) 685 (in the original German: '[Das Trennungsprinzip bezeichnet] die Nichtidentität und Nichtkongruenz […], die zwischen den Gesellschaftern einerseits und ihrer Gesellschaft als selbständiges Rechtssubjekt [sic!] andererseits bestehen').

[20] One need only refer to the recent article by Holger Fleischer: 'Idiosynkrasien im deutschen Personengesellschaftsrecht: Allmähliche Erosion oder erfolgreiche Exportartikel?' [2020] NZG 601, 602 et seq, 609 et seq (in German).

[21] For a historical perspective on the relationship between universitas and limitation of liability, see Meyer (n 14) 45 et passim. See below under c) on *universitas*.

[22] See above under I.2.a) after n 18. In this context, the debate as to whether the distinction between associations of persons with legal capacity and legal entities in German company law continues to make sense. For a more recent source, see Stefan Klingbeil, 'Der Begriff der Rechtsperson' (2017) 217 AcP 848 et seq (in German).

[23] For more details, see III.

[24] See eg Bainbridge and Henderson (n 2) 19 et seq.

[25] See immediately below 2.a).

1. Ancient References to Limited Liability

When searching for the ancient antecedents of limited shareholder liability, the legal literature typically focusses on (a) the *societas publicanorum* and (b) the *peculium*, two well-known institutions of Roman law.[26] However, particularly in Germany, (c) the *universitas* has also been taken into consideration repeatedly.

a) The societas publicanorum

The *societas publicanorum* was a form of association that performed public tasks delegated to it by the state. Some consider this form to have reached its zenith in the first century BC[27], while others assume it to have been during the early centuries of the Imperial Period[28]. The *societates publicanorum* undertook tasks on behalf of the state and consequently received assignments exclusively from the state.[29] Such assignments were commissioned by auction. Extensive assignments, such as the 'tax lease' of an entire province, required a correspondingly high level of capital and collateral, often beyond the means of any individual.[30] For this reason, the bidder (*manceps*) usually teamed up with other *socii* to form a *societas*. In addition to these 'main participants' who were also entrusted with management tasks, there was a group of 'sub-participants' called *adfines* who participated in the company only by providing capital.[31] According to a widely held view, the *socii* assumed unlimited personal liability[32] while the liability of the *adfines* was limited to the amount of their capital contribution.[33] *Karl Lehmann* therefore

---

[26] See, for example, Henry Hansmann, Reinier Kraakman and Richard Squire, 'Law and the Rise of the Firm' (2006) 119 Harv LRev 1335, 1356–1364 (also addressing, in connection with entity shielding (see n 9 above), the ordering of assets in the *familia*; with a focus on the *societas publicanorum* together with its Greek predecessors Lehmann (n 16) 12; also David Johnston, 'Limiting Liability: Roman Law and the Civil Law Tradition' (1995) 70 Chi-Kent LRev 1515, 1521–1524 on the *peculium* and the *actio de peculio*; Reinhard Zimmermann, *The Law of Obligations* (OUP 1996) 51 et seq; for details on the *societas publicanorum* and the *peculium*, see Andreas M Fleckner, *Antike Kapitalvereinigungen* (Böhlau 2010) 145 et seq, 217 et passim (in German) (analysing the simple *societas*). Bainbridge and Henderson (n 2) 21 et seq address, in addition to the general *societas*, mainly the *peculium*, but also the *nauticum fenus* (maritime loan).

[27] Fleckner (n 26) 327.

[28] Lehmann (n 16) 18.

[29] See Fleckner (n 26) 153 et seq, with further references, in particular against dissenting voices on p 167 with fn 119; briefly also Hansmann, Kraakman and Spire (n 26) 1361: 'One answer may lie in the fact that the societates publicanorum evidently provided services only to the state and not to private parties.'

[30] Fleckner (n 26) 188.

[31] See, for example, Lehmann (n 16) 12 et seq; Fleckner (n 26) 202 et seq.

[32] For details, see Fleckner (n 26) 325 et seq (assuming liability by virtue of participation only for tortious conduct, while liability for other causes would require more in the person of the respective *socius*).

[33] See, for example, Lehmann (n 16) 16 et seq (in German); also Hansmann, Kraakman and Spire (n 26) 1361 (speaking in this regard of 'general partners' and 'limited partners'). More

saw similarities to the liability of limited partners of later times.[34] *Hansmann*, *Kraakman*, and *Spire* also speak of 'limited partners' in connection with the *adfines*, and at the same time they establish a connection between influence and liability: 'Other investors could act either as general partners, who exercised control and were fully liable on firm debts, or as limited partners who lacked control but enjoyed limited liability.'[35]

b) The peculium

The *peculium* furthermore has been discussed intensively as featuring an ancient form of limited legal liability.[36] Comparative analysis of the *peculium* and modern corporations, already found in the literature of the nineteenth century,[37] is also a regular feature of recent treatises on the subject of limited liability.[38] To establish a *peculium*, the founder (head of household or *pater familias*) transferred certain assets to his subjects (his sons or slaves) for the purpose of running a business.[39] This could also be done by several founders, who for this purpose entrusted their property to a common slave (*servus communis*), thereby typically forming a *societas*.[40] While ownership of the transferred assets remained with the founder(s), the *peculium* led to a separation of those assets vis-à-vis their remaining assets. This asset separation also came with a liability shield for the founders, who were liable for debts incurred with respect to the business (run by the slave) only up to the value of the items contained in the *peculium*.[41] Thus, we see a decoupling of entrepreneurial opportunities on one hand and liability on the other. *Andreas Fleckner* describes this decoupling as follows:

---

recently, however, Fleckner (n 26) 333: 'The liability of the sub-participants (adfines, owners of partes, etc.) […] ultimately remains uncertain. There are a number of approaches to establishing a purely financial participation in which only the loss of the contribution is to be feared in the external and internal relationship. However, none of these alternatives can be verified with more certainty.' (In the original German: 'Die Haftung der Unterbeteiligten (adfines, Inhaber von partes, etc.) […] bleibt letztlich ungewiß. Es gibt einige Ansätze, eine rein finanzielle Beteiligung zu begründen, bei der im Außen- wie im Innenverhältnis lediglich der Verlust der Einlage droht. Es läßt sich jedoch keine dieser Möglichkeiten genauer verifzieren.')

[34] Lehmann (n 16) 17; cf also Meyer (n 14) 30.

[35] Hansmann, Kraakman and Spire (n 26) 1361.

[36] See, for example, Fleckner (n 26) 217 et seq and more often; see also Bainbridge and Henderson (n 2) 22; Pistor (n 7) 54.

[37] Fleckner (n 26) 227: 'The reason why the Romanists in the nineteenth century[…] used the peculium to explain and legitimise trading companies lies in the peculium's asset structure.' (In the original German: 'Der Grund, warum sich die Romanisten im neunzehnten Jahrhundert […] des peculium bedienten, um die Handelsgesellschaften zu erklären und zu legitimieren, liegt in der Vermögensverfassung des peculium.') With regard to the joint stock company, however, focusing solely on the *societas publicanorum*, Lehmann (n 16) 12 et seq.

[38] See the following contemporary sources.

[39] Fleckner (n 26) 227; see also Hansmann, Kraakman and Spire (n 26) 1358.

[40] Fleckner (n 26) 335.

[41] Fleckner (n 26) 227.

'If someone wants to run a business, but is afraid of the associated risk, he can entrust the objects to a person subject to his authority and thus limit the risk of loss to the value of the *peculium*, but still take advantage of the economic opportunities. In this way, a commercial enterprise can be organised with a limited risk of liability.'[42]

This limitation of liability seems to be the flip side of the founder's lack of control over the business conducted with the *peculium*.[43] *Bainbridge* and *Henderson* therefore conclude that the 'limitations in liability arose not from the identity or status of the parties, but rather from an instrumental view about the linkage between liability and control'.[44]

c) The universitas

In Ancient Rome, the *universitas* was a corporative structure that pursued public or religious purposes. According to a famous dictum of *Ulpian*, the obligations of the *universitas* were to be distinguished from those of its members.[45] Admittedly, the extent of legal independence of the *universitas* and – particularly relevant here – whether it exempted its members from liability – remains controversial to this day.[46] The *universitas* is in any case regarded as the 'main root of the concept of the legal person'.[47] German jurisprudence has repeatedly attempted to establish an explanatory link between an association's nature as a 'legal person' and the limited liability of its members.[48] However, these attempts may be regarded as a failure today. The claim of a genetic, conceptual or even a logical link between the two concepts has been refuted.[49]

2. Instrumental Explanations of Medieval and Early Modern Forms of Limited Liability

In the economy of the Middle Ages and the early modern period, forms of limited liability were found primarily where high-risk ventures required a high level of capital to be undertaken at all.[50] The prime example and main practical appli-

---

[42] Fleckner (n 26) 228 (in the original German: 'Möchte jemand ein Gewerbe betreiben, scheut allerdings das damit verbundene Risiko, kann er die Gegenstände einem Gewaltunterworfenen anvertrauen und so die Verlustgefahr grundsätzlich auf den Wert des peculium begrenzen, aber wirtschaftlich alle Chancen wahrnehmen. Auf diese Weise lässt sich eine wirtschaftliche Unternehmen mit beschränkter Haftungsgefahr organisieren.').

[43] Fleckner (n 26) 218.

[44] Bainbridge and Henderson (n 2) 23.

[45] D. 3,4,7,1: *Si quid universitati debetur, singulis non debetur, nec quod debet universitatis singuli debent.*

[46] One need only refer to Meyer (n 14) 23 et seq, with further references.

[47] Meyer (n 14) 45 (in the original German: 'Hauptwurzel des Begriffs der juristischen Person').

[48] See also the following text.

[49] See Meyer (n 14) 45, 207 et passim for details and emphasis.

[50] Cf, with regard to the functional predecessors of the stock corporation, Lehmann (n 16) 24: 'speculative enterprise on the one hand' (in the original German: 'spekulative Unterneh-

cation of the principle is in maritime trade.[51] The Italian *commenda*, which was designed for this purpose, is regarded as the forerunner of (a) today's limited partnerships;[52] the trade companies of the seventeenth and eighteenth centuries are regarded as the archetypes of (b) today's joint stock companies.[53] These trade companies were the subject of later criticism by *Adam Smith*, the repercussions of which continue to influence the debate on limited liability to this day.[54]

a) Medieval Italy: commenda, colonna, accomandita

After the fall of Rome, centres of long-distance trade increasingly concentrated around the Mediterranean rim, most notably in the Italian port cities, followed later on by important urban trading centres in the Italian inland area.[55] In order to raise funds for risky long-distance trade, financiers had to be able to limit their liability. For this purpose, the *commenda* was developed in the early Middle Ages[56] and at that time served as the main vehicle for capital investment in those centres.[57] However, the *commenda* was a purely contractual arrangement[58] that we would classify merely as an 'internal partnership' (*Innengesellschaft*).[59] In order

---

mung einerseits') and 'pooling of large amounts of capital through contributions by many on the other' (in the original German: 'Zusammenfassung grösserer Kapitalien durch Zuschüsse Vieler andererseits').

[51] On the Italian banking companies of the late Middle Ages and the early modern period, in particular the Genoese St. George's Bank, one need only refer to Lehmann (n 16) 42 et seq (in German) (describing it as the 'first secure joint stock company').

[52] See, for example, Holger Fleischer, '§ 1: Personengesellschaften im Rechtsvergleich: Vergangenheit – Gegenwart – Zukunft' in Holger Fleischer (ed), *Personengesellschaften im Rechtsvergleich* (CH Beck 2021) para 91 et seq (in German) with references to dissenting opinions in para 107; see also Hansmann, Kraakman and Spire (n 26) 1372–1374, which deal with the *commenda* under the heading 'Limited Partnerships'. On the precursors of *commenda*, see once again Fleischer, ibid, para 101 (in German), with further references.

[53] I would recommend the description in Meyer (n 14) 200 et seq (in German), within the chapter 'Haftungsbeschränkung im Recht der Kapitalgesellschaften' (Limited liability in the law of corporations).

[54] Thomale (n 3) 687 (in German), for example, also refers to Adam Smith. See below under IV.3.a).

[55] See, for example, the brief remarks in Hansmann, Kraakman and Spire (n 26) 1364.

[56] As the successor to the Roman *societas*, the *compagnia* was unsuitable for these purposes as it did not limit the liability risk. After all, in the event of a partner's insolvency, creditors had to first get hold of the company's assets in order to satisfy their claims arising from transactions with the *compagnia* before they could get at the partners' personal assets. See Hansmann, Kraakman and Spire (n 26) 1367, with further references from the Italian literature. On the *compagnia* in general, see the instructive overview in Fleischer (n 52) para 130 et seq.

[57] Thus Fleischer (n 52) para 98 with reference to a quotation from Silberschmidt.

[58] See also Lehmann (n 16) 27; also Fleischer (n 52) para 105: 'The *commenda* exhausted itself in a *bilateral contract*' (emphasis in original) (in the original German: 'Die commenda erschöpfte sich in einem *zweiseitigen Vertrag*').

[59] Fleischer (n 52) para 100, with further references; see also Lehmann (n 16) 27 (referring to the *commendator* as a 'silent partner').

to set up a *commenda*, a *tractator* (also known as *socius procertans*), who would organise the voyage and also invest, contracted with a *commendator* (also known as *socius stans*), who would finance (a large part of) the voyage as a passive investor. The *tractator* acted as an external agent and had no legal power to bind the *commendator*. If the *tractator* collected capital from several *commendatores*, the latter were usually not legally bound to each other, but rather each had an independent contractual relationship with the *tractator*.[60] The consequence for liability was that while the *tractator* assumed unlimited liability for debts associated with the business, the *commendatores* were liable only up to the amount of their contributions.[61] The *commenda* was 'a creature of commercial practice, not of legal theory'.[62] This is also true of its liability regime, or rather, of the limitation of the passive investor's liability. Hansmann, Kraakman and Spire describe the functional design of the *commenda* driven by the interests involved as follows:

> '[T]he commenda reflected the tradeoffs among control, incentives, and liability typical of limited partnerships in general. The reason that this tradeoff of limited liability for lack of control first appears in seagoing ventures is presumably that the passive partner's renunciation of control was made particularly credible by the fact that the firm's assets were at sea or in foreign ports for the life of the venture.'[63]

The merely contractual *commenda* evolved over time into true forms of association. These included the *colonna*, which was a combination of the *commenda* and the *societas navalis*.[64] The next major step towards modern limited partnerships was the *accomandita*, which was codified in a statute of the Republic of Florence dated November 31, 1408.[65] According to this statute, registering the *accomandita* was a prerequisite for its investors to enjoy limited liability.[66]

b) The trade companies of the seventeenth and eighteenth centuries and Adam Smith's critique

The trade companies of the seventeenth and eighteenth centuries have generally been regarded as an important intermediate step on the way, not so much to limited partnerships, but rather to the genesis of the modern stock corporation with

---

[60] See Lehmann (n 16) 27 with reference to Goldschmidt; for more recent literature, see, for example, Fleischer (n 52) para 106: '[…] the *tractator* was faced with a large number of mostly isolated depositors' (in the original German: '[…] stand der tractator einer Vielzahl meist isolierter Geldeinleger gegenüber').

[61] Cf Lehmann (n 16) 27.

[62] Thus Fleischer (n 52) para 95, with further references (in the original German: 'ein Geschöpf der kaufmännischen Praxis, nicht der juristischen Theorie').

[63] Hansmann, Kraakman and Spire (n 26) 1372–1373.

[64] See, for example, Lehmann (n 16) 28 et seq; more briefly Meyer (n 14) 53 et seq.

[65] See, for example, Fleischer (n 52) para 107; Meyer (n 14) 58 et seq.

[66] Fleischer (n 52) para 107; Meyer (n 14) 58 et seq.

its limited shareholder liability.[67] From a legal-historical (or genetic) point of view, depicting the development and features of these trade companies requires distinguishing between England and the Continent. The trading companies of France, Portugal, Denmark, Sweden, and the Margraviate of Brandenburg can be traced back to Dutch models, the first of which was the Dutch East India Company of 1602.[68] In these companies, limited liability of the simple members was a regular (albeit not mandatory) feature.[69] Admittedly, limited liability seems to have applied only to external liabilities towards the company's creditors. Internally, however, claims were made (at least in individual cases) against simple members for additional payments into the company's asset pool.[70] Some have attributed this limited external liability to the old *commenda* rules[71].[72] Others, however, see it at least in part as a consequence of the corporate structure of the company.[73] Finally, the shipping company (Dutch: *rhederei*) is said to have had a decisive influence on the organisation of Dutch trading companies and thus also on liability, which was typically limited, including waiver rights in the event of claims for additional payments.[74] To make this case, *Karl Lehmann* refers to *Hugo Grotius*, who, in his *Inleydinge Tot de Hollandsche Rechts-Geleertheyt*, on the question of liability, simply states that

'According to Roman law, many co-owners of a ship, or others engaged in joint merchant trading, suffered from being held liable by their directors with the entirety of their assets: but this is not our law because that would be detrimental to trade. According to Dutch law the merchants are only bound with their share in the business.'[75]

---

[67] Fundamental to this assessment is Lehmann (n 16) 51 et seq; cf also Achilles Renaud, *Das Recht der Actiengesellschaften* (2nd edn, 1875) § 2 (p 21 et seq) (in German); merely descriptive Meyer (n 14) 199.

[68] Lehmann (n 16) 53; cf also Meyer (n 14) 207, 212.

[69] Lehmann (n 16) 54.

[70] See Meyer (n 14) 207; also Lehmann (n 16) 58: 'However, the internal obligation of additional payments also remained in principle for shareholders of a corporation. Its elimination required explicit stipulation in the charter.' (In the original German: 'Wohl aber blieb die interne Zuschusspflicht im Prinzip auch bei der Korporation bestehen. Ihre Beseitigung bedurfte besonderer Festsetzung.')

[71] See a) above.

[72] With emphasis Meyer (n 14) 207 et seq; cf also Lehmann (n 16) 59.

[73] Lehmann (n 16) 58; cf also, Meyer (n 14) 207: The liability regime cannot be explained by references to the *universitas*.

[74] Cf Lehmann (n 16) 56: 'Above all, however, it should be borne in mind that among the Frisian seafaring people, the *Rhederei* was the authoritative model for commercial enterprises, especially with regard to the question of liability.' (In the original German: 'Vor allem aber ist im Auge zu behalten, dass bei dem seetreibenden friesischen Volke die Rhederei gerade mit Bezug auf die Haftungsfrage das maassgebende Vorbild für kaufmännische Unternehmungen gewesen ist.')

[75] Hugo de Groot, *Inleydinge Tot de Hollandsche Rechts-Geleertheyt* (1727) III § 31 (p 260) (in the original Dutch: 'Na de Roomsche rechten plagen veel mede-reeders van een schip, ofte andere t'zamen koop-handel dryvende, elk uyt de daed van hare bewind-hebbers in't geheel

The great humanist *Grotius* can apparently think of no better justification for limited liability than that unlimited liability 'would be detrimental to trade'. All the same, the purely functional (and consequentialist) reasoning in a source like *Grotius* is something to ponder when one is confronted with arguments for or against limited liability based on considerations of natural law.

The octrois of the French trade companies contained provisions very similar to those of the Dutch companies. In the statutes of the Compagnie des Antilles of 1635 or the Compagnie pour le voyage de la Chine of 1660, the internal liability of the members is expressly provided for by a combination of the obligation to make additional payments and the right of abandonment.[76] While the latter also creates a quasi-restriction on internal liability, the octroi of the Compagnie des Indes Orientales of 1664 goes a step further. Its Article 2 (also) rules out any obligation to make additional payments.[77] *Justus Meyer* sees the underlying reason for such a liability regime in the mercantilist economic strategy of the French state. More specifically, sufficient incentives were needed to stimulate the sluggish flow of private capital into state-dominated enterprises.[78]

For English trade companies, on the other hand, it is stated that in the course of the seventeenth century, 'not even a legal rule limiting the external liability [!] of the members of the company had developed'[79]. There is in any case no hard evidence for such a rule to have been established. The question of liability – so the assumption – simply was of no import at that time.[80] Theoretical musings on the question of liability can be found in *Thomas Hobbes*' famous 1651 work *Leviathan*. However, there is no mention of limited liability; instead, *Hobbes* advocates for unlimited contractual liability of the members, proportional liability for tax debts, and tort liability for those involved in the tort.[81] One hundred twenty-five years later, *Adam Smith* described the Royal African Company (1672),

aengesproken te werden: maer by ons is zulks niet aengenomen, als den koop-handel zynde schadelyk. Over zulks werden de koop-luyden alleen verbonden elk voor haer aendeel in de koop-handel').

[76] See Lehmann (n 16) 57; Meyer (n 14) 209.

[77] See Du Fresne de Francheville, *Histoire Generale et Particulière des Finances, ou l'on voit l'origine, l'etablissement, la perception & la Régie de toutes les Impositions: dressée sur les pièces authentiques* (1738) 28; Meyer (n 14) 209.

[78] See Meyer (n 14) 209 et seq, see also ibid 211et seq on the companies in the Margraviate of Brandenburg. His conclusion: 'A uniform liability constitution of the companies did not develop in Germany at that time.' (In the original German: 'Eine einheitliche Haftungsverfassung der Kompagnien hat sich nach alledem in Deutschland seinerzeit nicht entwickelt.')

[79] Meyer (n 14) 202 (in the original German: 'Es ist allerdings nicht feststellbar, daß sich im Zuge dieser Entwicklung eine Rechtsregel über die Beschränkung der Außenhaftung der Kompagnie-Mitglieder herausgebildet hätte').

[80] Meyer (n 14) 203, 205; likewise Ron Harris, 'A New Understanding of the History of Limited Liability: An Invitation for Theoretical Reframing' (2020) 16 J Inst Econ 643, 650: 'non-issue'.

[81] See Thomas Hobbes, *Leviathan* (1651) ch XXII, 120 (rev Student Edn 1996/2022). See also Meyer (n 14) 202 et seq.

the Hudson's Bay Company (1670), and the South Sea Company (1711) all as joint stock companies characterised not only by the free transferability of shares but also by shareholder liability limited to the value of the respective share.[82] *Smith* criticised the latter in no uncertain terms:

'This total exemption [of the proprietors of a joint stock corporation] from trouble and from risk, beyond a limited sum, encourages many people to become adventurers in joint stock companies, who would, upon no account, hazard their fortunes in any private copartnery. Such companies, therefore, commonly draw to themselves much greater stocks than any private copartnery can boast of. [...] The directors of such companies, however, being the managers rather of other people's money than their own, it cannot well be expected, that they should watch over it with the same anxious vigilance with which the partners in a private copartnery frequently watch over their own. [...] Negligence and profusion, therefore, must always prevail, more or less, in the management of the affairs of such a company.'[83]

Adam Smith thus links limited liability to the separation of ownership and control and points to the associated incentive problems, which we know today as 'agency costs'. It is hard to overestimate the impact of this argument, as various forms of it are invoked with great reliability whenever criticism is levelled at limited liability, the corporation, or capitalism in general. From a German perspective, Smith's line of thought can be found, for example, in *Walter Eucken*'s critique of limited shareholder liability.[84]

Finally, analysing the large trading companies of the seventeenth and eighteenth centuries with a view to justifying and explaining limited shareholder liability has brought yet another aspect into the debate: while the proponents of such limited liability argue that it was necessary in order for shares to be traded on the stock exchange, others point out that shares of English and Dutch companies were traded on the London and Amsterdam exchanges in the seventeenth century 'without the need for special rules on the limitation of liability.'[85]

3. *Preliminary Findings*

The development from ancient times until the end of the eighteenth century, as sketched out above, shows that limitations on the liability of shareholders and other investors were established primarily where such capital providers were unable to control the risk of the financed enterprise themselves due to a lack of sufficient means of control. This is particularly evident in the practically important

[82] Adam Smith, *The Wealth of Nations* (1776) ch I part III, 799 (Modern Library Edn 1994).

[83] Smith (n 82) 800.

[84] See Walter Eucken, *Grundsätze der Wirtschaftspolitik* (1952, 7th edn, utb 2004) 279 et seq (in German); see IV.1.a) below.

[85] Meyer (n 14) 205 (England) and 208 (Netherlands), with further references (in the original German: 'Diese Anteile wurden – auch an der Börse – gehandelt, ohne daß es dazu besonderer Haftungsbeschränkungsregeln bedurft hätte'); also Harris (n 80) 647, with further references; see also Walter Samuel, *Die Effektenspekulation im 17. und 18. Jahrhundert* (Spaeth & Linde 1924) 24 et seq and 76 et seq (in German). See once again under IV.3.b).

example of maritime trade, in which the company's assets, in the form of ships and cargo, were not only far away at sea but also exposed to considerable risks.[86] Willingness to invest thus hinged on the limitation of liability. The broad limitation of liability in the octroi of the Compagnie des Indes Orientales of 1664 was apparently also the necessary 'price' by which potential investors could be sufficiently induced to invest.[87] With respect to English trading companies, *Adam Smith* was one of the first to point out the incentive problems limited liability could cause (keywords: adventurism and agency problems due to the separation of ownership and control).[88] At the same time, the history of the trading companies of the seventeenth and eighteenth centuries unfolds as a 'natural experiment' that weakens the assumption that the public marketability of company shares could not be achieved without limited shareholder liability.[89] It is also noteworthy that the institution's roots in Roman law and considerations of formal-dogmatic continuity in general have played no significant role in the emergence of new forms of limited liability in corporate law. This is particularly true for the Roman *universitas* and the question of the corporate character of a business organisation.[90]

III. The Debates around the Codification of Limited Liability in the Nineteenth Century

The French Code de Commerce of 1807 marked a decisive step in the evolution of modern corporations.[91] It not only laid down rules for the *société commandite par actions* and the *société anonyme* (ie, the joint stock company), but it also contained one provision (art 33) that introduced limited liability for shareholders for the first time.[92] This code had a significant influence on other European jurisdictions such as Spain, Belgium, Italy, the German territories, and the Netherlands, which all adopted legislation on joint stock companies at various times during the nineteenth century.[93] Not even contemporary English law could escape the

---

[86] See above, in particular in 2.a) in n. 64.

[87] See n 80 above.

[88] See above under 2.b), in n 84.

[89] See above under 2.b), in n 85.

[90] On the relationship between the legal personality of the association and the limited liability of its members for the period up to 1800, see also Harris (n 80) 650: 'The implication of the legal personality attribute of the corporation was that the corporation formed asset partitioning. […] But without debt finance, without a procedure for dissolving insolvent corporations, without the legal ability to determine whether shareholders would bear liability in insolvency, owner shielding was a non-issue and limited liability in the modern sense could not yet exist.'

[91] See, for example, Lehmann (n 16) 3: 'most important stage in the development of stock corporation law' (in the original German: 'wichtigste Etappe in der Entwicklung des Aktienrechts'); more recently, see, for example, Meyer (n 14) 216 et seq.

[92] On this, one need only refer to Meyer (n 14) 217.

[93] See, for example, Bainbridge and Henderson (n 2) 26 et seq.

emanations of the Code de Commerce, and all the legislating was accompanied by a theoretical debate about the advantageous as well as the disadvantageous aspects of limited liability, discussions often more political than academic. The respective debates were mostly national; that is, each country mostly debated its own legislation. However, there is repeated reference to foreign developments. It therefore seems appropriate to speak of this 'limited liability revolution' as a transnational phenomenon[94] or a transnational joint debate, so to speak, with the various national debates contributing in different ways.

The following account is limited to debates which took place in (1) France, (2) England, and (3) Germany. For reasons of space, the contemporary US debate is omitted.[95] France's effort in the Code de Commerce of 1807 is worth considering because it was pioneering. The English made a particularly substantial (and at the time, innovative) contribution. The German debate tended to follow arguments put forward elsewhere and in some cases attempted to introduce formal and doctrinal considerations. However, what stands out is the GmbH, a project of the end of the century, which was highly innovative at the time. The debate accompanying the GmbH is thus outlined here as well.

1. The Code de Commerce of 1807: A Pioneering Achievement

a) The provisions of the Code de Commerce

The Code de Commerce provided for two types of limited liability companies. The law had already recognised the limited liability of limited partners or shareholders in both the *société en commandite simple* and its variant, the *société en commandite par actions*,[96] which the code now expressly codified.[97] Limited liability was tied to the prohibition of interference by limited partners or shareholders in the management or representation of the company (art 27 and 28)[98]

---

[94] From an economic and socio-historical perspective, see also Marie-Laure Djelic, 'When Limited Liability was (Still) an Issue: Mobilization and Politics of Signification in 19th-Century England' (2013) 34 (5–6) OS 595, 616: 'Our understanding of limited liability revolution would benefit from exploring the debates that took place elsewhere – and particularly in France, Prussia and the United States. In fact, the story of limited liability is in part a transnational story. Beyond a simple cross-country comparison, we need to identify the transnational mechanisms and challenges that connected national debates and developments.'

[95] See, however, the overview in Holger Fleischer, 'Die geschlossene Kapitalgesellschaft im Rechtsvergleich: Vorüberlegungen zu einer internationalen Entwicklungs- und Ideengeschichte' (2016) 45 ZGR 36, 50 (in German); on the US contributions to the debate in the twentieth century, see IV.2.

[96] See Meyer (n 14) 219 with reference to Henri Lévy-Bruhl, *Histoire juridique des sociétés de commerce en France aux XVIIe et XVIIIe siècles* (Domat-Montchrestien 1938) 45 et seq and 243 et seq.

[97] Meyer (n 14) 75 et seq, 224. Code de commerce 1807, art 26 reads: 'L'associé commanditaire n'est passible des pertes que jusqu'à concurrence des fonds qu'l a mis ou dû mettre dans la société'.

[98] See also Meyer (n 14) 76, 224.

and was available without government approval.[99] Article 33 of the Code de Commerce stipulated rules for the *société anonyme*[100] and provided limited shareholder liability: 'Les associés ne sont passibles que de la perte du montant de leur intérêt dans la société.'[101] However, it was the statutory provision as such that was new. Limitation of shareholder liability was in line with the common contractual practices at the time even though courts did not invariably recognise its legality.[102] The associated risks of limited liability to creditors and investors were addressed by art 36, which tied the founding of a *société anonyme* to permission from the state.[103]

b) The (lack of) debate

As impactful as the Code de Commerce of 1807 was in regard to the limited liability of limited partners and shareholders, no significant debate on the subject was seen in the run-up to codification. The inclusion of the *société anonyme* in the codification project was based on a proposal by a commission chaired (and heavily influenced) by the judge and politician *Gorneau*.[104] The legal literature of the late eighteenth century had largely ignored it,[105] and the authorities[106] consulted during the legislative process made only occasional references to the liability regime of the *société anonyme* without fundamentally questioning it. Instead, the debate focused on the issue of the state licensing requirement to set up a *société anoyme*.[107] Today, the lack of discussion about limiting shareholder liability is explained by the fact that the Code de Commerce, in regard to both the *société en commandite par actions* and the *société anonyme*, merely stipulated what was already common practice.[108] The reason for the codification was contradictory legislation enacted during the revolutionary years, which oscillated between strict prohibition and liberal laissez-faire, leaving legal uncertainty in its wake.[109]

---

[99] Meyer (n 14) 224.

[100] For a brief outline of the relevant regulations, see Lehmann (n 16) 68 et seq.

[101] Translated: Partners are only liable for the loss of the amount of their interest in the company.

[102] One need only refer to Lehmann (n 16) 67 (quoting from the treatise of the contemporary Vincens in fn 2); cf also Meyer (n 14) 220 et seq.

[103] Cf Meyer (n 14) 224: the limitation of liability thus remained 'under lock and key' (in the original German: 'unter Verschluss').

[104] See Meyer (n 14) 221 et seq, with further references.

[105] See the evidence in Lehmann (n 16) 66.

[106] See Observations des Tribuneaux de Cassation et d'Appel, des Tribuneaux et Conseils de commerce, etc. sur le Projet de Code du commerce, Tomes I et II, An XI (1802/1803).

[107] See the summary in Lehmann (n 16) 70; also Meyer (n 14) 222.

[108] Again, one need only refer to Lehmann (n 16) 67, 70; Meyer (n 14) 222.

[109] Lehmann (n 16) 67; similarly Meyer (n 14) 221.

c) The aftermath of codification

Due to restrictive licensing practices in the following decades, the Code de Commerce's rules on limited shareholder liability in the *société anonyme* were initially of little practical significance.[110] Businesses therefore resorted to the *société en commandite par actions*, often using a straw man as a general partner.[111] The economic boom of the 1830s led not only to new, vastly capitalised *sociétés en commandite par actions* but also to unbridled speculation ('fièvre des commanditistes').[112] The abuses led to an 1838 bill that sought to ban them altogether, but it failed. Another speculative boom in the mid-1850s was countered by the law of 17 July 1856 on the *société en commandite par actions*, which tightened the reins by introducing rules for raising capital and linking the transferability of shares to compliance with these rules.[113] The concessions system in France also came under increasing pressure under the influence of English legislation.[114] First, the law of 23 May 1863 introduced the unlicensed *société à responsabilité limitée*. Then, with the *loi des sociétés* of 24 July 1867, came a complete turnaround that allowed a *société anonyme* to be formed even without the prerequisite of a license.[115]

2. The English Debate: A Treasure Trove of (Early) Economic Arguments

While the French Code de Commerce of 1807 spurred the codification of limited liability stock corporations across Europe, the English legislator brought about a decisive breakthrough in freeing the joint stock company from the requirement of permitting by the state. Only when the 'shackle' of permitting was removed were joint stock corporations able to become a broadly impactful form for doing business.

a) Nineteenth-century english legislation on Joint Stock Companies

The situation in England in the first half of the nineteenth century did not favour unlicensed limited liability companies. The Bubble Act of 1720 attempted to enforce the traditional rule of regarding all associations formed without government permission as common-law partnerships with unlimited liability of the part-

---

110 For details, Meyer (n 14) 224 et seq; also Bainbridge and Henderson (n 2) 26 et seq.

111 Lehmann (n 16) 71.

112 Lehmann (n 16) 71 mentions the figure of 1000 SCpA with a capital of over one billion francs for 1838; following on from this, Meyer (n 14) 226 et seq.

113 These rules were later adopted in the law of 1867 and also served as a model for later German stock corporation legislation; see Meyer (n 14) 229.

114 See 2.a) below.

115 See Bainbridge and Henderson (n 2) 27: 'Not until France passed a general incorporation statute in 1867 did the modern idea of limited liability as a general rule for all corporate activity take root in France.'; in general, Lehmann (n 16) 71 et seq; Meyer (n 14) 229 et seq, with further references.

ners.[116] The broad repeal of the Bubble Act in 1825 provided some relief, but joint stock companies formed without government permission still qualified as partnerships.[117] Ultimately it took legislative action to overcome the courts' conservative and sometimes even hostile attitude towards joint stock companies that were founded without the permission of the state.[118] A key step was the Joint Stock Companies Regulation and Registration Act of 1844, which was heavily influenced by *William Ewart Gladstone*, then the president of the Board of Trade, who later became prime minister.[119] The Registration Act ended the system of government permitting and moved to a normative system of compulsory registration, but it did not change the principle of unlimited shareholder liability.[120] The 'formal breakthrough' was the Limited Liability Act of 1855,[121] which (except in certain industries) granted limited liability under certain conditions (at least 25 members holding shares of at least £10 and having paid up 20% of the capital contribution; company designation as 'limited'; dissolution and liquidation in the event of a loss of 75% of the capital).[122] However, the practical impact of the Limited Liability Act was modest.[123] This changed with the Joint Stock Company Act of 1856, which liberalised the incorporation process and eliminated capital requirements,[124] and with the Companies Act of 1862,[125] which reduced the minimum number of members to seven.[126] Subsequent crises, notably the 'Panic of 1866' triggered by the collapse of the London bank Overend, Gurney & Company, gave rise to criticism of this liberal legislation, but limited liability as a component of English company law was not seriously questioned.[127]

---

[116] Lehmann (n 16) 84; Bainbridge and Henderson (n 2) 29.

[117] Lehmann (n 16) 84.

[118] See, in particular on the role of the then Lord Chancellor Eldon, HA Shannon, 'The Coming of General Limited Liability' (1931) 41 The Economic Journal 267, 271 with fn 4; Meyer (n 14) 240, with further references.

[119] See the Gladstone report, 1844 P.P.R., vol VII, 119 et seq; and once again, Meyer (n 14) 240, with further references.

[120] 7 & 8 Victoria I c 110; see Lehmann (n 16) 84 et seq; Meyer (n 14) 241.

[121] 19 & 20 Victoria I c 133.

[122] See, for example, Meyer (n 14) 246; Lehmann (n 16) 84. However, for a different classification see, recently, Harris (n 80) 660: '[T]he Limited Liability Act 1855 in Britain was not a watershed in the history of this attribute.'

[123] Christine E Amsler, Robin L Bartlett and Craig J Bolton, 'Thoughts of Some British Economists on Early Limited Liability and Corporate Legislation Available to Purchase' (1981) 13 Hist Pol Econ 775, 787: 'was largely a dead letter owing to the defectiveness of the 1844 act.'

[124] 19 & 20 Victoria I c 47.

[125] 21 & 22 Victoria I c 91.

[126] On the Stock Company Act of 1856, see, for example, Amsler, Bartlett and Bolton (n 123) 788 (on the weaknesses of the registration regime); see also, generally, Meyer (n 14) 246.

[127] See Djelic (n 94) 616. For later criticism, see below under d).

b) Early economic arguments for and against Limited Liability

The early resistance to limited shareholder liability in England received strong argumentative support from *Adam Smith*.[128] In the previously quoted passage on joint stock companies, from his magnum opus The Wealth of Nations[129], he warns of the incentive problems arising from the separation of ownership and control ('negligence and profusion') and from the limited liability of investors ('adventurers').[130]

The Belleden Ker Report of 1837, commissioned by the UK Parliament, gave new impetus to the economic debate on limited liability. The commission's task was

'to inquire into the present state of the Law of Partnership [...] and to consider whether it would be expedient to introduce a law, authorising persons to become partners in trade with a limited responsibility, similar to the French Law of partnership *en commandite* [...].'[131]

With regard to limited liability, the opinions of *Thomas Tooke* and *Nassau William Senior* are of particular interest.[132] *Tooke* considered it a 'practical question' whether or not the law should allow for free access to partnerships *en commandite*. Ultimately, he was against such free access. If limited liability was an option for family firms, he argued, it could not in earnest be denied to joint stock companies. Such limited liability companies would subsequently replace companies with unlimited liability because the former would find it easier to raise capital. The reduced risk-sensitivity of investors in such limited liability entities would, in turn, necessitate costly regulation and divert capital away from business forms that could attract investors with lower exposure to liability even without such regulation.[133] Although *Tooke* conceded that limited liability could mobilise private savings for productive purposes, he did not consider it a necessary factor in ensuring that English business had an adequate supply of capital.[134] Therefore, his overall conclusion was that

---

[128] See also Amsler, Bartlett and Bolton (n 123) 780–781: 'The starting point of all subsequent assessments of joint-stock companies by the classicals is found in Book V of The Wealth of Nations. [...] An examination of the writings of British economists for the half-century following Smith discloses no serious attention to questions of either joint-stock-companies or limited liability arrangements. Any passing comments concerning these issues were entirely Smithian.'

[129] Smith (n 82) ch I, part III, 799–800. See above under 2.b) in fn 82.

[130] Also summarising, Amsler, Bartlett and Bolton (n 123) 780–781.

[131] Quoted from Jean du Plessis, 'Corporate Law and Corporate Governance Lessons from the Past: Ebbs and Flows, but far from "the End of History" – Part 1' (2009) 30 Company Lawyer 45, 50; also, summarising the Ker-Report, Amsler, Bartlett and Bolton (n 123) 781–784.

[132] For the following, see the summary in Amsler, Bartlett and Bolton (n 123) 781–784.

[133] See Amsler, Bartlett and Bolton (n 123) 781–783 (on the argumentation of Tooke, who also relied on Smith's line of reasoning).

[134] Again, see the reproduction in Amsler, Bartlett and Bolton (n 123) 783.

'the privilege would operate as a distinct inducement to individuals for the preference of a mode of business which in its tendency might be less advantageous to the general interests of the trade than that which it superseded. The privilege might operate in the way of a premium sufficient to induce a use of the inferior, instead of the better instrument, for carrying on the trade of the country.'[135]

Nassau William Senior, on the other hand, argued in favour of broad access to limited liability companies. He emphasised their positive effect on the supply of capital, in particular the mobilisation of small savings for productive purposes. This, he argued, was bound to be more significant than creating incentives to closely monitor the business through unlimited liability, and mobilising small investors could also strengthen competition by providing financing to new market entrants with high capital requirements.[136]

A nuanced, generally sympathetic analysis of limited liability can be found in *John Stuart Mill*'s Principles of Political Economy, published in 1848.[137] In clear contrast to *Smith*, *Mill* praises the advantages of joint stock companies, especially in mobilising large sums of capital.[138] *Mill* acknowledged the disadvantages *Smith* put forward in regard to the separation of management and ownership[139] but considered them to be exaggerated ('over-statements of a true principle').[140] *Mill* proposed that financial incentives would remedy the agency problem: 'There are modes of connecting more or less intimately the interest of the employés with the pecuniary success of the concern'. He thought attractive compensation schemes might help fill managerial positions with candidates whose skills were superior to those of the owners.[141] Otherwise, *Mill* advocated free competition among different kinds of business organizations:

'[W]henever competition is free its results will show whether individual or joint stock agency is best adapted to the particular case, since that which is most efficient and most economical will always in the end succeed in underselling the other.'

The third edition, published in 1852, added thoughts on creditor protection and limited liability:

'If a number of persons chose to associate for carrying on any operation of commerce or industry, agreeing among themselves and announcing to those with whom they deal that the members of the association do not undertake to be responsible beyond the amount of the subscribed capital; is there any reason that the law should raise objections to this proceeding, and should impose on them the unlimited responsibility which they disclaim? For whose sake? […]

---

[135] Quoted from Amsler, Bartlett and Bolton (n 123) 783.

[136] For a reproduction of Senior's argument, see, once again, Amsler, Bartlett and Bolton (n 123) 784.

[137] See also Amsler, Bartlett and Bolton (n 123) 784–785.

[138] John Stuart Mill, *Principles of Political Economy* (1st edn, 1848) book I ch IX § 2 (p 164–165).

[139] Mill (n 138) book I ch IX § 2 (p 165–168).

[140] Mill (n 138) book I ch IX § 2 (p 168–169).

[141] Mill (n 138) book I ch IX § 2 (p 168–169).

It must […] be for the sake of third parties; namely, those who may have transactions with the association, […]. But nobody is obliged to deal with the association: […]. The class of persons with whom such associations have dealings are in general perfectly capable of taking care of themselves, and there seems no reason that the law should be more careful of their interests than they will themselves be […].'[142]

Mill's work thus presages the contractarians' insights into limited shareholder liability.[143]

John Ramsey McCulloch, on the other hand, was an avowed opponent of limited liability. As a member of the Ricardian school inspired by *Smith*, he condemned limited liability both before and after the fundamental legal reforms of the 1850s and -60s.[144] However, even his later work ignores arguments in favour of limited liability; for example, in his *Considerations on Partnerships with Limited Liability*, from 1856, he states, echoing Smithian thinking,

'Most people engaged in business, as at present carried on, are impressed with the well-founded conviction that their interests will be best promoted by their preserving an unblemished reputation. And as they all act under the heaviest responsibility, the chances are ten to one that they will behave discreetly, fairly and honourably. But we can have no such guarantees for the conduct of partners in a society *en commandite*.'[145]

c) The political debate surrounding the 1855 and 1856 Acts

How did limited liability succeed politically against such strong opposition drawn upon arguments of the widely revered *Adam Smith*? In the words of the organisational and economic sociologist *Djelic*, the statutory limitation of liability in joint stock companies was ensured by a 'coalition of the unlikely', in which (economic) liberals and the labour and social movements of the Chartists and Christian Socialists[146] acted upon widespread sentiment that the existing legal situation hampered investment.[147]

---

[142] John Stuart Mill, *Principles of Political Economy*, ed by WJ Ashley (1936) book V ch IX § 6 (p 900).

[143] See below under IV.2.b).

[144] On McCulloch's early and late work, see the references in Amsler, Bartlett and Bolton (n 123) 786–788.

[145] John Ramsey McCulloch, *Considerations on Partnerships with Limited Liability* (1856) 16.

[146] Djelic (n 94) 614 et passim.

[147] See, for example, Djelic (n 94) 607 et seq; also Meyer (n 14) 243: 'The momentum for the Limited Liability Act was therefore not caused by a shortage of capital in industrial companies […]. Rather, the lack of profitable investment opportunities was lamented, and in some cases even individual investment-seeking circles are seen as the driving force behind the legislation.' (In the original German: 'Der Anstoß des Limited Liability Act war also nicht etwa eine Kapitalknappheit in den Industrieunternehmen […]. Vielmehr wurde das Fehlen rentabler Kapitalanlagemöglichkeiten beklagt, und teilweise werden sogar einzelne anlagesuchende Kreise als treibende Kraft der Gesetzgebung gesehen.')

On the political stage, the Chartists initially took the lead advocating for limited liability particularly in regard to the partnership *en commandite*.[148] In his motion for the appointment of a commission, of 17 February 1852, MP *Robert Aglionby Slaney* sought 'to suggest measures to remove the obstacles which impede the investments of the humbler classes.'[149] Others, such as *Cobden*, expressed slight doubts about the idea that the working class should assume a capitalist role. He nevertheless argued in favour of limited liability

> 'because he thought it would diffuse capital in this country. It would attract capital from the wealthy into the hands of the deserving and meritorious persons who could give profitable employment to that capital. […] The complaint of the present law was, that it […] prevented the marriage of skill and capital by means of limited liability'[150].

The Mercantile Laws Commission, established in 1853, circulated a 31-question questionnaire to more than 150 interested and well-informed persons to ascertain their attitudes toward the issue of liability.[151] It received 74 responses, mainly from merchants, chambers of commerce and lawyers, as well as six from academics.[152] In total, 43 respondents favoured limiting liability; 31 were against it. The majority of responses referred to the introduction of a partnership *en commandite*, but some also dealt with the issue of limited liability in joint stock companies.[153]

The commission was also divided, favouring limited liability by a margin of five to three. In its 1854 report, it confesses that it is

> 'much embarrassed by the great contrariety of opinion. […] Gentlemen of great experience and talent have arrived at conclusions diametrically opposite and in supporting these conclusions have displayed reasoning of the highest order.'[154]

The report's arguments for and against limited liability resembled those already presented by *Smith*, *Mill* and the contributors to the Belleden Ker report.[155] The objections can be summarised as follows:[156] (1) unlimited liability is based on individual responsibility as a natural principle of justice; those who share in the profits as owners are also obliged to bear the losses;[157] merely derivative of this imbalance in the relationship between risk and opportunity are the dangers of (2) cheating creditors, (3) excessive speculation, and (4) an unfair advantage over

---

[148] See Djelic (n 94) 605.

[149] HC Deb 7 August 1919, vol 119, col 668 (Hansard), where the debate is conducted under 'Working Classes – Law of Partnership'.

[150] HC Deb 7 August 1919, vol 119, cols 681–682 (Hansard). See also RA Bryer, 'The Mercantile Laws Commission of 1854 and the Political Economy of Limited Liability' (1997) 50 Econ Hist Rev, 37, 40–41.

[151] For more details, see Bryer (n 150) 42.

[152] See the table in Bryer (n 149) 43.

[153] Bryer (n 150) 43 with references.

[154] Report of the Commission on Mercantile Law 5, cited in Djelic (n 94) 609.

[155] See above under b).

[156] See in particular Bryer (n 150) 45–52; also Meyer (n 14) 245.

[157] According to commission member Lord Curriehill. See Bryer (n 150) 43.

companies with unlimited shareholder liability.[158] (5) Finally, it was argued that it would harm the reputation of British entrepreneurs to no longer be personally liable for the debts of their business.[159] Proponents of limited liability, on the other hand, pointed to (1) improved investment incentives from limiting the risk of passive investment[160] and (2) private autonomy on the part of partners/shareholders and creditors, who were not to be constrained by legal obstacles.[161] The fear of excessive speculation was countered by the argument that (3) risky investments with a positive expected value could also be socially desirable.[162] In his statement (4), Liberal MP *Robert Lowe* countered the objection of unfair competition with *Mill*'s[163] well-known argument:

> '[Unrestricted competition by allowing for limited liability] would break down one great obstacle to the competition of capital with capital. As a free-trader I can see nothing but good in increased competition, and if the result of it should be [...] to drive small traders and partnerships with unlimited liability out of the field, this could only be by cheapening production, from which the public would gain far more than individuals would lose.'[164]

That a majority on the commission voted against the introduction of limited liability did not however decrease the momentum in favour of such liability maintained by Liberal politicians, among whom the already-mentioned *Robert Lowe*, regarded as the most important supporter of limited liability, was later dubbed 'the father of modern company law'.[165] The political opportunity to enact a major reform of company law arose when the Liberal government of *Lord Palmerston* came to power in January 1855. Four bills were introduced in two stages, two of which (on joint stock companies) were successful, resulting in the Limited Liability Act 1855 and the Joint-Stock Companies Act of 1856. The other two bills, however, which dealt with partnerships (*en commandite*), failed.[166]

---

[158] For more on this see Bryer (n 150) 47–48.

[159] See Meyer (n 14) 245.

[160] JS Mill had already commented on this, linking it to a better credit rating for investors, and turning against Adam Smith in general: '[Unlimited liability – so the argument – had] the effect of preventing prudent and cautious persons who would be the best managers [...] from entering into [an association. ... In contrast], supposing a dozen individuals were to associate together, if they could show that they were not at the mercy of any dishonest member of the association, they could offer better security for advances of capital than they can now.' [quoted from Djelic (n 94) 606.].

[161] See once again Bryer (n 150) 48–49, with reference to statements by Bramwell and Lowe. Meyer (n 14) 245, describes the latter idea as 'laissez-faire', which was due to the 'liberalist attitude' of the time (in the original German: 'liberalistischen Grundhaltung'). In fact, there are echoes of Mill here (see n 140).

[162] Bryer (n 150) 49–50 (connecting it to the modern portfolio approach).

[163] See above at n 141.

[164] Thus Lowe in the Commission Report on p 84, cited in Bryer (n 150) 51.

[165] John Micklethwait and Adrian Woolridge, The Company: A Short History of a Revolutionary Idea (Modern Library 2003).

[166] For a summary, see Djelic (n 94) 612–613.

d) Reaction to the legal reforms of 1855/56 and beyond

The enactments of 1855/56 and subsequent legislation of course did not settle the controversy over limited liability. In response to the act of 1856, the *Law Times*, a contemporary conservative weekly for lawyers, complained that

'The new joint stock companies Act not merely introduces a novelty into morals and commerce – it is as strange in form as it is monstrous in conception […]. Every protection, which the former law had provided against fraud, folly and abuse, has been swept away.'[167]

Undeterred, many new joint stock companies had been formed by the mid-1860s,[168] a development slowed only by the aforementioned contemporary crisis triggered by the collapse of Overend, Gurney & Company (the 'Panic of 1866').[169]

3. The German Debate Between Legal Doctrine, Economic Functionality, and Political Interests

The reforms underway in France and England and the debates that accompanied them were not lost on the German territories.[170] These foreign influences encountered home-grown debates on interterritorial legal unification (including in commercial law) and, by the end of the nineteenth century, certain elements of company law for the new Reich. Reform movements were abundant in nineteenth-century Germany, but the following remarks are limited to the particularly important debates on or elements of (a) the Prussian Stock Corporation Act of 1843, (b) the 1884 amendments to the General German Commercial Act, and, finally, (c) the introduction of the GmbH at the end of the nineteenth century.

a) The Prussian Stock Corporation Act of 1843

The General Law for the Prussian States (Allgemeines Landrecht für die Preußischen Staaten, the 'ALR') said little about limited liability.[171] However, in most territories of the Rhineland (which belonged to Prussia as a result of the Congress

---

[167] Law Times (1856) 205, cited in Djelic (n 94) 615.

[168] See the figures in Meyer (n 14) 246.

[169] See once again Djelic (n 94) 616 (this already came up at the end of III.2.a).

[170] Going further, Werner Schubert, 'Die Abschaffung des Konzessionssystems durch die Aktienrechtsnovelle von 1870' (1981) 10 ZGR 285, 289 (in German), according to which 'the early German stock corporation legislation was entirely under the spell of foreign models' (in the original German: '[…] die frühe deutsche Aktiengesetzgebung [stand] ganz im Banne der ausländischen Vorbilder […]'); also Baums (n 14) 23 et seq, 36; on the influence of the Code de Commerce also Meyer (n 14) 81 et seq, with further references.

[171] See the concise overview in Baums (n 14) 15 et seq; Meyer (n 14) 249 et seq (pointing out in particular that under the ALR, '[t]he limitation of liability […] was not derived from the internal corporate structure of the company, but was regarded as an exception to general law' (in the original German: 'Die Haftungsbeschränkung wurde danach nicht aus der inneren körperschaftlichen Struktur der Gesellschaft abgeleitet, sondern als Ausnahme vom allgemeinen Recht angesehen […]').

of Vienna), the Code de Commerce, including its provisions on the *société en commandite (par actions)* and the *société anonyme*, was applicable law.[172] The application of French law in parts of Prussia intensified competition with Prussian law and spurred legal modernisations and unification aimed at abolishing the Code de Commerce in the Prussian territories.[173] The reform efforts finally resulted in the Prussian Stock Corporation Act of 9 November 1843.[174] The road to this act was, however, long and winding.[175]

(1) The opinion of the elders of the Berlin Merchants of 1829

Of early importance in regard to the issue of limited shareholder liability was an 1829 report by the elders of the Berlin Merchants' Association that argued in favour of limited liability.[176] According to the report,

> 'the basic idea and, therefore, the essence of the joint stock company lies in the pooling of several assets brought about by contract, without, as in other associations, the members also combining their intellectual activity, their work and their efforts to achieve the common ultimate purpose, and without being personally liable for the transactions undertaken or liable beyond the capital invested.'[177]

Limited liability is emphasised as an 'essential condition of [the stock corporation's] existence', 'without which it would almost never come into being'.[178] The authors saw a doctrinal basis for this in the commercial partnership, with the peculiarity that 'all the members are in fact silent partners; no one is liable to a greater or lesser extent than the amount of his share'.[179] They conceded that the German joint stock corporation therefore lacked the disciplinary effect of personal liability on the individual members, which could endanger the public. However,

> 'the safety of the public could certainly be ensured by making the disclosure of the articles of association mandatory for every stock corporation. The endowment with the rights of a moral

[172] See, for example, Baums (n 14) 26.

[173] Baums (n 14) 26.

[174] Gesetz-Sammlung für die Königlichen Preußischen Staaten, 1843, no 31 (in German; reprinted in Baums (n 14) 211 et seq.

[175] For details, see Baums (n 14) 29 et seq; also Meyer (n 14) 255 et seq.

[176] Reprinted in Eduard Gans (ed), *Beiträge zur Revision der Preußischen Gesetzgebung* (1832) 177 et seq (in German); see also Meyer (n 14) 255 et seq.

[177] Gans (n 176) 177 et seq (in the original German: 'Die Grund-Idee, und mithin das Wesen der Actien-Gesellschaft, besteht also in der durch Vertrag bewirkten Vereinigung mehrerer Geldmittel, ohne daß, wie bei anderen Gesellschaften, die Gesellschafter zugleich ihre geistige Thätigkeit, ihre Arbeiten und Bemühungen zur Erlangung des gemeinschaftlichen Endzwecks, vereinigen und ohne daß sie für die übernommenen Geschäfte persönlich oder weiter als mit dem eingelegten Capital haften').

[178] Gans (n 176) 179 (in the original German: 'Die wesentliche Bedingung ihrer Existenz, […] ohne welche sie fast nimmer zu Stande kommen würde […]').

[179] Gans (n 176) 181 (in the original German: 'Bei der Actien-Gesellschaft sind dagegen alle Mitglieder eigentlich stille Gesellschafter; keiner haftet höher und anders, als mit dem Betrag der Actie').

person […] does not correspond to the purpose as laid down here, and would therefore achieve nothing more than facilitating the legal capacity of the company being represented by representatives'.[180]

In addition, the authors recommended that 'no individual shareholder should have the right to interfere in the company's business […]'.[181] *Justus Meyer* summarises their view as follows:

'[T]he limitation of liability was, therefore, not based on a corporation, fiction or cooperative theory. Rather, the limitation of liability was seen primarily as an economically necessary condition and was derived on the basis of general partnership law […]'.[182]

(2) Controversy on the Law Commission

Appearing before the Council of State on 14 June 1843 (thus on the home stretch toward the enactment of the Stock Corporation Act), the great legal scholar *Savigny*, in his capacity as minister for the revision of laws, came very close to the Berlin merchants' report, stating that 'shareholders' associations' were less related to 'corporations […] than to partnerships in which silent partners were involved. All shareholders considered themselves to be silent partners, with the proviso that there was no commercial partnership of which they were members'.[183] This was against the backdrop of an internal controversy on the Law Commission as to whether limited liability should be granted only to companies serving the public good by way of special state privilege. The opposing position (which ultimately prevailed) also advocated that an association that was supposed to be granted greater rights and powers than an ordinary commercial partnership should be subject to a privilege or state license. But such a license was not to be tied to a de-

---

[180] Gans (n 176) 182 (in the original German: 'Es kann auch füglich wohl dadurch für die Sicherheit des Publici gesorgt werden, daß man die Publicität des Gesellschaftsvertrages jeder Actien-Gesellschaft zur Pflicht macht. Die Erlangung der Rechte einer moralischen Person, wie das Landrechte letztere bestimmt, entspricht dem hier ausgedeuteten Zweck nicht, und es würde also dadurch nichts weiter erreicht seyn als Erleichterung der rechtlichen Möglichkeit, daß die Gesellschaft durch Vertreter repräsentiert werde').

[181] Gans (n 176) 187 (in the original German: 'Kein einzelner Actionair hat das Recht, in den Geschäftsbetrieb sich zu mischen […]'); Meyer (n 14) 255.

[182] Meyer (n 14) 256. (in the original German: '[D]ie Haftungsbeschränkung leitete [das Gutachten …] dementsprechend nicht auf der Basis einer Korporations-, Fiktions- oder Genossenschaftstheorie ab. Die Haftungsbeschränkung wurde vielmehr in erster Linie als wirtschaftlich notwendige Vorbedingung gesehen und eher auf der Basis des allgemeinen Sozietätsrechts abgeleitet […]').

[183] Friedrich Carl von Savigny, Protokoll der 43. Sitzung des Königlichen Staatsrats (in the original German: 'Mit den letzteren [scil. Korporationen] hätten aber die Aktienvereine eine geringere Verwandtschaft als mit den Sozietäten, bei denen stille Gesellschafter beteiligt seien. Alle Aktionäre dächten sich als stille Gesellschafter mit der Maßgabe, daß neben ihnen keine offene Gesellschaft, an welche sie sich angeschlossen, bestehe'), reprinted in Baums (n 14) 168, 170 et seq; in more detail Baums (n 14) 32 et seq.

termination by the authorities that the company 'served the public good'.[184] The Prussian state ministers *Mühler* and *Graf von Alvensleben* took the stricter stance; they believed that it

'could not possibly be left to the discretion of a number of profit-hungry interested parties to enter into extensive ventures and to seek profit without having to meet the legitimate demands directed at them in the event of a flawed foundation or poor management of the company. This would encourage reckless speculation at the expense of sound industry and open the door to fraud.'[185]

But also in regard to 'well-founded stock corporations', there was a fear that they,

'due to their superior capital resources, would be able to completely crush the individual tradesmen and merchants [...], eliminate all competition and, thus, acquire a monopoly to the detriment of trade and commerce and the public as a whole, as has already been complained about in Belgium'.[186]

The majority of the Commission countered these concerns by arguing that whether stock corporations 'served the public good' was not relevant, since the issue was not whether such corporations possessed personhood but rather 'only of giving them those characteristics without which they cannot achieve their purposes'.[187] This view was buttressed by a comparative legal survey that referred not only to French law but also to more liberal company law in Spain and the Netherlands. This was followed by an (early) argument against too strict a regime for reasons of regulatory competition.[188] In addition, personal liability would

---

[184] Cf Motive zum Kommissionsentwurf vom 31.1.1840 (in German), reprinted in Baums (n 14) 54 et seq.

[185] Cf Motive zum Kommissionsentwurf vom 31.1.1840, reprinted in Baums (n 14) 57 (in the original German: 'Es könne unmöglich in die Willkühr einer Zahl gewinnlustiger Interessenten gestellt werden, mit ausgedehnten Unternehmungen aufzutreten und Gewinn zu suchen, ohne bei mangelhafter Begründung oder schlechter Verwaltung des Unternehmens, denjenigen gerecht werden zu müssen, welche Anforderungen an sie zu richten hätten. Es würde dadurch auf Kosten der soliden Industrie dem Hange zu unbesonnener Spekulation Vorschub geleistet und Betrügereien Thor und Thür geöffnet').

[186] Cf Motive zum Kommissionsentwurf vom 31.1.1840, reprinted in Baums (n 14) 57 (in the original German: 'Namentlich könnten sich in der Hinsicht Bedenken ergeben, daß die Aktiengesellschaften vermöge ihres Übergewichts an Kapital die einzelnen Gewerb- und Handeltreibenden [...] ganz zu erdrücken, jede Konkurrenz zu beseitigen, und so zum Nachtheil des Gewerbe- und Handelsstandes wie des gesamten Publikums ein Monopol zu erlangen wissen möchten, wie hierüber in Belgien sich schon Klagen hätten vernehmen lassen').

[187] Cf Motive zum Kommissionsentwurf vom 31.1.1840, reprinted in Baums (n 14) 64 (in the original German: '[...] da es eigentlich nicht davon handelt, die Aktiengesellschaften zu Korporationen im Sinne des Landrechts zu machen, sondern nur davon, ihnen diejenigen Eigenschaften zuzugestehen, ohne welche sie ihre Zwecke nicht erreichen können'); see also Meyer (n 14) 259.

[188] Cf Motive zum Kommissionsentwurf vom 31.1.1840, reprinted in Baums (n 14) 65 et seq: 'A state which prevents this is working against its own advantage in two ways. On the one hand, capital which would have been invested at home in shares of such companies goes abroad; on the other hand, many articles which could be produced at home are imported from abroad,

'defeat the whole purpose of stock corporations. If the individual shareholder is liable with all his assets beyond the amount of his share, the relationship between the shareholders will no longer be one of equals. The danger then is great for the rich and small for the less rich. Under such conditions, however, a large number of members cannot associate with each other'.[189]

The 'tendency to speculation' as the main objection to a general principle of limited liability admittedly deserved attention. However, since 'the proposed measure would, for the reasons stated above, make it impossible for joint-stock associations to come into existence at all, other means would have to be chosen to achieve this end […]'.[190]

(3) Other statements and outcome

Expert opinions submitted later in the legislative process[191] contain other arguments. State minister *Schön*, for example, pointed to the limited ability of the shareholders to control the directors, which made it necessary to limit liability.[192] Senior state officer ('Oberregierungsrat') *Hoffmann*'s report argued that limited liability was necessary to ensure liquidity in the secondary market for shares:

'Stock corporations can only have a widespread and prosperous effect if the government grants them corporate rights with the power to issue bearer shares or otherwise easily alienable securities, from which it follows cogently that each member remains liable to the corporation only up to the amount of the share's value.'[193]

---

because they are either not produced at all or are produced at a higher price by individuals at home.' (in the original German: 'Ein Staat, welcher dies hindert, wirkt in doppelter Beziehung seinem eigenen Vortheil entgegen. Einmal nämlich entsteht die Folge, daß Kapitalien, die sonst im Inlande auf Aktien zu derartigen Unternehmungen angelegt seyn würden, in's Ausland gehen; sodann aber werden mehrere Artikel, die hier produziert werden könnten, aus dem Auslande eingeführt, weil sie im Inlande von Einzelnen entweder gar nicht oder zu einem höheren Preise fabrizirt werden').

[189] Cf Motive zum Kommissionsentwurf vom 31.1.1840, reprinted in Baums (n 14) 68 (in the original German: 'Der ganze Zweck der Aktienvereine wird damit vereitelt. Haftet der einzelne Aktionair auch über den Betrag der Aktie mit seinem ganzen Vermögen; so hört das Verhältniß der Aktionaire auf, ein gleichmäßiges zu seyn. Die Gefahr ist dann für die Begüterten groß, für die Unvermögenden gering. Auf solche Bedingungen hin kann aber nicht eine große Anzahl von Mitgliedern zusammentreten').

[190] Cf Motive zum Kommissionsentwurf vom 31.1.1840, reprinted in Baums (n 14) 69 (in the original German: '[Weil] die vorgeschlagene Maaßregel aus den obenerwähnten Gründen das Entstehen der Aktienvereine überhaupt unmöglich machen würde, [müsse] man zur Erreichung jenes Zweckes andere Mittel wählen […]').

[191] For a more detailed overview of the legislative process, see Baums (n 14) 30 et seq.

[192] Schön, Gutachten vom 23.12.1841 (in German), reprinted in Baums (n 14) 111.

[193] Hoffmann, Gutachten vom 30.12.1841 (in the original German: 'Aktienvereine können überhaupt nur dann eine weit umfassende und gedeihliche Wirksamkeit äußern, wenn die Regierung ihnen Korporationsrechte mit der Befugniß ertheilt, auf Inhabern oder doch sonst leicht veräußerlich gestellte Bescheinigungen der Theilnahme an ihnen auszugeben, wovon folgerecht unzertrennlich ist, daß jeder Theilnehmer nur mit dem Betrage des Werthes dieser Bescheinigung der Anstalt verhaftet bleibt'), reprinted in Baums (n 14) 126.

At the aforementioned meeting of the Council of State, *Savigny* also stated that a limitation of shareholder liability could even be achieved 'without the approval of the State and without privilege', namely through a corresponding limitation of the powers of management.[194] Nevertheless, *Savigny* advocated for a general licensing requirement for corporations. The dangers thereby averted were 'not on the part of the creditors, who could also be disadvantaged in the [... other] ways described, but on the part of gullible shareholders, who could be tempted by speculators to sacrifice their assets.'[195]

The Stock Corporation Act of 1843 ultimately did provide a licensing requirement (s 1). This licensure bestowed legal personhood upon the stock corporation (s 8). The liability of shareholders was limited to their respective contributions (s 15), and shareholders were only liable to the corporation (s 16). This regime was secured by rules on raising and maintaining capital (ss 11ff, 17ff) together with director liability (s 20).[196]

b) Insights and developments from 1843 until amendment of the General German Commercial Code in 1884

(1) From mandatory licensing to the system of normative requirements

The nineteenth century in Germany and elsewhere was marked above all by struggles over the licensing requirement. As we have seen, the rationale for mandatory licensure for limited liability was threefold: to protect the (1) creditors, (2) investors, and (3) competitors of such companies.[197] Strict licensing practices, for example in Prussia, prevented a robust increase in the number of stock corporations and sometimes led to evasive strategies, most notably the formation of partnerships limited by shares.[198] Nevertheless, the defenders of mandatory licensing retained the upper hand for the time being. The legislative materials behind the draft Commercial Code of 1848/49[199] refer to all three rationales, but only creditor and investor protection are linked to limited liability.[200] The General German Commercial Code (Allgemeines Deutsches Handelsgesetzbuch or the

---

194 Savigny (n 183) 168, 170 et seq (in the original German: 'Den Zweck ihrer Verbindung, den Gläubigern nur mit dem eingeschlossenen Kapital zu haften, könnten sie aber ohne Genehmigung des Staates und ohne Privilegium [...] erreichen. [...]').

195 Savigny (n 183) 168, 171 (in the original German: 'Die Gefahren seien aber nicht auf seiten der Kreditoren, die auch auf den [...] bezeichneten Wegen benachteiligt werden könnten, sondern auf seiten der leichtgläubigen Aktionäre, die durch Spekulanten verleitet werden könnten, ihre Kapitalien zu opfern').

196 See also Meyer (n 14) 261.

197 See n 160 above and Hans Würdinger (ed) *Das Recht der Personalgesellschaften, 1. Teil: Die Kommanditgesellschaft, 1. Arbeitsbericht* (Beck 1939) 33 et seq (in German).

198 Meyer (n 14) 270 et seq.

199 For an overview, see Theodor Baums, *Entwurf eines allgemeinen Handelsgesetzbuches für Deutschland (1848/49)* (RuW 1982).

200 Reprinted in Baums (n 199) 153 seq.

'ADHGB') of 1861 thus required licensure not only for stock corporations (art 207) but also for partnerships limited by shares (art 174). However, exemptions from the licensure requirement were permitted under state law (art 249(1)), which Hamburg, Bremen, Lübeck, Baden, Württemberg and Saxony made use of (but Prussia only exempted partnerships limited by shares).[201] The principle of mandatory licensing, thus already under pressure, was finally abolished with the 1870 amendment of the Commercial Code. In view of the liberal laws of the German coastal cities and the abolition of licensure in England and France,[202] the Prussian trade minister *von Itzenplitz* proposed also abolishing it for the stock corporation. He sought the advice of *Paul Eck*, law professor in Giessen, and *Karl von Achenbach*, reporting officer in the Prussian Ministry of Trade and affiliate professor at the University of Bonn. *Eck*'s call for liberalisation prevailed; his main arguments, directed against the three main rationales behind mandatory licensing, were later adopted by the legislature and laid down in the materials to the legislative reform.[203] Only the first reason was legal in nature: the personhood that the Prussian government regarded stock corporations as possessing[204] could only be created by permission of the state (ie, licensure). But now the legislative materials referred to commercial partnerships that did not require a license and to which the law 'attache[d] all the essential rights of a legal person to exactly the same extent as to the stock corporation'.[205] The second reason – protecting the public as well as creditors against fraud and unsound formation of entities – was countered by an argument that appears rather outdated from today's perspective: experience had shown that such a 'highly benevolent intention' on the part of the state was 'unfortunately! unattainable'. That the public relied on the state for protection and therefore believed that it could dispense with its own diligence meant that this unfulfillable promise was downright harmful.[206] For example, a gullible public suffered considerable losses – in spite of the licensure requirement – during two periods of fraud and hucksterism of company shares in Prussia

[201] See Werner Schubert, Vom Konzessions- zum Normativsystem (ZGR Special Issue 22, De Gruyter 2017) 2 (in German).

[202] See Schubert (n 170) 289 et seq (in German).

[203] See Schubert (n 201) 3.

[204] See below under (3) on the debate about the legal nature of the AG.

[205] Motive für die Einbringung des preußischen Entwurfs zu einer Aktienrechtsnovelle [Motives for the Prussian Draft of an Amendment to Stock Corporation Law] (BR-Drucks 86/1869 of 31 May 1869) (in the original German: '[…], weil das Deutsche Handelsgesetzbuch allen übrigen, an die Staatsgenehmigung nicht geknüpften Handelsgesellschaftsformen […] alle wesentlichen Rechte einer juristischen Person in genau demselben Umfange beilegt, wie der Aktiengesellschaft […]'), reprinted in Schubert (n 201) 54, 55.

[206] Motives for the Prussian Draft of an Amendment to Stock Corporation Law (n 205) 55 (in the original German: 'Wenn […] der Staat dem Publikum […] Schutz gewähren will, so ist diese an sich höchst wohlthätige Absicht […] leider! unerreichbar. […] [Die] vom Staate […] verheißene Fürsorge […] *vermehrt* die Opfer des Schwindels und der Unsolidität, statt sie zu *verhüten*').

in 1855 and 1857. The investor's own diligence was regarded as the only protection.[207] The third reason for the licensing requirement – the competitive superiority of the stock corporation – was deemed unpersuasive in light of the availability of partnerships limited by shares without a license.[208] And while the advocates of liberalisation were well aware of the ensuing danger of fraud and rampant speculation, the concern was shrugged off nonchalantly: 'A transitional crisis may occur, but it will have to be endured'.[209]

The reaction to the crisis of 1873 (*Gründerkrach*) was not so sanguine. In a notorious harangue, *von Jhering* lamented that

> '[u]nder the eyes of our legislators, the stock corporations have changed into institutions of organized robbery and fraud whose secret history contains more perfidy, dishonour and villainy than many a penitentiary, except that the robbers and swindlers here sit in gold instead of irons.'[210]

With this in mind, some (like *Perrot*) called for abolishing the stock corporation altogether;[211] others pleaded for doing away with limited liability (!) (*Tellkampf*);[212] and still others saw advantages in the partnership limited by shares (*Goldschmidt*)[213].[214] At the 11th *Deutscher Juristentag* in 1873, it was proposed that there should be oversight in the form of a 'Reichsamt für das Aktienwesen' that would monitor the conduct of stock corporations.[215] A return to mandatory licensing was not considered feasible.[216] The amendments of 1884 ultimately stipulated a strict liability regime for those involved in the incorporation process (*Gründerhaftung*).[217]

---

207 Motives for the Prussian Draft of an Amendment to Stock Corporation Law (n 205) 56.

208 Motives for the Prussian Draft of an Amendment to Stock Corporation Law (n 205)4, 56 et seq.

209 Motives for the Prussian Draft of an Amendment to Stock Corporation Law (n 205) 57 (in the original German: 'Möglich ist das Eintreten solcher Übergangskrisis allerdings; sie muss dann aber eben durchgemacht werden').

210 Rudolf von Jhering, *Der Zweck im Recht*, vol 1 (1877) 222 (in the original German: 'Unter den Augen unserer Gesetzgeber haben sich die Actiengesellschaften zu organisierten Raub- und Betrugsanstalten verwandelt, deren geheime Geschichte mehr Niederträchtigkeit, Ehrlosigkeit, Schurkerei in sich birgt, als gar manches Zuchthaus, nur daß die Räuber und Betrüger hier statt in Eisen in Gold sitzen').

211 Franz Perrot, *Der Bank-, Börsen- und Actienschwindel* (1876) 120 et seq (in German).

212 Johann Ludwig Tellkampf, *Vorschläge zur Verbesserung des Actien-Gesellschaftswesens* (1876) 30 (in German).

213 Levin Goldschmidt, 'Gutachten über das Actiengesellschaftswesen' in *Zur Reform des Actiengesellschaftswesens: Drei Gutachten auf Veranlassung der Eisenacher Versammlung zur Besprechung der socialen Frage* (1873) 28, 31 (in German).

214 On the whole Großfeld (n 10) 143 et seq; briefly Meyer (n 14) 281.

215 *Wachtel*, Verhandlungen des 11. Deutschen Juristentages, vol 1 (1873) 110 et seq (in German).

216 Adolph Wagner, 'Das Actiengesellschaftswesen. Referat in der Versammlung des Vereins für Socialpolitik in Eisenach (October 1873)' (1873) 21 Jahrbücher für Nationalökonomie und Statistik 271 et seq; on the whole again Großfeld (n 10) 145.

217 Once again Großfeld (n 10) 147 et seq.

(2) The distinction between limited and silent partnership

In adopting the Commercial Code of 1861, German doctrine arrived at an important systematic clarification in connection with limited liability about the relationship between limited partnerships and silent partnerships.[218] The Prussian Commercial Code draft of 1857 refers only to a 'silent partnership'. In regard to limited shareholder liability, the legislative materials state that '[t]he provisions […] correspond to the general legal principles applying to the silent partnership […]'.[219] This uncertain distinction between silent partnerships (in the modern sense) and limited partnerships was now resolved. *Levin Goldschmidt*, in his critique of the Prussian draft,[220] introduced a theoretical distinction between the two forms. Despite much criticism, the Commercial Code finally provided separate rules for limited partnerships and silent partnerships.[221] However, limited shareholder liability took a different path that deviated from what the Prussian draft of 1857 actually intended (and in spite of the reference to 'silent partnerships').

(3) Once again: corporate personhood and limited liability

The question of whether the corporation's status as a legal entity is of any relevance to the assumption of limited liability of its members[222] was the subject of a lengthy debate, not only in the nineteenth century. As we have seen, *Savigny* regarded the corporation as a special form of partnership.[223] Privy councillor of justice and law professor *Johann Heinrich Thöl*[224] never tired of pointing out, across several editions of his textbook on commercial law, that the stock corporation was 'not a legal person' but 'the Roman societas, only modified'.[225] The draft German Commercial Code of 1848/49 in which *Thöl* had played a decisive role had deliberately refrained from classifying the stock corporation as a legal

---

[218] For details see Achilles Renaud, *Das Recht der Commanditgesellschaften* (1881) § 7 (p 42 et seq) (in German); more recently, Rüdiger Servos, *Die Personenhandelsgesellschaften und die stille Gesellschaft in den Kodifikationen und Kodifikationsentwürfen vom ALR bis zum ADHGB* (1984) 276 et seq (in German).

[219] Prussian HGB draft, 1857, Motives to art 188 et seq. See Meyer (n 14) 276 (in the original German: 'Die Bestimmungen dieses Artikels entsprechen den allgemeinen Rechtsgrundsätzen über die stille Gesellschaft […]').

[220] Levin Goldschmidt, 'Der Entwurf eines Handelsgesetzbuchs für die Preußischen Staaten' (1857) 4 KritZgR 289, 322 et seq (in German).

[221] On the whole, see the description in Servos (n 218) 284 et seq (in German).

[222] This already came up in a).

[223] This already came up in a) at fn 183.

[224] A brief outline of the person of Heinrich Thöl can be found in Baums (n 200) 38 et seq

[225] Johann Heinrich Thöl, *Das Handelsrecht*, vol 1 (6th edn, 1879) § 150 (p 466 et seq) (in German); previously, for example, Johann Heinrich Thöl, *Das Handelsrecht*, vol 1 (4th edn, 1862) § 44 (p 274) (in the original German: 'nicht eine juristische Person […] die römische societas, aber diese modificiert'); numerous references to the debate can be found in ibid (6th edn, 1879) § 87 in fn 3 (p 305).

entity.[226] Instead, art 80(1) stated that '[t]he stock corporation is as such, and apart from its shareholders, the subject of rights and obligations'[227]. This provision was taken up unchanged in the General German Commercial Code of 1861 (cf art 213(1) item 1).[228] However, *Achilles Renaud* took the opposite view; contrary to *Thöl* and in line with today's understanding, he classified the stock corporation as a legal entity (*juristische Person*).[229] Limited shareholder liability did not play a significant role in his analysis, though; he merely stated that the 'corporation' could also be a debtor and that the shareholders 'have neither unlimited nor limited liability for such liabilities [of the corporation], but only for the full payment of their shares'.[230] Later, in the mid-1880s, *Laband* took a different approach. From the statement that 'a legal person can have debts, a partnership cannot', he deduced that

> 'associations in which the objective law exempts the members from liability for the debts incurred for the achievement of the common purposes [...] are legal persons; associations in which the members as such are liable for the debts incurred for the achievement of the common purposes, [on the other hand ...] are legal relationships'.[231]

However, this 'link between legal personality and limited liability'[232] met with resistance, not only from *Thöl* but also from other contemporaries such as *Bekker* and *Stobbe*, neither of whom saw any compelling reason why corporate personhood should be regarded as incompatible with holding its members personally liable for the company's debts.[233] *Bekker* expressly referred to 'foreign jurisdic-

---

[226] See Motives for the draft HGB 1848/49 (there on art 80), reproduced in Baums (n 200) 157 (in German).

[227] In the original German: 'Die Aktien-Gesellschaft ist als solche, und abgesehen von den einzelnen Aktionären, Subjekt von Rechten und Verbindlichkeiten.'

[228] It states: 'The stock corporation as such has its rights and obligations independently' (in the original German: 'Die Aktiengesellschaft als solche hat selbstständig ihre Rechte und Pflichten'). On the dispute over the interpretation of these provisions, see ROHG 17 April 1877, 1585/76, (1878) 22 ROHGE 239 et seq (indeterminate). In historical retrospect, see also Meyer (n 14) 279 et seq (in German).

[229] Renaud (n 67) § 9 et seq (p 133 et seq) (in German).

[230] Renaud (n 67) § 12 (p 154) (in the original German: 'Debitoren sind hier nicht die Actionäre, welche weder einzeln noch zusammen aus solchen Verbindlichkeiten [des Actienvereins...] belangt werden können, und die daraus weder unbeschränkt, noch beschränkt, nämlich für den unbezahlten Betrag ihrer Actien, haften').

[231] Paul Laband, 'Beiträge zur Dogmatik der Handelsgesellschaften' (1885) 30 ZHR 469, 498 et seq, 502 et seq (in the original German: 'Vereinigungen, bei welchen das objektive Recht die Mitglieder von der Haftung für die zur Erreichung der Gemeinschaftszwecke eingegangenen Verbindlichkeiten befreit, sind juristische Personen; Vereinigungen bei welchen Mitglieder als solche für die zur Erreichung der Gemeinschaftszwecke eingegangenen Verbindlichkeiten haften, sind Rechtsverhältnisse').

[232] This is from Meyer (n 14) 34 (in the original German: 'Junktim zwischen juristischer Persönlichkeit und beschränkter Haftung').

[233] Ernst Immanuel Bekker, *System des heutigen Pandektenrechts*, vol 1 (1886) 216 et seq (in German); Otto Stobbe, *Handbuch des Deutschen Privatrechts*, vol 1 (3rd edn, 1893) 454 et seq (in German). Both expressly against Laband.

tions' that provided for stock corporations in which the shareholders were subject to personal liability. *Laband*'s contemporaries had thus already recognised that it was misguided to justify limited shareholder liability by referring to the concept of corporate personhood.[234] No subsequent revival has overcome the weakness of this analysis.

In regard to Anglo-Saxon law, *Ron Harris* notes that 'the liability attribute was separated from the personality attribute and conceptualized' much earlier – namely '[i]n the transition to Period II [ie, 1800–1900]'.[235] The discussion of the relationship between corporate personhood and limited liability in Germany at the end of the nineteenth century thus appears delayed.

c) The introduction of the GmbH: limited liability with unlimited control

With the introduction of the GmbH in 1892, the German legislator proved capable of creating an innovative corporate form that combined limited liability with active shareholder participation in the management of the company.[236]

(1) From Oechelshäuser's proposal to the GmbH Act of 1892

The driving force behind this legislative project was *Wilhelm Oechelhäuser*, an industrialist and member of parliament who had already pushed for limited liability to be made available to 'individualistic companies' in the course of enacting the reforms of 1884. He cited a practical need, in that stock corporations were not well suited for associations of small numbers of shareholders.[237] *Oechelhäuser* thus introduced a now-famous piece of legislation, modelled on the law of the commercial partnerships, that stipulated joint and several liability on the part of the partners in the amount of the share capital published in the commercial register.[238] Like the other proponents of such an 'individualistic' GmbH, he was aware that this went against traditional principles. *Goldschmidt*, for example, saw it as a 'natural principle' that unlimited liability applied to the extent that the shareholder or partner exercised control over the actions of the association.[239] A few

234 See also, for example, O Bähr, 'Gesellschaften mit beschränkter Haftung' (1892) 51 Die Grenzboten 210, 221 (in German) in his criticism of the draft of the GmbHG: 'Exaggeration based on the Roman doctrine'.

235 Harris (n 80) 654.

236 From among the contemporary literature, see, for example, Levin Goldschmidt, *Vermischte Schriften*, vol 2 (1901) 321, 332 (in German); furthermore, on the position of the GmbH in a legal comparison, refer to Holger Fleischer (n 95) (in German).

237 Werner Schubert, 'Das GmbH-Gesetz von 1892 – „eine Zierde unserer Reichsgesetzsammlung". Das historische Geschehen um die GmbH von 1888 bis 1902' in Markus Lutter, Peter Ulmer and Wolfgang Zöllner (eds), *Festschrift 100 Jahre GmbH-Gesetz* (Schmidt 1992) 1, 5 (in German).

238 The draft can be found in Holger Fleischer, in Holger Fleischer and Wulf Goette (eds), Münchener Kommentar zum GmbHG (5th edn, CH Beck 2025) 'Einleitung' para 56 (in German).

239 Levin Goldschmidt, 'Erwerbs- und Wirthschafts-Genossenschaften' (1882) 27 ZHR 1, 79 (in the original German: 'Die unbeschränkte Verantwortlichkeit ist ein natürliches und sitt-

years after the introduction of the GmbH Act (Gesetz betreffend die Gesellschaft mit beschränkter Haftung, the 'GmbHG'), *Karl Wieland* stated that the legislator had abandoned the 'guiding principle of current company law', according to which 'limited responsibility [...] appears as the correlate of a predominantly passive participation in the company'.[240] The departure from this 'guiding principle' was justified by the 'growth of modern business' and the associated 'increased scope of business'.[241] In a memorandum to the Prussian chambers of commerce and trade associations, *Oechelhäuser* put it in the following words:

> 'The scope and turnover of business have increased enormously compared to earlier times. To the same extent, concerns about entering into associations were bound to increase, since the stroke of a pen by a careless co-partner or signatory can destroy the private wealth, and indeed the commercial and civic honour, of a partner. In fact, for these and other reasons, joint and several liability increasingly discourages the creation of new business ventures.'[242]

As is well known, this view, with the description of a corresponding need for an intermediate form between the mining company (*Berggewerkschaft*) and the stock corporation on one hand and commercial partnerships on the other, finally led to the adoption of a new corporate form, ie, the GmbH. Following *Oechelhäuser*'s initiative in 1884, a legal solution for the German colonial companies was put into force in 1888.[243] This legislative activity was accompanied by extensive analytical elaborations (see, eg, *Esser*,[244] *Simon*[245] and *Ring*[246]). In the immediate aftermath of the reform of 1888, members of parliament saw a need for reform with

---

liches Prinzip [... Es ...] geht nur dahin: Unbeschränkte Verantwortlichkeit soweit die Möglichkeit eigenen Handelns oder doch eigener ausreichender Aufsicht reicht').

240 Karl Wieland, 'Die Gesellschaften mit beschränkter Haftung' (1895) 14 ZSR 205, 206 (in the original German: 'leitender Grundsatz des geltenden Gesellschaftsrechts', 'Korrelat einer vorwiegend passiven Beteiligung an Unternehmen'); similarly, Bähr (n 234) 220 (in German).

241 See Wieland (n 240) 219 et seq (in the original German: 'Anwachsen des modernen Geschäftsbetriebs', 'vermehrte[r] Geschäftsumfang').

242 Oechelhäuser, 'Schriften des Vereins zur Wahrung der wirtschaftlichen Interessen von Handel und Gewerbe', no. 25, 53 (in German), quoted from Wieland (n 240) 219 et seq (in the original German: 'Der Umfang und Umsatz der Geschäfte haben sich gegen frühere Zeiten enorm gehoben. In gleichem Masse mussten die Bedenken gegen das Eingehen von Verbindungen steigen, wobei der Federstrich eines leichtsinnigen Kompagnons oder Prokuristen weit über das Gesellschaftsvermögen hinaus das Privatvermögen, ja die kaufmännische und bürgerliche Ehre eines Teilhabers vernichten kann. Thatsächlich hält aus diesen und noch anderen Gründen die Solidarhaft in grossem stets steigenden Umfang von der Gründung neuer geschäftlicher Unternehmungen ab').

243 Gesetz wegen Abänderung des Gesetzes betreffend die Rechtsverhältnisse der deutschen Schutzgebiete vom 17.4.1886 (RGBl p 74) vom 15.3.1888 (RGBl p 71) (in German).

244 Robert Esser, *Die Gesellschaft mit beschränkter Haftbarkeit. Eine gesetzgeberische Studie* (1886) (in German).

245 Hermann Veit Simon, 'Deutsche Kolonialgesellschaften. Rechtliche Erörterungen und Vorschläge' (1888) 34 ZHR 85 et seq (in German).

246 Viktor Ring, 'Eine Rechtsform für Kolonialgesellschaften. Betrachtungen und Vorschläge' (1988) 48 Buschs Archiv 26 (in German).

a view to business in the German homeland as well.[247] As a result, the Prussian Ministry of Trade and Industry (headed by *von Bismarck*) surveyed the Prussian chambers of commerce and the Prussian Trade Congress[248] and found a vast majority in support of reform and in favour of *Oechelhäuser*'s draft, which had been backed by the Council of Elders of the Berlin Merchants' Association.[249] However, a subsequent bill drafted by an official in the Reich Ministry of Justice named *Eduard Hoffmann*[250] was modelled after an alternative, 'collectivist' concept that had been authored by another member of parliament, *Friedrich Hammacher*.[251] *Hoffmann*'s draft was essentially unchanged[252] when it was forwarded to the parliament in October 1891.[253] The actual legislative process lasted only a few months,[254] leaving little time for the legal profession to react to the draft. Requests by academics that the draft be published early were rejected.[255] Otto Bähr was the only one who managed to submit his fundamental criticism in time.[256] In the end, however, he too had no influence on the outcome.

The official comments to the draft justified the reform by referring not to the general considerations put forward by *Oechelhäuser*[257] but to specific scenarios: sugar factories, corporate succession in family businesses, creditor companies in restructuring cases and real estate companies.[258] Regardless of this rather unim-

---

[247] See Wieland (n 240) 209.

[248] Jakob Rießer, *Zur Revision des Handelsgesetzbuchs*, Beilagenheft zu Band 35, in: ZGH 36 (1889), 651 et seq (in German).

[249] See Wieland (n 240) 212 et seq.

[250] On Hoffmann's prominent role in the development of the GmbH Act, one need only refer to Fleischer (n 236) 41, with further references.

[251] See Wieland (n 240) 210, 212: 'Nonetheless, the draft drawn up by the Reichsjustizamt adhered in the main to the proposals made by Hammacher' (in the original German: 'Nichtsdestoweniger hielt sich der vom Reichsjustizamte ausgearbeitete Entwurf in der Hauptsache an die von Hammacher gemachten Vorschläge'). Goldschmidt (n 236) 321, 333 (in German), on the other hand, speaks of a 'kind of compromise' between Oechelhäuser's and Hammacher's concepts.

[252] See also Hans Crüger, 'Einleitung' in Ludolf Parisius and Hans Crüger (eds), Das Reichsgesetz, betreffend die Gesellschaften mit beschränkter Haftung (16th edn, De Gruyter 1923) 15 (in German); Wieland (n 240) 212 in fn 2.

[253] Entwurf eines Gesetzes betr. die Gesellschaften mit beschränkter Haftung, 1892 (in German). It was forwarded to the Bundesrat, the Reich's other legislative organ besides the Reichstag.

[254] See Fleischer (n 236) 41; Wieland (n 240) 213.

[255] As reported in Peter Koberg, *Die Entstehung der GmbH in Deutschland und Frankreich* (O Schmidt 1992) 123 in fn 282 (in German); on this, and quoted from, Meyer (n 14) 303.

[256] Bähr (n 234) published his critique shortly before the first reading in the Reichstag on 19 February 1892. Goldschmidt's lecture before the legal society in Berlin, on the other hand, did not take place until 19 March 1892, only two days before the third reading in the Reichstag. See Meyer (n 14) 303 in fn 652 and 304 in fn 660.

[257] See n 240 above.

[258] See, for example, Fleischer (n 236) 40 et seq; Meyer (n 14) 308; from the contemporary literature and in more detail, Wieland (n 240) 216.

pressive justification in the official comments, some German scholars today believe that the GmbH legislation expressed a 'belief in progress' and the 'expansive spirit' of the time.[259]

(2) Legal academia's belated critique

Whereas political forces had practically prevented academic debate prior to the GmbH Act,[260] academics took the opportunity to submit their critique afterwards.[261] *Otto Bähr* sharply declared that it would 'destroy the foundations of the existing law' if a company 'with the power to independently acquire assets and with limited liability [...] could be freely formed for any legal purpose [...]'.[262] He saw the creditor protections as too weak and thought limited liability would be used to 'pass on the damage' to creditors in the event of poor company performance.[263] The 'most effective countermeasure against fraudulent enterprises', *Bähr* stated, was therefore unlimited shareholder liability.[264] Only a short time later, however, in a speech to the Jurists' Association of Berlin, *Levin Goldschmidt* rejected this assessment.[265] Though he was 'quite sympathetic' to the proposed legislation, he called for 'great caution'[266] and questioned the need for the new corporate form.[267] In contrast to *Bähr*, he 'by no means abhor[red] the principle of limited liability'. Instead, his main concern was that the new entity might 'displace the generally more solid partnerships'.[268] He firmly believed that

[259] Meyer (n 14) 295 (in the original German: 'Fortschrittsgläubigkeit' and 'der expansive Geist').

[260] See, for example, Fleischer (n 236) 41: 'no role' (in the original German: 'keine Rolle'); Meyer (n 14) 303: 'An academic discussion comparable to that of the stock corporation has not taken place' (in the original German: 'Eine der aktienrechtlichen vergleichbare wissenschaftliche Diskussion hat nicht stattgefunden').

[261] For an overview of the 'most important criticism', see Meyer (n 14) 303 et seq.

[262] Bähr (n 234) 217 (in the original German: 'Man wird unbedenklich aussprechen können, daß er [scil. der Entwurf] dem bestehenden Rechte den Boden aufschlüge. Eine Gesellschaft mit der Befugnis selbständigen Vermögenserwerbs und beschränkter Haftung soll sich für jeden gesetzlichen Zweck frei bilden können!').

[263] Bähr (n 234) 223 seq, especially 225 with the addition: 'That's the whole point of it.' (in the original German: '[...] wollen die Unternehmer den Schaden [...] auf ihre Gläubiger überwälzen. Das ist der Witz von der Sache').

[264] Bähr (n 234) 225 (in the original German: 'das wirksamste Gegengewicht gegen schwindelhafte Unternehmungen').

[265] Goldschmidt (n 236) 333.

[266] Goldschmidt (n 236) 333 (in the original German: ' [...] stehe ich der Gesetzesvorlage durchaus sympathisch gegenüber [...]. Aber immerhin scheint mir große Vorsicht geboten').

[267] Goldschmidt (n 236) 333 et seq.

[268] Goldschmidt (n 236) 334 et seq (in the original German: 'Obwohl ich [...] das Prinzip der beschränkten Haftung keineswegs perhorrescire [...]' and '[I]n der Gefahr der Verdrängung dieser prinzipiell solideren Gesellschaftsformen [...] möchte ich die Hauptbedenken gegen die Gesetzesvorlage finden').

'where there [was] the possibility of constant personal intervention, supervision and performance, there [was] no reason to deviate from the principle of unlimited liability, including for the actions of authorised third parties and fellow members'.[269]

A few years later (and from a Swiss perspective), *Karl Wieland*, later a professor of commercial and civil law at the University of Basel, presented an in-depth analysis of the German GmbH, in particular its liability regime.[270] He explicitly acknowledged the need for an 'individualistic' limited liability company, as advocated by *Oechelhäuser*.[271] He also considered *Oechelhäuser*'s proposal – joint and several liability of the shareholders limited to the amount of the share capital published in the commercial register[272] – to be a superior conception of liability compared to what was implemented with the GmbH Act.[273] *Wieland*'s comments of 1895 contained an early, and quite elaborate, incentive-based analysis of shareholder liability. As a result, he considered the German GmbH liability regime to be inadequate, because it granted limited liability but lacked the security mechanisms of the stock corporation, which included strict rules at the formation stage, a 'contrast' between 'administration and shareholders', and the 'periodic publication of the business results'. For Wieland, the resulting risk to the company through 'alienation of assets' could be contained by a limited joint and several liability, as defined in the *Oechelhäuser* draft, that would limit the number of shareholders, who in turn would be compelled to 'keep themselves constantly informed of the course of the company's affairs and to exercise sufficient supervision over their fellow shareholders'.[274]

Some of today's commentators display a certain reservedness towards the contemporary project of enacting GmbHs at the end of the nineteenth century. *Justus Meyer*, for example, describes the GmbH as the result of a mentality 'of this period of advanced industrialisation' in which 'liberal ideas were combined with a widespread confidence in progress and practically unlimited growth'.[275] However, the GmbH must have had qualities that transcended this zeitgeist, because

[269] Goldschmidt (n 236) 336 (in the original German: '[…] wo die Möglichkeit des stets eigenen Eingreifens, der eigenen Aufsicht und Leitung besteht, kein Grund vorliegt, von der prinzipiell unbeschränkten Haftung auch für die Handlungen beauftragter Dritter und Genossen abzugehen').

[270] Wieland (n 240) 205 et seq.

[271] See n 240 above.

[272] See n 244 above.

[273] Wieland (n 240) 222 et seq.

[274] Wieland (n 240) especially 247 et seq (in the original German: 'Trotz des Wegfalls des illimitierten Risiko ist die Verantwortlichkeit, welcher der einzelne Teilhaber unterliegt, noch eine strenge: sie nötigt ihn, sich über den Gang der Gesellschaftsangelegenheiten fortwährend auf dem Laufenden zu erhalten und eine genügende Ueberwachung der Mitgesellschafter auszuüben').

[275] Meyer (n 14) 312 (in the original German: 'liberales Gedankengut mit einem weitverbreiteten Vertrauen in den Fortschritt und praktisch unbegrenztes Wachstum').

without them, the subsequent 'international triumph of the GmbH'[276] cannot be explained.

IV. Theorisation and Critique of Limited Liability from the Twentieth Century to the Present

1. The Ordoliberal Creed of the Indivisibility of Control and Liability: The Long Shadow of Adam Smith

The severing of the 'natural link' between control and liability with the GmbH Act occupied German legal scholars and economists alike well into the twentieth century (and in some ways still does). It appears that the reservations about this paradigm shift formed in the long shadow of *Adam Smith*'s scepticism.[277]

a) The postulation of the indivisibility of control and liability

After the turn of the century, the idea of the indivisibility of control and liability in company and partnership law was initially associated with the Munich professor *Rudolf Müller-Erzbach*,[278] who defended it into the 1950s.[279] During the Nazi era, the Academy of German Law took up his ideas about unlimited liability on the part of a limited partner exercising control over management. Its working group on partnership law recognised an 'ethical principle of law' in liability being coupled to monitoring of risks.[280] This view was supported and promoted by representatives of ordoliberal school of economics, who advocated for the unification of control and liability. The legal scholars *Franz Böhm* and *Hans Großmann-Doerth* were very outspoken in their opposition to the GmbH in the 1930s, to the point of wanting to abolish it.[281] But their arguments were not new;

---

[276] Meyer (n 14) 313 (in the original German: 'der internationale Siegeszug der GmbH').

[277] See above at II.2.b) for his contribution to the debate.

[278] On this and the following, see the comprehensive description in Holger Fleischer and Jakob Hahn, '§ 7 – Rektor' in Holger Fleischer and Jan Thiessen (eds), Gesellschaftsrechts-Geschichten (Mohr Siebeck 2018) 264 et seq (in German).

[279] Of Müller-Erzbach's writings, see, for example, Rudolf Müller-Erzbach, 'Die Haftung und die Vermögensbcteiligung des Kommanditisten und des stillen Gesellschafters, besonders im Falle ihrer Anteilnahme an der Unternehmensverwaltung' in Fiedrich Klausing and Hans Carl Nipperdey (ed) *FS Heymann – Beiträge zum Wirtschaftsrecht*, vol 2 (Elwert 1931) 737 et seq (in German); 'Das Erfassen des Rechts aus den Elementen des Zusammenlebens, veranschaulicht am Gesellschaftsrecht' (1955) 154 AcP 299, 342 et seq (in German); 'Die Verbandsmacht – eine unbekannte Welt: Einblicke in die höchstrichterliche Einstellung zum Leben' [1956] JZ 705, 708 (in German).

[280] Hans Würdinger (ed), *Das Recht der Personalgesellschaften, 1. Teil: Die Kommanditgesellschaft, 1. Arbeitsbericht* (Beck 1939) 32 et seq (in the original German: 'rechtsethisches Prinzip'). For more details, see Fleischer and Hahn (n 278) 255, 265 et seq.

[281] See Hans Großmann-Doerth, Gutachten zum 5. DJT in der Tschechoslowakei (Sudetendt Verl 1931) 165, 239 (in German); Großmann-Doerth, 'Sinnlosgewordenes Wirtschaftsrecht'

they fell back on the principle of unlimited personal liability and criticised how limited liability shifted risks to creditors. The ordoliberal critique coincided with scepticism on the part of the Nazis, who perceived the GmbH as an expression of the 'prevailing liberal economic view'[282] at the end of the nineteenth century and seriously considered abolishing it.[283]

The economist *Walter Eucken*, the figurehead and main proponent (along with *Franz Böhm*) of the ordoliberal 'Freiburg School', also dealt with the issue of limited liability in his posthumous *Grundsätze der Wirtschaftspolitik*.[284] He, too, begins with the 'liability principle', according to which 'the person who is responsible for the plans and actions of the enterprises […] is liable'.[285] *Eucken* combined this with the idea of responsibility as a correlate of reaping the benefits ('He who reaps the benefits must also bear the injury')[286]. The link between control and liability is justified, according to *Eucken*, by the 'macroeconomic function' of liability: in a competitive system, he argues, (unlimited) liability enables and facilitates the selection of companies and managers; it encourages prudence and discourages wastefulness; it counteracts harmful corporate concentration.[287]

Subsequently, lawyers in the tradition of ordoliberalism also called for liability to be linked to control, in particular *Ernst-Joachim Mestmäcker* and his student *Ulrich Immenga*, who considered the principle to be binding and even valid *de lege lata*.[288]

b) Rejection by the Federal Court of Justice in the Rektor case and scholarly response

In terms of its practical impact, the ordoliberal creed of the indivisibility of control and liability was rejected by the Federal Court of Justice (the BGH). In the

HansRGZ 1934 19, 40 (in German); Großmann-Doerth, 'Vom Kampf um die GmbH' [1938] HansRGZ 209, 211 (in German); Franz Böhm, *Die Ordnung der Wirtschaft als geschichtliche Aufgabe und rechtspolitische Leistung* (Kohlhammer 1937) 102 (in German).

282 See, for example, Helmut Vollweiler, 'Wirtschaftliche und rechtliche Probleme der G.m.b.H.-Reform' (1938) 147 Jahrbücher für Nationalökonomie und Statistik 189, 192 (in the original German: 'herrschende liberalistische Wirtschaftsauffassung').

283 On the National Socialist criticism of the GmbH and resistance from the Cologne lawyer Otto Schmidt, see the overview in Fleischer (n 238), 'Einleitung' para 89 et seq (in German), with further references.

284 Walter Eucken, *Grundsätze der Wirtschaftspolitik* (1952; 7th edn, Mohr Siebeck 2004) 279 et seq.

285 Eucken (n 284) 281 (in the original German: 'Wer für Pläne und Handlungen der Unternehmen (Betriebe) […] verantwortlich ist, haftet (Haftungsprinzip)').

286 Eucken (n 284) 279 (in the original German: 'Wer den Nutzen hat, muß auch den Schaden tragen').

287 Eucken (n 284) 280 et seq.

288 Cf Ernst-Joachim Mestmäcker, *Verwaltung, Konzerngewalt und Rechte der Aktionäre* (Mueller 1958) 25 (in German); Ulrich Immenga, *Die personalistische Kapitalgesellschaft* (Athenäum 1970) 117 et seq (in German); again Fleischer and Hahn (n 278) 267.

famous *Rektor* case, the justices ruled that the link between managerial control and personal liability was not a 'cogent principle of economic constitutional law'.[289] The court argued from a genuinely juridical point of view, pointing to the non-mandatory nature of the relevant provisions of limited partnership law and the legal uncertainty that would otherwise arise,[290] adding that

> '[a]s the legal development of the last 50 to 60 years shows, the management of a commercial business with limited liability by one or more natural persons has become an integral part of our legal life. In this respect, one need only refer to the legal concepts of the one-man company and the GmbH & co.'[291]

The *Rektor* decision was largely well received by legal academics. Their reactions echoed earlier criticisms about the ordoliberal creed's validity from a legal perspective,[292] which eminent authors such as *Karsten Schmidt*, *HP Westermann*, and *Rudolf Wiethölter* pointed out with great clarity and unbridled ridicule.[293] In his seminal work on company law, *Herbert Wiedemann* concluded that '[w]ithout further specification [...] the parallelism of control and liability does not even present itself as a legal principle[; ...] the discussion of catchwords leads nowhere.'[294] From a more functional, economic point of view, it is argued today that the ordoliberal school overemphasised the disciplinary effect of the 'inexorable atonement' of poor performance through losses and bankruptcy[295] and did not sufficiently appreciate the investment-promoting effect of limited liability.[296] Moreover, *Eucken*'s other arguments are perceived as ultimately unconvincing. It has been argued, eg, that the nature of liability is not an exogenous factor but rather properly belongs to competition; the risk of default is reflected in the price

---

289 BGH 17 March 1966, II ZR 282/63, 45 BGHZ 204, 205 et seq (in the original German: 'kein zwingender wirtschaftsverfassungsrechtlicher Grundsatz'); see details at Fleischer and Hahn (n 278) 255 et seq.

290 BGH 17 March 1966 (n 289) 206. On the significance of the preliminary considerations of then-presiding justice Robert Fischer, see Fleischer and Hahn (n 278) 273.

291 BGH 17 March 1966 (n 289) 205, 207 (in the original German: 'wie die Rechtsentwicklung der letzten 50–60 Jahre lehrt, ist die Führung eines Handelsgeschäfts mit einer nur beschränkten Haftung durch eine einzelne oder durch mehrere natürliche Personen aus unserem Rechtsleben überhaupt nicht mehr fortzudenken. Man braucht insoweit nur auf die Rechtsfiguren der Einmanngesellschaft und der GmbH und Co. zu verweisen').

292 For a summary, Fleischer and Hahn (n 278) 274 et seq.

293 For criticism, see Karsten Schmidt, *Zur Stellung der oHG im System der Handelsgesellschaften* (Röhrscheid 1972) 111 et seq (in German); Harm Peter Westermann, *Vertragsfreiheit und Typengesetzlichkeit im Recht der Personengesellschaften* (Springer 1970) 273 (in German); Rudolf Wiethölter in Centrale für GmbH (ed.), *Aktuelle Probleme der GmbH & Co. KG* (Dr. Otto Schmidt 1970) 36 (in German).

294 Herbert Wiedemann, *Gesellschaftsrecht*, vol 1 (Beck 1980) 543 et seq (in German), especially 544 (in the original German: 'Der Gleichlauf von Herrschaft und Haftung stellt sich ohne nähere Festlegung [...] noch nicht einmal als Rechtsprinzip dar, [... d]ie Diskussion um Schlagworte führt nicht weiter').

295 Eucken (n 284) 281 (in the original German: 'unerbittliche Sühne').

296 See, for example, Fleischer and Hahn (n 278) 275, with further references.

(ie, in the interest rate).[297] Finally, antitrust law is perceived to be more effective at curbing market power than unlimited liability.[298]

2. Greetings from America: Analysing Limited Liability Through the Lens of Law and Economics

In terms of innovation and maturation, the debate about limited liability experienced its greatest boost in the United States during the twentieth century. Corporations featuring limited shareholder liability took root as business vehicles in the first half of the nineteenth century[299] during a quite rapid phase nowadays attributed, at least in part, to the states having retained jurisdiction over corporate law. The resulting regulatory competition led to a liberalisation of the incorporation process, not to mention limited shareholder liability.[300] As early as 1832, *Joseph K Angell* and *Samuel Ames*, in their *Treatise on the Law of Private Corporations*, stated that

> '[n]o rule of law we believe is better settled, than that, in general, the individual members of a private corporate body are not liable for the debts, either in their person or in their property, beyond the amount of property which they have in the stock.'[301]

a) Limited shareholder liability as a building block of an economically inspired 'theory of corporations'

When analysing the debate about limited liability, one must be aware that the American debate is characterized in general by great scepticism toward traditional formalistic legal doctrine; instead, it leans toward socio-economic analysis and theorisation. This socio-economic bent began as early as the end of the nineteenth century, when the great thinker and federal judge *Oliver Wendell Holmes, Jr* devised his famous prediction theory of law.[302] Later on, in the 1920s and 1930s, legal realism turned to empirical methods for gaining legal insights.[303] One of the most influential books on corporate law of this period – *The Modern Corporation and Private Property* published in 1932 – was written by two economists, *Adolf Berle* and *Gardiner Means*. Admittedly it did not address the subject of

---

[297] Hans Christoph Grigoleit, *Gesellschafterhaftung für interne Einflussnahme im Recht der GmbH* (Beck 2006) 27 (in German); cf also Philipp S Fischinger, *Haftungsbeschränkung im Bürgerlichen Recht* (Mohr Siebeck 2015) 270 et seq (in German)

[298] Fischinger (n 297) 265 et seq.

[299] Bainbridge and Henderson (n 2) 31: 'Within 50 years of the Founding, over 20,000 corporations were formed […] and "America became the world's leader in […] the number of corporations and the sophistication and flexibility of its innovative corporate law".'

[300] Bainbridge and Henderson (n 2) 32.

[301] Joseph Kinnicut Angell and Samuel Ames, *Treatise on the Law of Private Corporations Aggregate* (1832) 349 referencing the case law; see also Bainbridge and Henderson (n 2) 38.

[302] Cf Oliver Wendell Holmes, *The Common Law* (1881).

[303] See, for example, the overview in Bruce A Ackerman, 'Law and the Modern Mind by Jerome Frank' (1974) 103 Daedalus 119–130.

limited shareholder liability. Rather, it focused on the change in 'ownership', as control was transferred to professional managers.[304]

In contrast, *Henry G Manne*, in a 1967 journal article,[305] presented an economically inspired 'theory of the corporation' in which limited shareholder liability played a central role. The 'economic turn' in U.S. law is already clearly discernible in this piece.[306] *Manne* distinguished between publicly traded and close corporations. He saw the former as a capital pool ('function of the corporate form to amass the funds of investors'). This economic function 'logically' led him to the concept of limited shareholder liability, which makes it broadly attractive (especially for wealthy investors) to acquire small shareholdings in companies. In *Manne*'s assessment, the alternative – liability on a pro-rata basis – is undermined by practical enforcement difficulties. *Manne* concluded that '[l]imited liability, of course, obviates all these questions, and directly shifts an easily recognizable risk to the corporation's creditors.'[307] According to *Manne*, it also makes sense to transfer to them the risk of insolvency. What are potentially prohibitively high costs to investors are 'probably relatively low' costs to creditors, and in any case 'the risk of insolvency [is] regularly understood and, where significant, treated as any other cost' by contract creditors. Other mechanisms protected statutory (involuntary) creditors (*Manne* refers employees to bankruptcy law and unemployment benefits). He thought '[t]he solution to the industrial accident problem was simply shifted out of the corporate arena, and its modern counterpart, the auto accident, seems to place no special pressure on the limited liability concept.'[308] Finally, limited liability would significantly increase the liquidity of corporate shares, which in turn would create positive investment incentives. *Manne* applied this analysis to public companies; but when he turns to the close corporation, the issue of limited liability falls away, and his theory draws a blank.

Thirteen years later, *Paul Halpern*, *Michael Trebilcock* and *Stuart Turnbull* of the University of Toronto took up *Manne*'s remarks on the legal and economic justifications of limited liability and added certain arguments on the efficiency of capital markets. Their key point was that without limited liability, the value of a company, and thus the price of its shares, would depend on the financial endowment of its shareholders. Therefore, no uniform price could be achieved, and prices would depend on the respective financial situations of buyers and sellers.[309]

---

[304] See Adolf Augustus Berle and Gardiner C Means, *The Modern Corporation and Private Property* (1932; rev edn, Harcourt 1968) viii. There is no entry on the keyword 'liability' in the index of the work.

[305] Henry G Manne, 'Our Two Corporation Systems: Law and Economics' (1967) 53 Va LRev 259.

[306] Genuinely legal contributions are dismissed by Manne right at the beginning: 'To attribute the success of the modern corporation specifically to law and lawyers is a professional conceit which will not bear scrutiny.'

[307] Manne (n 305) 262.

[308] Manne (n 305) 263 (1967).

[309] Paul Halpern, Michael Trebilcock and Stuart Turnbull, 'An Economic Analysis of Limited Liability in Corporation Law' (1980) 30 UTLJ 117; summarised in Harris (n 80) 659.

b) Limited shareholder liability in the contractarian theory of corporate law

Shortly before *Halpern*, *Trebilcock* and *Turnbull* published their article, the economists *Michael C Jensen* and *William H Meckling*, had shown in their seminal contribution on the 'Theory of the Firm'[310] that *Manne*'s analysis was incomplete. According to them, *Manne* had overlooked that limited liability does not eliminate the risk of the firm defaulting on its debts but merely shifts it (to the creditors), which they justify by the comparatively high costs to shareholders of monitoring the corporation's finances.[311]

(1) The contractarian theory of corporate law

Following *Jensen* and *Meckling*'s theory of the firm, *Frank H Easterbrook*, a federal judge and lecturer at the University of Chicago Law School, and Professor *Daniel R Fischel*, a professor at the same university, developed what became known as the contractarian theory of corporate law.[312] This theory quickly came to dominate corporate law in the U.S. and still does. Its rise completely marginalised the traditional concession theory, which understood incorporation as a government privilege and limited shareholder liability as an associated subsidy (a 'social subsidy').[313] Contractarian theory understands the corporation as a legal construct, that is, as a complex network of contractual relationships between various stakeholders who contribute to the productive processes of the corporation.[314] The corporation is therefore nothing more than a 'nexus of contracts'. In this context, corporate law appears as an enabling law that, much like boilerplate language in a contract, provides default rules that facilitate private ordering in the face of otherwise prohibitively high transaction costs.[315]

---

[310] Michael C Jensen and William H Meckling, 'Theory of the firm: Managerial behavior, agency costs and ownership structure' (1976) 3 J Fin Econ 305 et seq.

[311] Jensen and Meckling (n 310) 331. This is reminiscent of the idea already expressed by AEF Schäffle in his Nationalökonomie of 1861 (which today seems almost modern) that the information costs with regard to the company's financial situation are lower for its creditors than for the shareholders. See AEF Schäffle, *Die Nationalökonomie* (1861) 209 (in German); see also Meyer (n 14) 985.

[312] Frank H Easterbrook and Daniel R Fischel, 'The Corporate Contract' (1989) 89 Colum LRev 1416; for a monograph, see Frank H Easterbrook and Daniel R Fischel, *The Economic Structure of Corporate Law* (Harv UP 1991); see also Thomas S Ulen, 'The Coasean Firm in Law and Economics' (1993) 18 J Corp L 301, 318–328.

[313] See the overview in Bainbridge and Henderson (n 2) 68 et seq, with further references to current attempts to reactivate the concession theory. It serves not least to require companies to behave in a manner compatible with the common good in return for the 'subsidy'.

[314] As summarised in Bainbridge and Henderson (n 2) 54, with further references.

[315] This is the summary in Bainbridge and Henderson (n 2) 54. Easterbrook and Fischel, 'Corporate Contract' (n 312) 1444, say the same thing: 'Corporate codes and existing judicial decisions supply the terms "for free" to every corporation, enabling the venturers to concentrate on matters that are specific to their undertaking.'

(2) *Justification and criticism of limited liability in public corporations*

In contractarian theory, limited shareholder liability, at least in public corporations, appears to be a majoritarian default rule, a hypothetical bargain between creditors and shareholders. Creditors, the argument goes, agree because they have comparative advantages over rationally apathetic shareholders in monitoring the corporation's activities, for which reason they are believed to be the 'cheapest cost avoider of monitoring services'.[316] However, this assumes that negotiations between creditors and shareholders lead to socially desirable outcomes because there are no significant externalities to third parties.

With a view to statutory creditors, particularly tort creditors, this argument in favour of limited liability did not go unchallenged for long. In their article 'Toward Unlimited Liability for Corporate Torts' from the early 1990s, professors *Henry Hansmann* (Yale Law School) and *Reinier Kraakman* (Harvard Law School) argued for pro-rata shareholder liability for torts of the corporation in order to force them to internalise the risks of mass torts.[317] Objections were swift: Some scholars pointed -to the sometimes prohibitively high costs of enforcing such a liability regime (*Cooper Alexander*, *Grundfest*).[318] *Mark R Manning*, pointed out that unlimited liability would reduce the company's equity cushion, which he deems to be the superior mechanism for compensating corporate creditors.[319] Others criticised *Hansmann* and *Kraakman* for not sufficiently explaining why the nexus-of-contracts theory meant that shareholders should be liable for mass torts. Or, to put it another way, 'little would be gained by eliminating limited liability. The core argument for doing so must be that shareholders monitoring managers will reduce the risk of mass torts.'[320]

(3) *Justification and criticism of limited liability in the close corporation*

The close corporation remains as sore a point for contractarians as it was for *Manne*, because the shareholders of a close corporation typically control the business, making them directly involved in decisions that can lead to risks being externalised.[321] Moreover, the cost to creditors of enforcing liability against the (usually few) shareholders of a close corporation is relatively low.[322] In spite of these

[316] See the details in Bainbridge and Henderson (n 2) 56 et seq, with further references.

[317] Henry Hansmann and Reinier Kraakman, 'Toward Unlimited Shareholder Liability for Corporate Torts' (1991) 100 Yale LJ 1879.

[318] Janet Cooper Alexander, 'Unlimited Shareholder Liability through a Procedural Lens' (1992) 106 Harv L Rev 387; Joseph A Grundfest, 'The Limited Future of Unlimited Liability: A Capital Markets Perspective' (1992) 102 Yale LJ 387; summarising Bainbridge and Henderson (n 2) 71 et seq.

[319] Mark R Manning, 'There's a Change in the Status Quo: Corporate Veil Piercing in Ohio after *Dombroski v. WellPoint*' (2010) 5 Entrepreneurial Bus LJ 315, 325; see also Bainbridge and Henderson (n 2) 72.

[320] Bainbridge and Henderson (n 2) 73 et seq, 75.

[321] Bainbridge and Henderson (n 2) 77 et seq, with further references. This objection is reminiscent of the criticism of the GmbHG in Wieland, see n 240 above.

[322] Bainbridge and Henderson (n 2) 78.

issues, Yale Law School professor *Ian Ayres* does not question limited liability per se but looks at exceptional rules that result in unlimited liability (particularly veil piercing in cases of deficient capitalisation), understanding them to be default penalties intended to foster negotiation.[323] *Bainbridge* and *Henderson*, on the other hand, interpret the principle of limited liability in close corporations itself as a penalty default rule, and consider the incentive for genuine negotiations between shareholders and contract creditors to be sufficiently high in this scenario.[324]

The contractarian theory of limited liability seems even less convincing vis-à-vis statutory and, especially, tort creditors. Here, its proponents either resort to veil-piercing[325] or to the idea that statutory creditors are collaterally protected by the monitoring of contractual creditors.[326]

In general, veil-piercing appears to the contractarian as a legal tool that, as an exception to the rule, ignores the corporate entity in order to prevent otherwise-occurring welfare losses. However, *Bainbridge* and *Henderson* argue that the doctrine as applied in practice by the courts is not equal to the task.[327]

3. The Current Debate in the Shadow of the Political Zeitgeist

The debate over limited liability has never completely abated in Germany. The debate sparked in the U.S. by *Hansmann* and *Kraakman* quickly spread to Germany via an article by Harvard Law professor *Detlev Vagts*.[328] *Justus Meyer* also built on their critique in his *Haftungsbeschränkung im Recht der Handelsgesellschaften*, published in 2000,[329] which remains the standard reference on the subject and is characterised by a critical tone. *Meyer* suggests a 'much more general restriction' of limited liability for entrepreneurial shareholders[330],[331] and proposes

---

[323] Ian Ayres, 'Making a Difference: The Contractual Contributions of Easterbrook and Fischel (reviewing The Economic Structure of Corporate Law by Frank H. Easterbrook, Daniel R. Fischel)' (1992) 59 U Chi L Rev 1391, 1398–1399; fundamentally, on the concept of penalty default rules, Ian Ayres and Robert Gertner, 'Filling Gaps in Incomplete Contracts: An Economic Theory of Default Rules' (19889) 99 Yale LJ 87; Bainbridge and Henderson's assumption (n 2) 80 with fn 118, that Ayres interprets the principle of limited liability as a penalty default rule, seems to be based on a misunderstanding.

[324] Bainbridge and Henderson (n 2) 80 et seq with fn 118.

[325] See Easterbrook and Fischel, 'Economic Structure' (n 312) 55 et seq, 58 et seq; see also Bainbridge and Henderson (n 2) 83.

[326] Bainbridge and Henderson (n 2) 83.

[327] Bainbridge and Henderson (n 2) 302 et seq. On the German debate on recourse in control situations (*Abhängigkeit*) – not examined in detail here – one need only refer to Meyer (n 14) 663 et seq (in German); Georg Bitter, *Konzernrechtliche Durchgriffshaftung bei Personengesellschaften* (Heymann 1999) (in German).

[328] Detlev Vagts, 'Wohin mit der beschränkten Haftung der Aktionäre? Neue Strömungen im amerikanischen Gesellschaftsrecht' (1994) 23 ZGR 227 et seq (in German).

[329] Meyer (n 14) 2–5.

[330] He includes the parent company of a corporate group into his considerations. Limited liability in the corporate group is, however, not dealt with in this article. See I.1. above.

[331] Meyer (n 14) 1117 (in the original German: 'sehr viel weitergehende allgemeine Einschränkung geboten').

a rule that permits entrepreneurial shareholders to be ordered to make additional payments in the event of corporate insolvency.[332]

a) Anti-capitalist sentiments after the financial crisis of 2007

In the aftermath of the 2007 financial crisis, occasional scepticism (such as from *Justus Meyer*) mounted into a veritable chorus – not least due to growing anti-capitalist sentiment at large but also among legal scholars – and has been further fuelled by the shadow of climate change. *Thomas Piketty*'s 2013 work *Le Capital au XXI siècle* particularly appealed to this zeitgeist in academia, the title alone an unmistakable reference to *Karl Marx*. However, the concept of limited liability did not figure significantly in his argument that comparatively fast growth in capital gains had resulted in greater material inequality.[333] In 2019, *Katharina Pistor*, a German-educated law professor at Columbia Law School, analysed the significance of law in relation to undesirable developments in the capitalist system. Her treatise *The Code of Capital – How the Law Creates Wealth and Inequality* features limited shareholder liability ('loss shifting') alongside entity shielding as minions of the great villain of 'capitalism'.[334] Nor could some in Germany resist referring to *Marx*: *Chris Thomale*, law professor at the University of Vienna, titled his 2017 postdoctoral thesis *Kapital und Verantwortung*. A précis of his work, unfortunately not yet published, develops a fundamental critique of limited shareholder liability:

> 'All in all, the institutional limitation of liability [...] proves unfounded in very essential respects. The principle of the separate entity, whether in terms of historical development of the legal principle or legal positivism, is unable to support it, and the nexus-of-contracts doctrine upon critical analysis not only provides no basis for it but, quite the opposite, formulates the central objection to it: in economic terms, limited shareholder liability is a negative externality, a contract at the expense of third parties. [...] Put as a social critique: in the corporation, capital evades its responsibility to society as a fund for compensating those aggrieved by companies whose profits it wants to privatise while socialising the losses.'[335]

With this verdict, *Thomale* sees himself in the tradition of *Adam Smith*, *Walter Eucken*, and the duo of *Henry Hansmann* and *Reinier Kraakman*. The 'socio-criti-

---

[332] Meyer (n 14) 1118 et seq.

[333] Cf Thomas Piketty, *Capital in the Twenty-First Century* (Harv UP 2014) 203 (briefly referencing the concept).

[334] See Pistor (n 7) 54 et seq, 59 et seq.

[335] Thomale (n 3) 687 (in the original German: 'In der Summe erweist sich die IH [scil. institutionelle Haftungsbeschränkung] als in ganz wesentlicher Hinsicht unfundiert. Das Trennungsprinzip kann sie weder in dogmengeschichtlicher noch in rechtspositivistischer Hinsicht stützen, und die Nexus-of-contracts-Lehre liefert ihr bei kritischer Analyse nicht nur keine Grundlage, sondern formuliert umgekehrt den zentralen Einwand gegen sie: Die IH ist, ökonomisch gesprochen eine negative Externalität, ein Vertrag zu Lasten Dritter. [...] Sozialkritisch gewendet: In der Kapitalgesellschaft entzieht sich das Kapital seiner gesamtgesellschaftlichen Verantwortung als Haftungsmasse für die Geschädigten derjenigen Unternehmen, deren Gewinne es privatisieren, deren Verluste es jedoch sozialisieren will').

cal' impetus expressed here is also evident in *Andreas Conow*'s 2015 doctoral thesis, which reads in part like a political manifesto. He even expresses constitutional doubts about § 5(1) of the GmbH Act, and calls for § 13(2) of the GmbH Act to be supplemented by additional creditor protections.[336] In his postdoctoral thesis on limitation of liability in civil law (published the same year), *Philipp Fischinger* adopts a completely different tone while also advocating for a tighter regime of shareholder liability. He states – completely in line with the prevailing view in business law – that

'Contrary to the criticism particularly of the [ordoliberal] Freiburg School, the limitation of liability to the GmbH's assets is in principle legitimate in terms of legal policy and doctrine as well as constitutional law, because it strengthens, in a macroeconomic sense – and thus in line with the common good – entrepreneurial initiative and willingness to invest […] by promising to protect the shareholders' private assets. However, this only holds as long as effective creditor protections are guaranteed by the legislature and the judiciary.'[337]

Fischinger considers the creditor protection regime of the GmbH to be deficient and makes suggestions for its improvement, including mandatory insurance for the GmbH, a tightening of § 64 of the GmbH Act, or the turnover-dependent obligation to convert the GmbH into a stock corporation.[338]

b) Lacunas in the standard narrative

The prevailing narrative of limited shareholder liability actually has serious lacunas, particularly for liability in close corporations. The debate over the revised GmbH Act as well as criticism of the contractarian theory of corporate law have clearly identified weak points. The factual observation that 'the wish and the reality of limited liability' often diverge, given regular demands from creditors that shareholders provide personal guarantees,[339] could be interpreted in line with the penalty default theory.[340]

In regard both to close and public corporations, however, the traditional narrative that limited liability is what drove capital markets and industrialisation has recently been called into question. As *Justus Meyer* already pointed out, 'for the period of the Bubble Act [1720–1825], it can be concluded that England's indus-

---

[336] Conow (n 3); see the review by Schmolke (2016) 180 ZHR 136 et seq.

[337] Fischinger (n 297) 768 et seq (in the original German: 'Die mit einer GmbH verbundene Haftungsbeschränkung auf das Gesellschaftsvermögen ist entgegen der Kritik vor allem der Freiburger Schule im Grundsatz sowohl rechtspolitisch und -dogmatisch legitim wie verfassungskonform, weil sie im volkswirtschaftlichen – und damit Allgemeinwohl- – Interesse durch das „Versprechen" einer Verschonung des Privatvermögens die Unternehmerinitiative und Investitionsbereitschaft samt der damit verbundenen Vorteile zu stärken verspricht. Das kann allerdings nur gelten, solange durch Gesetzgeber und Rechtsprechung ein effektiver Gläubigerschutz gewährleistet wird').

[338] Fischinger (n 297) 769 et seq.

[339] See Fleischer (n 238) 'Einleitung' para 20 (in the original German: 'Wunsch und Wirklichkeit der Haftungsbeschränkung').

[340] See IV.2.b) in n 324.

trial development – the most advanced in the world – was not driven by business entities with limited liability'.[341] Furthermore, given lively trading in the shares of the big trading companies on English and Dutch exchanges in the sixteenth century, it cannot be said with certainty that the concept of limited liability was absolutely necessary to a functioning stock market.[342] Legal historian *Ron Harris* has recently made a similar point.[343]

Finally, recent legal (and factual) changes may require adjustment of the narrative that limited liability is justified by the comparative cost advantages of contractual creditors over shareholders when it comes to monitoring the company's finances.[344] From a legal perspective, for example, we have seen reforms in the wake of the financial crisis that call for shareholder engagement, ie, for the return of the shareholder who for too long was an 'absentee landlord'. If at least some shareholders are called upon to monitor the company's activities, it is likely to shift the cost calculus. Given an increasingly digitised business world, the same may be true in regard to the enforcement costs of personal (unlimited) shareholder liability, which may decrease significantly from applications of digital technology.

V. Bottom Line: Analytical Achievements and Ongoing Discourse

The history of the debate outlined in this contribution shows vigorous discussion of the concept of limited liability since the end of the eighteenth century. For a long time, by looking for 'genetic links' between ancient business arrangements and modern business entities, legal scholars tried to argue for limited liability based on ancient Roman law. From a legal policy perspective, the early debate was characterised by regulatory competition between European jurisdictions, and therefore also by comparative law. The breakthrough of limited liability in the nineteenth century, both in public and in close corporations, was mostly driven by liberal-minded politicians or commercial interests. At least in England, theoretical arguments were mostly provided by (proto-)economists. In Germany, jurisprudence at this time was considerably embroiled in doctrinal controversies that ultimately led nowhere. But by the end of the nineteenth century, the German debate over the then-novel GmbH was at the cutting edge of contemporary jurisprudence.

By the twentieth century, even German legal scholars had come to realise there was nothing to be gained from trying to justify limited liability by establishing

---

[341] Meyer (n 14) 239 (in the original German: 'Für die Zeit des Bubble Act ergibt sich damit insgesamt, daß die – weltweit am weitesten fortgeschrittene – industrielle Entwicklung Englands nicht von haftungsbeschränkenden Rechtsformen getragen war').

[342] Meyer (n 14) 205, 208. See II.2.b) above.

[343] Harris (n 80) 659 et seq, 661.

[344] See II.3. above.

a 'genetic link' to business arrangements of the distant past. *Bernhard Großfeld* described this succinctly in his post-doctoral thesis, published in 1968:

'[l]imited liability does not have the historical significance often attributed to it in legal discussions. It is not an expression of ancient natural necessity, but rather the result of recent, positive, purposive decision-making.'[345]

Unlike German jurisprudence in the twentieth century, U.S. jurisprudence radically broke with traditional legal doctrine and focused instead on socio-economic arguments and concepts as the theoretical basis for legal institutions. For company law in general, and on limited liability in particular, economists as well as lawyers with backgrounds in economics still set the tone. Since the 1980s and -90s, the contractarian theory of corporate law (also known as the nexus-of-contracts theory) is dominant among corporate law scholars. This theory provides a mathematically modellable framework to justify limited shareholder liability, using social welfare maximisation as its normative standard to make cost-benefit comparisons that are, in principle, empirically verifiable. The analytical and theoretical boost to academic debate from this framework has attracted worldwide attention from legal scholars today. This historical review shows that arguments similar to those of today's contractarians were already being exchanged in the nineteenth century, but without an elaborate conceptual framework to tie them together. Regardless of the achievements of contractarian theory in corporate law, it, too, has obvious weaknesses when it comes to justifying limited liability in close corporations. Ultimately, the proponents of limited liability trust that the incentives to entrepreneurial activity result in welfare gains that exceed the costs to creditors.

Abandoning the idea that modern law may be explained through 'genetic links' to the past has the advantage of freeing us from the doctrinal idiosyncrasies of individual jurisdictions. This helps to focus the debate on substantive arguments and also facilitates international exchange. However, if we concede that limited shareholder liability is the 'result of positive purposive decision-making', then, as *Bainbridge* and *Henderson* put it,

'limited liability is not inherent to the corporate form, but rather depends upon the ends to which that form is applied. At times, whether in Ancient Rome or Modern America, that application demands the isolation of liabilities in the corporate entity, while at other times, the concept of shareholder liability for a corporation's creditors is a more sensible one.'[346]

However, 'what the times demand' is a highly political question that resurfaces time and again. Therefore, even though the forces of international regulatory competition are strongly in favour of limited shareholder liability, an end to the debate is not in sight.

---

[345] Großfeld (n 10) 105 (in the original German: 'Die beschränkte Haftung hat daher historisch nicht die Bedeutung, die ihr in der juristischen Diskussion oft beigemessen wird. Sie ist nicht Ausdruck uralter Naturnotwendigkeit, sondern Ergebnis junger, positiver Zwecksatzung').

[346] Bainbridge and Henderson (n 2) 20.

Director Liability in Stock Corporation Law

*Dörte Poelzig**

I. Introduction

The liability of directors of stock corporations is a favourite issue in recent German corporate law literature. The number of monographs, commentaries and papers on the topic has grown to be unmanageable. But this was not always the case. The increased relevance is evident from a comparison of older and newer commentaries on § 93 of the German Stock Corporation Act (the 'AktG'): whereas the 50-year-old commentary by *Schilling*[1] contains 75 recitals and few references, the current edition by Hopt and Roth has grown to more than 700 recitals and contains a bibliography of more than 14 pages.[2] Other commentaries are similar. *Jens Koch*'s manual, the current edition of which was released this year,[3] is five times the size of the 1st edition by *Hüffer* from 1993. The number of monographs being published on director liability has exploded since the mid-1990s.

* All translations into English are by the author.

[1] Wolfgang Schilling, in Carl H Barz and others (eds), *Aktiengesetz. Großkommentar* (3rd edn, De Gruyter 1971/1973) § 93.

[2] Klaus J Hopt and Markus Roth, in Heribert Hirte, Peter O Mülbert and Markus Roth (eds), *Aktiengesetz. Großkommentar*, vol 4/2 (5th edn, De Gruyter 2015) § 93.

[3] Jens Koch, *Aktiengesetz* (17th edn, CH Beck 2023) § 93.

The academic debate over director liability has also had an impressive run. Disputed is not whether directors may be held liable but how, under what circumstances, and for how much. That directors must be civilly liable for breaches of duty was recognised even before the principle was codified; however, then as now, there is a constant struggle over the individual prerequisites for and the legal consequences of director's liability. The discussion moves back and forth like a pendulum between expanding and enforcing liability on one hand and limiting liability on the other. But where do the decisive impulses come from, and which voices swing the debate about the right form of director liability?

In this paper, I first take a brief look at the history of directors' liability (II.). Then I will trace the course of the debate and will analyse the voices and methods in their approach to directors' liability (III.). Finally, I will discuss some current impulses in the debate (IV.).

II. History of Director Liability

1. Development of the Law

a) From Code de Commerce to ADHGB and AktG

The history of the law on director's liability started in 1807 with the Code de Commerce, which initially referred to the principle of contract law by which contractors were held liable for breaches of duty. The first specific regulation on director's liability was found in the German General Commercial Code (the 'ADHGB') of 1861. Article 241(2) of this code provided for joint and several liability of the board members for breaches of duty. With the Zweite Aktienrechtsnovelle of 1884 the law on director's liability became more restrictive, authorising minority shareholders to compel the corporation to enforce claims against directors. Moreover, creditors received the right to claim damages against directors in specific cases. The legislator argued that stricter liability was necessary because of the 'unpleasant fraud that had arisen in the organisation, administration and business operations of joint-stock companies'.[4]

After the First World War, the world economic crisis of 1929–1931 sent the discussion of stock corporation law generally in a new direction. Spectacular scandals in stocks and corporate collapses had also sharpened the focus on the responsibilities of directors. To restore public confidence in stock corporations, an emergency ordinance (a 'Notverordnung') was issued to strengthen the rights of minority shareholders to enforce claims for damages against the directors.

This *Notverordnung* provided no more than temporary calm. Lasting reform had to wait until 1937. Directors were given a much more influential role in § 84 of the AktG: an 'elevated position' that was supposed to correspond to 'increased

[4] 'Gutachten des Reichs-Oberhandelsgerichts (1877)', printed in Werner Schubert and Peter Hommelhoff, *Hundert Jahre modernes Aktienrecht* (ZGR Special Issue 4, De Gruyter 1985) 157, 159.

responsibility'.[5] Expanded above all was the directors' liability towards creditors. At the same time, however, the legislator codified the principle of fault on the justification that holding a director liable for the success of management without regard to fault would risk that 'directors' willingness to assume responsibility would be considerably reduced and [they] would be deprived of any courage to act'.[6] In addition, the wording of the statute included for the first time a shifting of the burden of proof to establish a breach of the duty of care in § 84(2)2 of the AktG of 1937 (today § 93(2)2 of the AktG). However, since it had already been consistently established in the case law that directors bear the burden of proof to establish that they observed their duty of care, the effect of this codification was clarifying only. This burden-shifting was justified on the presumption that the director stood in greater proximity to and could be held accountable for the evidence. That this burden-shifting provision ultimately found its way into the 1937 reform of the AktG can probably be attributed to a compromise between the introduction of liability for the corporation's success on the one hand and the retention of liability for fault on the other; the codification thus presented itself as the right balance. This regulation on directors' liability pursuant to sec 84 of the AktG of 1937 was adopted largely unchanged into sec 93 of the AktG.

b) Recent Reforms

This rule on the liability of directors remained untouched for several years until 1998, when enforcement of director liability by minority shareholders was further facilitated. In 2004, the legislator presented a draft act called the 'Capital Market Information Liability Act'.[7] Although it ultimately failed, this proposal was the legislator's reaction to mismanagement and corporate collapses on the capital market at the turn of the millennium. It was based on preliminary work in the law literature as well as on the fundamental German legal policy platform of the Deutscher Juristentag of 2002.[8] To improve investor protections, it was envisaged to hold external directors liable to investors for disseminating false information on the capital market. However, in view of considerable criticism from practitioners, especially lawyers,[9] this particular piece of legislation was abandoned.

[5] Peter Hommelhoff, 'Eigenkontrolle statt Staatskontrolle' in Schubert and Hommelhoff (n 4) 71, 73.

[6] *Amtliche Begründung zu § 84 AktG 1937* (official explanatory statement), printed in Friedrich Klausing, *Gesetz über Aktiengesellschaft und Kommanditgesellschaften auf Aktien* (Heymann 1937) 71.

[7] *Federal Ministry of Finance*, 'Diskussionsentwurf eines Gesetzes zur Verbesserung der Haftung für falsche Kapitalmarktinformationen (Kapitalmarktinformationshaftungsgesetz – KapInHaG)' [2004] NZG 1042.

[8] Holger Fleischer, 'Empfiehlt es sich, im Interesse des Anlegerschutzes und zur Förderung des Finanzplatzes Deutschland das Kapitalmarkt- und Börsenrecht neu zu regeln? Gutachten F' in *Gutachten zum 64. DJT 2002* (CH Beck 2002) F 101ff.

[9] See above all Handelsrechtsausschuss des DAV, 'Zum Gesetz über die Haftung für fehlende Kapitalmarktinformationen' [2004] NZG 1099; Johannes Semler and Stephan Gittermann,

One year later, in 2005, the business judgment rule was codified after the German Federal Court of Justice (the 'BGH') had recognised it a few years earlier. The business judgment rule insulates directors from liability for business decisions if they acted on an informed basis, in good faith, and in the honest belief that the action was in the best interest of the company. At the same time – as a counterweight to the safe harbour of the business judgment rule and in view of the corporate scandals on the capital markets at turn of the millennium – the legislator also adopted a derivative shareholder action in an attempt to bolster the enforcement of director liability. And in 2009, the financial crisis finally also gave rise to stricter rules on director liability as mandatory deductibles were enacted and the limitation period for claiming director liability was extended. All in all, however, German law on director's liability itself has remained exceptionally stable for the well over 100 years since its codification in the ADHGB (and later the AktG). It can be said that the legislator has been prompted to take action and amend laws mainly by scandals and crises.

2. *Practical Significance*

Although the law on director liability is relatively old, it was considered to be a dead letter until the mid-1990s.[10] This was in no small part because the large German stock corporations had been closely intertwined with one another since the end of the nineteenth century in the so-called 'Deutschland AG', involving members of the executive board of one corporation often serving on the supervisory boards of other corporations and vice versa.[11] Because the German two-tier system makes the supervisory board responsible for supervising the management board and thus for claiming damages against the management board on behalf of the corporation, this structure hindered an effective enforcement of director liability.[12]

'Persönliche Haftung der Organmitglieder für Fehlinformationen des Kapitalmarktes – Zeigt das KapInHaG den richtigen Weg?' [2004] NZG 1081; Eckart Sünner, 'Ungereimtheiten des Entwurfs eines Kapitalmarktinformationshaftungsgesetzes' [2004] DB 2460.

[10] Herbert Wiedemann, *Gesellschaftsrecht*, vol I (Beck 1980) § 11 III 2 a, p 624. See also Michael Adams, 'Stellungnahme zur Aktienrechtsreform 1997' (1997) 8 AG Special Issue 9, 10; Theodor Baums, *Empfiehlt sich eine Neuregelung des aktienrechtlichen Anfechtungs- und Organhaftungsrechts, insbesondere der Klagemöglichkeiten von Aktionären? Gutachten F für den 63. DJT* (CH Beck 2000) F 246ff; Marcus Lutter, 'BGH, 23.6.1997 – II ZR 132/93. Kapitalerhöhung unter Ausschluß des Bezugsrechts der Aktionäre' [1998] JZ 50, 52.

[11] See, eg, Bernhard Schwetzler and Marco O Sperling, 'Die Entflechtung der Deutschland AG' [2008] AG R 468ff; see also Michael Adams, 'Die Usurpation von Aktionärsbefugnissen mittels Ringverflechtung in der Deutschland-AG' [1994] AG 148ff; Heinz-Dieter Assmann, in Klaus J Hopt and Herbert Wiedemann (eds), Aktiengesetz Großkommentar, vol 1 (4th edn, De Gruyter 2004) Einl. para 322, 137; Marcus Lutter, 'Defizite für eine effiziente Aufsichtsratstätigkeit und gesetzliche Möglichkeiten der Verbesserung' (1995) 159 ZHR 287, 301.

[12] Eberhard Vetter, 'Der Aufsichtsrat – Spagat zwischen gesetzlichen Vorgaben und wachsenden Herausforderungen' in Holger Fleischer and others (eds), *50 Jahre Aktiengesetz* (De Gruyter 2016) 105.

The literature ascribed to the supervisory board an 'inhibition to bite' (*Beißhemmung*) when it came to enforcing director liability.[13]

This changed starting in the early 1990s. Mainly due to pressure from the capital markets, an unbundling of the Deutschland AG took place such that institutional investors have replaced large companies as the owners of other companies; these investors hold the majority of the share capital in many large companies and are interested in maximum returns on their investments.[14] In addition, more than half the shares in Germany's largest listed companies have since been in the hands of foreign investors. The collapse in capital markets at the turn of the millennium, the financial crisis of 2008, and several instances of corporate scandals have led to a change in public awareness.[15] The internet and social media have also done their part to widely expose misconduct by directors. And last but not least, the recognition of D&O insurance has been an important reason for the increased practical importance of the topic of director liability. D&O insurance remained unusual until the mid-1990s but is now common. Yet coverage creates liability, as the saying goes, and much litigation is conducted that would not take place without such insurance; from 2002–2020, almost 50 cases received media coverage.[16]

III. Course of the Debate

1. Beginnings

The actual beginning of the latest debate over director liability dates to 1997 with a landmark BGH decision known as *ARAG/Garmenbeck*. In it, the court expressly established, for the first time, a duty of the supervisory board to sue members of the executive board for damages on behalf of the company.[17] The BGH thereby thrust director liability not only into the corporate consciousness but also, and

---

[13] Peter Ulmer, 'Strikte aktienrechtliche Organhaftung und D&O-Versicherung – zwei getrennte Welten?' in Andreas Heldrich and others (eds), *Festschrift für Claus-Wilhelm Canaris*, vol 2 (CH Beck 2007) 451; similarly: Martin Peltzer, 'Die Haftung des Aufsichtsrats bei Verletzung der Überwachungspflicht' [1981] WM 346, 348f: 'Bisssperre'.

[14] Christian Andres, André Betzer and Inga van den Bongard, 'Das Ende der Deutschland AG' (2011) 44 Kredit und Kapital 185ff.

[15] For details see Gregor Bachmann, *Reform der Organhaftung? Materielles Haftungsrecht und seine Durchsetzung in privaten und öffentlichen Unternehmen. Gutachten E zum 70. DJT* (CH Beck 2014) E 19; Klaus J Hopt, 'Die Verantwortlichkeit von Vorstand und Aufsichtsrat: Grundsatz und Praxisprobleme – unter besonderer Berücksichtigung der Banken' [2013] ZIP 1793ff; Hopt and Roth (n 2) 39ff; Koch (n 3) fn 1; Walter G Paefgen, 'Organhaftung: Bestandsaufnahme und Zukunftsperspektiven: ein kritischer Werkstattbericht vor dem Hintergrund der Beratungen des 70. Deutschen Juristentages 2014' [2014] AG 554ff

[16] Oliver Lange, *D&O-Versicherung und Managerhaftung* (2nd edn, CH Beck 2022) Rec. 831ff.

[17] BGH 21 April 1997, II ZR 175/95, 135 BGHZ 244.

above all, into the academic spotlight. Since then, the number of publications and monographs on director liability has exploded.[18]

2. The Pendulum Between Liability Extension and Limitation

The foregoing description of the history of director liability has already shown a debate characterised by a constant struggle between expansion and limitation. Legislators – especially in the aftermath of crises and scandals – have raised the level of liability, only to have restrictions follow hot on the heels of reform (or at least be demanded by moderating voices). This swaying and oscillation back and forth between the poles of expanding and limiting liability is also evident in the academic debate. It is remarkable that many of the same issues were already discussed during the early stages of the law on director liability at the end of the nineteenth century.

a) Limiting liability based on director discretion

After the BGH set the pendulum swinging in the direction of aggravating liability by establishing the supervisory board's right to sue for damages, however, the discussion in the literature initially took the opposite turn and was devoted to elaborating the discretionary powers of management in business decisions. But while the debate over the business judgment rule may not have begun until 1997 with the BGH's decision in *ARAG/Garmenbeck*, the need to distinguish breaches of the duty of care from mere failures and errors had in fact been recognised very early on, and with it the existence of discretion on the part of the directors. As early as the end of the nineteenth century, the legislator had realised that directors, who represent the company in an executive capacity, should not be held liable for any commercial failure within their responsibility. The fact that the business judgment rule was not explicitly recognised until more than 100 years later by the BGH in *ARAG/Garmenbeck* and was even later to be codified was due in no small part to work in the literature on comparative law. In the Festschrift for Mestmäcker, *Klaus Hopt* set forth the prerequisites and consequences of discretion in making business decisions on the basis of the business judgment rule in the United States.[19] The attention paid in the academic literature to the BGH's recognition of director discretion following the *ARAG/Garmenbeck* decision verged on the explosive, which is surprising, because the court had merely repeated what had already been said a long time before, and indeed in quite similar terms.[20]

---

[18] Holger Fleischer, 'Gesellschaftsrecht im Spiegel seiner Habilitationsschriften' (2022) 51 ZGR 191, 202.

[19] Klaus J Hopt, 'Die Haftung von Vorstand und Aufsichtsrat – Zugleich ein Beitrag zur corporate governance-Debatte' in Ulrich Immenga (ed), *Festschrift für Ernst-Joachim Mestmäcker* (Nomos 1996) 919ff.

[20] Jens Koch, '§ 14 – ARAG/Garmenbeck. AG – Geltendmachung von Schadensersatzansprüchen gegen den Vorstand' in Holger Fleischer and Jan Thiessen (eds), *Gesellschaftsrechts-Geschichten* (Mohr Siebeck 2018) 477.

Scholars also played a central role in the subsequent 2005 codification of the business judgment rule. *Peter Ulmer* in particular asked the legislator to codify it and submitted an initial proposal.[21] After the Deutscher Juristentag of 2000 (in Leipzig) endorsed his proposal, in 2005 the legislator took it up and, indeed, codified the business judgment rule. Despite warnings in the literature not to prematurely interrupt the dialogue between scholars and courts, the codification of the business judgment rule is today widely considered successful.[22] Evidence of this is that there have been only very few requests for changes. The debate over the business judgment rule is thus an impressive example of the interplay of scholars, courts and the legislator.

b) Extension of liability

After the court in *ARAG/Garmenbeck* recognised a safe harbour for directors in the business judgment rule, the pendulum of the debate swung back in the direction of stricter liability.

(1) Stricter enforcement

Now began an intensive discussion about bolstering the enforcement of director liability based on the belief that director liability, while strict, was too rarely pursued. Leaving the enforcement of director liability solely in the hands of the supervisory board appeared to be insufficient because typically no one, certainly not the supervisory board, could be expected to file a lawsuit if it would expose their own misconduct. Therefore, there arose a debate over whether to enhance enforcement by strengthening shareholder rights of action. Back in 1884, the legislator deliberately refrained from codifying shareholder rights of action, fearing that

> 'complete anarchy would endanger the stability of the organisation [and] the activity of the corporate bodies and encourage blackmail of all kinds [and] paralyse the energy and responsibility of the executive board and the supervisory board'.[23]

However, after the literature began to clamour loudly for more effective enforcement of director liability, shareholder derivative actions were codified in § 148 of the AktG in 2005. The enactment was based on preparatory work in the legal

---

[21] Peter Ulmer, 'Die Aktionärsklage als Instrument zur Kontrolle des Vorstands- und Aufsichtsratshandelns. Vor dem Hintergrund der US-Erfahrungen mit der shareholders' derivative action' (1999) 163 ZHR 290, 299

[22] Gregor Bachmann, 'Reformbedarf bei der Business Judgement Rule?' (2013) 177 ZHR 1; Holger Fleischer, in Stilz/Veil (eds) *beck.online Großkommentar* (CH Beck 2nd ed 2022) § 93 AktG, para 86; Peter Hemeling, 'Organisationspflichten des Vorstands zwischen Rechtspflicht und Opportunität' (2011) 175 ZHR 368, 379ff; Hans-Christoph Ihrig and Carsten Schäfer, *Rechte und Pflichten des Vorstands* (Schmidt 2014) para 1528.

[23] Allgemeine Begründung ('General Reasoning') printed in Schubert and Hommelhoff (n 4) 404, 469.

literature, including in comparative law examining derivative suits in the U.S.[24] And this codification again was accompanied by dire predictions of non-meritorious strike suits, 'liability tourism', and cries of 'opening Pandora's box'[25] similar to those in the early stages of the ADHGB. However, contrary to these expectations the shareholder derivative action has turned out to be effectively meaningless and is thus still merely 'law on the books'.[26] Therefore, it is not surprising that after the financial crisis, more effective enforcement and especially more robust shareholder actions were again called for. Despite intensive debate over this issue at the Deutsche Juristentag conferences of 2010 and 2014, each specific proposal to enhance shareholder actions failed. The issue of effective enforcement of director liability has been described as an 'unsolvable task'[27] or a 'squaring of the circle'.[28]

(2) External liability

In addition to making enforcement more effective, there has also been discussion about expanding director liability towards third parties. Director liability vis-à-vis investors came into focus with the scandals on the German capital market at the turn of the millennium, in which large numbers of investors were harmed by erroneous promises. There were calls for (among other things) holding directors liable to investors for disseminating false information on the capital market. Corresponding demands, expressed both in the literature and at the 64th Deutscher Juristentag in 2002, which were based on an expert opinion by *Holger Fleischer*[29] and supported by a narrow majority,[30] resulted in the (ultimately doomed) Capital Market Information Liability Act (see above at a)). Again, this discussion was not entirely new; even under the ADHGB, holding executive bodies liable to third parties was controversial. While the courts were regularly holding defendants externally liable to third parties in view of the broadly worded statutory provision in Art 241(2) of the ADHGB of 1861, the legislator restricted third party

---

[24] For a closer examination see Klaus Ulrich Schmolke, 'Die Aktionärsklage nach § 148 AktG' (2011) 40 ZGR 398, 411; Mathias M Siems, 'Welche Auswirkung hat das neue Verfolgungsrecht der Aktionärsminderheit?' (2005) 104 ZVglRWiss 376, 378; *Ulmer*, supra note 21, 290ff.

[25] Ulrich Seibert, 'Berufsopponenten – Anfechtungsklage – Freigabeverfahren – Haftungsklage. Das UMAG, eine Rechtsfolgenanalyse' [2007] NZG 841 (on sounding the alarm).

[26] Schmolke (n 24) 399.

[27] Bachmann (n 15) E78.

[28] Martin Peltzer, 'Das Zulassungsverfahren nach § 148 AktG wird von der Praxis nicht angenommen! Warum? Was nun?' in Ulrich Burgard and others (eds), Festschrift für Uwe H. Schneider (De Gruyter 2011) 964; Karsten Schmidt, 'Verfolgungspflichten, Verfolgungsrechte und Aktionärsklagen: Ist die Quadratur des Zirkels näher gerückt? Gedanken zur Reform der §§ 147–149 der AktG vor dem Hintergrund der Juristentagsdiskussion des Jahres 2000' [2005] NZG 796.

[29] Fleischer (n 8).

[30] Cf Beschluss 1. 11 in: Verhandlungen des vierundsechzigsten DJT, vol 2/1 (CH Beck 2002) P 88 (27 Yes-Votes and 26 No-Votes).

liability with the second major revision (the 'Zweite Aktienrechtsnovelle') of the ADHGB in 1884. The preparatory work for these amendments recognised that

> 'the acts and declarations of the directors, in particular those which are made public […] have an impact on the decision of persons to first enter into a legal relationship with the corporation, be it through the purchase of shares or entry into a creditor relationship'.[31]

However, general external director liability was not ultimately included in the ADHGB of 1884 because 'mere oversight [would] be capable of creating useless obligations'.[32] The legislator thus deliberately opted for director liability to be restricted to internal liability, since 'the law should not deter careful persons from assuming the functions of directors'.[33]

But since then, external director liability has snuck in through the back door via tort law.[34] The *Baustoff* case (1989) is considered to be the 'nightmare of external director liability'.[35] In *Baustoff*, the 11th Senate of the German BGH found that the director of a GmbH is liable to third parties under tort law pursuant to § 823 (1) of the German Civil Code (the 'BGB') if he has harmed a third party through his own tortious act.[36] Both the 2nd Senate of the BGH as well as large portions of the literature on the subject disagreed with this opinion and rejected director liability in torts for breaches of duty in the course of their activities as directors; in general, the argument was that external liability of directors contradicts the principle of limited liability in the company as laid down in the AktG, and therefore it could at best be an 'exception requiring justification'.[37] Despite numerous so-called crises – such as the scandals on the German capital market at the turn of the millennium, the financial market crisis or the Wirecard accounting scandal a few years ago – the legislator so far has not found the resolve to codify external director liability for disseminating incorrect or misleading information on capital markets. Third-party liability is thus one of the 'evergreens' in the debate over director liability, and the topic remains controversial.

c) Limitation of director liability

Some time ago, after a long period of focus on bolstering the enforcement of director liability, the debate shifted again, and the pendulum has now swung back, and for several years there has been intensive debate about limiting director liability. The main reason for this has been the increased duties of directors in the

---

[31] Gutachten des Reichs-Oberhandelsgerichts von 1877, printed in Schubert and Hommelhoff (n 4) 208, 218.

[32] Gutachten des Reichs-Oberhandelsgerichts von 1877, printed in supra note 4, 208, 219.

[33] Gutachten des Reichs-Oberhandelsgerichts von 1877, printed in supra note 4, 208, 218.

[34] Jan-Erik Schirmer, *Das Körperschaftsdelikt* (Mohr Siebeck 2015) 131ff (recounting historical developments).

[35] Bachmann (n 15) E118: the 'große Schreckgespenst der Organaußenhaftung'.

[36] BGH 5 December 1989, VI ZR 335/88, 109 BGHZ 297; Andreas Dieckmann, '30 Jahre „Baustoff-Entscheidung" und ihre Relevanz für die Organaußenhaftung von heute' (2020) 49 ZGR 1039 (on the 30th anniversary).

[37] Fleischer (n 22) para 392.

context of corporate compliance. Although it became very clear early on that directors have to abide by the rules, the relevance of compliance to questions of director liability was not recognised until the beginning of the 2000s, when the *Siemens* global corruption case made the significance (and liability risks) to directors obvious.[38] Since then, the regulatory requirements for companies, and with them the duties and liability risks that directors face – in areas such as antitrust, securities, banking and insurance law – have increased. Against this background, it is clear why the discussion has shifted toward limiting director liability. It has been discussed, for example, whether there is a 'legal judgment rule' analogous to the business judgment rule,[39] or if directors are shielded from culpability if they can establish that they relied on advice of counsel.[40] Although the BGH has had several opportunities to decide on the validity of advice of counsel as a liability shield, not until 2011 did it decide the issue and specify the requirements in the *ISION* case.[41] This decision attracted much attention in the literature. Numerous monographs and essays on the subject followed.

Discussion of limiting director liability escalated even more after another landmark decision in 2013 – not, it is worth noting, one by the BGH but instead by the Landgericht of Munich I, a higher district court – which held a former member of the management board of Siemens AG, Heinz-Joachim Neubürger, liable for more than 15 million euros in damages because he breached his duty to comply with the law and thereby incurred fines, payable by Siemens, in the wake of the already-mentioned global corruption scandal.[42] This decision was regarded as a 'thunderbolt'[43] and an 'iconic case'.[44] Not only did a civil court explicitly recog-

---

[38] See <https://www.spiegel.de/international/spiegel/a-swamp-of-bribes-siemens-forced-to-battle-internal-corruption-a-451105.html>.

[39] See Nicolas Ott, 'Anwendungsbereich der Business Judgment Rule aus Sicht der Praxis – Unternehmerische Entscheidungen und Organisationsermessen des Vorstands' (2017) 46 ZGR 149, 158 et seq; Gerald Spindler, 'Die Haftung von Vorstand und Aufsichtsrat für fehlerhafte Auslegung von Rechtsbegriffen' in Heldrich (n 13) 414ff; Gerald Spindler, in Wulf Goette and Mathias Habersack (eds), *Münchener Kommentar zum Aktiengesetz*, vol 2 (6th edn, CH Beck 2023) § 93 para 95. See also Fleischer (n 22) para 40ff.

[40] Rafael Harnos, *Geschäftsleiterhaftung bei unklarer Rechtslage* (Duncker & Humblot 2013) 129ff, 149ff, 253ff; Philipp Maximilian Holle, Legalitätskontrolle im Kapitalgesellschafts- und Konzernrecht (Mohr Siebeck 2014) 62ff; Jens Koch, 'Die Legal Judgment Rule: ein Fall für die Wolfsschlucht' in Meinrad Dreher and others (eds), *Festschrift für Alfred Bergmann* (De Gruyter 2018) 413ff; Dirk A Verse, 'Organhaftung bei unklarer Rechtslage – Raum für eine Legal Judgment Rule?' (2017) 46 ZGR 174.

[41] BGH 20 September 2011, II ZR 234/09, [2011] AG 876 para 16; furthermore BGH 28 April 2015, II ZR 63/14, [2015] NZG 792 para 28.

[42] LG München I, 10 December 2013, 5 HK O 1387/10, [2014] NZG 345.

[43] Gregor Bachmann, 'Anmerkung zum Urteil des LG München I vom 10.12.2013 – 5 HK o 1387/10 – Zur Haftung des Vorstands für Mängel des Compliance-Systems Kurzreferat' [2014] ZIP 579.

[44] Holger Fleischer, 'Aktienrechtliche Compliance-Pflichten im Praxistest: Das Siemens/Neubürger-Urteil des LG München I' [2014] NZG 321.

nise a director's duty to comply with the law for the first time in history – which is why the decision is considered to be the '"zero hour" of German compliance'[45] – but the ruling also made it clear that a breach of the director's duties can have severe financial consequences. The decision is therefore deemed to have been a turning point in the debate over director liability, not least because of its tragic extrajudicial ending[46] in Mr. Neubürger's suicide shortly afterwards.

Various approaches to limiting liability risks have been discussed since *Siemens/Neubürger*. One is to relax the supervisory board's duty to seek damages that the BGH established in *ARAG/Garmenbeck* (see III. 1.) and thus to partly alleviate director liability.[47] There are also various proposals to substantively limit director liability, for example by applying labour law principles on the liability of employees,[48] by codifying liability limits,[49] or by granting a statutory freedom to mitigate liability.[50] The 70th Deutsche Juristentag in 2014 conducted a fundamental discussion about whether and how to reform director liability. A large majority declined to support codified limitations on director liability, but a majority was in favour of granting statutory freedom on this issue.[51] So far none of these impulses has been implemented.

---

[45] Bachmann § 22 Siemens/Neubürger – LG München I NZG 2014, 345 in Holger Fleischer and Jan Thiessen (eds), *Gesellschaftsrechts-Geschichten*, 2018, 691, 722.

[46] Bachmann (n 45) 722.

[47] Critical of this Jens Koch, 'Die schleichende Erosion der Verfolgungspflicht nach ARAG/Garmenbeck' [2014] NZG 934.

[48] For details see Jens Koch, 'Beschränkungen des gesellschaftsrechtlichen Innenregresses bei Bußgeldzahlungen' in Michael Hoffmann-Becking, Uwe Hüffer and Jochem Reichert (eds), *Liber amicorum für Martin Winter* (O Schmidt 2011) 327ff; Jens Koch, 'Beschränkung der Regressfolgen im Kapitalgesellschaftsrecht' [2012] AG 429ff.

[49] See, eg, Walter Bayer and Philipp Scholz, 'Haftungsbegrenzung und D&O-Versicherung im Recht der aktienrechtlichen Organhaftung. Grundsatzüberlegungen zum 70. DJT 2014' [2014] NZG 926, 930ff; Peter Hemeling, 'Reform der Organhaftung? Erwartungen an den 70. Deutschen Juristentag' (2014) 178 ZHR 221, 224; Johannes Semler, 'Überlegungen zur Praktikabilität der Organhaftungsvorschriften' in Mathias Habersack and Peter Hommelhoff (eds), *Festschrift für Wulf Goette* (CH Beck 2011) 510; Martin Peltzer, 'Mehr Ausgewogenheit bei der Vorstandshaftung' in Gerd Krieger, Marcus Lutter and Karsten Schmidt (eds), *Festschrift für Michael Hoffmann-Becking* (CH Beck 2013), 861, 865; Gerald Spindler, 'Organhaftung in der AG – Reformbedarf aus wissenschaftlicher Perspektive' [2013] AG 889, 895.

[50] See Bachmann (n 15) E 58ff, E 62ff; Barbara Grunewald, 'Haftungsvereinbarungen zwischen Aktiengesellschaft und Vorstandsmitgliedern' [2013] AG 813, 815ff; Wilhelm Haarmann and Michael Weiß, 'Reformbedarf bei der aktienrechtlichen Organhaftung' [2014] BB 2115, 2116; Mathias Habersack, 'Perspektiven der aktienrechtlichen Organhaftung' (2013) 177 ZHR 782, 804; Spindler (n 49) 895ff; Eberhard Vetter, 'Aktienrechtliche Organhaftung und Satzungsautonomie. Überlegungen de lege ferenda' [2014] NZG 921, 923ff.

[51] Cf DJT, Beschlüsse der Abteilung Wirtschaftsrecht des 70. DJT 2014, I. 1–3.

d) The current state of affairs

In summary, the current state of affairs is that the ongoing debate over director liability is a constant struggle to find the right balance between severe liability and effective enforcement on the one hand and reasonable limitations, of substantive law, in order to avoid having unmanageable liability risks on the other hand. Especially in the aftermath of corporate crises and scandals, there have always been calls for stricter rules on director liability. For example, at the end of the nineteenth century, fraud and irregularities in the organisation, administration and operation of joint stock companies let to restrictions in the Zweite Aktienrechtsnovelle of 1884). Similarly, after the stock scandals and corporate collapses of the Great Depression, at the end of the 1920s, minority shareholders received enhanced rights to force the company to sue directors. The collapse of the capital markets at the turn of the millennium prompted a debate on third-party liability of directors (such as towards investors). And last but not least, stricter substantive rules on director liability were adopted after the financial market crisis of 2008.

However, these tendencies to want to subject directors to greater liability are always accompanied by cautionary voices against going too far. This is seen as early as in the preparatory materials to the Zweite Aktienrechtsnovelle of 1884, which say that 'the law should not deter conscientious persons from taking over the function of directors'.[52] Similar considerations will be repeated later on: in 1937, the legislator codified the already recognised fault requirement in order to ensure that directors would not be deprived of 'all courage to act' by virtue of the tremendous financial consequences of failure. It goes to show that the debate over director liability moves, like a pendulum, between raising and limiting liability. If liability goes too far, the pendulum swings back, as *Siemens/Neubürger* especially tragically demonstrated.

3. Methods and Contestants in the Debate

a) Contestants

The central contestants influencing the debate over director liability are legal scholars, judges and justices, and the legislator. But their roles have not been static and indeed have shifted over time. While the debate over director liability was originally dominated by the legislator, more recently it has been significantly shaped and decisively influenced by fundamental court decisions such as *ARAG/Garmenbeck*, *ISION* or *Siemens/Neubürger*. But legal scholars have nonetheless also played a central role even if law scholarship admittedly is 'no source of law in its own right, but rather merely a source of legal knowledge'.[53] Even though

---

[52] 'Gutachten des Reichs-Oberhandelsgerichts von 1877' (n 4) 217ff.

[53] Holger Fleischer, 'Gesellschaftsrechts-Honoratioren: Schlüsselfiguren im Gesellschaftsrecht und ihr diskursives Zusammenwirken' [2019] NZG 921, 927.

scholars such as *Levin Goldschmidt* or *Heinrich Wiener* were involved in early legislation, 'legal science' – though late to discover its enthusiasm for the duties and liability of directors – has studied it all the more intensively. Whereas the legislator is motivated to take action above all after corporate scandals and crises, scholars on the other hand have reacted mainly to the important jurisprudence on which the debate has turned: *ARAG/Garmenbeck* was the starting point for the academic debate on effective enforcement of director liability; *Siemens/Neubürger* initiated a turnaround and brought ways of limiting liability into focus.

While the legal scholarship, jurisprudence and legislation that have significantly shaped the development of director liability has been in the foreground, commercial and business interests in particular have influenced the debate in the background as well (see also in connection with ESG *Koch*, in this book, p 215). Thus the public in no small regard, as well as practitioners, has exerted significant influence over the debate about director liability. The public influence is particularly evident in connection with scandals that have attracted public attention, often significantly pressuring the legislator to act following corporate scandals and crises. The significant influence of practitioners is exemplified by the fate of the failed 'Capital Market Information Liability Act' that provided for external liability of corporate bodies for disseminating incorrect or misleading information on the capital market. That draft legislation, which was based essentially on preliminary work by legal scholars[54] and which was also generally positively received by them,[55] failed in no small part due to considerable criticism from practitioners, especially in the legal profession.[56]

b) Methods

In addition to those relevant actors, methodological impulses have also influenced the debate. Impulses have come primarily from comparative law and the economic analysis of law.

(1) Comparative law

Although corporate law has been diagnosed as 'lacking foreign sensitivity',[57] the same cannot be said of the academic debate on director liability. Director liabili-

[54] Especially the expert opinion by Fleischer (n 8).

[55] Thomas MJ Möllers, 'Der Weg zu einer Haftung für Kapitalmarktinformationen' [2005] JZ 75, 79ff; Carsten Schäfer, 'Effektivere Vorstandshaftung für Fehlinformation des Kapitalmarkts?' [2005] NZG 985ff; Rüdiger Veil, 'Die Haftung des Emittenten für fehlerhafte Information des Kapitalmarkts nach dem geplanten KapInHaG' [2005] BKR 91, 92ff. Anders Gerald Spindler, 'Persönliche Haftung der Organmitglieder für Falschinformationen des Kapitalmarktes' [2004] WM 2089, 2093.

[56] See above all Handelsrechtsausschuss des DAV (n 9) 1099.

[57] Marc-Philippe Weller, 'Zukunftsperspektiven der Rechtsvergleichung im IPR und Unternehmensrecht' in Reinhard Zimmermann (ed), *Zukunftsperspektiven der Rechtsvergleichung* (Mohr Siebeck 2016) 210.

ty is a good example of comparative law in action and is a playing field for legal transplants. Comparative law played a central role early on – for example, in the run-up to the 1884 amendments to the German Stock Corporation Act, where the focus was primarily on French and Belgian law.[58] Later, the focus turned to U.S. law – as shown, above all, by the business judgment rule[59] or by the recognition of D&O insurance. The special reference to U.S. law is not coincidental. Since many director liability cases were first initiated by U.S. authorities,[60] it seems only logical if the expansion of director liability is compensated for by limitations of liability under U.S. law – as in the context of the business judgment rule.[61]

(2) Economic analysis of law

With the advance of economic legal analysis as a recognised method in corporate law, the economics of director liability have become increasingly suspect. Based on agency theory, which views the relationship between shareholders and management as a classic principal-agent relationship, director liability is now also recognised as an instrument of prevention and behavioural control, and considerations of the law from an economic perspective are now a customary part of the debate.[62] Accordingly, the discussion is conducted not only by and among lawyers, but rather it is interdisciplinary. For example, the 67th Deutscher Betriebswirtschafter-Tag (Conference of German microeconomists) in 2013 joined in under the title 'Uncertainty by Directors' Liability'.[63]

c) Interim result

The debate over director liability is based on the fruitful interplay of various contributions by scholars, courts, and the legislator and is a good example of the sophisticated culture of discourse involving those three poles, which Holger Fleischer has described as the 'German approach'.

---

58 See *Verhandlungen des Vereins für Socialpolitik am 12. und 13. October*, vol IV (1874) 60ff; and later, 'Gutachten des Reichs-Oberhandelsgerichts von 1877' (n 4) 208, 214ff.

59 See Regierungsbegründung, BT-Drs. 15/5092, 11; Hanno Merkt, 'Rechtliche Grundlagen der Business Judgment Rule im internationalen Vergleich zwischen Divergenz und Konvergenz' (2017) 46 ZGR 129 (from a comparative law perspective).

60 *Siemens/Neubürger* as well as the Volkswagen emission affairs are examples. See Bachmann (n 22) 724.

61 Bachmann (n 22) 724.

62 Bachmann (n 15) E21ff, E73ff, is a good example.

63 67. Deutscher Betriebswirtschafter-Tag, 'Unternehmenssteuerung in unsicheren Zeiten'. On this see <https://www.presseportal.de/pm/66303/2533197>.

IV. (No) End in Sight

The debate on director liability continues unabated. New impulses are already emerging that could keep the pendulum swinging between limitation and expansion of director liability. These include the major issues of our time: sustainability, digitalisation and globalisation.

1. Sustainability

Currently there has been a focus on director liability in connection with sustainability and ESG. Primarily driven by non-governmental organisations and by particularly tragic incidents involving the German retail chain kik (on which see Koch, in this book, p 215), corporations have been taken to task to do more toward climate change mitigation and other environmental and social goals. This development, which has crossed the external boundaries of the corporation to affect the internal duties and liability of directors, reached a temporary apex with the European legislator's inclusion in the draft Corporate Sustainability Due Diligence Directive of a provision according to which

> 'Member States shall ensure that, when fulfilling their duty to act in the best interest of the company, directors of companies […] take into account the consequences of their decisions for sustainability matters, including, where applicable, human rights, climate change and environmental consequences, including in the short, medium and long term.'[64]

This regulation has attracted a great deal of attention from scholars and practitioners alike. According to some, it is nothing short of a 'paradigm shift'.[65] Even though this particular provision – which the Commission only intended to have a clarifying effect anyway[66] – was withdrawn, the pendulum has already started to swing, and a lively debate has been triggered about a 'duty of sustainability'[67] both *de lege lata* and *de lege ferenda*.[68] Since practitioners in particular have begun to fear a noticeable increase in liability, calls for modification of the business judgment rule in the interest of sustainability were not long in coming; for ex-

[64] Art 25 Proposal for a Directive of the European Parliament and of the Council on Corporate Sustainability Due Diligence and amending Directive (EU) 2019/1937 <https://eur-lex.europa.eu/legal-content/EN/TXT/?uri=CELEX:52022PC0071>.

[65] Marc-Philippe Weller and Tim Fischer, 'ESG-Geschäftsleitungspflichten. Unternehmenstransformation zur Klimaneutralität' [2022] ZIP 2253; Anne-Christin Mittwoch, *Nachhaltigkeit und Unternehmensrecht* (Mohr Siebeck 2022) 240; see also Gregor Bachmann, 'Zielsetzung und Governance von Unternehmen im Lichte der Klimaverantwortung' (2023) 187 ZHR 166, 195ff (a softer version of the same position).

[66] Recital 63 (n 64).

[67] Bachmann (n 65) 196 ('Nachhaltigkeitspflicht').

[68] See Weller and Fischer (n 65) (favouring a duty of care to observe sustainability goals); Stephan. Harbarth, '„Corporate Sustainability Due Diligence"-Richtlinie. (Kein) Systemumbruch im deutschen Aktienrecht?' [2022] AG 633 para 1ff (favouring a merely procedural duty to take sustainability into account).

ample, there have been calls for an addition to the business judgment rule according to which the board of directors should receive safe-harbour protection 'only after adequately identifying and assessing environmental and social sustainability risks'. Given the past course of the debate, it would not be surprising to see another struggle over tightening and limiting liability in this context in the near future.[69]

2. *Digitalisation*

The second impulse currently affecting the debate on director liability is digitalisation, for example through the extensive use of information technologies, modern forms of comprehensive data generation and evaluation, or the use of artificial intelligence. Since digitalisation not only offers opportunities but also poses risks and as a management issue entails increased duties for executive bodies, it also affects the liability of corporate executive bodies and directly affects the debate about the structure of director liability. There have been calls for legislation to repeal the burden-shifting provision at § 93(2)(2) of the AktG, or at least to limit it to cases of fault or to current board members. Justification for repealing outright or at least weakening the burden-shifting provision is seen in a belief that in the digital age, board members or directors (particularly retired ones) are no longer in a better position than the corporation itself to monitor their own activities, and thus the original justification for shifting the burden of proof (see a)) no longer applies. Accordingly, a majority of those attending the 70th Deutscher Juristentag favoured revisiting the rule. Other, more cautious voices rejected a change. It remains to be seen how this debate will develop.

3. *Globalisation*

Globalisation is another trend of our time alongside digitalisation and sustainability and a third potential turning point in the debate over director liability. However, according to some of the literature, internationalisation is the Achilles' heel of corporate law.[70] Especially 'for the mega-topic of compliance', there is a considerable backlog of issues related to globalisation, since (and on this there is probably unanimity) – in 'the cross-border context [...] practically everything is still unclear here'.[71] Although dealing with questions of the board's responsibili-

[69] Sustainable Finance Beirat (SFB), Shifting the Trillions: Ein nachhaltiges Finanzsystem für die Große Transformation – 31 Empfehlungen des Sustainable-Finance Beirats an die Bundesregierung (2021) 96. See also Fraktion Bündnis 90/Die Grünen from 2012 (BT-Drs. 17/11686) (similar proposal by a German political party). See also Bachmann (n 65) 200ff (dismissive); Mathias Habersack, 'Gemeinwohlbindung und Unternehmensrecht' (2020) 220 AcP 594, 645 (dismissive); Marc-Philippe Weller and Nina Benz, 'Klimaschutz und Corporate Governance' (2022) 51 ZGR 563, 586 (sceptical).

[70] Cf Weller (n 57) 191, 210.; Markus Lieberknecht, *Die internationale Legalitätspflicht* (Carl Heymanns 2021) 4ff.

[71] Weller (n 57) 191, 210; Lieberknecht (n 70) 4 (discussing initial findings).

ty for complying with foreign law is reality for many transnational corporations and is of particular practical relevance, the debate over director liability has been surprisingly slow to focus on it. That *Siemens/Neubürger* dealt with bribery in Nigeria (i.e., with violations of foreign law) no more than slightly increased the salience of compliance issues. Whether compliance issues will set the pendulum of director or 'executive body' liability swinging again remains to be seen.[72]

V. Summary

1. Director liability has been a favourite topic in German corporate law for almost 30 years. The debate is characterised by a fruitful interplay among scholars, courts, and the legislator. While the legislator primarily gets involved after corporate scandals and crises, scholars contribute primarily in response to cases, in particular to decisions by the Federal Court of Justice.
2. The debate focuses mainly on comparative law and economic considerations. The early debates mainly referred to French law, but more recently the debate refers above all to U.S. law.
3. The debate over director liability moves like a pendulum between stricter liability to combat abusive business practices and limiting liability to avoid overreach in the name of deterrence. Since the 'right' balance is very much influenced by economic and social circumstances, this balancing process never seems to reach a conclusion.
4. Even if case law and legislation have supplied many of the details on the law of director liability, there is no end in sight to the policy debate about what it should be. Every corporate scandal brings corporate liability into focus again. Digitalisation, globalisation and sustainability, or ESG as a 'moving target' also influences the discussion of director liability. Potentially, the issue of director liability may never be settled.

---

[72] For a good starting point see Lieberknecht (n 70).

New Legal Forms and Rules for Italian Innovative Enterprises

Peter Agstner[*]

I. Introduction

Innovative start-ups, conventionally defined as rapid-growth firms with outside investors and an IPO or trade sale as an exit event, have been a major force in commercializing innovative science and revolutionizing the world we live in.[1] Innovative start-ups that survive, and then scale-up, create jobs and wealth.[2] Old

[*] An earlier version of this article appeared in (2024) 35 EBLR 1065ff, published by Kluwer Law International. The present version includes revisions and updates by the author.

[1] On the issue of 'causal links' and in particular whether the driver of the development of innovative enterprises is the presence of innovative ideas as such (the innovation-first hypothesis) or the presence of venture capitalists willing to finance them, cf, Bernard S Black and Ronald J Gilson, 'Venture Capital and the Structure of Capital Markets: Banks Versus Stock Markets' (1998) 47 J Fin Econ 243; John Armour and Douglas Cumming, 'The Legislative Road to Silicon Valley' (2006) 58 Oxf Econ Pap 596; Masayuki Hirukawa and Masako Ueda, 'Venture Capital and Innovation: Which is First?' (2011) 16 Pac Econ Rev 421.

[2] For a general account of the VC-world, see Mahendra Ramsinghani, *The Business of Venture Capital* (Wiley & Sons 2021); Sebastian Mallaby, *The Power Law: Venture Capital and the Making of the New Future* (Penguin Press 2022). For the unique corporate governance aspects of start-ups, cf Robert P Bartlett III, 'Venture Capital, Agency Costs, and the False Dichotomy of the Corporation' (2006) 54 UCLA L Rev 37; Ronald J Gilson, 'Engineering a Venture Capital Market: Lessons from the American Experience' (2003) 55 Stan LRev 1067; Jesse M Fried and Mira Ganor, 'Agency Costs of Venture Capitalist Control in Startups' (2006) 81 NYU

Europe, when compared with the U.S., where most unicorns are created,[3] is still lagging behind.[4] For several years now, European institutions have been trying to ignite a start-up revolution through public initiatives and coordination measures like the Start-up and Scale-up Initiative,[5] and finally through the proposed framework for innovative companies known as the 28th Regime.[6]

In order to create a more favourable legal environment for innovative start-ups, some national legislators have adopted targeted policy interventions, for instance in Slovakia and Polen, where respective amendments to the commercial codes in 2017 and 2021 led to the introduction of a simplified joint-stock company with the objective of, among other things, encouraging the establishment and development of innovative companies financed by venture capitalists (VCs).[7] The Spanish legislator has taken a similar path, introducing a *ley de startups* in 2022 with significant tax incentives and a more flexible corporate law regime applicable to *empresas emergentes*.[8] Austria seems to be moving in the same direction with the recent introduction of a new type of company, the so-called *Flexible Kapitalgesellschaft* (a variant of the traditional *GmbH*), specifically aimed at supporting innovative start-ups in their early stage.[9] In contrast, other policymakers,

---

L Rev 967; Elizabeth Pollman, 'Startup Governance' (2019) 168 U Pa LRev 155 (2019); Thilo Kuntz, Gestaltung von Kapitalgesellschaften zwischen Freiheit und Zwang (Mohr Siebeck 2016) 43ff.

[3] The most prominent examples are Apple, Alphabet, Microsoft, Amazon, and Tesla.

[4] Among the European unicorns are BlaBlaCar (France); CureVac and DeepL (Germany); and Yoox, Scalapay and Satispay (Italy). Satispay is financed mainly by prominent foreign VC funds such as Tencent, Tiger Global, Greyhound Capital and Coatue.

[5] European Commission, 'Europe's next leaders: the Start-up and Scale-up Initiative' COM (2016) 733 final. For literature on the role of corporate law in promoting a VC market, see Casimiro A Nigro and Alperen A Gözlügöl, 'Building an EU Venture Capital Market: What About Corporate Law?' in Gabriella Gimigliano and Valentino Cattelan (eds), *Money Law, Capital, and the Changing Identity of the European Union* (Hart 2022) 165ff.

[6] Communication from the Commission to the European Parliament, the Council, the European Economic and Social Committee and the Committee of the Regions, A Competitiveness Compass for the EU, 29.1.2025, COM(2025) 30 final.

[7] On the Slovak jednoduchá spoločnosť na akcie, see Mária Patakyovà and others, 'Slovak Simple Joint Stock Company – Critical Review and Preliminary Assessment' (2020) 17 ECFR 205; on the Polish *Prosta Spółka Akcyjna* (*P.S.A.*), see Adam Opolski and others, 'The Simple Joint Stock Company: Emergence of a New Close Company in Poland' (2024) 21 ECFR 604.

[8] Ley 28/2022, de 21 de diciembre, de fomento del ecosistema de las empresas emergentes. For a comment on the preliminary draft, see Enrique Moreno Serrano, 'Anteproyecto de Ley de fomento del ecosistema de las empresas emergentes' (2021) 63 Rev derecho de sociedades 351.

[9] See art 1 of the Gesellschaftsrechts-Änderungsgesetz 2023 (GesRÄG 2023), which entered into force on 1 January 2024 and contains 29 paragraphs. For an assessment see Elke Heinrich-Pendl and Matthias Pendl, 'Flexible Kapitalgesellschaft – Entwurf einer Start-up-Rechtsform für Österreich' [2023] GmbHR R224; Holger Fleischer and Matthias Pendl, 'Die Flexible Kapitalgesellschaft als österreichische Rechtsformneuschöpfung: Genese – Grundlagen – Gesamtwürdigung' [2024] GmbHR 174; Susanne Kalss, 'Die flexible Kapitalgesellschaft – eine neue Rechtsform für Österreich' [2023] NZG 1437. Similar initiatives have also been

such as in Belgium, have failed to consider the specific needs of start-up firms despite extensive overhauls of general corporate law.[10]

Broadly speaking, Italy stands out in this regulatory competition as the first European country to introduce tailor-made rules for innovative start-ups. This was achieved not by introducing a new corporate form but by turning the traditional limited liability company, the *società a responsabilità limitata* (the '*s.r.l.*'), on its head.[11] In fact, although some regulatory innovations also affect public companies, ie, the joint-stock corporation or *società per azioni* (the '*s.p.a.*') and co-operatives, the major impact of reform has certainly been on the private limited liability company, which has been profoundly remodelled. Apart from the novelties in corporate law that will be the main focus of the present analysis (sec III), and besides the newly accessible digital incorporation option (sec IV), innovative start-ups now enjoy tax and labour benefits as well as special treatment in the event of insolvency (sec VI).

I will analyse the discreet stages of this 'disruptive revolution',[12] starting from the general overhaul of corporate law in 2003 (sec II).[13]

II. The Corporate Law Reform of 2003

The policy approach started to change with the 2003 company law reform.[14] At the time of its introduction in 1942, the *società a responsabilità limitata* was considered to be a 'simplified' or 'minor' public corporation, as emblematically ex-

discussed by U.S. scholars, who have proposed a custom-made business entity, ie, the 'venture corporation' or 'v-corp', designed to serve start-ups' distinctive character as exit-driven entities: see Gad Weiss, 'The Venture Corporation' (25 January 2023) <https://ssrn.com/abstract=4338030> or <http://dx.doi.org/10.2139/ssrn.4338030> accessed 18 September 2023.

[10] For a general comment and criticism of the lack of this 'missing piece', see Hans De Wulf, 'An Introduction to and Evaluation of the 2019 Belgian Companies Act – Preparing for the Previous War?' (2023) 20 ECFR 109, 159 ('Today, a reform of the law of private companies should probably also be about actively catering to the capital and governance structures desired by venture capital and private equity investors').

[11] Paolo Giudici and Peter Agstner, 'Startups and Company Law: The Competitive Pressure of Delaware on Italy (and Europe?)' (2019) 20 EBOR 597ff.

[12] An expression here employed in the Kuhnian sense (Thomas S Kuhn, *The Structure of Scientific Revolutions* (3rd edn, UCP 1996)) to descsribe a true paradigm shift that is still underway.

[13] For a first good overview, see Gaetano Presti, 'Vent'anni vissuti pericolosamente. TUF e codice civile: una convivenza difficile' (2019) 2 An giur econ 473, 478ff; also, from a *Typuslehre* perspective, see Alessio Diego Scano, 'Il "tipo"' in Carlo Ibba and Giorgio Marasà (eds), *Le società a responsabilità limitata* (Giuffrè 2020) 51ff.

[14] Marco Cian, 'Il tipo s.r.l.?' (2021) 44 Nuove leggi civ comm 293, 302ff; Paolo Spada 'Classi e tipi di società dopo la riforma organica' (2003) 49 Riv dir civ 496; also Giudici and Agstner (n 11) 610–611; for an in-depth account on the historical evolution of the regulation of Italian *s.r.l.*'s, see Mario Stella Richter, 'Antecedenti e vicende della società a responsabilità

pressed in the phrase 'small *s.p.a.* without shares'.[15] The 2003 law was to radically reform this type of corporation. Indeed, on the occasion of the reform the legislator emphasized that *s.r.l.*'s and *s.p.a.*'s were distinct organizational forms, each under its own autonomous, organic set of rules.[16] This was a substantial dismissal of the public corporation-centric view in favour of a quotaholder-centric perspective.[17] In fact, the leitmotif of the reform was to enhance the central role of the quotaholder as an important element of modernization in governance structures.[18] Numerous provisions set forth distinctive features of the newly designed *s.r.l.*, allowing (among other things) the attribution of special rights to individual quotaholders[19] as well as optional different management structures[20] or granting quotaholders an inalienable right to participate in decisions on specific resolutions (eg, on the appointment and removal of directors and auditors, dividend payments, charter amendments, or fundamental corporate transactions).[21]

The result was the construction of a corporate form that primarily facilitated the conduct of the business by actively involved, entrepreneurial quotaholders (*soci imprenditori*)[22] and expressed the central importance of the shareholder as set out in art 3 of the Delegated Law of 3 October 2001, no 366. A direct consequence of this focus was the elimination of the option for the private company to raise capital by soliciting 'public savings', both on the equity and debt side.[23] Also banned was the issuance of different classes of shares or the carrying out

limitata' in Aldo Angelo Dolmetta and Gaetano Maria (eds), *S.r.l. Commentario dedicato a G.B. Portale* (Giuffrè 2011) 1ff.

15 Gian Carlo Maria Rivolta, 'Profilo della nuova disciplina della società a responsabilità limitata' (2003) 56 Banca borsa tit cred 683ff.

16 Cf Aldo Angelo Dolmetta, 'Sul "tipo" s.r.l.' in Aldo Angelo Dolmetta and Gaetano Maria (eds) (n 14) 15ff; Paolo Spada, 'Classi e tipi di società dopo la riforma organica (guardando alla "nuova" società a responsabilità limitata)' in Giorgio Cian (ed), *Le grandi opzioni della riforma del diritto e del processo societario* (CEDAM 2004) 31ff. In spite of this, the applicable law still makes frequent reference to the rules governing the *s.p.a.*; for a critical account, see Giuseppe Zanarone, *Della società a responsabilità limitata*, vol 1, in Francesco D Busnelli (ed), *Il Codice Civile. Commentario* (Giuffrè 2010) 19 and fn 24.

17 I refer here to quotaholders instead of shareholders in order to stress that persons participating in an *s.r.l.* are somewhere between partners and shareholders.

18 Vincenzo Buonocore, 'La società a responsabilità limitata' in Amedeo Bassi, Vincenzo Buonocore and Salvatore Pescatore (eds). *La riforma del diritto societario* (Giappichelli 2003) 170; Gian Franco Campobasso, *Diritto commerciale. 2. Diritto delle società* (10th edn, UTET 2020) 561ff.

19 CC, art 2468(3).

20 CC, art 2475.

21 CC, art 2479(2). For a good overview of these novelties, see Campobasso (n 18) 562–563.

22 Carlo Angelici, *La riforma delle società di capitali* (CEDAM 2006) 7ff.

23 CC, art 2468(1): The shareholders' quotas can neither be represented by shares nor be offered to the public as financial instruments. Also, the newly permitted ability to issue debt securities (CC, art 2483) suffers important limitations in the *s.r.l.* For comment, see Francesco Brizzi, *S.R.L. PMI e offerta al pubblico di quote di partecipazione* (Giappichelli 2022) 69ff; Maurizio Sciuto, 'Le quote di partecipazione' in Ibba and Marasà (eds) (n 13) 531ff.

of transactions in the company's own shares.[24] This regulatory approach did not adequately accommodate the needs and aspirations of investors whose interest in the company was merely financial (*soci finanziatori*), who typically are angel investors and venture capital funds that represent the 'backbone' of innovative start-up activities.

III. The Reforms of 2012–2017: Introductory Remarks

The reforms implemented in the five-year period from 2012–2017 were part of a broader phenomenon of competition between legal systems.[25] This competition, under the auspices of the European Commission,[26] focused precisely on SMEs, which are generally identified as the primary field in which interventions should be concentrated in order to facilitate the formation of new enterprises and the growth of existing ones.[27] The outcome of these policy initiatives consisted in a general relaxation of regulatory constraints in their various national guises.

The first area affected by the march of reform was minimum share capital. Until the beginning of the 21th century, lawmakers generally required, even for private companies, the paying up of a minimum share capital that varied between 7,500 (France), 10,000 (Italy), 18,000 (Netherland), 25,000 (Germany) and even 35,000 (Austria) euros. Nowadays, however, most of these countries permit an ordinary or simplified private limited liability company to be formed with a share capital of 1 euro (or even less).[28] Another aspect under review that is considered an obstacle to the creation of new companies is the formalities of registration; the policy objective of easing the requirements has now been realized through the

[24] CC, art 2474.

[25] For a general overview, cf Holger Fleischer, 'Internationale Trends und Reformen im Recht der geschlossenen Kapitalgesellschaft' [2014] 17 NZG 1081ff; Mette Neville and Karsten Engsig Sørensen, 'Promoting Entrepreneurship – The New Company Law Agenda' (2014) 15 EBOR 545ff; for empirical data see Reiner Braun and others, 'Does Charter Competition Foster Entrepreneurship? A Difference-in-Difference Approach to European Company Law Reform' (2013) 51 JCMS 399.

[26] Small Business Act for Europe (COM (2008) 394 final).

[27] See in France the *Loi Dutreil pour l'initiative économique* of 2003; in Italy the Reform of 2003; in Germany the *Gesetz zur Modernisierung des GmbH-Rechts und zur Bekämpfung von Missbräuchen* of 2008; in Spain the *Ley de la sociedad limitada Nueva Empresa* of 2003; in the Netherlands the *Wet vereenvoudiging en flexibilisering bv-recht* of 2012.

[28] Two prominent exceptions are Austria and Switzerland, where the respective laws require 35,000 euros (§ 6(1) of the GmbHG, but now with the recent reform of the *GmbH* law following the introduction of the 'Flex-Co' with a reduction to 10,000 euros) and 20,000 Swiss francs (§ 773 of the OR) as minimum capital for the incorporation of a *GmbH*. For detailed comparative references, cf Michael Grimm, *Die Finanzverfassung der kleinen Kapitalgesellschaft. Eine rechtsvergleichende Untersuchung der Reformdiskussion in Europa* (Duncker & Humblot 2013) 51ff; Alessio Bartolacelli, 'Almost Capital-less Companies in Europe: Trends, Variations, Competition' (2017) 14 ECFR 187.

generalized provision of online incorporation procedures.[29] Special emphasis was initially placed also on the establishment of subtypes of private companies for the purpose of setting up new businesses; these organizational forms are characterized by the simplification, if not standardization, of internal governance features;[30] today, however, several national legislators have backtracked, abolishing the new corporate vehicles introduced at the time.[31]

Although all Member States made significant efforts to promote entrepreneurship and competitiveness, the lack of a specific approach to the needs and problems of innovative enterprises was apparent.[32] The change in Italy came between 2012 and 2017. In this quinquennium, the Italian legislator, in a curious and totally unexpected turn of events, transformed the *s.r.l.* by implementing a special regulation outside the Civil Code that differs remarkably from the two company forms available under general corporate law (ie, the public and private company types). This intervention demolished an old legal institution of continental Europe, the *Gesellschaft mit beschränkter Haftung*-model – Germany's most important and successful legal export product[33] – which the majority of European countries embraced between the end of the nineteenth and the first half of the twentieth century.[34] Influential scholars have called the end result a phenomenon of hybridization of company types (*ibridazione dei tipi* or *Grundtypenvermischung*).[35]

---

[29] Directive (EU) 2019/1151 of 20 June 2019 amending Directive (EU) 2017/1132 as regards the use of digital tools and processes in company law [2019] OJ L186/80.

[30] Cf Fleischer (n 25) 1088–1089; Giuseppe B Portale, 'Società a responsabilità limitata senza capitale sociale e imprenditore individuale con "capitale destinato" (Capitale sociale quo vadis?)' (2010) 55 Riv soc 1237.

[31] Take Spain, with the *sociedad limitada nueva empresa*, which was introduced in 2003 and abolished in 2022 (*Ley* 18/2022, *de 28 de septiembre, de creación y crecimiento de empresas*); in Belgium, the *société privée à responsabilité limitée-starter*, introduced in 2010 and now abolished by the general corporate law reform of 2019; in Denmark, the *ivaersaetterselskab*, established in 2014 as a domestic version of the German *Unternehmergesellschaft*, abolished in April 2019.

[32] In Austria, as mentioned, precisely this policy rationale underlies reform efforts that led to the recent introduction of the 'Flex-KapG'.

[33] Markus Lutter, 'Die Entwicklung der GmbH in Europa und der Welt' in Markus Lutter, Peter Ulmer and Wolfgang Zöllner (eds), *Festschrift 100 Jahre GmbH-Gesetz* (Otto Schmidt 1992).

[34] Giudici and Agstner (n 11) 607ff; Peter Agstner, Antonio Capizzi and Paolo Giudici, 'Business Angels, Venture Capital e la nuova s.r.l.' (2020) 8 Riv ODC 353, 363ff.

[35] Cf Giuseppe Zanarone, *La s.r.l. A vent'anni della Riforma del diritto societario* (Giuffrè 2023); Paolo Benazzo, 'Categorie di quote, diritti di voto e governance nella "nuovissima" s.r.l.: quale ruolo e quale spazio per la disciplina azionaria nella s.r.l.-PMI aperta?' (2018) 63 Riv soc 1441, 1458ff; Marco Cian, 'Le start-up innovative a responsabilità limitata: partecipazioni, altri rapporti partecipativi e nuovi confini del tipo' (2014) 37 Nuove leggi civ comm, 1178, 1179 (2014); Scano (n 13) 82ff (qualifying the *s.r.l.* emblematically as 'forma senza tipo'); Marco Speranzin, 'S.r.l. piccole-medie imprese tra autonomia statutaria e ibridazione dei tipi (con particolare riferimento alle partecipazioni prive del diritto di voto)' (2018) 63 Riv soc 335; in the German scholarship, Harm Peter Westermann, *Vertragsfreiheit und Typengesetz-*

1. The Restart, Italia! Report

The profound changes undergone by Italian company law in the five-year period from 2012–2017 are a response to the almost zero growth in productivity and very low rate of innovation and development in the Italian economy.[36] It is for this reason that the Ministry of Economic Development (today the Ministry of Enterprises and Made in Italy) appointed a task force of twelve experts in the field of start-ups, business developers (incubators, accelerators, etc.) and venture capital, which concluded its work with a report called 'Restart, Italia!'[37] that contained proposals for an 'i(nnovative) *s.r.l.* package' (as it was termed in the document) envisaging almost all the instruments used in VC financing: work-for-equity and a less restrictive regime of legal capital for start-ups, convertible notes, and different classes of shares – performance shares for the founders and team and seeding shares for investors – with all the rights typically given to investors in VC financing, such as tag-along and drag-along rights, liquidation preferences, nomination rights, etc.[38] The report also envisaged amendments to the regulation of asset management companies in the area of venture capital,[39] a specific regulatory regime for crowdfunding,[40] and a more favourable insolvency law regime.[41]

2. Decree Law of 18 October 2012, no 179 ('Growth Decree 2.0')

In 2012, following the 'Restart, Italia!' report, the government enacted a legislative package called the 'Growth Decree' (art 25–32, Decree Law of 18 October 2012, no 179, converted into the Law of 18 December 2012, no 221). The relevant provisions, entitled 'measures for the creation and development of innovative start-ups' (sec IX), aim to foster sustainable growth, technological development, and new entrepreneurship and employment (particularly amongst the young), including through the creation of a more innovation-friendly environment.[42]

---

lichkeit im Recht der Personengesellschaften (Springer 1970); recently, Holger Fleischer, 'Der numerus clausus im Gesellschaftsrecht: Rechtsdogmatik – Rechtsvergleichung – Rechtsökonomie – Rechtspolitik' (2023) 52 ZGR 261.

[36] Matteo Bugamelli and others, 'Productivity Growth in Italy: A Tale of a Slow-motion Change' (2018) 422 Questioni di economia e Finanza della Banca d'Italia (Occasional Papers) <https://www.bancaditalia.it/pubblicazioni/qef/2018-0422/QEF_422_18.pdf> accessed 28 December 2023.

[37] *Restart, Italia!, Rapporto della Task Force sulle startup istituita dal Ministro dello Sviluppo Economico* (2012) <www.mise.gov.it/index.php/it/per-i-media/pubblicazioni/2030418-rapporto-restart-italia> accessed 28 December 2023).

[38] *Restart, Italia!* (n 37), 51–52.

[39] *Restart, Italia!* (n 37) 53–54, under the section 'Simplifying the organizations that invest in startups'.

[40] *Restart, Italia!* (n 37) 79–81.

[41] *Restart, Italia!* (n 37) 97–101.

[42] Stated in such terms is art 25(1) of Decree Law 179/2012.

An innovative start-up is defined as an entity incorporated in the form of a(n) (even unipersonal) private company, public company, or co-operative whose shares or quotas are not traded on a regulated market or multilateral trading facility.[43] To qualify, companies may be no more than five years old (four years by 2015);[44] not the result of an extraordinary corporate transaction (ie, a merger, de-merger, or business transfer); and must have headquarters in Italy (or if in another Member State, a branch in Italy). Additional conditions are: total annual revenues no higher than 5 million euros starting from the second year of activity; non-distribution of profits since incorporation; company activities consisting exclusively or predominantly in the development, production or trading of innovative products or services having a high technological value. Finally, the innovative start-up must meet at least one of the following requirements: (a) minimum threshold of research and development (R&D) expenses,[45] (b) minimum number of highly qualified employees,[46] or (c) holder of at least one intellectual property right. If the above qualifications for an 'innovative start-up company' are satisfied, the company is registered in a special section of the company register.[47] Registration is automatic and based on certification by a legal representative who attests to the satisfaction of the requirements.[48] According to data provided by the Ministry of Enterprises and Made in Italy, as of 31 December 2023 there were 13,394 innovative start-ups registered in the special section of the company register, of which 93.9% are incorporated as an *s.r.l.*[49]

The above conditions are a prerequisite for the recognition of the benefits envisaged by the special regulatory regime, but they do not affect the validity of the company's articles of incorporation and/or the continued existence of the com-

---

[43] Decree Law 179/2012, art 25(2).

[44] This means that innovative start-up status is designed to automatically sunset. Companies already established at the date of entry into force of the law converting Decree 179/2012 are considered to be innovative start-ups for purposes of this decree if they file, on the company register, a declaration attesting that they meet the relevant requirements. They then fall within the special regulation for four years from the date of entry into force of the decree if the innovative start-up was established within the previous two years; or for three years if established within the previous three years; or for two years if established within the previous four years (art 25(3)).

[45] Research and development expenses must be greater than or equal to 15% of the company's production costs or the company's production value, whichever is higher.

[46] At least one-third of the personnel must have a doctorate, be enrolled in a doctoral degree program, or have completed a degree with a research program of 3 years at a public or private research entity in Italy or abroad. Alternatively, at least two-thirds of the workforce must have a master's degree.

[47] Decree Law 179/2012, art 25(8).

[48] Decree Law 179/2012, art 25(9).

[49] Ministro delle Imprese and Made in Italy, *Relazione annuale al Parlamento 2024 sullo stato di attuazione e le policy a sostengo di Startup e Pmi innovative* <https://www.mimit.gov.it/images/stories/documenti/RELAZIONE_ANNUALE_2024-finale.pdf> (accessed 25 November 2025).

pany.[50] In fact, the loss of the aforesaid requirements simply determines the removal of the innovative start-up from the special section of the company register; conversely, the company's registration in the ordinary section remains untouched.[51] Still, for innovative start-ups established as an *s.r.l.*, any clauses included in the articles of incorporation pursuant to art 26(2), (3) and (7) remain effective even upon termination of innovative-company status, but only with respect to the quotas already subscribed and the participatory (hybrid) financial instruments already issued.[52]

While the innovations are in fact negligible for innovative start-ups organized as public companies, certainly the greatest impact has registered in reference to companies incorporated as private companies (*s.r.l.*'s).[53] The relevant provision is art 26 of the earlier-mentioned Growth Decree of 2012, no 179, entitled 'exemption from corporate law and reduction of start-up burdens'.[54] According to the initial wording of this provision, an innovative start-up organized as an *s.r.l.* is allowed to:

(a) issue classes of quotas with different rights and, within the limits imposed by the law, freely determine the content of said rights;[55] hence, in order to diversify the investment options, it is legitimate to grant corporate rights disproportionate to the holding in the company or to assign special rights to the class of quotas (instead of only to single shareholders), thereby derogating from the general rules set forth for private companies in art 2468(2–3) of the Civ. Code.[56]

---

[50] Zanarone (n 35) 524, 533.

[51] Decree Law 179/2012, art 25(16). For case law see Tribunale Rome 5 April 2019, (2019) 38 Le Società 1375, with comment by Elisabetta Codazzi, 'Cancellazione di start up innovativa dalla sezione speciale del registro delle imprese per perdita del requisito di innovatività'.

[52] Decree Law 179/2012, art 31(4).

[53] Scano (n 13) 74; Silvia Guizzardi, *L'accesso al capitale di rischio delle società innovative a responsabilità limitata* (Giuffrè 2022) 39.

[54] For a general overview, cf, for example, Paolo Benazzo, 'Start-up e PMI innovative' in *Digesto Discipline Privatistiche – Sezione Commerciale – Ottavo aggiornamento*, vol 8 (UTET 2017) 467ff; Marco Cian, 'S.r.l. PMI, s.r.l., s.p.a.: schemi argomentativi per una ricostruzione del sistema' (2018) 63 Riv soc 818ff; Monica Cossu, 'Le start up innovative in forma di società a responsabilità limitata. Profili privatistici' in Mario Campobasso and others (eds), *Società, banche e crisi d'impresa. Liber amicorum Pietro Abbadessa*, vol 2 (UTET 2014) 1705ff; Elena Fregonara, *La start up innovativa* (Giuffrè 2013) 21ff; Carlotta Rinaldo, 'La multiformità della s.r.l.' (2020) 65 Riv soc 1513ff; Guizzardi (n 53) 35ff; Zanarone (n 35) 523ff, 536ff.

[55] Decree Law 179/2012 art 26(2). For example, it is possible to create classes of quotas without withdrawal rights (Notary Bar of Florence-Pistoia-Pisa, Guideline no 39/2014) or inspection rights (idem, Guideline no 41/2014); on the contrary, it would not be possible to create a class of quotas with no right to share in profits, since this would constitute a violation of the ban against *societas leonine* clauses (CC, art 2265).

[56] This means that unless otherwise stipulated, the rights incorporated in the class(es) of quotas circulate with the transferred class(es) of quotas, whereas the transfer of individual quotas does not normally entail the transfer of any special rights to which the seller quotaholder may be entitled. See Notary Bar of Milan, Guideline no 171/2018 (27 November 2018).

Furthermore, it is possible to create classes of quotas without voting rights or with multiple voting rights or voting rights limited only to resolutions on particular matters;[57]

(b) offer their quotas to the public, including by means of online equity crowdfunding campaigns.[58] Currently, the legislative decree of 10 March 2023, no 30, implementing Regulation (EU) 2020/1503 of 7 October 2020 on European crowdfunding service providers for business,[59] extends the possibility of raising equity capital via crowdfunding to *all* limited liability companies, including non-SMEs.[60] In this case, opting for an alternative regime permits subscription of *s.r.l.* quotas through authorized financial intermediaries who carry out this mandate in their own name and on behalf of the subscribers or purchasers who have participated in the crowdfunding offer. Within 30 days of the closing of the offer, the authorized intermediaries must file with the company register a certificate attesting to their ownership of quotas on behalf of third parties bearing the related cost. The subsequent disposal of the quotas by the subscriber or purchaser carried out by simply annotating the transfer in the registers kept by the authorized intermediary, without the need for a written contract as normally prescribed by art 2470(2) CC and art 36(1-*bis*) of Decree Law of 25 June 2008, no 112, converted into the Law of 6 August 2008, no 133;[61]

(c) carry out transactions (buy-backs) on their own quotas functional to implementing vesting schemes for the allocation of quotas to directors and employees;[62]

(d) issue participatory financial instruments (*strumenti finanziari partecipativi*) that provide property rights or even administrative rights, with the exclusion of the right to vote in the general meeting of quotaholders;

---

[57] Decree Law 179/2012, art 26(3). For an in-depth analysis, see Sciuto (n 23) 415ff; Speranzin (n 35) 335ff; Zanarone (n 35) 540ff; for a different opinion affirming the impossibility of creating classes of quotas with multiple voting rights, see Rinaldo (n 54) 1535. For the effectiveness of such clauses even upon termination of innovative company status, see n 52 above and corresponding text.

[58] Decree Law 179/2012, art 26(5), 30; Consolidated Financial Securities Act (CFSA) of 1998, no 58, art 100-*ter* and National Commission for Companies and the Stock Exchange (CONSOB), Regulation no 18592 of 26 June 2013. For comments on the previous regulatory framework, cf Siliva Corso, *Le s.r.l. "aperte" al mercato tra governance societaria e diritti dei soci investitori* (Giuffrè 2021) 43ff; Enrico Ginevra, 'Le società di capitali "aperte", tra codice civile e t.u.f.' (2022) 75 Banca borsa tit cred 868, 887ff; Piergiuseppe Spolaore, *S.r.l. e offerta al "pubblico" di partecipazioni sociali* (Giuffrè 2022). In Germany, the relevant provisions on *Schwarmfinanzierung* are in §§ 32b–32f of the Wertpapierhandelsgesetz (WpHG).

[59] Johannes Öhmann, *Die Verordnung über Europäische Schwarmfinanzierungsdienstleiste* (Duncker & Humblot 2023) 112ff.

[60] See the newly amended art 100-*ter*(1) CFSA. Whether this implies an implicit abrogation of art 2468(1) CCis not yet clear, and Italian scholars have not adequately studied the question.

[61] CFSA, art 100-*ter*(2).

[62] Decree Law 179/2012, art 26(6), thus derogating from the general rule set forth in art 2474 CC.

(e) enjoy more favourable rules with regard to the reduction of share capital for losses.[63] In particular, the relevant provision grants a 'grace period' of one additional year (thus of two years in total) in the event of losses affecting the share capital by more than one third; likewise, in the event of losses reducing the capital below the legal minimum, as an alternative to immediately reducing the capital and simultaneously increasing it to an amount not less than the legal minimum – thus avoiding the company's dissolution (ie, the 'recapitalize or liquidate' rule) – the innovative start-up may resolve to postpone such decisions until the end of the following financial year.[64]

Most of these provisions merely introduce a special regulatory framework distinct from the general codified law by recalling legal concepts embedded in joint-stock corporation law. Apart from this formal reference, nothing specific is said as to the applicable substantive law. Thus it is uncertain, for example, whether limits on the issue of shares without voting rights or with limited voting rights under art 2351(2) CC (ie, face value may not exceed a total of half of the share capital) also extend to an SME organized as an *s.r.l.*; similarly, it is unclear whether they are subject in the same way to the ten-vote-per-share maximum under art 2351(4) CC;[65] finally, it is unclear whether the limits on the purchase of the company's own shares (expenditure must not exceed available reserves and dis-

---

[63] The general provisions on reducing the share capital for losses are contained in art 2446–2447 CC (for the *s.p.a.*) and in art 2482-*bis* – art 2482-*ter* CC (for the *s.r.l.*).

[64] Decree Law 179/2012, art 26(1).

[65] The competitiveness bill ('*Legge Capitali*': for more details, see below at part V) raised the three-vote limit to ten votes per share, with maintenance of these shares even after the initial public offering (art 13, modifying art 2351(4) CC). Current Italian regulations, as amended in 2014, prohibit listed companies from issuing shares with multiple voting rights, except in the form of a loyalty share program that gives long-term shareholders (holding uninterrupted for at least 24 months) double voting rights. Now, the current wording of art 14(1)(b) of the Law 5 March 2024, no 21, by modifying art 127-*quinquies* of the CFSA, allows companies adopting the increased voting mechanism to provide, in their articles of association (opt-in), that in addition to the ordinary double-voting right, such rights may be further increased to the extent of one vote per share for each 12 month-period of continuous share ownership up to a maximum total of 10 votes per share (step-up mechanism); in such case, dissenting shareholders have a withdrawal right. For critical commentary see CONSOB, 'Memoria tecnica relativa agli articoli 12, 14 e 19' (16 November 2023) <www.consob.it> accessed 4 December 2023); Giuseppe A Rescio, 'Gli "azionisti stabili": voto plurimo e voto maggiorato' (2024) 18 Riv dir soc 193. For Germany, following the proposal at the EU-level for a directive on multiple-vote share structures (COM (2022) 761 final) as part of the 'Listing Act' package, see the *Zukunftsfinanzierungsgesetz* (ZuFinG), which amends §§ 12 and 134 of the *Aktiengesetz* (AktG). For literature on this issue, see Klaus J. Hopt and Susanne Kalss, 'Mehrstimmrechtsaktien – Grundsatzprobleme, Regelungsbausteine, Praxisfragen' (2024) 53 ZGR 84; Susanne Kalss, 'Das Kommen, Gehen und Wiederkommen des Mehrstimmrechts' (2023) 187 ZHR 438; Matthias Casper, 'Das Zukunftsfinanzierungsgesetz' (2023) 187 ZHR 5; Philip Denninger and Daniel von Bülow, 'Mehrstimmrechtsaktien im Recht der öffentlichen Übernahmen' (2023) 68 AG 417; Sebastian Mock and Jean Mohamed, 'Goodbye One Share One Vote? – Welcome Dual-Class Shares! Ein komparativer Überblick zu rechtspolitischen Reformüberlegungen' (2022) 25 NZG 1275.

tributable profits pursuant to art 2357 CC) apply to buybacks functional to the implementation of vesting schemes.[66]

In any case, the regulatory gap between the public and the private company, especially with respect to financial flexibility, was reduced, and the *GmbH*-like tradition was broken thanks to measures with no full equivalents in the comparative landscape.

3. *From Exception to Rule: The Legislative Interventions of 2015 and 2017*

The significance of identifying the exact contours of the 'innovativeness' embedded in the relevant rule is much diminished, because almost all the innovations originally envisaged (solely) for innovative start-ups have since been extended to virtually all Italian companies operating in the form of an *s.r.l.*

In fact, what were supposed to be temporary exceptions to an established system have instead rapidly spread. They first spread to all innovative SMEs (Decree Law of 24 January 2015, no 3, converted into Law of 24 March 2015, no 33 – the 'Investment Compact'), as defined in accordance with Recommendation 2003/361/EC[67] and subject to some further requirements. In particular, all innovative SMEs are required to have their latest financial statement and any consolidated financial statement drawn up by an certified auditor or auditing firm (art 4(1)(b)); while the trading on growth markets or multilateral trading facilities is allowed (art 4(1)(c)), innovative SMEs in the form of an *s.p.a.* cannot trade their shares on a regulated market; furthermore, innovative SMEs cannot be registered in the special section of the company register reserved (only) for innovative start-ups (art 4(1)(d)); finally, while certain minimum thresholds of (indirect) innovativeness must be met (R&D expenses, employment of research staff, holding intellectual property rights), they are less stringent than those envisaged for innovative start-ups (art 4(1)(e)).

The most striking differences between the regulatory framework for innovative SMEs and that for innovative start-ups are that (*i*) innovative SMEs, with some minor exceptions, are not subject to any time limit, while innovative start-ups cannot have been established for more than 60 months; (*ii*) the only size limit for innovative SMEs is 50 million euros (the EU parameter), while total annual revenues for innovative start-ups cannot exceed 5 million euros beginning in the second year of activity; (*iii*) innovative SMEs are not subject to any constraints on the distribution of profits; (*iv*) the corporate purpose of an innovative SME is not limited to activities in the development, production and trading of products

[66] In favour of application of the *s.p.a.* regulatory regime, see generally Benazzo (n 35) 479; Oreste Cagnasso, 'Start up e P.M.I. innovative: inquadramento' (2016) 168 Giur it 2285ff; Cian (n 35) 1180ff; contra Agstner, Capizzi and Giudici (n 34) 401.

[67] The category of SMEs is made up of enterprises which employ fewer than 250 persons and which have an annual turnover not exceeding 50 million euros and/or an annual balance sheet total not exceeding 43 million euros (see Annex, art 2 of the Commission Recommendation 2003/361/CE of 6 May 2003 [2003] OJ L124/36).

or services of high technological value. Once the relevant legal conditions are met, innovative SMEs benefit from essentially the same favourable regulatory regime as innovative start-ups (art 4(9)), except that the more favourable rules on labour law and insolvency law do not apply.[68]

Finally, in 2017, these novelties were extended to all SMEs even if they do not qualify as innovative in the specified sense; thus, *de facto* they were applied to all *s.r.l.*'s (art 57, Decree Law of 24 April 2017, no 50, converted into Law of 21 June 2017, no 96), which in Italy amounts to more than one and a half million organizations (as opposed to just over thirty thousand *s.p.a.*'s).[69] This was achieved by simply replacing, in art 26 of Decree Law 179/2012, the phrase 'innovative start-up' with the abbreviation 'SME'.[70] The only significant exceptions are that it is impossible for non-innovative SMEs to issue hybrid securities (*strumenti finanziari partecipativi*) and that the more favourable rules regarding the reduction of legal capital for losses do not apply. Surprisingly, only a few 'big' *s.r.l.*'s have preserved their traditional closely-held characterization – an outcome of systematic incongruity.[71]

The exact definition of an SME is debated, given that the decree of 2017, by amending art 26 of Decree 179/2012 – unlike the decree of 2015, which expressly refers to the relevant EU provision – gives no indication in this regard. Most scholars refer to the parameters provided in Recommendation 361/2003, but others refer, less convincingly, to the definition of SMEs envisaged in the Consolidated Financial Securities Act (CFSA) (TUF, Testo unico della finanza),[72] which in turn refers to the EU Prospectus Regulation 2017/1129 (art 2(1)(f)). The difference is not totally marginal. In fact, notwithstanding the equal thresholds (average number of employees less than 250; total balance sheet not exceeding 43 million euros; annual net turnover not exceeding 50 million euros), this definition of an SME differs from the one in Recommendation 361/2003 because in the latter, the threshold number of employees must never be exceeded, whereas under the Italian capital market rules, a company with 250 or more employees still qualifies as an SME if its balance sheet and net annual turnover are both below the respective threshold.[73]

---

[68] For an accurate examination of the differences, see Marco Cian, 'Società start-up innovative e PMI innovative' (2015) 42 Giur comm 969; Oreste Cagnasso, 'La s.r.l. piccola e media impresa (P.M.I.)' in Ibba and Marasà (eds) (n 13) 87ff.

[69] This statistical data was provided by *Infocamere*, which manages the company register on behalf of the single Chambers of Commerce (*Camere di Commercio*).

[70] See Benazzo (n 35) 469 (criticizing such extension).

[71] Benazzo (n 35) 470.

[72] Cf CFSA, art 61(1)(h); and CFSA art 1(5-*novies*); art 50-*quinquies*, art 100-*ter*, now repealed or substituted by Legislative Decree 2023, no 30, implementing the mentioned EU Crowdfunding Regulation of 2020.

[73] For a complete summary of the debate, see Zanarone (n 35) 589ff. See also (though it is not applicable to the *s.r.l.*) the definition of an SME contained in the MiFID II Directive (UE) 2014/65 (art 4(1) point 13 (companies that had an average market capitalization of less than

IV. Digital Incorporation of Innovative Start-up *s.r.l.*'s (Now All *s.r.l.*'s)

Pursuant to art 4(10-*bis*) of Decree Law 3/2015[74] and the executing ministerial decrees,[75] for the sole purpose of favouring the establishment of new enterprises, the articles of incorporation and eventual amendments are to be drawn up by public (notarial) deed – as mandatorily required for the 'ordinary' *s.r.l.* (CC, art 2463(2), 2480) – *or* by a deed digitally signed in the manner provided by the digital administration code (the 'DAC', enacted by the Legislative Decree of 7 March 2005, no 82); the digital signature may either be simple (DAC, art 24) or notarized (DAC, art 25). In incorporation by a digitally signed document, the articles of incorporation and their amendments shall be drawn up in accordance with a uniform standard model provided by the responsible ministry.[76] Digital incorporation was available for innovative start-up *s.r.l.*'s from July 2016 to March 2021, when the State Council, in decision no 2643 of 29 March 2021, declared the above-mentioned two ministerial decrees void,[77] with the corresponding legal proceeding initiated by the National Council of Notaries (Consiglio Nazionale del Notariato).[78] However, art 39-*septies* of Decree Law 77/2021 provides that articles of incorporation (as well as by-laws and subsequent amendments thereto) of innovative start-up companies established as *s.r.l.*'s, registered as of 31 July 2021, and drafted in a manner alternative to a public deed remain valid and effective.[79]

Today, the dispute is no longer particularly relevant.[80] In fact, with the legislative decree of 8 November 2021, no 183 (art 2), implementing Directive (EU)

---

200 million euros on the basis of end-year quotes for the previous three calendar years)), recalled by the Prospectus Regulation of 2017.

[74] Converted into the Law of 24 March 2005, no 33.

[75] Ministerial Decrees of 17 February 2016 (to which was annexed 'model articles of incorporation/by-laws for innovative start-ups in the form of limited liability companies') and of 28 October 2016 (containing a model of the quotaholder resolution for the amendment of the company's articles of incorporation).

[76] For a complete overview, cf Zanarone (n 35) 564ff; Alessandra Zanardo, *Costituzione online e costituzione standardizzata di società di capitali* (Giappichelli 2022) 72ff, 99ff; Alessandra Zanardo, 'Costituzione online di società: uno strumento per il rafforzamento della libertà d'impresa?' (2021) 9 Riv ODC 1333.

[77] Published, *inter alia*, in (2021) Riv not 574.

[78] For comment on this decision, see Silvia Corso, 'La costituzione in modalità digitale delle s.r.l. start-up innovative: il Consiglio di Stato censura la disciplina ministeriale' (2022) 49 Giur. comm. 123.

[79] Zanarone (n 35) 575ff.

[80] Zanardo (2021) (n 76) 87 (remembering that art 4(10-*bis*) of Decree Law 3/2015 was implicitly abolished by Legislative Decree 183/2021); with significant historical references, see Federico M Mucciarelli, 'La costituzione digitale di società nell'evoluzione del diritto societario europeo' in Alessandro Pajno, Filippo Donati and Antonio Perrucci (eds), *Intelligenza artificiale e diritto: una rivoluzione?* (Mulino 2022) 371, 385ff; Federico M Mucciarelli, 'Cos-

2019/1151 as regards the use of digital tools and processes in company law,[81] the articles of incorporation of limited liability companies and simplified limited liability companies[82] having their registered office in Italy and with capital paid up in cash may be received by a notary by means of a digital public deed; in this case, all or some of the subscribed quotaholders participate via videoconference using a telematic platform set up and managed by the National Council of Notaries. The ministerial decree of 26 July 2022, no 155 provided standardized model articles of incorporation, with such templates also published in English on the websites of the chambers of commerce.[83]

V. The Law on the Competitiveness of Capital Markets: A New Frontier

Recently, with the Law on the competitiveness of capital markets (Law 5 March 2024, no 21 or '*Legge Capitali*'), a new frontier was reached in the regulation of private limited liability companies as well.[84] Of special interest here is the provision in art 3 of the *Legge Capitali*, which, by amending art 26 of Decree Law of 18 October 2012, no 179, states in the new par 2-*bis* that quotas issued by *s.r.l.*-SMEs that have equal value and confer equal rights may exist in dematerialized form (as book-entry securities) pursuant to the provisions of art 83-*bis* of the CFSA, thus allowing market trading in derogation of art 2468 CC. Hence, after the opening of the financial structure (at first only for *s.r.l.*-SMEs and now for all *s.r.l.*'s) to forms of capital-raising by means of crowdfunding, the aforementioned law today allows the dematerialization of standardized shares of *s.r.l.*-SMEs (with market capitalization of less than 1 billion euros); it is the latest step in this disruptive evolution. As a consequence, the phenomenon of private companies with

tituzione digitale delle società e interconnessione dei registri' in Nicolò Abriani and Renzo Costi (eds), *Diritto societario, digitalizzazione e intelligenza artificiale* (Giuffrè 2023) 27ff.

[81] Cf Marco Saverio Spolidoro, 'La s.r.l. semplificata e la s.r.l. a capitale ribassato' in Ibba and Marasà (eds) (n 13) 145ff; Nicola de Luca, 'La costituzione online delle società. Riflessioni sulla Direttiva 2019/1159/EU (Direttiva CorpTech)' (2020) 74 Riv not 415ff; Peter Kindler and Simon Jobst, 'Costituzione di società ed identificazione elettronica: il Company Law Package e la sua attuazione nell'ordinamento tedesco ed in quello italiano' (2019) 42 Nuove leggi civ comm 1556ff; Zanardo (2021) (n 76) 140.

[82] For example, the Belgian regulation implementing the Digitalization Directive (*Loi du 12 juillet 2021*) allows online incorporation even for public companies.

[83] Zanardo (2021) (n 76) 197ff.

[84] The regulatory impact has been substantial for public listed companies as well, especially on the issues of slate voting (the list voting system), loyalty shares, and mandatory bids. For a good first overview, see Piergaetano Marchetti and Marco Ventoruzzo (eds.), *Commentario alla Legge Capitali. Legge 5 marzo 2024, n. 21* (Pacini 2024).

quotas, to be qualified as securities, and capable of trading on MTF growth markets will no longer be heterodox.[85]

Furthermore, another significant innovation was introduced by art 28(2)(a-*bis*) of Decree Law 17 March 2023, no 25, converted into Law 10 May 2023, no 52, which adapts national legislation to Regulation (EU) 2022/858 on a pilot program for market infrastructure based on distributed ledger technology. This provision gives the public watchdog CONSOB the power to extend, by its own specific regulation, the applicability of the aforementioned decree (and thus the definition of digital securities) to, among other things, *s.r.l.* quotas, which would then become negotiable on DLT-based systems. The provision thereby also derogates from art 2470 CC, according to which the transfer of *s.r.l.* quotas takes effect vis-à-vis the company as soon as the deed of transfer is filed in the company register.[86]

VI. Other Benefits for Innovative Start-ups

Apart from the special corporate law status outlined here, innovative start-ups enjoy other significant benefits and exemptions. The relevant provisions in art 27ff envisage a series of tax and labour law benefits as well as privileged treatment in insolvency. The following aspects are of peculiar interest:

(i) Tax privileges for work-for-equity schemes. Article 27 of Decree Law 179/2012 provides that shares, quotas, and participatory financial instruments assigned to directors and employees as a form of remuneration are not attributable to them as taxable income for taxation or pension purposes, provided that such financial instruments are not repurchased by the innovative start-up or by entities it controls or is controlled by. The same privileged tax treatment applies if these financial instruments are issued in return for work or services rendered to the innovative start-up (work-for-equity or vesting schemes).[87]

---

[85] For details and comparative references, cf Peter Agstner, 'Le s.r.l. aperte: uno sguardo comparatistico' (2024) Riv ODC 198; Francesco Brizzi, 'La dematerializzazione delle quote di S.r.l. PMI' (2024) 44 Le Società 785; Marco Cian, 'Le quote dematerializzate di s.r.l.' (2024) 70 Riv dir civ 291. On the qualification of *s.r.l.* quotas as transferable securities (*valori mobiliari*), see Emanuele Cusa, 'Le quote di s.r.l. possono essere valori mobiliari' (2019) 72 Banca borsa tit cred 675.

[86] For comment, see Raffaele Lener, 'Cosa sta succedendo alle quote di srl?' (2023) 1 Quaderni Assosim 13ff; Silvia Corso and Aldo Laudonio, 'Le s.r.l. aperte al mercato tra crowdfunding e sperimentazione di nuovi ambienti digitali' (2024) 12 Riv ODC 119; see also the 'first' CONSOB resolution, no 22923 of 6 December 2023, on the issuance and circulation of financial instruments in digital form. For an instructive overview of the EU DLT pilot regime, see generally Philipp Maume and Finn Kesper, 'The EU DLT Pilot Regime for Digital Assets' (2023) 20 ECLJ 118.

[87] For comment see Claudio Sottoriva, 'Le imprese start up innovative: inquadramento tributario' in Oreste Cagnasso and Angelo Mambriani (eds), *Start up e P.M.I. innovative* (Zanichelli 2020) 935, 942ff.

(ii) Various tax incentives for investments in innovative start-ups and innovative SMEs. First, individuals investing in the share capital of innovative start-ups or innovative SMEs, either directly or through undertakings for collective investment in transferable securities (UCITSs) that invest predominantly in innovative start-ups or innovative SMEs, up to a maximum of 1 million euros in each tax period, are afforded a general income tax deduction of 30% (thus, the maximum deduction applicable is EUR 300,000). This investment in the company must be maintained for at least three years under penalty of forfeiture.[88] Alternatively, the rules allow a personal income tax deduction of 50% for individuals investing in the share capital of innovative start-ups or innovative SMEs; here the benefits are pursuant to the *de minimis* Regulation (Commission Regulation (EU) 1407/2013 of 18 December 2013). Again, the investment, either direct or made through UCITSs that invest predominantly in innovative start-ups or innovative SMEs, must be maintained for at least three years. For investments in innovative start-ups, the eligible investment amounts to a maximum of 100,000 euros in each tax period.[89] For investments in innovative SMEs, the eligible investment amounts to a maximum of 300,000 euros in each tax period. Beyond this limit, the investor may deduct 30% of the excess in each tax period.[90]

(iii) Special regulatory regime in the case of insolvency.[91] In particular, art 31 of Decree Law 179/2012 states that unlike innovative SMEs, innovative start-ups are not subject to insolvency proceedings other than those provided by the Law of 27 January 2012/3, now repealed and merged into the new Code of Business Crisis and Insolvency (*Codice della crisi di impresa e dell'insolvenza*, the 'CBCI'), which finally entered into force on 15 July 2022.[92] This means that innovative start-ups in a situation of over-indebtedness (*sovraindebitamento*), ie, in crisis or insolvency,[93] can access the 'simplified' procedures provided by art 65ff of the CBCI, ie, controlled liquidation of the debtor's assets *ex* art 268ff (*liquidazione controllata*) and minor arrangements with creditors *ex* art 74ff (*concordato minore*)[94]; but they are not subject to the main procedure of judicial liquidation *ex* art 121ff (*liquidazione giudiziale*), the term that now replaces *fallimento* (bank-

---

[88] Decree Law 179/2012, art 29 and executing Ministerial Decree of 7 May 2019.

[89] Decree Law 179/2012, art 29-*bis*, as introduced by Decree Law of 19 May 2020, no 34 (the 'Relaunch Decree', art 38(7)).

[90] Decree Law 3/2015, art 4(9-*ter*), as introduced by Decree Law of 19 May 2020, no 34 (the 'Relaunch Decree', art 38(8)).

[91] For general observations on the challenges posed by start-up failures, see Elizabeth Pollman, 'Startup Failure' (2023) ECGI Law Working Paper 729/2023 <https://ssrn.com/abstract=4535089> accessed 27 September 2023.

[92] The actual version is available at <www.altalex.com/documents/codici-altalex/2019/02/15/codice-crisi-impresa> accessed 25 September 2023).

[93] CBCI, art 2(c).

[94] The procedure called 'agreement' for the restructuring of consumer debt is not available for innovative start-ups *ex* art 67ff of the CBCI (*ristrutturazione dei debiti del consumatore*).

ruptcy).[95] Also available to innovative start-ups are certain out-of-court restructuring tools, ie, certified recovery plans (*piano attestato di risanamento*) *ex* art 56 of the CBCI and negotiated crisis resolutions (*composizione negoziata della crisi*) *ex* art 12ff of the CBCI.[96]

VII. Conclusions

The reforms in the five-year period from 2012–2017 reshuffled the organization of closed companies. Put more elegantly, these reforms effected a hybridization or even a standardization of company types. The result has been a gradual evaporation of the distinction between unlisted joint-stock corporations and *s.r.l.*'s (whether or not they are also SMEs).[97] Thus, in Italy the dual-class (ie, public vs. private) model of company law – historically related to and forged by the German *GmbH*-model – collapsed. Today, the real line of distinction runs in an overarching fashion between closed and open corporations. In each of these macro-types, we find both closed and open *s.r.l.*'s (whether SMEs or no) as well as closed and open *s.p.a.*'s. Conversely, the 'big' *s.r.l.* plays an 'outlier' role of systematic incoherence with negligible practical relevance. Some regulatory drawbacks remain, especially with respect to the open *s.r.l.* (again, whether an SME or no), resulting from a lack of clarity about which rules apply.[98] But the trend is clear, as witnessed by similar regulatory interventions across Europe (such as in Slovakia, Polen, Spain, and Austria), which is even more surprising considering that path dependency barriers have been overcome.[99] Here Italy received the necessary impulses from the U.S. VC-financing practice, and in that regard Italy was the trendsetter of this particular regulatory competition in the broad sense.[100]

---

[95] For a good overview, cf Marina Spiotta, 'Sulla non fallibilità delle start-up' (2023) 50 Giur comm 141ff; Giovanni B Nardecchia, 'Profili di diritto fallimentare' in Cagnasso and Mambriani (eds) (n 87) 951ff; for case law, see Corte di Cassazione 7 July 2022, no 32491; Tribunale Milan 8 April 2021, no 241.

[96] Spiotta (n 95) 143.

[97] On this opinion see also Roberto Sacchi, 'Note a margine del saggio di Aldo Dolmetta sul tipo S.R.L.' (2022) 120 Riv dir comm 569ff; critically Cian (n 14) 297, 304.

[98] On the argument that eventual regulatory gaps are to be filled by applying the rules provided for public (listed) companies, cf, *inter alia*, Benazzo (n 35) 1463ff; Oreste Cagnasso, 'S.r.l. aperta' (2020) 43 Nuove leggi civ comm 1208, 1223; Silvia Corso, 'S.R.L.-PMI aperte al mercato: scelte statutarie e diritti dei soci investitori' (2019) 72 Banca borsa tit cred 877; contra Agstner, Capizzi and Giudici (n 34) 391ff; Antonio Cetra, 'Le s.r.l.-p.m.i.: disciplina legale e autonomia statutaria' (2020) 73 Banca borsa tit cred 815, 826ff. For useful observations in the German literature on what rules apply to *Grundtypenvermischung*, see Marcus Lutter, 'Theorie der Mitgliedschaft – Prolegomena zu einem Allgemeinen Teil des Korporationsrechts' (1980) 180 AcP 84, 105ff.

[99] On path dependency and its implications, see generally Lucian Arye Bebchuk and Mark J Roe, 'A Theory of Path Dependence in Corporate Ownership and Governance' (1999) 52 Stan LRev 127.

[100] For extended discussion see Giudici and Agstner (n. 11) 597.

Sustainability and Corporate Governance

Shareholderism vs. Stakeholderism in the Italian Debate

Giulia Ballerini and Carlotta Rinaldo[*]

I. Introduction

The debate on corporate governance has been characterised by a contrast between shareholder and stakeholder orientation ever since the issue of the internal balance of power within the company arose as a concept and a problematic area. Especially from a comparative perspective, which traditionally considers different approaches, the question has been thoroughly analysed, and the discussion has developed along strikingly similar lines in Anglo-American jurisdictions as well as in continental Europe.[1]

---

[*] Sections I and II were written by Carlotta Rinaldo; sections III to VII by Giulia Ballerini. All translations of texts, statutory provisions and legislative titles are freely rendered by the authors.

[1] The literature on the subject is by now very extensive. The following notes only mention some of the main general literature on the subject. Considering only literature in English, see especially Klaus J Hopt, 'Comparative Corporate Governance: The State of the Art and International Regulation' (2011) 59 AJCL 1, 3ff; Klaus J Hopt, 'Corporate Purpose and Stakeholder Value – Historical, Economic and Comparative Law Remarks on the Current Debate, Legislative Options and Enforcement Problems' (2023) ECGI Law Working Paper 690/2023, 2ff; Holger

It is well known that the purpose of a company determines the kind of corporate governance that needs to be implemented and thus the duties, powers, and responsibilities of the directors in their discretionary activities. According to a widespread shareholder approach, a director's only duty is to the company's 'owners' and to maximising their investment. In recent years, however, there has been a clear tendency to steer corporate governance in the direction of sustainability. The aim is to develop a legal basis for governance that harmonises corporate capitalist activity on one hand with protecting other interests, such as those of communities, the environment, or workers' well-being on the other hand. A stakeholderist approach seeks to reconcile profit maximisation (the primary interest of the company's 'owners') with the pursuit of non-owners' interests and those of society as a whole in the business activity.

The main question, therefore, is whether directors must protect the interests of shareholders at all costs, such that a failure to do so exposes them to liability, or whether they are free to take into account the interests of other stakeholders impacted by the company's activity.[2] Given the new trend in the European Union Member States as well as at the EU level,[3] it may no longer be possible to say that the shift towards stakeholderism and a broader interpretation of directors' duties in a more socially responsible environment can be summed up as 'much ado about little'[4].

Indeed, the question of whether companies should exclusively aim at profit-making or also have a social purpose has early antecedents, and it has accompanied the history of joint-stock companies since their inception, when incorporating required state approval.[5] However, the contrast between 'shareholder capitalism' and 'stakeholder capitalism' has gained momentum over the last twenty years and is trending especially in the most recent corporate governance debate. Amid growing conviction that profit-driven capitalism is responsible for many

Fleischer, 'Corporate Purpose: A Management Concept and its Implications for Company Law' (2021) 2 ECFR 161ff.

[2] In the Italian literature, see Eugenio Barcellona, 'La sustainable corporate governance nelle prospettive di riforma del diritto europeo. A proposito dei limiti strutturali dello stakeholderism' [2022] Riv soc 3ff, Eugenio Barcellona, *Shareholderim versus stakeholderism. La società per azioni contemporanea dinanzi al "profitto"* (Giuffré 2022) 57ff; Umberto Tombari, *"Potere" e "interessi" nella grande impresa azionaria* (Giuffré 2019) 23ff.

[3] See, eg, Luca Enriques, 'The European Parliament Draft Directive on Corporate Due Diligence and Accountability; Stakeholder-Oriented Governance on Steroids' [2021] Riv soc 319ff; Marco Libertini, 'Sulla proposta di Direttiva UE su "Dovere di diligenza e responsabilità delle imprese"' [2021] Riv soc 325ff; Piergaetano Marchetti, 'Il bicchiere mezzo pieno' [2021] Riv soc 336ff; Federico M Mucciarelli, 'Perseguire un diritto societario "sostenibile": un obiettivo sincero?' [2021] Riv giur lav 521ff; Piero Guido Alpa, 'Responsabilità degli amministratori di società e principio di "sostenibilità"' [2021] Contr impr 721ff; Barcellona, 'La sustainable corporate governance' (n 2) 1ff.

[4] See Andrew R Keay, 'Moving Towards Stakeholderism? Constituency Statutes, Enlightened Shareholder Value, and More: Much Ado About Little?' (2021) 22 EBLR 1ff.

[5] See especially Fleischer (n 1) 167ff.

of the problems affecting contemporary society – starting with the current environmental crisis – stakeholder capitalism is particularly relevant in the context of corporate social responsibility ('CSR'), ESG values and corporate sustainability.[6] Sustainability is undoubtedly one of the greatest challenges for corporate, accounting and financial market law today, and it will be tomorrow.

As for Italy, the problem of the purpose of corporate action and the duties of directors has been debated starting with the general concept of *interesse sociale*, the pursuit of which is the objective of every director of a company, just as in German legal culture the starting point is generally the *Unternehmensinteresse*.[7] The Italian debate on company purpose has evolved over time in a direction similar to that in the United States, where the issue has been (more pragmatically) to identify the fiduciary duties of directors.[8]

Among Italian scholars, theories at the opposite ends of a spectrum, ie, the 'institutional' and the 'contractual' approaches, have had different practical functions and ideological implications depending on the historical period and the purposes for which they were used.[9] It thus seems useful to preface the most recent developments with a brief description of their evolution in Italian legal culture.

II. The Italian Debate on Corporate Purpose: Roots of Institutional and Contractarian Approaches to Company Law

Italian authors first discussed the question of the nature and concept of the 'corporate purpose' (*interesse sociale*) in the 1930s, when liberal ideas and the political legitimacy of profit were under attack from both the Catholic Church and contemporary 'socialist' culture. Institutional approaches that emphasised the social relevance of companies clearly dominated.[10] Companies were supposed to pursue profit not as an end in itself but as a means generating collective wealth.

[6] See, eg, Carlo Angelici, 'Divagazioni sulla "responsabilità sociale" di impresa' [2018] Riv soc 3ff; Umberto Tombari, 'L'organo amministrativo di S.p.A. tra "interessi dei soci" ed "altri interessi"' [2018] Riv soc 20ff; Tombari (n 2) 64ff; Guido Ferrarini, 'Redifining Corporate Purpose: Sustainability as a Game Changer' (November 2020) EUSFiL Research Working Paper 1/2020; Marco Cian, 'Sulla gestione sostenibile e i poteri degli amministratori: uno spunto di riflessione' [2021] Riv ODC 1131ff; Mario Stella Richter jr, 'Corporate social responsibility, social enterprise, benefit corporation: magia delle parole?' [2017] Vita not 953ff; Mario Stella Richter jr, 'Long-termism' [2021] Riv soc 21ff; Giuseppe B Portale, 'La Corporate Social Responsibility alla ricerca di effettività' [2022] Banca borsa tit cred I 947.

[7] On this concept, see, eg, Claudia Schubert, *Das Unternehmensinteresse – Maßstab für die Organwalter der Aktiengesellschaft. Unter besonderer Berücksichtigung der Nachhaltigkeit und sozialen Verantwortung von Unternehmen* (Nomos 2020) (with extensive references).

[8] Barcellona, *Shareholderism versus stakeholderims* (n 2).

[9] Gastone Cottino, 'Contrattualismo e istituzionalismo (Variazioni sul tema da uno spunto di Giorgio Oppo)' [2005] Riv soc 693 (especially at 696ff); Mucciarelli (n 3) 526ff.

[10] See Giorgio Oppo, 'Le grandi opzioni della riforma e le società per azioni' [2003] Riv dir civ 477ff; Cottino (n 9) 693ff.

There was, of course, a clear ideology behind this recognition of firms as 'institutions' that are part of other hierarchically superior entities, notably the state.

The idea that enterprises, as part of a larger whole, should aim to create social benefits was clearly articulated by Asquini,[11] who was early to recognise a contrast between an institutional and a contractual understanding of the company.[12] Referring to the German theory of the *Unternehmen an sich*, he rejected the idea that companies should be reduced to the contractual regulation of the relations between individual members; they should serve more than the individual interests of the shareholders in a narrow sense and should not purely pursue profits.

The provisions of the 1942 Civil Code clearly contain an ambiguity: recognising the social function of private enterprise so as to allow for public intervention in the economy; fully legitimising the pursuit of profit at the same time. This normative text was imbued with the corporate-fascist culture that was prevalent at the time, in which the social relevance of enterprises was underlined by the possibility of public intervention in the economy.[13]

The first few decades of the Italian Republic saw lively debate between 'institutional' positions and liberal, market-oriented theories.[14] There were indeed opposing views regarding whether company directors could reinvest profits, ie, in excess of normal market returns on equity, in the company. At issue were limits on shareholders' rights to receive an annual dividend and, by extension, the legitimacy of the majority shareholders' decision to reinvest over the minority's vote to the contrary. No one sought to deny that companies should aim at producing profit, as was and still is stated in art 2247 CC. Rather, the dispute was about different interpretations of the relationship between the (profit-oriented) firm and the market, and about who can decide more efficiently where and how the wealth created by the company should be distributed.[15]

Debate on this issue was particularly intense the 1950s and the 1960s,[16] and it should be noted that the debate already involved whether short- or long-term timeframes should govern the administration of the business.

---

[11] Alberto Asquini, 'Profili dell'impresa' [1943] Riv dir comm I 1ff. In later years, Alberto Asquini, 'I battelli del Reno' [1959] Riv soc 617ff, recalled a famous line, attributed to the director of the Hamburg company Norddeutscher Lloyd, that the purpose of the company is not to distribute profits but to sail its ships on the Rhine.

[12] See also Ariberto Mignoli, 'L'interesse sociale' [1958] Riv soc 726ff.

[13] See Francesco Galgano, *Storia del diritto commerciale* (Il Mulino 1976) 103ff, Barcellona, Shareholderim versus stakeholderism (n 2) 60ff.

[14] For a reconstruction of this debate, see, eg, Stella Richter jr, Long-termism (n 6) 16ff.

[15] Especially Asquini, I battelli del Reno (n 11) 619ff, Tullio Ascarelli, 'La disciplina delle società per azioni e legge antimonopolistica' [1955] Riv trim proc civ 273ff. See also Stella Richter jr, Long-termism (n 6) 20ff.

[16] Guido Rossi, *Utile di bilancio riserve e dividendo* (Giuffré 1957) and Domenico Pettiti, *Contributo allo studio del diritto dell'azionista al dividendo* (Giuffré 1957), naturally come to mind. See also, around the same time, Giovanni E Colombo, 'Riserve facoltative e riserve occulte nel bilancio delle società per azioni' [1960] Riv dir comm 176ff and Giuseppe Ferri, 'Diritto agli utili e diritto al dividendo' [1963] Riv dir comm 405ff.

Asquini resolved this issue by referring to the concept of good faith, both as a limit to be respected by the majority shareholders and as a restraint on certain excesses of contractualism. Asquini states that the common goal of the company is to achieve socially desirable outcomes that go beyond individual objectives and individual profit.[17] For Ascarelli,[18] on the other hand, the question of self-financing in companies was to be resolved by identifying the limits within which private individuals can be entrusted to choose how to allocate profits not their own that could be allocated either to private consumption or investment. His well-known answer is that profits should be allocated to dividends (formally, 'passed on to capital') following a 'contractual' position and considering the market as the most efficient mechanism for the allocation of financial resources.

However, it is important to note[19] that according to Asquini, the problems of the shareholder's right to a dividend and the legitimacy of self-financing are not necessarily linked to the conceptualisation of the company as a contractual organisation or as an institution. Nor are they linked to the notion of its object and purpose.[20]

In the 1960s, a clear predominance of the 'contractual' school of thought began to emerge. Particularly influential at the time was Pier Giusto Jaeger, who argued strongly in favour of the idea that there is no room in Italian companies for assigning legal relevance to interests other than those of the actual shareholders, such that directors need only consider the shareholders' interests when making decisions regarding the company.[21] He addressed the issue of the conflict between different visions of the company's interest – whether long-term or short-term – and entrusted shareholders with the task of reconciling these different interests through resolutions that would determine whether profits should be distributed or set aside as reserves to be reinvested in the company.[22]

For a long time, this was the dominant view among Italian authors: shareholder value from a purely economic point of view should play a decisive role in the

---

[17] Asquini, Profili dell'impresa (n 11), 143–144; Asquini, I battelli del Reno (n 11) 619, 628ff. For a similar institutional approach from a different ideological background, see Lorenzo Mossa, *L'impresa nell'ordine corporativo* (Sansoni 1935); Lorenzo Mossa, 'Il diritto del lavoro, il diritto commerciale ed il codice sociale' [1945] Riv dir comm 39ff. For a detailed discussion on these institutional theories, see Barcellona, Shareholderism versus stakeholderism (n 2) 58ff.

[18] Especially Tullio Ascarelli, 'Tipologia della società per azioni e disciplina giuridica' [1959] Riv soc 995ff; Ascarelli (n 15) 273ff; Tullio Ascarelli, 'I problemi delle società anonime per azioni' [1956] Riv soc 3ff.

[19] See also Stella Richter jr, Long-termism (n 6) 21.

[20] Asquini, I battelli del Reno (n 11).

[21] Pier Giusto Jaeger, *L'interesse sociale* (Giuffré 1963). Later, Pier Giusto Jaeger, 'L'interesse sociale rivisitato (quarant'anni dopo)' [2000] Giur comm I 796ff.

[22] On the impact of this position and its relevance in Italian law, see Francesco Galgano, 'Società in generale: c) diritto privato' in *Enciclopedia del diritto*, vol XLII (Giuffré 1990) 865ff; Angelici (n 6) 3ff. In case law see, for example, Cass 18 March 1986, no 1839; Cass 11 March 1993, no 2959.

identification of the corporate purpose.[23] More 'institutionalist' positions were only aimed at supporting targeted solutions, in particular with regard to company-worker relations.[24]

With the establishment of a growing relationship between company law and financial market law, and in particular with the development of listed companies, the concept of shareholder value and its relevance to decision-making has become increasingly prominent in corporate governance.[25] If the purpose of the corporation is only to serve the interests of the shareholders, the directors' duties are confined to maximising the company's growth for their benefit. And in listed companies, if the value of the shares is (or should be) equal to the value of the company itself, then the duty of directors is to maximise the value of the shares. 'Shareholder value' thus corresponds to the notion of profit, which according to art 2247 CC is one of the main elements of companies. This was clearly stated in the first version of the *Codice di autodisciplina* for listed companies of 1999, according to which (at point 1.3) the main objective that directors of listed companies should pursue is the creation of value for the generality of shareholders.

The limitation of a corporation's purpose to shareholder value was then questioned from a different perspective around the same time as the phenomenon of corporate groups began to be regarded as a problem area.[26] To dwell on this in depth would take us too far from the purpose of this paper, but the discussion of corporate purpose had to take into account that corporate law had left the 'atomic age' and had entered the 'molecular age'; It had to consider that 'solitary stars no longer exist in the corporate firmament, only constellations'[27]. It was therefore necessary to supply legal relevance to a broader purpose, separate but compatible with the corporate purpose, that took into account the purpose of the group itself, rather than the purpose(s) of its constituent entities alone.

---

[23] This approach never made universalistic claims. Jaeger, L'interesse sociale rivisitato (n 21) 796ff. According to Floriano d'Alessandro, 'Il diritto delle società da i "battelli del Reno" alle "navi vichinghe"' [1988] Foro it V 55, 'la dottrina italiana ha condotto una lunga e tutto sommato vittoriosa battaglia contro di essa, contro l'idea che lo scopo della società non si identifichi con il prosaico interesse comune dei soci a riscuotere dividendi, ma con qualcosa di diverso e apparentemente più alto e nobile, sia esso la navigazione fluviale o altra intrapresa' ('the Italian literature has waged a long and all in all victorious battle against the idea that the purpose of the company is not to be identified with the prosaic common interest of the shareholders in collecting dividends, but with something different and apparently higher and nobler, be it river navigation or some other enterprise').

[24] See Barcellona, Shareholderism versus stakeholderism (n 2) 65.

[25] Cf Jaeger, L'interesse sociale rivisitato (n 21) 798ff; Mucciarelli (n 3) 527ff.

[26] An extensive body of literature on this flourished, especially in the last two decades of the last century. See Giuliana Scognamiglio, *Autonomia e coordinamento nella disciplina dei gruppi di società* (Giappichelli 1996). Specifically on the present question, see d'Alessandro (n 23) 48ff (with further references).

[27] 'Non si scorgono più nei firmamenti societari stelle solitarie, ma solo costellazioni', d'Alessandro (n 23) 49. Similarly, Ariberto Mignoli, 'Interesse di gruppo e società a sovranità limitata' [1986] Contr impr 733.

It is undisputed that the existence of a group is substantially relevant to determining the corporate purpose of the companies in the group, especially when there is a conflict between an individual company and the group as a whole[28]. The purpose of the group must therefore be recognised *per se* within the limits of compensatory benefits (art 2497(1) CC). The Italian system would therefore assign relevance to interests other than those of the shareholders, such as those of the group's constituent companies or the stability of the economic system, thus leading to a kind of 'group institutionalism'.[29]

Over time, legal doctrine began to overcome the crystallisation of the opposing positions that characterised this debate on the nature and legal construction of the enterprise, which as we have seen was theoretical but not without practical implications.[30] It was moreover generally acknowledged that the interests of shareholders may well be directed towards making a profit in the long term,[31] but that this does not preclude the pursuit of short-term goals or the case-by-case evaluation of directors' choices.[32]

This brings us to the current debate on corporate purpose: after several crises and in the face of several, potentially even more critical challenges, both social and climatic, the question of what companies should do has taken on new contours and new perspectives.[33] Topics trending 'like a widespread refrain'[34] include

---

[28] Jaeger, L'interesse sociale rivisitato (n 21) 810ff.

[29] For a critical perspective see d'Alessandro (n 23) 49. See also Jaeger, L'interesse sociale rivisitato (n 21) 811.

[30] Oppo (n 9) 477ff; Cottino (n 9) 693ff; Paolo Montalenti, 'L'interesse sociale: una sintesi' [2018] Riv soc 305ff; Umberto Tombari, 'Lo "scopo della società": significati e problemi di una categoria giuridica' [2023] Riv soc 338ff.

[31] Especially Paolo Montalenti, 'Interesse sociale e amministratori' in *Società per azioni corporate governance e mercati finanziari* (Giuffré 2011) 89ff; Paolo Montalenti, 'Interesse sociale, interesse di gruppo e gestione dell'impresa nei gruppi di società' in *Impresa società di capitali e mercato finanziari* (Giuffré 2017) 215ff.

[32] On the ambiguity of "long-termism" in the Italian literature and for further references, see Stella Richter jr, Long-termism (n 6) 38ff; Angelici (n 6) 3ff (underscoring that it has no legal basis in the Italian legal system) and more recently Mario Campobasso 'Gli amministratori, il successo sostenibile e la pietra di Spinoza' [2024] Banca borsa tit cred I 1ff.

[33] The topic has been revived in Italy, especially with articles by Carlo Angelici, 'Nonte minime sull'interesse sociale' [2014] Banca borsa tit cred I 255ff; Angelici (n 6) 3ff, Vincenzo Calandra Bonaura, 'Funzione amministrativa e interesse sociale' in *L'interesse sociale tra valorizzazione del capitale e protezione degli stakeholders, Studi in ricordo di Pier Giusto Jaeger* (Quaderni di giurisprudenza commerciale 342, Giuffrè 2020) 101ff; Francesco Denozza, 'Logica dello scambio e "contrattualità": la società per azioni di fronte alla crisi' [2015] Giur comm I 5ff; Francesco Denozza, 'La frammentazione del soggetto nel pensiero giuridico tardo-liberale' [2014] Riv dir comm I 13ff; Francesco Denozza, 'Quattro variazioni sul tema: "contratto, impresa e società nel pensiero di Carlo Angelici"' [2013] Giur comm I 480ff; Guiseppe Guizzi, 'Appunti in tema di interesse sociale e *governance* nelle società bancarie' [2017] Riv dir comm I 241ff; Montalenti (n 30) 303ff.

[34] Francesco Denozza, 'Lo scopo della società: dall'organizzazione al mercato' [2019] Riv ODC 615.

corporate social responsibility, sustainability of enterprises and corporations, sustainable corporate governance, and enlightened shareholder value or stakeholder value.[35] Indeed, only systematic scrutiny of the legal provisions and rationale behind a particular regulatory framework can lead us to adopt one perspective rather than another. This means that an in-depth analysis of the Italian statutory law is necessary.

III. Two Premises

Before turning to an analysis of the debate on shareholderism versus stakeholderism in current Italian corporate law, two premises are needed.

First, when we talk about the duties of companies or their directors towards those affected in various ways by the business activity (commonly referred to as stakeholders), it is crucial to emphasise that the core question is whether the company or its directors can or should pursue the interests of stakeholders *even beyond* what the law requires. Indeed, when an environmental law or a consumer protection law constitutes an external limit to the business activity, it is not in dispute that companies or their directors must comply. In the shareholderism versus stakeholderism debate, the key issue is therefore whether companies or their directors should do more for the benefit of the stakeholders than what the law already requires.

Second, for the purpose of the following discussion we do not consider companies that by nature (*società benefit)*[36] or in their bylaws choose to adopt a multistakeholder approach through the insertion of a common benefit or sustainability clause.[37] Instead, we consider 'common' companies (namely joint-stock compa-

---

[35] The references here only represent a very broad literature on the subject. In addition to the literature already cited, see Edward B Rock, 'For Whom is the Corporation Managed in 2020?: The Debate over Corporate Purpose' (2020) ECGI Law Working Paper 515/2020; Ferrarini (n 6) *passim*; Tombari (n 2) *passim*.

[36] See the Law of 28 December 2015, no 208. On *società benefit* see, *inter alia*, Carlo Angelici, 'Società benefit'; Francesco Denozza and Alessandra Stabilini, 'La società benefit nell'era dell'investor capitalism'; Giorgio Marasà, 'Scopo di lucro e scopo di beneficio comune nella società benefit'; Serenella Rossi, 'L'impegno multistakeholder della società benefit'; Mario Stella Richter jr, 'Società benefit e società non benefit'; Andrea Zoppini, 'Un raffronto tra società benefit ed enti non profit: implicazioni sistematiche e profili critici', all published in (2017) 2 Riv ODC 1ff. See also Angelici (n 6) 8ff; Giuseppe B Portale, 'Diritto societario tedesco e diritto societario italiano in dialogo' [2018] Banca borsa tit cred I 597ff; Tombari (n 6) 20ff; Stefano Prataviera, 'Società benefit e responsabilità degli amministratori' [2018] Riv soc 919ff; Francesco Corazza, 'Società "benefit", discrezionalità e limitazione della (ir)responsabilità degli amministratori' [2024] Nuove leggi civ 498ff.

[37] See Marco Cian, 'Clausole statutarie per la sostenibilità dell'impresa: spazi, limiti e implicazioni' [2021] Riv soc 475ff; Marco Ventoruzzo, 'Osservazioni sulle conseguenze applicative dell'adozione di clausole statutarie (e di autodisciplina) sul "successo sostenibile"' [2024] Riv soc 129ff.

nies[38] and LLCs[39]) and ask to what extent their directors *can* or *should* consider the interests of stakeholders and, in general, the demands of sustainability, in the actual legal framework.

IV. Some Terminological Clarifications

As already pointed out in section I, the shareholderism versus stakeholderism debate has gained new life in recent years due to the emergence of a 'new paradigm', ie, the sustainability of business activity.[40] For context, it may be useful to delve briefly into the interconnection between these concepts.

First of all, it should be noted that the term 'sustainability' can have multiple meanings. In the Italian literature, it is used in at least two senses: economic sustainability and environmental and social sustainability[41]. Economic sustainability means the ability of the company to maintain business continuity, including its capacity to regularly fulfil its obligations. Environmental and social sustainability – the only sense that matters in this paper – is understood as attending to the company's impact on the environmental and social level, ie, to the negative externalities of the business. While there are several examples in Italian positive law where the meaning is clear,[42] other cases remain ambiguous. Take for example art 123-*ter*(3-*bis*) of the Consolidated Financial Law,[43] which states that the directors' 'remuneration policy contributes to the company's strategy, the pursuit of long-term interests, and the sustainability of the company, explaining how it provides this contribution'. Here, the term 'sustainability' can theoretically be understood in either sense, with different implications for the remuneration policy.

That clarified, it should be emphasised that today's 'great debate' on sustainability appears to have evolved from the debate in Italian commercial law scholarship a few decades ago on CSR,[44] which itself could be considered an outgrowth (at least in terms of the implications) of the debate on contractualism versus institutionalism (see II).[45] The debate on CSR then evolved into a debate on the inclusion of ESG factors in the management function,[46] which in turn evolved into the debate on sustainability. However, slogans (contractualism versus institutionalism; CSR; ESG factors; sustainability) aside, it is important to highlight

---

[38] See CC, art 2325ff.

[39] See CC, art 2462ff.

[40] Vincenzo Cariello, 'Per un diritto costituzionale della sostenibilità (oltre la "sostenibilità ambientale")' [2022] Riv ODC 413, 424, links sustainability to a proper paradigm.

[41] Stella Richter jr, Long Termism (n 6) 30.

[42] See, eg, art 21 of the new Italian Insolvency Code (Legislative Decree 12 January 2019, no 14).

[43] Legislative decree of 24 February 1998, no 58.

[44] On this debate, see Serenella Rossi, 'Il diritto della Corporate Social Responsibility' [2021] Riv ODC 99ff.

[45] On the opposing views, see Jaeger, L'interesse sociale (n 21) 13ff.

[46] On the acronym 'ESG' as merely a lexical update of 'CSR', see Portale (n 6) 947.

that the fulcrum of the debate remains unchanged. It is a matter of understanding how the interests of investors (shareholders) are reconciled with the interests of stakeholders, or of those in some way affected by the company's activities.[47] This is the reason for our focus on shareholderism versus stakeholderism.

The meaning of these terms, however, needs to be clarified in light of diverse nuances in the doctrinal discourse.

In addition to the meaning already mentioned in section I (shareholderism as 'maximizing the overall value of the shareholding'[48]), the term shareholderism can indeed also be used in a further sense, namely that of 'enlightened shareholderism', a term that was taken from the common law debate[49]. Enlightened shareholderism refers to the idea that given two options that would both maximise shareholder value, directors should choose the one that better protects the stakeholders' interests. That is, directors should choose the one that maximises the interests of shareholders and stakeholders *at the same time*. The shareholderism model also encompasses the concept of 'opportunistic sustainability',[50] which emphasises that sometimes, maximising shareholder value may mean pursuing sustainability goals and stakeholder interests, for example when a company's pursuit of sustainability enhances its reputation and attracts more customers.[51]

In the Italian debate and elsewhere, the notion of stakeholderism (also called 'disinterested sustainability'[52]) is also used in at least two meanings, one strong and one light.[53] 'Light stakeholderism' refers to the idea that the directors of a company can freely choose to pursue the interests of stakeholders, even possibly sacrificing the interests of shareholders. This perspective allows, but does not impose, the sacrifice of shareholder profits in favour of stakeholder interests. Evidently, however, the consequence of this approach is that no one can complain, and therefore that directors are essentially unaccountable.

'Strong stakeholderism' on the other hand refers to the idea that directors *must* pursue the interests of stakeholders, even at the expense of the shareholders. This

---

47 See Marco Ventoruzzo, 'Brief Remarks on Prosperity by Colin Mayer and the Often Misunderstood Notion of Corporate Purpose' [2020] Riv soc 43, 45 ('although in different forms and terms, the question of the balance among the interests of different stakeholders is at least as old as the history of corporate law, and actually older').

48 See, eg, Cass 17 July 2007, no 15950 and Cass 12 December 2005, no 27387 (clarifying that among the common interests of shareholders as parties to the company contract, which therefore qualify as social interests, is the maximisation of 'profit', understood as the maximisation of the overall value of shares or quotas.

49 In the Italian literature, see Sabrina Bruno, 'Il ruolo della s.p.a. per un'economia giusta e sostenibile: la Proposta di Direttiva UE su "Corporate Sustainability Due Diligence". Nasce la stakeholder company?' [2022] Riv dir comp 303, 335–336.

50 See Cian (n 6) 1131ff.

51 The concept is also referred to as "instrumental stakeholderism".

52 Cian (n 6) 1131ff.

53 See Barcellona, La sustainable corporate governance nelle proposte di riforma del diritto europeo (n 2) 3ff; id, Shareholderism versus stakeholderism (n 2) 6ff.

perspective imposes the sacrifice of shareholder profit for stakeholder interests. Carried to its logical conclusion, this model implies that stakeholders could have a cause of action against directors if they fail to pursue the stakeholders' interests. This is precisely where the greatest interpretive doubts lie.

V. Majority Position in Italy: Shareholderism (Possibly Enlightened)

The current majority position in Italy favours shareholderism or at most enlightened shareholderism.[54] The interests of stakeholders are thereby taken into account (i) through the need to comply with certain laws (environmental, worker protection, consumer protection laws, etc.), or (ii) by virtue of enlightened shareholderism, ie, directors pursuing stakeholder interests to the extent they align with the interests of shareholders.

Here one may recall the Italian Corporate Governance Code of 2020[55], which speaks of 'sustainable success', defined by the Code itself as the 'objective that guides the action of the managing body and is embodied in the creation of value over the long term for the benefit of shareholders, *taking into account* the interests of other *stakeholders* relevant to the company'[56] – as distinct from the previous version of the Code, which assigned to management 'the primary objective of creating value for the shareholders over a medium to long-term horizon'.[57]

In the Italian system, the arguments in favour of shareholderism and against stakeholderism (strong or weak) are manifold. For the purpose of this paper – as well as more generally – they can be divided into three categories: (i) arguments from the specific regulation of companies in the Italian Civil Code or special laws; (ii) arguments from either constitutional or general principles; (iii) legal policy arguments from the impracticality and dangers of stakeholderism (both strong and weak). The rest of the paper looks at each of these arguments in more detail.

---

[54] Montalenti (n 30) 303ff. For a highly critical view of stakeholderism, see Floriano d'Alessandro, 'Il mantello di San Martino, la benevolenza del birraio e la Ford modello T, senza dimenticare Robin Hood (divagazioni semi-serie sulla c.d. responsabilità sociale dell'impresa e dintorni)' [2022] Riv dir civ 409ff.

[55] It is worth pointing out that this is a soft law instrument. Adherence to the code is voluntary and is made explicit in the report on corporate governance and ownership structure.

[56] On the notion of sustainable success and its implications see, eg, Niccolò Abriani, 'Successo sostenibile e regole statutarie: il ruolo del board nel Codice di Corporate Governance' [2021] Riv corp gov 7ff; Enrico Ginevra, 'Il Codice di "Corporate Governance": Introduzione e Definizioni (con un approfondimento sul "Successo sostenibile")' [2023] Riv soc 1017ff; Campobasso (n 32) 1ff.

[57] See art 1.P.2. of the previous version of the Corporate Governance Code, launched in July 2018.

1. Arguments from Corporate Law as Regulated in the Italian Civil Code and Special Laws

The first and principal argument in favour of shareholderism refers to art 2247 CC, which states that by virtue of the company contract, two or more persons confer goods or services for the joint exercise of an economic activity for the purpose of *dividing the profits thereof*. This is the first article pertaining to companies in the Italian Civil Code and, as its title states, it contains the definition of a 'company contract'. The reference to the 'purpose of dividing the profits' is taken as an indication that the purpose of the company must be in line with the shareholders' interests. In this regard, one author has pointed out that the rule is meant to prohibit conduct by the directors that would violate the shareholders' interest in the profitability of their investment.[58]

Other authors, however, have suggested a 'progressive' interpretation of art 2247 CC, arguing that the historical context of 1942, when the code was drafted, was vastly different from today's corporate landscape.[59] Considering the evolving nature of the system and the alignment of European law with the pursuit of a more sustainable corporate paradigm, these authors suggest that the term 'profit' in art 2247 CC could be redefined as 'fair profit'[60]. In this context, profit is not meant to be pursued recklessly but rather should be directed towards achieving a harmonious balance between the interests of shareholders and stakeholders, particularly when fundamental interests are at stake. More specifically, 'fair profit' refers to the idea that shareholder profit need not be pursued to the maximum at all times. In some cases, especially when constitutionally protected fundamental interests may be excessively harmed, the interest in maximising profits can be sacrificed for other interests (even beyond what the law requires). This means profits,

[58] Marco Maugeri, '"Pluralismo" e "monismo" nello scopo della s.p.a. (glosse a margine del dialogo a più voci sullo Statement della Business Roundtable)' [2019] Riv ODC 637, 639.

[59] Of course, the statement applies to the Italian Civil Code as purged of elements that can be traced back to fascist corporatism. In fact, as already mentioned in section II, it should be considered that the Italian Civil Code of 1942, drafted during the fascist era, contained several references to the corporative regime (see, eg, art 2088 to 2092) and to the fact that the enterprise, understood as an organism producing new wealth, was recruited to the higher interest of the national economy. However, in practice, the recruitment of the enterprise to the higher interest of the national economy never found application, first due to the lack of the implementing corporate rules and later due to the abolition of the corporate regime. On this point see Giorgio Marasà, 'L'imprenditore – art 2082–2083' in *Il Codice Civile – Commentario* (Giuffrè 2021) 11. In any case, the functionalisation of enterprise was not an absolute novelty on the European scene in 1942. It was also reflected in the German Aktiengesetz of 1937 (not coincidentally, given the regimes then in power in Germany and Italy). See Jaeger, L'interesse sociale (n 21) 42ff.

[60] Daniele Stanzione, Liquidazione dell'attivo e interessi degli stakeholders (ESI 2023) 47ff. For a similar interpretative result, see Anna Genovese, *La gestione ecosostenibile dell'impresa azionaria. Fra regole e contesto* (il Mulino 2023) 142ff.

just not the maximum conceivable. Through this lens, art 2247 CC could be interpreted in a manner consistent with a form of stakeholderism.[61]

A second argument in favour of shareholderism appeals to the general power of shareholders to appoint and especially to remove directors. Within the Italian legal framework, shareholders can remove directors at any time without being required to provide specific reasons (*revoca ad nutum*).[62] This principle applies even to directors particularly committed to sustainability. The argument therefore posits that sustainability is irrelevant to the standard to which the managerial function must adhere.[63]

A similar line of reasoning emerges in the third argument against stakeholderism, which centres on the authority of shareholders to initiate the liquidation of the company at their discretion.[64] The ability of shareholders to opt for liquidation at any time,[65] even when the company is notably commendable in its commitment to furthering the interests of stakeholders, underscores that stakeholderism holds no substantial significance in terms of a 'duty' incumbent upon the company or its directors.

Further statutes that can be used to argue for shareholderism can be found in art 2392–2393 CC on directors' liability toward the company. According to these provisions, if the directors perform an act of mismanagement (*mala gestio*), the company (*rectius*, the shareholders' meeting)[66] can claim damages from the direc-

---

[61] According to some authors, shareholderism seems to have been embodied in another provision of the Italian Civil Code, ie, art 2497. According to this rule, companies or entities that act in their own or others' entrepreneurial interests by exercising the management and coordination of other companies in violation of the principles of proper corporate and entrepreneurial management are directly liable to the shareholders of those companies for the 'damage caused to the profitability and value of the shareholding'. Within this context, the emphasis on the profitability and value of the shareholding could be viewed as a clear indication of the Italian legislature's explicit endorsement of shareholderism. See, eg, Maugeri (n 58) 638. On the impact of the debate on the notion of the "group interest" with respect to the topic examined here, see section II.

[62] As regards joint-stock companies, see CC, art 2383(3). Just cause for removal is relevant only for the purpose of compensation for damages, which, except in special cases (reputational damage), generally corresponds to the remaining compensation under the management contract (on this principle see Cass 26 January 2018, no 2037). Moreover, it should be considered that the new Italian Insolvency Code has stipulated that, as of the registration in the business registry of a decision to access a crisis-and-insolvency regulatory instrument and until sanction, the removal of directors without just cause is ineffective. Also, filing an application to access a crisis-and-insolvency regulatory instrument when the conditions of the law are met does not constitute just cause, and the removal resolution must be approved by decree of the specialised section of the competent business court after it has heard the interested parties (Italian Insolvency Code, art 120-*bis*(4)).

[63] Maugeri (n 58) 639.

[64] Maugeri (n 58) 639.

[65] See CC, art 2484(1)(6) (joint-stock companies, limited partnerships with shares, and LLCs are dissolved by resolution of the general meeting).

[66] In addition to the claim submitted by the majority (art 2393), there exists a claim that may be pursued by a qualified minority (art 2393-*bis*). It is nonetheless worth noting that mi-

tors, understood as impoverishment of the company's assets or failure to earn a profit.[67] The fact that shareholders can demand that directors who have harmed the company in violation of their duties must restore the company's assets could be considered an indication in favour of shareholderism.

A further argument is rooted in the 2015 establishment in Italy of benefit corporations.[68] According to art 376 of the Law of 28 December 2015, no 208, 'società benefit' are those companies that in carrying out an economic activity, in addition to the purpose of dividing its profits, pursue one or more purposes of common benefit and operate in a responsible, sustainable and transparent manner towards people, communities, territories and the environment, cultural and social goods and activities, bodies and associations and other stakeholders.[69] Some scholars contend that the creation of this distinct model, designed to harmonise the interests of shareholders with those of stakeholders, confirms that the prevailing and default 'rule' is the pursuit of shareholder interests.[70] However, other authors believe that the introduction of benefit companies in the Italian legal system should be interpreted as supportive of stakeholderism, as it illustrates compatibility between the corporate model and the direct pursuit of interests beyond the shareholders.[71]

Lastly, another argument against stakeholderism arises from the absence of a robust enforcement mechanism to safeguard the alleged right of stakeholders to have their interests pursued by the directors.[72] In Italian corporate law, the recourse available to stakeholders to address the failure of company directors to advocate for the stakeholder's interests would be art 2395 CC, which grants individual shareholders *or third parties* who have incurred direct harm due to the

---

nority shareholders are afforded the opportunity to act on behalf of the company, with the legal action primarily directed towards the restoration of the company's assets.

[67] See, eg, Cass 20 October 2021, no 29252.

[68] Italy became the first European state to establish a new legal status for *società benefit* (benefit companies), a concept reminiscent of the U.S. benefit corporations outlined in the Model Benefit Corporation Legislation. See Marco Speranzin, 'Benefit Legal Entities in Italy: An Overview' (2022) 19 ECL 142.

[69] The common benefit objective should be explicitly articulated in the statement of the corporate purpose and actively pursued through management practices that strike a balance between the interests of the shareholders and the interests of those who may be impacted by the company's activities. According to paragraph 384 of Law no 208/2015, if a benefit legal entity fails to actively pursue its common benefit purpose, it becomes subject to the regulations governing misleading advertising (as defined in Legislative Decree no 145 of 2 August 2007) and the provisions outlined in the consumer code (Legislative Decree no 206 of 6 September 2005). This includes regulations related to unfair commercial practices, encompassing anti-competitive practices as well.

[70] Elisabetta Codazzi, 'Scopo di lucro e di beneficio comune nel passaggio da società non benefit a società benefit' [2021] Riv ODC 1243, 1248ff.

[71] See, eg, Marasà (n 36) § 3ff; Prataviera (n 36) 946ff.

[72] Marco Maugeri, in Andrea Perrone (ed), 'Lo statement della Business Roundtable sugli scopi della società. Un dialogo a più voci' [2019] Riv ODC 589, 599–600.

negligent or malicious actions of directors the right to seek compensation.[73] This form of liability is generally rooted in tort liability under art 2043 CC, which stipulates that 'any intentional or negligent act, which causes unjust damage to others, obliges the person who committed the act to compensate for the damage'[74]. The problem here is that since the essence of stakeholderism entails actions beyond what the law mandates, any damage a stakeholder might have incurred cannot, by its very nature, be deemed unjust. For example, if the directors of a company cause pollution (resulting in harm to stakeholders) but do so within the legal limits, the remedy proves ineffectual due to the absence of the requisite 'unjust' element, since the directors have actually complied with the law.

2. Arguments from Constitutional or General Principles

The arguments against stakeholderism from the Civil Code and special laws are joined by others from constitutional and general principles.

First, one could question – along the lines of Milton Friedman more than fifty years ago[75] – whether it is legitimate for private enterprises (and thus their directors), given that they lack democratic legitimacy, to decide how, and how much, to pursue interests of common benefit (like environmental interests). Some authors think that only the legislature, which enjoys political legitimacy, ought to be able to make such decisions.[76] To expect private individuals to be responsible for (i) selecting the interests of common benefit and (ii) choosing how and to what degree they will pursue them may be inconsistent with the Italian constitutional system as envisioned and described in Part II of the Constitution (art 55–139).

Second, some have highlighted the inherent contradiction in mandating that private companies and their directors behave in a more virtuous manner than what the law prescribes.[77] These authors argue that if the legislature intends to elevate environmental or worker protections, it has the capacity to enact such changes through new legislation. However, in the absence of such legislative action, it becomes paradoxical to impose this requirement on companies (and their directors), as it would imply acknowledging the existence of two inherently conflicting rules within the system. For example, if an environmental standard permits

---

[73] In the Italian corporate system, a distinction is made between direct and indirect or "reflected" harm. Direct harm means harm directly suffered by the individual shareholder or a third party and does not reflect a loss of the company's assets. Reflected harm 'passes through' the company's assets and reduces the value of the shareholdings as a consequence of the reduction of the company's assets. Reflected harm entitles the shareholders to bring a corporate liability action under art 2393 and 2393-*bis* CC, whereas direct harm is actionable under art 2395 CC.

[74] See Massimo Franzoni, 'Fatti illeciti' in Giorgio De Nova (ed), *Commentario del Codice Civile e codici collegati Scialoja-Branca-Galgano* (Zanichelli 2020) 26ff.

[75] Milton Friedman, 'The Social Responsibility of Business is to Increase its Profits', *The New York Times Magazine* (New York, 13 September 1970).

[76] Roberto Sacchi, 'La capacità propulsiva della s.p.a. quotata è andata esaurendosi?' [2021] Riv ODC 581, 600.

[77] See Barcellona, La sustainable corporate governance (n 2) 15ff.

the emission of up to 100 units of pollution, then to hold that stakeholders have a claim against the company and its directors if the company (indeed) emits less than 100 units of pollution would mean admitting that the system contains two conflicting rules, one express and one inferred from the multistakeholder approach; in other words, you both can and cannot emit 100 units of pollution. Among other things, this would be contrary to the typical principle of Italian law that 'legal certainty' is understood as the accessibility of legal provisions whose addressees are capable of effectively understanding their meaning.[78]

Third, reducing shareholder profit in the name of pursuing other interests (besides what is required by law) could be construed as a form of expropriation without compensation to the detriment of shareholders in violation of art 42 of the Italian Constitution (protecting private property).[79] In this regard, it is worth noting that in Italy as elsewhere, the ownership of shares of a company is within the scope of constitutional guarantees of private property.[80] In this perspective, if it is determined that under the shareholderism model a profit of x would have been realised, but the adoption of the stakeholderism model resulted in a profit of $x - n$, then n could be perceived as an expropriation of private property without the provision of due compensation, contravening the principles outlined in art 42 of the Italian Constitution.

Such a reduction in profits could also be viewed as an imposition of an additional tax on businesses, which, in turn, would constitute a violation of art 53 of the Constitution.[81] According to this article, everyone is required to contribute to public expenses according to his or her ability to contribute. The problems here are twofold. First, under the stakeholder approach only shareholders would bear the burden to contribute, rather than 'everyone' as stipulated in art 53. Furthermore, in accordance with Italian tax law, taxes must be certain and predictable;[82] a tax on shareholders under the stakeholderist approach may not meet these criteria, as it is at the discretion of directors to decide how and to what extent they pursue the interests of stakeholders.

---

[78] Gianmarco Gometz, *La certezza giuridica come prevedibilità* (Giappichelli 2005).

[79] This argument – like the one rooted in art 53 of the Italian Constitution – was mainly articulated in the 1980s by Floriano d'Alessandro, 'Interesse pubblico alla conservazione dell'impresa e diritti privati sul patrimonio dell'imprenditore' [1984] Giur comm I 53, 58ff. However, he focused on the relationship between the interests of creditors and stakeholders, particularly workers, during times of business crisis. D'Alessandro's argument also appears to be applicable to safeguarding the proprietary rights of shareholding.

[80] Maugeri (n 58) 639; Marco Maugeri, 'Banche popolari, diritto di recesso e tutela costituzionale della proprietà azionaria' [2016] Riv soc 991, 1010ff; Niccolò Abriani, 'La proprietà come diritto dell'individuo: tra diritto internazionale, diritto comunitario e disciplina interna' [2010] Giur it 2226, 2228.

[81] See supra n 79.

[82] Gianni Marongiu, 'Lo statuto dei diritti del contribuente' [2016] Riv trim dir trib 579ff.

A final area of concern pertains to art 41 of the Italian Constitution and the principle of freedom of private economic initiative.[83] The issue of the scope of art 41 of the Italian Constitution is much debated and will be assessed in more detail in section VI.

3. *Unfeasibility and Perils Associated with the Stakeholderist Approach*

Finally, a number of arguments based on legal policy implications need to be considered.

As previously mentioned, stakeholderism operates on the premise that private companies and their directors should go beyond what the law requires. If this is true, then there is, by definition, no benchmark against which directors must behave. This has the consequence that directors of companies will be the arbiters of identifying this parameter. This, in turn, can result in (i) their total unaccountability, since judges would lack parameters by which to review directors' decisions; or, alternatively – especially where the practical application of the business judgement rule in the case law is sometimes characterised by purely formal adherence, as is the case in Italy[84] – (ii) an invasiveness of judicial authority *ex post*.[85]

These implications are particularly worrisome when viewed in light of three additional considerations.[86]

First, the concept of stakeholders is exceptionally broad and encompasses a wide range of entities, including employees, members of local communities, consumers, and more. In the absence of well-defined regulatory guidelines, the discretion exercised by directors in determining which stakeholders are pertinent to a specific enterprise can be subjective, prone to arbitrariness, and frequently impervious to judicial review.

Second, within the overarching category of 'stakeholder interests', conflicts can emerge among these interests.[87] Consider, for instance, the decision of whether to shut down a polluting operation that nonetheless sustains certain levels of employment. Without a legal hierarchy in place, this opens the door to justifying any choice by emphasising the advantage of one group of stakeholders over another, with the consequent risk of opportunistic behaviour and increased agency costs. As a result, directors under the stakeholderist model are faced not only with

---

[83] Mario Libertini, 'Impresa e finalità sociali. Riflessioni sulla teoria della responsabilità sociale dell'impresa' [2009] Riv soc 27ff.

[84] See Sacchi (n 76) 591–592.

[85] As regards the first risk, see, eg, Franceso Denozza and Alessandra Stabilini, 'CSR and Corporate Law: The Case for Preferring Procedural Rules' (2008) <http://papers.ssrn.com/sol3/papers.cfm?abstract_id=1117576>, 5. As regards the second risk, see Umberto Libertini, in Perrone (n 72) 602.

[86] For broader analysis, see Giulia Ballerini, 'Spunti problematici su sostenibilità, modifiche alla Costituzione italiana e Proposta di Direttiva europea sulla dovuta diligenza' [2022] Studium Iuris 999ff.

[87] Stella Richter jr (n 6) 32ff.

the challenge of reconciling the conflicts between profit-driven objectives and stakeholder interests but also with navigating conflicts that may arise among different groups of stakeholders with their own conflicting interests.

Additionally, it is important to recognise that conflicts can arise even within a single category of stakeholder interest.[88] Take environmental concerns, for instance. The decision to pursue organic farming, while environmentally friendly, may require more land and consequently lead to deforestation, undermining forest ecosystems.[89] In the absence of regulatory guidance, the director would once again be an arbiter whose decision could hardly be reviewed in court.

In this context, the concern is that such elevated insulation from oversight and diminished accountability would lead to heightened managerial discretion and higher agency costs. Along the lines of what U.S. scholars *Lucian A. Bebchuk* and *Roberto Tallarita* have affirmed,[90] some Italian scholars believe that stakeholderism masks the potential for promoting a managerialist agenda, possibly ushering in a new era of managerial dominance.[91]

VI. Possible Arguments in Favour of Stakeholderism (Strong or Weak) and Their Rejection

At this point, it is also worth indicating potential arguments for stakeholderism (strong or weak) in light of the peculiarities of the Italian system.

One provision that may be invoked in favour of stakeholderism is art 41(1) and (2) of the Italian Constitution, which in its current form provides that free private economic initiative cannot contravene social utility or be harmful to health, the environment, security, liberty, or human dignity.[92] Under this provision, it could be argued that when company directors recognise that a decision might have a detrimental impact on one of the values enshrined in art 41 of the Constitution, they should voluntarily constrain their actions beyond what is mandated by law.

However, it is important to note that this argument hinges on a minority interpretation of the provision. Indeed, the prevailing view among scholars is that art 41 is directed at the legislature, not at citizens or market operators. According to this majority interpretation, art 41 commands the legislature to establish boundaries on the freedom of private economic initiative. Within those established lim-

[88] See Ballerini (n 86) 1007.

[89] L Ciccarese and V Silli, 'Agricoltura biologica, una scelta giusta per l'ambiente, la sicurezza alimentare e la salute?' [2015] Energia, ambiente e innovazione 57.

[90] See Lucian A Bebchuk and Roberto Tallarita, 'The Illusory Promise of Stakeholder Governance' (2020) 106 Cornell L Rev 91, 101.

[91] Ventoruzzo (n 47) 50.

[92] When referring to art 41 of the Constitution, it is important to acknowledge that Constitutional Law no 1 of 11 February 2022 modified this provision, explicitly adding references to the protection of the environment and public health.

its, anything is considered legitimate, regardless of whether it conflicts, in practical terms, with principles such as social utility or human dignity.[93]

In contrast, the minority interpretation of art 41 posits that market operators themselves should voluntarily limit their economic activities to ensure they do not run counter to social utility, human dignity, and other such principles.[94] Under this perspective, courts are empowered to review whether economic activities were in violation of art 41(2), allowing for judicial intervention and scrutiny. It is essential to underscore that even if this were the correct interpretation of art 41, the rule nevertheless *limits* private economic initiative, rather than imposing *ends* to be pursued by it, as the stakeholder approach would require.

Another possible argument in favour of treating the interests of stakeholders as directly relevant may be found in reformed art 2086 CC, which refers to the duty of directors to 'establish an organizational, administrative and accounting structure appropriate to the nature and size of the enterprise, *also* in function of the timely detection of the enterprise's crisis and the loss of business continuity' (emphasis added). According to this thesis, the last-mentioned provision (and art 3 of the new Italian Insolvency Code) would indicate that 'business continuity' has changed from a 'means-value' to an 'end-value';[95] business continuity would be preserved as a value in itself. This would confirm – the argument posits – the direct relevance of the interests of stakeholders (and thus also of the principle of sustainability) in the regulation of businesses. This reasoning, however, is premised on the idea, questioned by many, that business continuity equals business sustainability.[96] In fact, it is not necessarily the case that the continuation of business activity guarantees sustainability. In addition, it seems reasonable to assume that art 2086 CC was designed to protect creditors, who in the crisis phase can be regarded, from an economic point of view, as the new shareholders of the company, compared to whom other interests are not relevant.

Supporters of the stakeholder approach also contend that since the interests of shareholders are not uniform and may often conflict, directors are already accustomed to managing delicate balances among competing interests even under shareholderism. This would imply that concerns about directors having excessive discretionary powers under stakeholderism are equally applicable in the context of shareholderism, which would undermine the validity of relying on the negative effects of excessive director discretion to argue against stakeholderism (see V.3).

In this regard, it is worth mentioning the position of one Italian author who believes that the pursuit of sustainable choices even at the cost of reduced profits (ie, the pursuit of 'disinterested sustainability') may fall within the scope of mana-

---

93 Raffaella Niro, 'art 41' in Raffaele Bifulco, Alfonso Celotto and Marco Olivetti (eds), *Commentario alla Costituzione*, vol 1 (Utet 2006) 853–854.

94 Ugo Natoli, *Limiti costituzionali dell'autonomia privata nel rapporto di lavoro, I, Introduzione* (Giuffrè 1955) 97.

95 Edgardo Ricciardiello, 'Sustainability and going concern' [2022] Riv soc 53, 64.

96 See Giulia Ballerini, 'La sostenibilità nel diritto della crisi: problemi e prospettive' [2023] Riv ODC 486, 519 (with further references).

gerial discretion in shaping business strategies.[97] The argument is that while directors cannot disregard the general profit motive, pursuit of *the maximum legally achievable profits* does not appear to be necessary. In fact, if it were, it would imply that directors have a duty to comparatively evaluate any business strategy or initiative against any number of others in view of realising the greatest possible gain. The author, finding no obligation to comparatively assess all potential strategies in the Italian legal system, therefore concludes that just as directors are free to pursue less profitable strategies for the company, they are also free to pursue sustainability goals that themselves consist in sacrificing profits. In other words, as part of a strategy that is generally coherent with the pursuit of profit, in some cases less profitable choices are permitted in order to pursue sustainability goals.

One counterargument to this thesis would be that while directors may not be strictly or explicitly required to evaluate all potential choices and select the most profitable one in every instance, shareholders still have the opportunity to seek compensation from directors for any harm to the company's assets under art 2393–2393-*bis* and 2476 CC. More specifically, shareholders can in principle pursue such claims if they can prove that an alternative was available that would have led to higher profits than what was ultimately achieved. Of course, this presupposes that the directors' decision is reviewable, considering that the business judgment rule also applies in Italy.[98]

'Solidarity' as an Alternative to Sustainability

Recently the Italian doctrinal landscape has seen an alternative attempt to assert the direct relevance of stakeholder interests in corporate governance. This approach draws upon the principle of solidarity enshrined in art 2 of the Constitution,[99] according to which the republic recognises and guarantees the inviolable rights of humans, both as individuals and in the social organisations in which their personalities unfold, and requires the fulfilment of the mandatory duties of political, economic and social solidarity[100].

---

[97] Cian (n 6) 1144ff.

[98] It has become a well-established principle in Italy that directors cannot be held liable for economically inopportune choices as these evaluations fall within entrepreneurial discretion and are beyond the scope of judicial scrutiny unless entirely irrational and, in any case, subject to an examination of the adequacy of the process through which they were made. See, eg, Cass 28 April 1997, no 3652; Cass 23 March 2004, no 5718; Cass 12 February 2013, no 3409; Cass 22 June 2017, no 15470.

[99] Stefano A Cerrato, 'Appunti per una "via italiana" all'ESG. L'impresa "costituzionalmente solidale" (anche alla luce dei "nuovi" artt. 9 e 41, comma 3, Cost.)' [2022] An giur econ 63, 101ff.

[100] On the definition of 'solidarity', see Luigi Mengoni, 'Fondata sul lavoro: la Repubblica tra diritti inviolabili e doveri inderogabili di solidarietà' [1998] Jus 49, who speaks of solidarity in the sense of taking charge, in the exercise of an individual right to freedom, and also in terms of the common good, at least in the minimal sense of not pursuing one's own selfish interest as opposed to social utility and the general interest in respect for security, freedom and human dignity.

According to this theory, the legal system could infer from art 2 of the Constitution – even in the absence of primary laws implementing such a principle – a duty upon entrepreneurs (and in the case of companies, their directors) to direct their activities according to principles of proportionality, reasonableness, and balance between their individual self-interest and the interests of those who may, even in the future, suffer the effects of the company's activities.[101] This duty would stem from the direct application of the constitutional principle of solidarity in the form of judicial review of *whether* and *how* the entrepreneur or the directors concretely reconcile the freedom of enterprise with the duty of solidarity.[102] It would require that company directors adequately consider other constitutionally recognised and protected legal interests in their decision-making,[103] in pursuit of 'solidary management', which would translate into managerial decisions that, while potentially affecting the interests and rights of different categories of persons or subjects, do not unreasonably or disproportionately sacrifice any of them.[104]

It is important to note that this approach does not question the centrality of the profit motive but simply argues that directors should adopt decision-making aimed at reasonably minimising (within the limits of an acceptable sacrifice of shareholder benefits) the harm to fundamental values such as health, the environment, safety, liberty, and human dignity.[105]

The argument in question is based on the current Italian jurisprudential trend that directly applies art 2 of the Constitution to private law relationships,[106] elevating the duty of (horizontal[107]) solidarity to ensure that private autonomy is exercised in accordance with constitutional precepts. This means regarding private autonomy not as the domain of individual selfish arbitrariness but rather as a tool for realising interests and functions deserving of protection. Such private autonomy – according to this line of reasoning – is also supposed to be exercised in a proportional and reasonable manner in regard to the individual interests at stake.[108] An example of this trend are cases that have recognised the judge's power (even

[101] Cerrato (n 99) 109.

[102] Cerrato (n 99) 106–107 and fn 105.

[103] Cerrato (n 99) 110.

[104] Cerrato (n 99) 111.

[105] Cerrato (n 99) 112.

[106] For an overview, including a historical perspective, see Giovanni d'Amico, 'Problemi (e limiti) dell'applicazione diretta dei principi costituzionali nei rapporti di diritto privato (in particolare nei rapporti contrattuali)' [2016] Giust civ 443ff (criticising the direct applicability of constitutional principles by judges outside exceptional cases in which it can be considered permissible). This author highlights the risk of combining – without a formal modification of our system of legal authority – "written" law (based on legislation) with a law of "jurisprudential" sources (based on equity), where the latter is considered capable of derogating from the former whenever the characteristics of the concrete case signal that the legislated outcome is "unfair".

[107] On the distinction between horizontal solidarity between citizens and vertical solidarity between citizens and the state, see Emanuele Rossi, 'art 2' in Bifulco, Celotto and Olivetti (n 93) 57–58.

[108] Cerrato (n 99) 104.

ex officio) to equitably reduce penalties under art 1384 CC[109] or that have declared termination at will (*recesso ad nutum*) to be abusive even though the parties' contract provided for it[110]. The proponent of this view would extend the rulings in this case law to business management activities and the related directors' liability.[111]

This thesis is commendable because it offers an alternative approach to corporate sustainability that avoids the inherent drawbacks of altering the purpose of the corporation by extending the range of interests that directors are required to pursue. However, it invites criticism on other points.

First and foremost, it is important to consider that direct, horizontal application (ie, between private parties) of constitutional norms, in the absence of primary legislative enactments, is disputed. Many authors believe that without legislative intervention in the form of specific legal obligations, the duty of solidarity cannot operate.[112] What is needed in this perspective is a law that would impose on corporate directors the duty to manage the company in line with the duty of social solidarity, meaning a duty to adopt measures in the decision-making process that reasonably minimize the harm caused to fundamental values.

Aside from this, the problem remains of the unpredictability of the effects of a parameter that, in the absence of specific criteria, leaves ample room for the personal sensibilities of judges, creating harmful uncertainties in markets and the economy.

Finally, the thesis of horizontal solidarity suggests that a violation of the duty of solidarity-based management could give rise to a liability for mismanagement (*mala gestio*),[113] but it is unclear how such an action could be constructed.

VII. Preliminary Conclusions and Future Debates

In light of all the above, it seems at this stage that shareholderism is the theory to be embraced in Italy on the level of both positive law and advisability. Acting to modify the duties of company directors or the corporate purpose by affirming stakeholderism (strong or weak) would appear to be a difficult means of pursuing the sustainability paradigm.

This conclusion finds confirmation on the level of European law. As is well known, the initial Proposal for a Directive on corporate sustainability due diligence (European Commission Proposal for a Directive of 23 February 2022, here-

[109] Cass 13 September 2005, no 18128. In relation to the court's power to equitably reduce the deposit under art 1385 CC if it is manifestly excessive, including in light of the principle of solidarity, see also Corte Cost 13 October 2013, no 248 and Corte Cost 2 April 2014, no 77.

[110] See the famous Renault case, Cass 18 September 2009, no 20106.

[111] Cerrato (n 99) 106–107.

[112] See, eg, Mengoni (n 100).

[113] Cerrato (n 99) 111.

after the 'Directive Proposal'[114]) originally extended directors' duties to include the pursuit of stakeholders' interests (art 25 Directive Proposal). The EU Council, in its General approach[115], has suggested eliminating it, perhaps in light of the critical issues involved in the technique of extending directors' duties and modifying corporate purposes. The final text of the Directive (Directive (EU) 2024/1760 of the European Parliament and of the Council of 13 June 2024 on corporate sustainability due diligence, hereafter CSDDD) does not contain such a duty.

In Italy, therefore, the discussion in the literature within the field of corporate governance is shifting from directors' duties and corporate purpose to due diligence strategies, on the model of the CSDDD just mentioned, and to issues of imposing civil liability on the *company* for harm it causes (including in the value chain) as a result of the failure to adopt an adequate due diligence strategy.

Furthermore, the discussion is also shifting from the level of corporate purpose to that of corporate organization, with proposals to introduce a kind of democratic governance of companies, in the sense that stakeholder representatives are to be included on boards of directors, or at least that directors are to be obligated to coordinate with stakeholders in elaborating strategic plans (stakeholder representative committees). This approach has been referred to by one Italian scholar as 'democratic stakeholderism'[116].

Regarding due diligence strategies, it seems that the most significant challenges in the context of Italian corporate law (and beyond) lie in the relationship between the duty of adequate due diligence and the business judgment rule. Indeed, the CSDDD essentially introduces an obligation to establish organizational structures adequate to prevent, mitigate, and eliminate adverse impacts on human rights and the environment throughout the value chain. In the Italian system, such organizational structures are governed by art 2086 CC. Yet this provision has long been the subject of debate, particularly concerning the applicability of the BJR. More specifically, it remains contested whether the BJR applies to directors' decisions on how to structure the organizational structures required under art 2086 CC[117]. If the answer is affirmative, courts would be precluded from undertaking

---

[114] 'Proposal for a Directive of the European Parliament and of the Council on Corporate Sustainability Due Diligence and amending Directive (EU) 2019/1937' COM (2022) 71 final.

[115] Available at <https://data.consilium.europa.eu/doc/document/ST-15024-2022-REV-1/en/pdf> accessed January 2024.

[116] Francesco Denozza, 'Due concetti di stakeholderism' [2022] Riv ODC 37ff.

[117] Some scholars are inclined to believe that the duty to establish adequate organisational structures is not subject to the application of the business judgment rule. This is because it constitutes a specific obligation whose execution is not subject to managerial discretion but rather is anchored in objective parameters (see Paolo Montalenti, 'La società quotata' in Gastone Cottino (ed), *Trattato di diritto commerciale*, vol IV/2 (Cedam 2004) 265; Carlo Amatucci, 'Adeguatezza degli assetti, responsabilità degli amministratori e Business Judgment Rule' [2016] Giur comm I 643, 667ff). For a contrary view, see Vincenzo Calandra Buonaura, 'Corretta amministrazione e adeguatezza degli assetti organizzativi nella Società per azioni' [2020] Giur comm I 439, 443–444; see also Trib Roma 8 April 2020 [2021] Riv dir soc 279ff.

a substantive review of those structures and could merely verify, in an abstract sense, that the directors have put them in place. If the answer is negative, by contrast, courts would be allowed to examine whether the structures adopted are in fact adequate.

Regarding democratic stakeholderism, the issues at stake – and the 'great debates' that may arise from them – are vast and cannot be thoroughly explored in this paper.

It is worth noting that the issue of stakeholders appointing a director involves reflecting on whether non-shareholder entities generally can nominate directors. A starting point for future analysis may be art 2351(5) CC, which grants voting rights on specific matters, including on the appointment of a board member, to holders of participatory financial instruments who are not shareholders under art 2346(6) and art 2349(2) CC. The question then arises as to whether this provision could extend to entities other than holders of financial instruments.

In any case, the inclusion of stakeholder representatives on the board of directors implies certain problematic choices that must be made upstream concerning (i) the identification of categories of stakeholders who should be empowered to designate the director(s); and (ii) these directors' weight on the board. If the bylaws assign these choices to the shareholders, then they are the arbiters of which stakeholders should be represented on the board and what weight should be given them. This has the consequence that such choices would be deferred to the preferences of the capital market.[118]

Finally, as for the establishment of a director's duty to coordinate with stakeholders or a stakeholder committee on the development of key corporate strategies, one of the main issues from an Italian corporate law standpoint is the compatibility of such an obligation with the principle enshrined in art 2380-*bis* CC, which dictates that the management of the company is *exclusively* reserved to the directors (at least in joint-stock companies).[119]

These are just a few of the issues at the frontier of sustainability in Italian corporate law that have the potential to generate *great debates* and are already doing so.

[118] Roberto Sacchi, 'Stakeholders, investitori istituzionali e nominee *directors*: note a margine della proposta di *Denozza*' in Roberto Sacchi (ed), *Conflitto di interessi e interessi in conflitto in una prospettiva interdisciplinare* (Giuffrè 2020) 489ff.

[119] See generally Marco Cian, 'I comitati rappresentativi degli stakeholders e l'organizzazione societaria' [2023] Banca borsa tit cred I 356ff.

ESG – A New Guiding Star in Corporate Strategy

Jens Koch[*]

I. Introduction

From an academic point of view, the title of this article should end with a question mark. In academic debate, it is highly controversial whether the managing board should pursue interests other than shareholder interests. However, the corporate reality is that a question mark would produce unnecessary vagueness, since corporate practice, public and political pressure, and (most recently) legislation have long settled any question. Today, ESG *is* a new lodestar for corporate strategy, and rather than a question mark, the phrase deserves an exclamation point.[1] Although the anti-ESG movement is also gaining ground politically in the United States,[2] so far no official statements have reflected it in Germany (behind closed doors is a different story). Of course, very lively discussions still await about how ESG concerns should weigh against shareholder interests. However, this article

---

[*] This article is based on the author's detailed paper in [2023] AG 553.

[1] See Jens Koch, 'ESG – Zündstufen zum Megatrend' [2023] AG 553 para 1ff.

[2] For a brief overview, see Andrea Böhringer and Karl Döding, 'Aktion und Reaktion – Anti-ESG-Aktivismus am Horizont' [2022] AG R304ff; for a radical counter-position to the European ESG debate, see, eg, Vivek Ramaswamy, *Woke, Inc.: Inside Corporate America's Social Justice Scam* (Center Street 2021). As a result of this counter-movement, BlackRock CEO Larry Fink has recently announced he is ending the use of the term ESG. See <https://nypost-com.cdn.ampproject.org/c/s/nypost.com/2023/07/03/esg-is-on-its-way-out-now-that-investors-have-been-forced-to-wise-up/amp/>.

will not dig into the details of the debate. Rather, it is about the debate itself. How has it unfolded? How did we get where we are today? What ingredients were necessary to create the ESG euphoria, or, as some might say, hysteria that we see today?

A satisfactory answer would require an international perspective. ESG is a global trend that is insufficiently described from a national perspective. Nevertheless, the following paper is limited to the national debate and will only highlight international aspects as impetus for the German discussion. Of course, this inevitably results in considerable incompleteness, a constraint of this format, which does not leave sufficient room for a global view.

II. An Old Debate in a New Guise

One of the first characteristics of this debate is that we are uncertain if it is new or very old. Today, ESG is the hottest topic in corporate law. However, it traces back to one of our oldest debates, which reaches its initial pinnacle during the Weimar Republic in the 1920s.[3] It was (and still is) about whether the managing board may exclusively pursue shareholder interests or may also pursue stakeholder interests.[4] Not surprisingly, we call the first approach the shareholder-value approach and the second the stakeholder-value approach. In Germany, prevailing opinion has always favoured the stakeholder-value approach. The reasons for this include a profound history:[5] the stakeholder-value approach was once laid down in the letter of the law,[6] and it is assumed that this tradition still prevails today. However, the shareholder-value approach gained significant favour, especially in the 1980s and 1990s, and it also had some persuasive arguments in its favour. Just to name the most compelling one: Accountability to everyone is accountability to no one. To measure board performance, responsibility, success, and liability, we need a clear benchmark, and that benchmark can only be the interest of shareholders. If we add too many other objectives, we lose this yardstick, and the board's accountability becomes blurred.[7]

---

3 Holger Fleischer in *BeckOGK*, § 76 AktG para 46 (as of 1 October 2023).

4 See the overview in Jens Koch, *Aktiengesetz* (18th edn, CH Beck 2024) § 76 para 63ff.

5 For an overview of historical reasons, see Koch (n 4) § 76 para 67ff; Mathias Habersack, 'Gemeinwohlbindung und Unternehmensrecht' (2020) 220 AcP 594, 603ff; Fleischer (n 3) § 76 AktG para 22ff, who takes a critical view of the persuasive power of these reasons.

6 In particular, § 70(1) of the AktG of 1937 obliged the managing board to manage the corporation under its own responsibility in accordance with the interests of the company and its employees and the common good of the people and the state.

7 Fleischer (n 3) § 76 AktG para 34; Holger Fleischer 'Unternehmensspenden und Leitungsermessen des Vorstands im Aktienrecht' [2001] AG 171, 177.

III. CSR: The Megatrend Before the Megatrend

The outset, at the dawn of the new millennium, was corporate social responsibility. However, the balance of power has shifted since the early 2000s. This shift did not occur in academic debate, it did not occur in legislature, but it occurred in corporate practice. All over the globe, companies were adopting CSR. In 2009, *Peter Mülbert* identified CSR as a new global megatrend.[8] This is striking because today, the exact same thing is being said about ESG.[9] Apparently, there was a megatrend before the megatrend, and it is interesting to note that the first megatrend emerged entirely voluntarily. Companies adopted CSR on their own initiative, whether driven by conviction or for reputational reasons. CSR reporting long preceded CSR reporting duties.[10] This raises the question of whether all our legislative endeavours in recent years, and the restrictions on entrepreneurial freedom that have come with them, might have been unnecessary. Maybe it would have been possible to leave the issue of sustainability to market forces, which could not have evaded it in view of the widespread change in public awareness.[11] This early development demonstrates that it is not only regulation that is capable of initiating change.

As a result of this widespread CSR commitment, the shareholder-value approach was in an increasingly difficult position because it contrasted with entrepreneurial reality. For our question of how the ESG debate unfolded, three lessons can be derived from this development.

The first lesson is that it is always difficult for an academic theory to argue against the facts. If the shareholder-value approach teaches that the managing board serves exclusively shareholder interests, but every website emphasizes the company's commitment to CSR, the shareholder-value approach seems increasingly implausible.[12] We observe something that *Georg Jellinek* once called the normative power of the factual.[13] Particularly in the wake of the financial crisis, which coincided with the election of Barack Obama as US president and led to the Occupy Wall Street movement, the idea of shareholder value was utterly discredited. Now even the most ardent proponents of the shareholder-value approach

[8] Peter O Mülbert, 'Soziale Verantwortung von Unternehmen im Gesellschaftsrecht' [2009] AG 766, 767.

[9] Petra Justenhoven, 'Der Megatrend Nachhaltigkeit verändert die Wirtschaftsprüfung – Warum Prüfer bei der gesellschaftlichen Transformation eine Schlüsselrolle spielen' [2023] WPg 344.

[10] Mülbert (n 8) 767 (referring to the portal <www.csrgermany.de> and its European counterpart <www.csreurope.org>).

[11] Wolfgang Schön, '„Nachhaltigkeit" in der Unternehmensberichterstattung' (2022) 8(2) ZfPW 207, 256.

[12] On this finding and the phenomenon of changing social values, see Koch (n 4) § 76 para 75, 77.

[13] Cf Georg Jellinek, *Allgemeine Staatslehre* (3rd edn, 7th repr 1960) 337ff.

would not dare to call it that. And it is tricky to propagate an idea without calling it by its proper name.

The second lesson is that one cannot deny corporate reality, especially in stock corporation law. In stock corporation law, those most affected by corporate malpractice – the shareholders – are not entitled to bring an action against the corporation. There is a famous and most accurate saying in German law: 'Wo kein Kläger, da kein Richter'. No plaintiff, no judge. The course of this debate strongly confirms this proverb.

The third lesson is that to spread an academic idea, it is always helpful to give it a catchy name, preferably in English or, even better, Latin.[14] In our case, this catchphrase was 'corporate social responsibility'. The debate formerly was between stakeholder and shareholder value, neither of which carries any charm. 'Corporate social responsibility', however, has another groove, another gravitas; it has an ethical component and casts a different spell. It is often observed that a term creates its own plausibility. That is what has happened here.

IV. Human Rights Due Diligence

The next twist in the ESG plot occurred around 2010, when some new and unexpected players entered onto the corporate stage. These were human rights activists and non-governmental organisations, who raised the following question: can German corporations be obliged to enforce human rights-compliant business policies in their subsidiaries, especially those abroad?[15]

Upon closer inspection, most academic commentators denied any such obligation.[16] And in the most prominent case, which involved a fire at a textiles facility in Pakistan, a German court rejected a civil action based on this very construction of the law.[17] However, the activists introduced something into the discussion that had not been there before: a very powerful, emotional narrative. Its proponents showed themselves quite unimpressed by subtle legal arguments. As mentioned above, it has always been difficult for the shareholder-value approach to

[14] On this observation – related to the business judgment rule – see Jens Koch, '§ 14 – ARAG/Garmenbeck' in Holger Fleischer and Jan Thiessen (eds), *Gesellschaftsrechts-Geschichten* (Mohr Siebeck 2018) 477ff.

[15] See Carsten Schäfer, 'Gesellschaftsrechtliche Implikationen bei der Durchsetzung einer menschenrechtskonformen Geschäftspolitik im Konzern' in Stefan Grundmann and others (eds), *Festschrift für Klaus J. Hopt. Unternehmen, Markt und Verantwortung*, vol 1 (De Gruyter 2010); Miriam Saage-Maaß and Maren Leifker, 'Haftungsrisiken deutscher Unternehmen und ihres Managements für Menschenrechtsverletzungen im Ausland' [2015] BB 2499; Thomas Voland, 'Unternehmen und Menschenrechte – vom Soft Law zur Rechtspflicht' [2015] BB 67; Gerhard Wagner, 'Haftung für Menschenrechtsverletzungen' (2016) 80 RabelsZ 717, 750ff; Bastian Brunk, *Menschenrechtscompliance* (Mohr Siebeck 2022).

[16] See Wagner (n 15) 750 (with further references).

[17] See LG Dortmund 10 Januar 2019, 7 O 95/15, [2019] IPRax 317 para 1ff.

argue against corporate realities. It turned out that it is even harder to argue against an emotional narrative, even if one's legal arguments may have been better.

Furthermore, the activists introduced new and unusual forms of controversy to voice their issues. They entered onto the public stage of the annual shareholder meeting, which, as a major, semi-public event, offers precisely the forum sought for the propagation of public concerns. This again is a forum where legal argumentation frequently loses against emotional appeals. The consequences are seen, for example, in the comprehensive question catalogues that used to be employed by predatory shareholders. A more recent manifestation is that larger, activist investors are adopting ESG concerns and supporting campaigns to win seats on administrative and supervisory boards.[18]

In the end, the activists did not succeed on the legal stage. But they have won the much more important battle at the legal policy level. Their initiatives have successfully anchored the issue in both the political and legal agendas. As to the political agenda, naturally it was a few years before the debate led to visible achievements, but ultimately these were resounding and particularly far-reaching: the Supply Chain Due Diligence Act (*Lieferkettensorgfaltspflichtengesetz*) has established precisely the human rights-related transnational and group-wide due diligence obligations that people had been trying so hard to derive from general company law, contract law, tort law, international law and international agreements. Regulation to date has been exclusively at the national level, but it is becoming apparent that a European Union-wide set of rules will follow.[19]

However, even before this law was passed, the discussion of ESG had already left visible traces in corporate law legal academia and even more traces in practice, which moreover remain relevant even beyond the issue of human rights. For the first time, the protagonists of the debate have succeeded in giving the topic of corporate social responsibility a completely different legal quality. That the discussion took place under the banner of due diligence obligations was crucial for the further course of the debate. Due diligence bridged social responsibility

---

[18] On these consequences of the ESG movement, see Ben W Fuhrmann and Karl Döding, 'Enkraft Capital vs. RWE AG – misslungener Auftakt des ESG-Aktivismus in Deutschland?' [2022] AG R168; Philipp Jaspers, 'Das Minderheitenrecht auf Bestellung eines besonderen Nachhaltigkeitsprüfers' [2022] AG R 240. Discussion of the commitment to human rights in the statutes is primarily conducted within the context of the law of German registered associations. See Koch (n 4) § 82 para 10; Sebastian Mock and Jean Mohamed, 'Say on Human Rights – zur Beachtung von Menschenrechten im aktienrechtlichen Organisationsgefüge' [2022] NZG 350, 356; Samy G Sharaf, 'Das Bekenntnis zu Menschenrechten in der Verbandssatzung' [2022] ZIP 1427 (all discussing LG München I 25 November 2021, 13 T 15372/21, [2022] NZG 371 (regarding a German registered association)).

[19] Cf the draft of a Corporate Sustainability Due Diligence Directive (Directive [EU] 2019/1937, COM (2022) 71 final); see also Sebastian Lutz-Bachmann, Kristin Vorbeck and Lenard Wengenroth, 'Nachhaltigkeitsbezogene Sorgfaltspflichten in Geschäftsbeziehungen – zum Entwurf der EU-Kommission für eine „Lieferkettenrichtlinie"' [2022] BB 835; Gerald Spindler, 'Der Vorschlag einer EU-Lieferketten-Richtlinie' [2022] ZIP 765.

and corporate compliance – another fashionable term at the time – to form 'human rights compliance responsibility'.[20] What previously had been a purely moral appeal, which provided cover but in no way obliged the board of directors, was now being discussed as a legal responsibility, possibly subject to liability, and thus it potentially indicated a duty to monitor the legality of the company's operations. This gave corporate social responsibility a completely different status. Even management boards that were not overly concerned with protecting human rights in other countries (or with other social issues) were encouraged to address the issue, not only to protect their reputations but also out of concern for liability.

V. Legislative Activities

The debate on human-rights-based due diligence was an important intermediate step towards the current dominance of the ESG issue. However, the discussion did not spread very far in the corporate law community. In the 2010s, human rights due diligence was an important topic in political circles but was not yet a major topic in corporate law.

This changed abruptly with the introduction of CSR sustainability reporting under EU law in 2013. It brought the issue of sustainability into company law from a somewhat surprising direction, namely via the auditing and reporting of annual financial statements. § 289b of the German Commercial Code (the HGB) now requires large capital market-oriented companies[21] to issue a non-financial statement that, in accordance with § 289c of the HGB, must also describe how they deal with environmental, employee and social issues, human rights, corruption, and bribery.[22]

The underlying idea is quite simple: If companies must report on their activities, they will design their activities so that the report does not make them look bad. Many authors identified this kind of law-making as a nudging mechanism,[23]

---

[20] In a contemporary context, see the monograph by Brunk (n 15).

[21] For a precise description of the scope of application, see Koch (n 4) § 170 para 2c.

[22] For a brief summary of these rules, see Koch (n 4) § 170 para 2cff; for a comprehensive account of the impact of disclosure obligations on the purposes of a stock corporation, see Patrick A Hell, *Offenlegung nichtfinanzieller Informationen* (Mohr Siebeck 2020) 257ff.

[23] Holger Fleischer, 'Corporate Social Responsibility – Vermessung eines Forschungsfeldes aus rechtlicher Sicht' [2017] AG 509, 522; Wolfgang Schön, 'Der Zweck der Aktiengesellschaft – geprägt durch europäisches Gesellschaftsrecht?' (2016) 180 ZHR 279, 282ff; Christoph Seibt, 'CSR-Richtlinie-Umsetzungsgesetz: Berichterstattung über nichtfinanzielle Aspekte der Geschäftstätigkeit' [2016] DB 2707, 2708; Birgit Spießhofer, 'Corporate Social Responsibility – „Indienstnahme" von Unternehmen für gesellschaftspolitische Aufgaben?' in Gesellschaftsrechtliche Vereinigung (ed), *Gesellschaftsrecht in der Diskussion 2016* (Otto Schmidt 2017) 69ff; see also Holger Fleischer, 'Gesetzliche Unternehmenszielbestimmungen im Aktienrecht – Eine vergleichende Bestandsaufnahme' [2017] ZGR 411, 425 (note).

referring to the famous book by *Richard Thaler* and *Cass Sunstein*.[24] On closer inspection, however, this legal mechanism goes far beyond nudging. Nudging means choice architecture that subtly pushes people to make good, healthy decisions without exercising pressure.[25] But this is not what happened here. This is not a free choice for companies. Instead they were obliged to report on specific issues that strongly affected their reputational concerns. No company can afford to publicly declare that its entrepreneurial success is based on child labour, and so they would have to stop these activities.

Regardless of this characterization, the approach undeniably proved highly successful and provided a strong new impetus for CSR. In Germany, a new discussion began on whether these duties obliged the managing board to pursue CSR activities.[26] The prevailing opinion rejected any such obligation.[27] However, it still made life more complicated for the shareholder-value approach. If everyone is discussing a duty to pursue CSR activities, it becomes more difficult to argue that doing so is not even allowed. From the perspective of how an academic debate unfolds, this stage of the debate exhibited two noteworthy features.

The first is more of a fun fact, because something very unexpected happened. Since the European legislator had introduced CSR in the form of accounting duties, it was accounting experts and auditors, of all people, who felt called to be CSR experts. This is striking because this is an area in which this group had been inconspicuous in terms of being particularly competent.

---

[24] Richard H Thaler and Cass R Sunstein, *Nudge: Wie man kluge Entscheidungen anstößt* (Econ 2008) 1.

[25] Thaler and Sunstein (n 24).

[26] Peter Hommelhoff, 'Nichtfinanzielle Ziele in Unternehmen von öffentlichem Interesse – Die Revolution übers Bilanzrecht' in Reinhard Bork, Godehard Kayser and Frank Kebekus (eds) *Festschrift für Bruno M. Kübler zum 70. Geburtstag* (CH Beck 2015); Peter Hommelhoff, 'Nichtfinanzielle Unternehmensziele im Unionsrecht – Zwanzig Bemerkungen zum Kommissionsvorschlag für die Novellierung der 4. und 7. Bilanzrichtlinie vom April 2013' in Burkhard Boemke, Mark Lembke and Rüdiger Linck (eds), *Festschrift für Gerrick Frhr. v. Hoyningen-Huene zum 70. Geburtstag* (CH Beck 2014); Peter Hommelhoff, 'CSR-Vorstands- und -Aufsichtsratspflichten' [2017] NZG 1361; Berrit Roth-Mingram, 'Corporate Social Responsibility (CSR) durch eine Ausweitung der nichtfinanziellen Informationen von Unternehmen' [2015] NZG 1341, 1343ff.

[27] Koch (n 4) § 76 paras 70, 80; Gregor Bachmann, 'CSR-bezogene Vorstands- und Aufsichtsratspflichten und ihre Sanktionierung' [2018] ZGR 231, 233ff; Fleischer, Corporate Social Responsibility (n 23) 522; Mathias Habersack, 'Gemeinwohlbindung und Unternehmensrecht' (2020) 220 AcP 594, 627ff; Stephan Harbarth, 'Nachhaltigkeit im Rahmen unternehmerischer Entscheidungen' in Boris P Paal, Dörte Poelzig and Oliver Fehrenbacher (eds), *Deutsches, Europäisches und Vergleichendes Wirtschaftsrecht: Festschrift für Werner F. Ebke zum 70. Geburtstag* (CH Beck 2021) 314ff; Hell (n 22) 257ff; Walter G Paefgen, 'Corporate Social Responsibility (CSR) als aktienrechtliche Organverantwortung' in Alfred Bergmann, Michael Hoffmann-Becking and Ulrich Noack (eds), Recht und Gesetz – Festschrift für Ulrich Seibert zum 65. Geburtstag (O Schmidt 2019) 649ff; Cornelius Simons, 'Corporate Social Responsibility und globales Wirtschaftsrecht' [2018] ZGR 316, 322ff; Dirk A Verse and Rachid René Wiersch, 'Die Entwicklung des europäischen Gesellschaftsrechts 2014–2015' [2016] EuZW 330, 334.

The second feature is even more important and generalizable. A debate takes on a whole new momentum when it establishes a business model for an important set of actors. This is what happened to CSR: auditors as well as lawyers identified CSR as a very promising business model and were thus especially incentivized to keep the debate going.

In Germany, another legislative process unfolded, and in a rather peculiar manner. In § 87(1)(2) of the Stock Corporation Act, the term 'sustainable' had long been established as compensation structures were predicated on it; here, 'sustainability' referred to remuneration aligned with the long-term success of the company.[28] During the implementation of the second Shareholders' Rights Directive, the term 'sustainable' was meant to be replaced with 'long-term' in an alignment with the terminology of the European legislator. In response, the German legislature was hesitant to eliminate the positively connoted term 'sustainability' from the law. As a result, the law still contained the term 'sustainability', with 'long-term' merely added alongside it. This in turn led to a situation in which systematic interpretation required that 'sustainability' no longer be understood as synonymous with 'long-term' because the term would otherwise have been duplicated.[29] Although the legislature explicitly did not intend to make a substantive change[30], since this terminological realignment a vigorous debate has ensued over whether the norm implies a corresponding legal obligation to incorporate ESG considerations. Given the broad scope for interpretation surrounding the term 'sustainability', this may have little practical relevance, yet it served as an entry point for corresponding expectations from the investor community.[31]

VI. Expansion of the Combat Zone

As it turned out, CSR reporting duties were only the prelude to an extensive list of legislative initiatives. One legislative approach that proved particularly influ-

---

[28] See also Jens Koch in Uwe Hüffer (found) and Jens Koch (ed), *Aktiengesetz* (13th edn, CH Beck 2018) § 87 para 11; Jan Dörrwächter, 'Nachhaltigkeit und Gesellschaftsinteresse – Zu den Pflichten des Vorstands im Zusammenhang mit ESG' [2022] NZG 1083, 1086; Fleischer, Corporate Social Responsibility (n 23) 523; Sebastian Mock, 'Berichterstattung über Corporate Social Responsibility nach dem CSR-Richtlinie-Umsetzungsgesetz' [2017] ZIP 1195, 1196ff; Klaus-Stefan Hohenstatt and Michael Kuhnke, 'Vergütungsstruktur und variable Vergütungsmodelle für Vorstandsmitglieder nach dem VorstAG' [2009] ZIP 1981, 1982; Christoph Louven and Malte Ingwersen, 'Wie nachhaltig muss die Vorstandsvergütung sein?' [2013] BB 1219, 1220ff; *Thüsing*, AG 2009, 507, 519ff.

[29] See also Tim Florstedt, 'Die wesentlichen Änderungen des ARUG II nach den Empfehlungen des Rechtsausschusses' [2020] ZIP 1, 3 ('kein Pleonasmus').

[30] The government's explanatory memorandum, BT-Drucks. 19/9739, 72, describes the change in wording planned by the ARUG II as an editorial adjustment that did not aim to make any substantive changes; cf Ulrich Seibert, 'Das VorstAG – Regelungen zur Angemessenheit der Vorstandsvergütung und zum Aufsichtsrat' [2009] WM 1489, 1490; see also Florstedt (n 29) 3.

[31] See Koch (n 1) paras 28ff (with further references).

ential was to extend reporting duties beyond the managing board to cover the company's owners and their helpers.[32] This phase began with the new shareholder rights directive. It introduced §§ 134a–134d of the Stock Corporation Act (the AktG), which oblige institutional investors, asset managers and proxy advisors to disclose the basis of their investment and advising strategy. These disclosure requirements aim to inform investors and ultimate beneficiaries about the exercise of shareholder rights and the intermediaries' involvement in corporate governance.[33] The mechanism is very similar to the CSR reporting duties; again, the European legislature instrumentalized the reputational concerns of the owners and their helpers, who then carry their influence to the board through their voting rights in the general meeting.[34]

Finally, the Disclosure Regulation[35] and Taxonomy Regulation[36] significantly increased pressures on owners and investors. Both pieces of legislation follow the omnipresent 'information model' of European banking and capital markets law.[37] The Disclosure Regulation obliges investment funds and portfolio managers to

---

[32] Predicted by Ulrich Seibert, 'Corporate Governance: The Next Phase – Die Corporate Governance Debatte schreitet weiter zu den Pflichten der Eigentümer und ihrer Helfer' in Gerd Krieger, Marcus Lutter and Karsten Schmidt (eds) *Festschrift für Michael Hoffmann-Becking zum 70. Geburtstag* (CH Beck 2013).

[33] See the government's explanatory memorandum, BT-Drs. 19/9739, 98; Jens Koch, 'Der Kapitalanleger als Corporate Governance-Akteur im Rahmen der neuen §§ 134 a ff. AktG' [2020] BKR 1.

[34] Cf Koch (n 33) 8ff.

[35] Regulation (EU) 2019/2088 of the European Parliament and of the Council of 27 November 2019 on sustainability-related disclosures in the financial services sector [2019] OJ L317/1.

[36] Regulation (EU) 2020/852 of the European Parliament and of the Council of 18 June 2020 on the establishment of a framework to facilitate sustainable investment, and amending Regulation (EU) 2019/2088 [2020] OJ L198/13. On both regulations, see Eckart Bueren, 'Die EU-Taxonomie nachhaltiger Anlagen, Teil I' [2020] WM 1611, 'Die EU-Taxonomie nachhaltiger Anlagen, Teil II' [2020] WM 1659; Robert Eberius, 'Verrechtlichung der ESG-Compliance: Pflichten für Fondsmanager und institutionelle Investoren' [2019] WM 2143; Harald Glander, Daniel Lühmann and Thomas Jesch, 'Nachhaltigkeitsbezogene Offenlegungspflichten im Finanzdienstleistungssektor unter der Offenlegungsverordnung (Teil 2)' [2020] BKR 545; Harald Glander, Christian Kropf and Daniel Lühmann, 'Praktische Umsetzung der Pflichten aus der Offenlegungs-VO' [2023] BKR 28; Harbarth (n 27) 310ff; Nils Ipsen and Lars Röh, 'Mysterium Taxonomie – Was ist eine ökologisch nachhaltige Wirtschaftstätigkeit?' [2020] ZIP 2001; empirical Peter Kajüter and Carl Wolff, 'Berichterstattung nach der EU-Taxonomie – Empirische Befunde zur Erstanwendung bei DAX-Unternehmen' [2022] DB 2041.

[37] *Harnos*, ÖBA 2022, 882, 883f; for details about the 'information model' as an instrument of the capital market law, see Rüdiger Veil, '§ 2 – Begriff, Ziele und Regulierungskonzepte' in Rüdiger Veil (ed), *Europäisches und deutsches Kapitalmarktrecht* (3rd edn, Mohr Siebeck 2022) para 27ff; Johannes Köndgen, 'Sustainable Finance: Wirtschaftsethik – Ökonomik – Regulierung' in Katharina Boele-Woelki and others (eds), *Festschrift für Karsten Schmidt zum 80. Geburtstag*, vol 1 (CH Beck 2019) 693ff; Thomas M J Möllers, 'Green Deal: Greenwashing, Information Overload und der vergessene Good Corporate Citizen als Investor' (2021) 185 ZHR 881, 893ff.

be transparent to their clients about their consideration of sustainability issues. To facilitate this task as well as to combat greenwashing, the Taxonomy Regulation establishes a classification system that determines whether activities and investments are sustainable. In addition, art 54 of Delegated Regulation (EU) 2017/565 obliges investment advisors and portfolio managers to inquire about the investor's sustainability preferences in addition to their investment purpose, risk tolerance, and risk preferences. Despite their intricate regulatory techniques, the austere terminology, and highly complex subject matter, the impact of these regulations on the investor side constitutes an innovation of significant legal consequence.[38] This is particularly evident in the role of the stock company as a 'capital reservoir', showcasing the profound implications.

VII. What are the Shareholders' Interests?

This recent development makes life even more complicated for proponents of the shareholder-value approach, because no one can confidently identify the shareholders' interests. The classical assumption underlying the shareholder approach has always been that the shareholder's interest is to maximize profits,[39] an assumption that was mitigated by consideration of the time horizon. Today, most proponents of the shareholder-value approach take a long-term rather than a short-term perspective, which allows for consideration of the stakeholders' concerns.[40] This leads to a strong convergence of the shareholder and stakeholder perspectives. The more customers, employees, and job applicants as well as the public expect a company to address CSR issues, the more lucrative these concerns may prove to be.[41] Combining these two facts – the time horizon and the new awareness of CSR – increasingly neutralizes the differences between stakeholder- and shareholder-value thinking. However, it even goes a step further: if all these stakeholders consider ESG to be a paramount priority, no one can tell for sure whether shareholders see things differently and are perhaps mainly interested in maximizing profits. This question shakes the shareholder-value approach to its foundations: if profits are no longer the primary motive of shareholders, the shareholder-value approach loses its foundation.[42]

On the other hand, the shareholder-interest approach also faced new challenges. The more the legislature uses 'sustainability' in its law-making, the more com-

[38] Jens Koch, 'ESG – Zündstufen zum Megatrend' [2023] AG 553 para 31ff.

[39] Jochen Vetter, 'Geschäftsleiterpflichten zwischen Legalität und Legitimität' [2018] ZGR 338, 360ff.

[40] See Fleischer (n 3) § 76 AktG para 32; for further examples and references, see Gregor Bachmann, 'Zielsetzung und Governance von Unternehmen im Lichte der Klimaverantwortung' (2023) 187 ZHR 166, 172; Vetter (n 39) 360ff.

[41] See Harbarth (n 27) 315ff.

[42] On this see Koch (n 4) § 76 para 75, 77 (with further references).

plicated it becomes to deal with sustainability issues in practice. That sustainability has such a good reputation is also because it is an empty signifier.[43] And so it was even more surprising when the bodies of the European Union, in agreement with many member states, categorized nuclear power – not popular in every member state – as sustainable. For the first time, the problem of the conflicting objectives inherent to the shareholder-interest approach now became visible to the public.[44]

VIII. Shift in Public Opinion

Shifts in the debate are easy to identify and categorize if they can be traced back to specific changes in the law, court decisions, or scholarship. Changes that result from a gradual shift in public awareness or the political mood are much more challenging to grasp. On this particular subject, however, these shifts cannot be ignored, as their political and social dimensions are much more pronounced here than they are in other discussions in this book.

While many citizens are stirred by human rights violations, their agitation is often triggered by individual incidents, and it subsides as soon as public interest and the media's focus turn to other topics. However, the discussion about climate change obviously follows other rules. Today, large segments of the population (especially the young) have identified climate change as one of the crucial challenges facing humanity. This new focus is reflected in an intensified political debate and, increasingly, by legislative interventions as well as by a shift in terminology from CSR to ESG, with a strong emphasis on the 'E'.

Even though this article has consistently referred to 'the sustainability debate' or 'the ESG debate', those buzzwords are by no means the headings under which the debate began. Instead, the course of the debate has been characterized by different designations and changing emphasis. Change first occurred very subtly within the concept of sustainability itself, because 'sustainability' in an early phase of the debate meant a company's long-term success. Today, it describes the company's responsibility for the entire ESG spectrum with little regard for the company's interests.

However, the shift in the political agenda becomes even more evident through the replacement of the term 'corporate social responsibility' with the buzzwords 'environmental, social and governance'. This change is intended to express that

---

[43] Jens Ekkenga, 'Investmentfonds als neue Kontrollagenten einer „nachhaltigen“ Realwirtschaft: Sinnvolle Instrumentalisierung oder schrittweise Demontage der Kapitalmärkte in Europa?' [2020] WM 1664, 1667.

[44] On the problem of conflicting objectives, see Koch (n 4) § 76 para 21, 84ff; Bachmann (n 40) 183, 193ff; Christoph Koch and Maxilmillian Kneflowski, 'Umgang mit Zielkonflikten in der Praxis – „New Corporate Governance“ als Lösungsmöglichkeit?' [2022] BB 1963; Schön (n 11) 243ff.

the political focus has shifted from human rights violations to climate protection.[45] At first glance, this triad of terms indicate that protecting the climate has taken its place alongside protecting human rights and social issues. However, there have been endeavours to assign a 'certain' priority to mitigating climate change, given its now overriding political importance within the various ESG objectives.[46] How this priority can be legally justified remains unclear; even if one accepts the priority, it is hard to imagine how it could be transferred into corporate practice. However, in this debate, which is more political than legal, the participants have become accustomed to this kind of dogmatic blurring, and so this new emphasis on climate will probably be accepted without major objections.

IX. From Discretionary Option to Managerial Duty

Today, the managing board of a stock corporation faces a significant thicket of duties primarily resulting from broader legal requirements. Without these requirements, the academic discussion between the shareholder- and stakeholder-value approaches would prevail. Most recent scholarship seems to regard it as settled that the board may consider public welfare interests. Authors may mention perennial debate while leaving no doubt that the interest-pluralist conception is broadly acknowledged.[47] Either the shareholder-value approach is recognized as an outdated reminiscence, or the authors point out that the results are no different because shareholder value is increasingly diluted by long-term perspectives.

Instead, the discussion has gradually shifted away from contemplation of the management's option to consider ESG concerns and toward management's duty to do so. Although initial attempts to construct such a duty gained no significant following,[48] there is now an unmistakable tendency to reinterpret the increasingly substantial number of legal initiatives, via an overall analogy, as a duty to consider ESG factors.[49]

This debate reached a preliminary climax with the Commission's proposal for a new Corporate Sustainability Due Diligence Directive (CSDDD), art 25 of which contained the following provision:

'Member States shall ensure that, when fulfilling their duty to act in the best interest of the company, directors of companies referred to in Article 2(1) take into account the consequences of

---

45 Marc-Philippe Weller and Tim Fischer, 'ESG-Geschäftsleitungspflichten: Unternehmenstransformation zur Klimaneutralität' [2022] ZIP 2253, 2254ff.

46 On the following considerations, see Weller and Fischer (n 45) 2254, 2262.

47 See Stephan Harbarth, '„Corporate Sustainability Due Diligence"-Richtlinie. (Kein) Systemumbruch im deutschen Aktienrecht?' [2022] AG 633 para 6ff.

48 Approaches from the debate on human rights-related due diligence obligations may be mentioned here (see notes 15 to 20) as well as approaches in the wake of CSR sustainability reporting (see notes 26 and 27).

49 For a similar finding, see Bachmann (n 40) 171 (the discussion 'is tilting').

their decisions for sustainability matters, including, where applicable, human rights, climate change and environmental consequences, including in the short, medium and long term.'[50]

Prominent German authors saw in this proposed amendment a very far-reaching shift in the objectives of the management board.[51] These authors believed that directors could even be obliged to pursue ESG concerns at the expense of profits. Here the underlying assumption was that the CSDDD would compound the obligations of management with ESG concerns, whereas previously there had only been a CSR reporting obligation. According to these voices, management would have been obligated to include ESG concerns as part of their consideration process even if they were economically disadvantageous. ESG concerns would not take precedence over economic considerations; however, they would have had to be weighed against economic considerations with a minimum weight. If a business administration measure had promised relatively little economic gain, it could not have outweighed a considerable disadvantage to an ESG factor.

Other authors refuted that interpretation,[52] instead interpreting art 25 of the CSDDD draft from a purely procedural perspective, in the sense that the managing board would have had to take ESG concerns into account. According to this understanding, the new provision would have been effortlessly integrated into the existing pluralistic understanding of the duties of management. However, these authors were unable to derive a result-related minimum weighting of ESG concerns.

In the meantime, this discussion has come to a provisional end after all, since the Council's General Approach deleted art 25 of the CSDDD without replacement.[53] Since the Council and the European Parliament reached a provisional deal on the CSDDD on 14 December 2023,[54] it can no longer be assumed that the directive will even include this provision (the final text of the directive is not yet available). However, the trend towards increasing legalization and materialization is unmistakable. For now, the dams of company law may still withstand this flood of EU law. Given the current state of the discussion, it is hardly foreseeable how long it will take for them to break down.

X. End of the Debate

A common way to end an article is with a conclusion or an outlook. Neither can be given for this particular topic. A conclusion cannot be drawn because develop-

---

[50] COM (2022) 71 final p 66.

[51] For the following, see Weller and Fischer (n 45).

[52] See Harbarth (n 47) para 1ff.

[53] Council of the European Union, General Approach, 30/11/2022 (15024/1/22).

[54] <https://www.consilium.europa.eu/en/press/press-releases/2023/12/14/corporate-sustainability-due-diligence-council-and-parliament-strike-deal-to-protect-environment-and-human-rights/> accessed 25 January 2024.

ments appear to be ongoing and even picking up speed. Nor is it possible to look ahead, on the other hand, because no one can predict the direction this journey will take. It is conceivable that the ESG train will continue to pick up speed on its journey. However, it cannot be ruled out that the anti-ESG campaign in the United States (see section I) will also spill over to Germany and significantly slow down the pace. In particular the investor side, whose outstanding role in the debate was recognized in section VI, could take a powerful impetus from this direction. If those developments prevail, the shareholder-value approach could experience a renaissance that one would hardly expect from today's national perspective.

So instead of a conclusion or an outlook, a simple snapshot must suffice. We see ESG issues having an impressive impact that, unlike in the United States, does not seem to be diminishing yet. In many areas, the academic debate about ESG has become increasingly obsolete as the political focus on ESG has born numerous legislative initiatives that oblige the board to take ESG objectives into account. In this case, managerial discretion is replaced by managerial duties.

But even without legal requirements, the long-term perspective and a new political awareness have diluted shareholder interests as a guidepost. If any grey areas remain, the business judgment rule eliminates any remaining accountability. As a result, the consideration of stakeholder interests has become possible to such a broad extent that most observers assume that the debate has been clearly decided in favour of the stakeholder-value approach.[55] But the discussion is actually gaining momentum towards reinterpreting ESG discretion into a duty to take ESG concerns into account as described in section IX.

In consequence, many prominent observers have declared an official end to the debate and announced the final defeat of the shareholder-value approach. But here comes the last lesson to be learned about academic debates, on an analogy to horror movies: all one needs to know is that whenever the monster seems to be dead, it is actually, most definitely, not dead. The monster always comes back, and that is exactly what has happened in this debate. Witness *Elon Musk*: 'Stop the outrageous false ESG assessments, where Tesla gets a bad grade, but an oil company can get a good grade. Total gaming of the system!'[56]

The reason for *Musk's* complaint is that, as mentioned above, the primary concern of the shareholder-value approach has always been that accountability to everyone is accountability to no one.[57] ESG's remarkable success is this prediction come true, and it snatches a victory for the shareholder-value approach at the very moment of its apparent complete defeat. ESG has become a catch-all term,

---

[55] See note 47.

[56] Elon Musk on Twitter on 7 May 2022: 'Yes! Stop the outrageous false ESG assessments, where Tesla gets a bad grade, but an oil company can get a good grade. Total gaming of the system!'. A detailed illustration of the background is available under <https://time.com/6180638/tesla-esg-index-musk/>: 'Why Tesla CEO Elon Musk is calling ESG a "Scam"'.

[57] Fleischer (n 3) § 76 AktG para 34.

representing increasingly important issues from Black Lives Matter to animal welfare, diversity, or climate change. This diversity of what ESG stands for ensures that every important aspect of the political agenda is transferred to the corporate agenda. However, it also ensures greater complication in simultaneously promoting all these concerns. Instead, the problem of conflicting goals emerges.[58] The board has not one but many lodestars. How should an executive board react when confronted with dozens of different 'E', 'S' or 'G' objectives that inevitably will not point it in the same direction? This lack of standards is precisely what the shareholder-value approach is intended to counteract: formulating a clear guideline in the form of profit maximization is a clear instruction to the managing board and offers a yardstick by which to measure the board's performance. In consequence, the sustainability movement is in danger of being overwhelmed by its success as it proves inoperable as a legal concept.

Given these doubts, this debate is not yet over. A formula for how greater corporate social responsibility can be translated into more precise actions and targets remains elusive.

[58] On the problem of conflicting objectives, cf Koch (n 4) § 76 para 21, 84ff; Bachmann (n 40) 183ff, 193ff; Koch and Kneflowski (n 44); Schön (n 11) 243ff.

Contributors

Peter Agstner
Associate Professor, Free University of Bozen-Bolzano

Vincenzo Antonini
Associate Professor, University of Padua

Giulia Ballerini
Tenure-Track Assistant Professor, University of Padua

Marco Cian
Full Professor, University of Padua

Holger Fleischer
Director, Max Planck Institute for Comparative and International Private Law; Affiliate Professor, Bucerius Law School

Jens Koch
Professor, University of Cologne; Executive Director, Institute of Labour and Commercial Law

Dörte Poelzig
Professor, University of Hamburg, Chair of Private Law and Trade and Company Law

Carlotta Rinaldo
Associate Professor, University of Padua

Claudia Sandei
Full Professor, University of Padua

Alexander Schall

Professor, Chair of German, European and International Private and Business Law, Leuphana Law School

Klaus Ulrich Schmolke

Professor of Private Law, Commercial and Business Law, Comparative Law, Johannes Gutenberg University Mainz

Marco Speranzin

Full Professor, University of Padua